UNIVERSITY OF NORTH CAROLINA AT CHAPEL HILL
DEPARTMENT OF ROMANCE LANGUAGES

NORTH CAROLINA STUDIES IN THE ROMANCE LANGUAGES AND LITERATURES

ESSAYS; TEXTS, TEXTUAL STUDIES AND TRANSLATIONS; SYMPOSIA

Founder: URBAN TIGNER HOLMES

Distributed by:

UNIVERSITY OF NORTH CAROLINA PRESS
CHAPEL HILL
North Carolina 27514
U.S.A.

NORTH CAROLINA STUDIES IN THE
ROMANCE LANGUAGES AND LITERATURES
Number 176

FIGURES OF REPETITION IN THE OLD PROVENÇAL LYRIC:
A STUDY IN THE STYLE OF THE TROUBADOURS

FIGURES OF REPETITION
IN THE
OLD PROVENÇAL LYRIC:
A STUDY IN THE STYLE OF THE TROUBADOURS

BY

NATHANIEL B. SMITH

CHAPEL HILL

NORTH CAROLINA STUDIES IN THE ROMANCE
LANGUAGES AND LITERATURES
U.N.C. DEPARTMENT OF ROMANCE LANGUAGES
1976

Library of Congress Cataloging in Publication Data

Smith, Nathaniel B
  Figures of repetition in the old Provençal lyric.

  (North Carolina studies in the Romance languages and literatures; 176)
  Bibliography: p.
  1. Provençal language—Style. 2. Troubadours.
I. Title. II. Series.

PC3275.S6   849'.1   76-22806
ISBN 0-8078-9176-2

I.S.B.N. 0-8078-9176-2

Depósito legal: V. 2.450 - 1976   I.S.B.N. 84-399-5236-8
Artes Gráficas Soler, S. A. - Jávea, 28 - Valencia (8) - 1976

*To my mother,
Martha B. Smith,
and the memory of my father,
Melville Smith.*

PREFACE

A study of the style of the troubadours, who were among the founders of modern western literature, has many ramifications relative to other periods and writers. Effort has been made to make the present work accessible and easy to consult despite its specialized nature. A detailed table of contents and indexes of subjects discussed and of troubadours' names and poems will help the reader to locate specific items of interest.

As a further convenience to the general reader, each poem mentioned in the less technical chapters I and II is identified in our text by its standard number from H. Pillet and A. Carstens, *Bibliographie der Troubadours* (abbreviated as P-C), plus the line number of references. For all troubadours for whom a "standard" edition exists, as indicated by an asterisk (*) in section B of our Bibliography, the editors' numbering is given in roman numerals in our text, and the text of these editions is adopted. For such poems in our more specialized chapters III to VI, the reader wishing to know P-C numbers or first lines can consult index 2. Where no "standard" edition exists, only the P-C number is given in our text, and such poems are quoted from Hill and Bergin's anthology or, if not found there, from Appel's *Chrestomathie* or from other anthologies or editions.

In a work devoted to stylistics, such as this one, it seems necessary to quote the texts discussed in the original; and for the reader needing translations from the Provençal, the relevant editions and anthologies will be of use. Other Romance languages are also left in the original, except in rare cases where there is a particular reason to translate in the text, and then the original is given in notes. As a further possible convenience, quotations from German are translated in the text, with the original in notes, although when a quotation is given only in the notes, it was thought unnecessary to furnish a translation.

Old Provençal nouns are referred to in the oblique case (e.g., *rim derivatiu*, singular; *rims derivatius*, plural). The following symbols have been used when relevant, especially in chapter VI, to indicate correspondences and repetitions of phonemes:

x́	a tonic vowel (in Provençal words)
x̱	a repeated phoneme
ẋ	a close vowel
x̣	an open vowel
x�	another repeated phoneme
xxxx	a repeated syllable, root or word.

I wish here to express my appreciation to Thomas G. Bergin, who was my advisor when this work was written in its original form as a PhD dissertation for the Department of Medieval Studies at Yale, and who has inspired countless classes with his love of the troubadours and of their art. My deep thanks are also due to my three dissertation readers at Yale, who gave generously of their advice, and in particular to Peter Haidu for unfolding to me the importance of justifying stylistic or statistical analysis by the effect in specific poetic contexts, to Howard Garey for his help including the compilation of an extensive list of written comments on the finished dissertation with a view to future publication, and to John Freccero for opening wider vistas into medieval literature, especially Dante.

This work has been quite extensively revised in places to take additional scholarly material into account. I am grateful to Charles Faulhaber of the University of California at Berkeley for making a large number of very helpful suggestions on chapter I; and to Frank M. Chambers of the University of Arizona and Yakov Malkiel, editor of *Romance Philology*, for encouraging me to move ahead with fulllength publication. And I wish to thank the editorial staff of the University of North Carolina Studies in Romance Languages and Literature for their collaboration.

Finally, I owe much to the encouragement of my wife, Anne G. Plimpton-Smith; and my mother, Martha Belknap Smith, supplied very welcome technical assistance in preparing the final manuscript, the bibliography and the indexes. I am also endebted to the Department of Romance Languages of the University of Georgia for supplying, the services of its research typist, Mrs. Kendra Weiss, who helped retype portions of the manuscript; and to my colleague Joseph Snow, who kindly read the manuscript and made many useful comments.

Athens, Georgia
October, 1973

CONTENTS

	Pages
PREFACE	9
INTRODUCTION: STYLE, STYLISTICS, AND THE TROUBADOURS	17
I. THE TROUBADOURS AND THE CONCEPT OF STYLE.	25
A. The *Vidas*	26
B. *Las Leys d'Amors*	29
C. Manuscripts, Popularity and Style	36
D. The Troubadours, Rhetoric and Literary Tradition	38
E. The Troubadours' Attitudes Toward Their "Craft"	54
II. FIGURES OF REPETITION	62
A. Classification of Old Provençal Means of Expression	62
B. Figures of Repetition and the Troubadours	64
C. Methods	68
III. WORD REPETITION	71
A. The Modern View	72
B. The Medieval Context	74
1. Traditional Rhetoric	74
2. The *Leys d'amors*	75
C. The Troubadours' Practice: Anaphora	78
1. Minimal Anaphora	78
2. Independent Anaphora	80
3. Architectural Anaphora	81
4. Melodic Identity	83
D. Internal Repetition	85
1. Functional Repetition	85
2. Repetition with Semantic Importance	86
3. Multiple Repetition	88
4. Structural Repetition	90
5. *Epizeuzi*	91
6. Epistrophe	92

14   FIGURES OF REPETITION IN THE OLD PROVENÇAL LYRIC

- E. Rime Word Repetition ... 93
    1. Importance of the Rime ... 93
    2. Minimal Effects ... 94
    3. Thematic Rime Words ... 94
    4. The Distance Factor ... 95
    5. Melodic Identity ... 97
    6. Refrain Words ... 99
    7. Refrain Lines ... 101
- F. Repetition in Different Positions Relative to the Verse ... 101
    1. Initial and Internal Repetition ... 101
    2. Internal and Final Repetition ... 104
    3. Initial and Final Repetition ... 105
- G. Repetition with Relation to the Stanza ... 106
- H. Repetition with Relation to Melody ... 108
    1. Position in Different Stanzas ... 108
    2. Rime Word Repetition with Relation to Melody ... 109
- I. Repetition in the Context of the Entire Poem ... 111
    1. Repetition at Extremities of the Poem ... 111
    2. Rime Word Repetition in Tornadas ... 113
- J. Grammatical Nature of Repetitive Groups ... 116
    1. Coordinated Repetition: Minor Words ... 117
    2. Coordinated Repetition: Major Words ... 119
    3. Uncoordinated Repetition ... 122
- K. Conclusion ... 122

IV. MORPHEMIC REPETITION ... 124
- A. Rhetoric and Morphemic Repetition ... 125
- B. The *Leys d'Amors*: *Paronomazia* and *Rim Derivatiu* ... 127
- C. Scholarship ... 128
- D. Morphological Relation Among Occurrences of One Root ... 131
    1. Etymological Figure ... 131
    2. Compounds ... 134
    3. Morphological Figure ... 135
    4. Non-etymological Morphological Figure ... 136
    5. Morphological Figure by Syntactical Phonetics ... 138
- E. Structural Relation Among Occurrences of One Root ... 141
    1. Morphemic Repetition in Enumeration ... 141
    2. Morphemic Repetition in Direct Grammatical Relation. 143
    3. Morphemic Repetition in Comparisons ... 146
    4. Morphemic Repetition in Hypotheses and Other Complex Sentences ... 147
    5. Morphemic Repetition in Unrelated Syntactical Structures ... 149
- F. Morphemic Repetition in Minor Parts of Speech ... 150
    1. Functional Monemes in Etymological Figure ... 150

CONTENTS

  2. Non-cognate Morphemic Repetition of Minor Words ... 151
  3. Minor Words in Parallel Structures 152
 G. Simple Internal Morphemic Repetition 154
  1. Cooperating Pairs 154
  2. Thematic Morphemic Repetition 157
  3. The Most Common Roots in Morphemic Repetition ... 159
  4. Dialectical Morphemic Repetition 162
 H. Multiple Unrimed Morphemic Repetition 164
  1. Triple Morphemic Repetition 164
  2. Multiple Non-etymological Morphological Figure 166
  3. Roots Repeated More than Three Times 167
  4. The Unrimed Refrain 170
 I. Simple Morphemic Repetition in the Rime 174
  1. Generalities 174
  2. Derivative Rime 175
  3. Compound Rime 178
 J. Multiple Rimed Morphemic Repetition 179
 K. Conclusion 181

V. SOUND EFFECTS 183
 A. Scholarship and Sources 184
  1. Scholarship 184
  2. The Problem of Sources 189
 B. Medieval Authority 193
 C. Values of Sounds 195
  1. Inherent Values 195
  2. Value by Association 198
  3. Strength of Repeated Sounds 200
 D. The Position of Sound Repetition 202
  1. Position with Relation to the Word 202
  2. Position with Relation to the Verse: in Different Verses. 206
  3. Position with Relation to Stanza, Poem and Music 209
 E. Consonance 211
  1. Consonance and Medieval Authority 211
  2. Consonant Alliteration: Scholarship 213
  3. Coordinated Alliteration 217
  4. Uncoordinated Alliteration 220
  5. Frequency and Effect of Alliteration 225
  6. Final Consonance 228
  7. General Consonance 230
 F. Vocalism 232
  1. Generalities 232
  2. Vocalic Alliteration 233
  3. Assonance in the Romance Tradition 234
  4. Assonance in the Troubadours 236

16   FIGURES OF REPETITION IN THE OLD PROVENÇAL LYRIC

    G. General Sound Repetition 241
        1. Combined Vocalism and Consonance 241
        2. Multiple Phonetic Correspondences Among Words 245
        3. *Homoeoteleuton, Homoeoptoton* and *Rim Fayshuc* 248
        4. *Rim Fayshuc* in the Troubadours 250
        5. *Rim Fayshuc* at the Cesura: *Vers Enpeutatz* 253
    H. Homophony 255
        1. Near-homophony 255
        2. Homophony or *Motz Equivocz* 259
        3. Equivocal Rime 259
        4. Puns 262
    I. Density and Duration 266
        1. Concentration of Sound 266
        2. The Time Factor 268
        3. Vocalic Density 269
    J. Conclusion 271

VI. CONVERGENCE OF FIGURES OF REPETITION 273
    A. Convergence: The Three Types 273
    B. Enumeration in the Troubadours 276
    C. Enumerative Convergence 279
    D. Free Convergence 282
    E. Convergence in an Illustrative Poem 286

CONCLUSION 293

BIBLIOGRAPHY OF WORKS CITED 299

INDEXES 308

CHARTS

1. Figures of Word Repetition in Medieval Rhetoric 75
2. Figures of Word Repetition in the *Leys d'Amors* 76
3. Average Frequency of Internal Repetition per Poem 86
4. Melodic Identity in Peire Vidal's Repeated Rime Words 98
5. Position of Peire Vidal's Repeated Rime Words 110
6. Position of Repeated Rime Words Within Peire Vidal's Poems. 112
7. Categories of Morphemic Repetition According to Density and Quantity 172
8. Categories of Sound Repetition 205
9. Frequency of Alliteration 225
10. Frequency of Vocalic Alliteration 234
11. Average Frequency of Assonance per Poem 240
12. Average Frequency of Enumeration per Poem and Part of Speech 279

Introduction

STYLE, STYLISTICS, AND THE TROUBADOURS

For eight centuries the troubadours have suffered under a curse of their own making: their preponderant subject, love in its infinite variety, is so provocative as to have devoured the major part of their admirers' interest. It was only human — but, for the modern critic, unfortunate — that the medieval Provençal biographers should have paid more attention to the troubadours' largely imagined love lives than to their real poetic accomplishments. This romanticizing influence of the chiefly thirteenth-century *vidas* and *razos* was compounded by the notorious sixteenth-century falsifier Jehan de Nostre-Dame, who made "Courts of Love" of uncertain authenticity into the supposed centers of Old Provençal culture and poetic life.

In times nearer our own, Stendhal's *De l'amour,* then Denis de Rougemont's *L'amour et l'occident* and Robert Briffault's *Les troubadours et le sentiment romanesque* [1] contributed further, along with a host of others, to establishing the ideological-sociological context in which the troubadours have, on the whole, been viewed. The "Big Questions" posed about the troubadours have not in general concerned their art but their lives and loves, for example: Did the troubadours really compose their poems for real, identifiable ladies? Was the love they expressed "platonic" or "physical," and do the troubadours form "realistic" and "idealistic" schools with respect to love? And whatever the nature of their love, was it learned from Arabic poets or from Christian thought, or did it spring full-bloomed into being in the land

---

[1] Stendhal: Paris, 1822. De Rougemont: Paris, 1939. Briffault: Paris, 1945.

of the troubadours? Though the answers to these questions have varied over the years, the same concerns have continued to motivate recent works such as René Nelli's *L'érotique des troubadours*, Moshé Lazar's *Amour courtois et "fin' amors*," and Charles Camproux's *Le "joy d'amor" des troubadours*. [2]

A number of other scholars, including Alberto del Monte, S. C. Aston, Erich Köhler, Leo Pollmann, and Ulrich Mölk,[3] have tended also to approach the troubadours from the point of view of ideology — the ideology of style as well as of love. Mölk in particular goes deeply into the troubadours' own pronouncements on *trobar clus* and *trobar leu* and into the "problem of Latin sources," the subject and title of his part II. The real problem, however, is that it is hard to elaborate on the troubadours' own stylistic theories until we have a foundation of methodical observations to build on. For example, the essential terms *trobar clus* and *trobar leu*, designating the "obscure" and the "easy" styles, have yet to receive the needed objective definition based on the figures of speech, the lexical frequencies, the structural techniques which actually characterize the work of the troubadours adhering to these schools. Such a foundation, of an almost statistical nature, would allow us to describe and classify the troubadours on the basis of their collective and individual styles more accurately than is possible at present.

Much still remains to be done, then, towards the formation of an eventual stylistic synthesis of the troubadours' art. The only comparative stylistic study of a large number of individual troubadours remains a series of sketches written by Alfred Pätzold in 1897. [4] And the most authoritative survey of the troubadours, Alfred Jeanroy's *La poésie lyrique des troubadours*,[5] is devoted chiefly to the externals

---

[2] Toulouse, 1963; Paris, 1964; and Montpellier, 1965, respectively; the latter hereafter Camproux, "*Joy d'amor*."

[3] Alberto del Monte, *Studi sulla poesia ermetica medievale* (Naples, 1953); S. C. Aston, "The Troubadours and the Concept of Style," *Stil-und Formproblem in der Literatur* (Heidelberg, 1959), pp. 142-147; Erich Köhler, *Trobadorlyrik und höfischer Roman* (Berlin, 1962); Leo Pollmann, "*Trobar clus*," *Bibelexegese und hispano-arabische Literatur* (Münster/Westfalen, 1965); Ulrich Mölk, *Trobar clus - Trobar leu: Studien zur Dichtungstheorie der Trobadors* (Munich, 1968; hereafter *Trobar clus - Trobar leu*).

[4] *Die individuellen Eigentümlichkeiten einiger hervorragender Trobadors im Minneliede* (Marburg, 1897).

[5] Paris, 1934, 2 vols. Hereafter *Poésie lyrique*.

— to biographies, courts, and dates — with little mention of style. What is badly needed, for the troubadours — and the present study is only a beginning toward this goal — is a work of the scope and quality of Roger Dragonetti's *La technique poétique des trouvères dans la chanson courtoise*,[6] giving, however, more stress than he does to the "figures of word" which were such a significant means of development for the medieval poets, including the troubadours.

Other models applicable to stylistic study of the troubadours are Helmut Hatzfeld's and Paul Zumthor's twin articles "Style 'roman' dans les littératures romanes" and " 'Roman' et 'Gothique': deux aspects de la poésie médiévale"; and above all Zumthor's remarkable books *Langue et techniques poétiques à l'époque romane* and *Essai de poétique médiévale*.[7] Also, a number of Old French textual studies such as Spitzer's or Auerbach's and many stylistic analyses of the *chanson de geste*, of Chrestien de Troyes, and of other Old French works and authors can well inspire the troubadour scholar.

At present, for concrete examination of the troubadours' artistic techniques, the best secondary sources remin a certain number of editions which devote two or three pages, typically, to "The Style of —." For excellence of stylistic comment one may cite Zenker's *Peire von Auvergne*, Almqvist's *Guilhem Adémar*, Pattison's *Raimbaut d'Orange*, Branciforti's *Lanfranco Cigala* and Toja's *Arnaut Daniel*;[8] and a few studies like Fassbinder's on Raimbaut de Vaqueiras and Ruffini's on Aimeric de Belenoi.[9] Most other "stylistic" discussions are in reality devoted to that small but significant section of style known as "form," including stanza length, syllabification and rime. A few other editors have given lists of selected metaphors and occasionally examples of anaphora or antithesis, but have not often made the connection be-

---

[6] Bruges, 1960. Hereafter *Technique poétique*.

[7] *Studi in onore di Italo Siciliano* (Florence, 1966), I, 525-540, and II, 1223-34; Paris, 1963 and 1972, respectively.

[8] Rudolf Zenker, ed., *Die Lieder Peires von Auvergne* (Erlangen, 1900); Kurt Almqvist, ed., *Poésies du troubadour Guilhem Adémar* (Uppsala, 1951); Walter T. Pattison, ed., *The Life and Works of the Troubadour Raimbaut d'Orange* (Minneapolis, 1952); Francesco Branciforti, ed., *Il canzoniere di Lanfranco Cigala* (Florence, 1954); Gianluigi Toja, ed., *Arnaut Daniel: canzoni* (Florence, 1960).

[9] Klara M. Fassbinder, "Der Trobador Raimbaut von Vaqueiras: Leben und Dichtung," *ZfRP*, XLVII (1927), 619-643; XLIX (1929), 129-190, 437-472; hereafter "Raimbaut von Vaqueiras." Mario Ruffini, *Il trovatore Aimeric de Belenoi* (Turin, 1951), hereafter *Aimeric de Belenoi*.

tween these stylistic features and a poem's particular meaning or the general context of the Provençal lyric.

A major impediment to the study of Provençal style has been the almost exclusively philological outlook of Romance scholarship as it developed in the nineteenth century. Provençal, the Romance vernacular with the earliest cohesive literature, has long been the practicing ground of the philology student. The study of Provençal has lain submerged under exercises in paleography and lexicography, under inventories of manuscripts and variants, under attempts to establish manuscript filiations and "definitive" texts; and these descriptions unfortunately include many troubadour editions. The expectation of nineteenth-century critics that their basic philological tasks would give way to synthesis on the level of literature and esthetics has not been fulfilled.

Study of the troubadours' style has suffered for other reasons as well. At first approach, the troubadours' poems, particularly those devoted to love, may seem to have a certain uniformity, which can lead the uninitiated to conclude that stylistic originality is rare. Yet this supposed uniformity is more apparent than real and has more to do with subject than with style. As Peter Dronke says: "Phrases such as 'the code of courtly love' or 'the conventions of troubadour lyric' have badly blunted the perception of what is poetically alive and individual in this world of songs." [10]

Even the general trend toward increasing formal complexity, far from precluding the possibility of stylistic originality, actually arose, in large part, from a real esteem for the individuality of expression. As Walter T. Pattison brings out,

> There is some attempt at complexity in every troubadour poem, if for no other cause than a desire for variety.... It follows that the element of complexity was the mark of the author's originality or genius, and that complexity became equated with genius. [11]

The same is true of all domains of Provençal style. As Dante says, "La bellezza [è] nell'ornamento delle parole"; [12] and this "ornamen-

---

[10] Peter Dronke, *The Medieval Lyric* (New York, 1969), p. 118.
[11] Pattison, *Raimbaut d'Orange* (see n. 8), p. 48.
[12] Dante Alighieri, *Convivio*, II, xii.

tation of words" is precisely that element most sought after by the troubadours in their pursuit of beauty. A more prosaic description of this ornamentation for the sake of beauty is simply "style," in Riffaterre's definition (which we will here adopt):

> Quel que soit le degré de spontanéité ou d'artifice qu'il comporte, *le choix entre les possibilités qu'offre la langue, dans une intention donnée ou en fonction d'une certaine attitude d'esprit*, constitue le style.[13]

Given the partial stylization of their subjects, it was all the more important for the troubadours to make profitable use of the "choice of possibilities" offered by the rich and sophisticated language at their disposal. This choice operated on two levels: the troubadour first chose a formal structure, generally unique and always suitable to the particular requirements of his subject, tone and melody; then, he made use of the very limitations imposed by that form to display his skill at choosing words, images, and all the other components of what we call style.

The motives for the troubadours' efforts at stylistic individualization have been described as follows by Hendrik van der Werf:

> In many of their poems the troubadours and trouvères strove to rise above the level of the ordinary everyday love songs. It is difficult to determine how conscious the authors were of this endeavor, but it appears that their motivations to do so ranged from a genuine desire to write about the beauty of love to a pedantic or fashionable attempt at being different, at appearing sophisticated and esoteric.[14]

This range from the "genuine" to the "pedantic or fashionable" is broad enough to include all troubadours in their striving to express themselves and their ideas as well, as beautifully, and as distinctively as they could.

Even formalism with its recherché rime schemes and syllabification — often considered the cause or at least a major symptom of the

---

[13] Michael Riffaterre, *Le style des "Pléiades" de Gobineau. Essai d'application d'une méthode stylistique* (New York, 1957), p. 15. Italics in original. Hereafter *Pléiades*.

[14] Hendrik van der Werf, *The Chansons of the Troubadours and Trouvères* (Utrecht, 1972), p. 21. Hereafter *Chansons*.

troubadours' downfall — is not only an essential element of their collective style, but also a stimulus to their individual styles. The restrictions of form are a seedbed and proving-ground of the poet's genius. In the pioneer Diez's words:

> A difficult form, as long as it is not a meaningless game, stimulates the poetically-inclined spirit to master it entirely, and challenges it to a contest through which, if the poet triumphs, nobility of expression is wont to profit. [15]

The importance of form, already considerable at the beginnings of the Old Provençal lyric, sprang in part from the necessities of an oral literature, which dictated a strong concern for structure and the various pattern of rhetoric. As H. J. Chaytor says:

> As readers were few and hearers numerous, literature in its early days was produced very largely for public recitation; hence it was rhetorical rather than literary in character, and rules of rhetoric governed its composition. [16]

The recurrence of metrical units and of other rhythms at fixed intervals contributes to the heard unity of a work, and above all to its "reproducibility" through oral transmission, which remained important for the troubadours' work even after a parallel written transmission began, probably about the middle of the thirteenth century. [17] Certainly in the "classic" era of the later 1100's, though a jongleur may well have carried about written notes or even copies of entire poems, there is no evidence that such written materials represented anything but a direct filiation from a troubadour to a contemporary jongleur, from a composer to the performer of his choice. That is, the jongleurs who sang songs of a troubadour with whom no personal contact was possible, either from distance or from death, must pre-

---

[15] Friedrich Diez, *Die Poesie der Troubadours*, 2d ed. (Leipzig, 1883, p. 85: "Eine schwierige Form, soferne sie nicht bedeutungsloses Spiel ist, reizt den poetisch gewandten Geist, sich ihrer ganz zu bemächtigen, und fodert ihn zu einem Wettstreit auf, durch welchen, wenn der Dichter siegt, der Adel des Ausdrucks zu gewinnen pflegt." Hereafter *Poesie*.

[16] H. J. Chaytor, *From Script to Print, an Introduction to Medieval Vernacular Literature* (Cambridge, England, 1945), p. 10. Quoted in van der Werf, *Chansons*, p. 29.

[17] This date according to van der Werf, *Chansons*, p. 28.

sumably have relied on a word of mouth tradition, much in the way that the oldest French *chansons de geste* are often held to have been perpetuated in their most primitive form. The difference, of course, is that no alteration of the troubadour's text was permitted, though extremely minor variations did inevitably arise over the years.

The largely oral character of the troubadours' work as it was conceived and transmitted, then, helps explain the importance to them of devices such as the various sorts of repetition which are central to their style. The recurrence of rhythmic or syllabic units and the presence of rime or, in the older epic literature, of assonance, form the framework of recited medieval literature; but repetition of words, roots, sounds, images, and ideas is equally essential if an oral poetry is to be fully comprehended, appreciated, and retained. For one thing, the troubadours' audience had to seize meanings without visual aid, so that repetition was needed simply to ensure that the audience would not be in the dark as to what the poet was trying to say.

As modern literature has found larger freedoms and taken on a more written character, such repetitions as we have mentioned have in general acquired an old-fashioned or artificial hue. But far from being merely utilitarian or, at the opposite extreme, merely ornamental, what we will call "figures of repetition" assumed almost a life of their own in the Middle Ages, and represent one of our most valuable keys to the literary esthetic of the earliest school of vernacular poets, the troubadours.

Chapter I

THE TROUBADOURS AND THE CONCEPT OF STYLE

Before approaching these figures of repetition directly, we must first ask what sort of attitude the troubadours themselves held towards their art. A rather high degree of stylistic consciousness is implied by the character of their own work and by later medieval evidence. A certain stylistic awareness can be found in the *vidas* and, to a much greater degree, in the slightly later *Leys d'amors*. Some features of the very manuscripts of the troubadours' poetry imply certain contemporary standards of literary taste; and the troubadours also partake of long-standing rhetorical traditions involving conscious literary analysis. Finally, the way in which the troubadours describe their "craft" again implies that they looked at it in a way not altogether foreign to the modern literary critic.

To the troubadours as to the critic, every word has its importance, and every literary device its identifiable function. The troubadours are among the best evidence for the accuracy of the view described as follows:

> No other epoch was so conscious of the ends it pursued and the means required to reach them as the medieval period. It had its poetry and its Arts of Poetry, its eloquence and its Arts of Rhetoric.[1]

Even more than most other medieval vernacular poets, the troubadours demonstrate an advanced awareness of poetic ends and means.

---

[1] Harry Caplan, citing Etienne Gilson, "Rhetorical Invention in Some Medieval Tractates on Preaching," *Speculum*, II (1927), 284.

A. THE "VIDAS"

The Old Provençal biographies or *vidas* were written or recorded from the early thirteenth century to the early fourteenth century by poets or scholars of whom two, Uc de Saint Circ and Miquel de la Tor, identify themselves by name. Almost all important troubadours have their *vidas*, and many have *razos* ("situations" or "narratives") purporting to describe the conditions and reasons which led to the composition of particular poems. As one might expect, the *razos*, as narrative, show interest chiefly in adventure and romance, while the *vidas*, as biography, dwell more on the externals of a troubadour's life than on his poetic character. And yet, a number of stylistic comments do find expression in the *vidas*.

It is only natural for poetry to undergo evaluation on the part of its audience; the *vidas* show that Old Provençal society was no exception. A large number of *vidas* show at least some degree of stylistic comment. Numerous troubadours receive either criticism or, more often, praise for their verbal composition (*trobar*, in technical language), choice of vocabulary and particularly of rime words (*motz*), musical composition (*sos*), oral delivery (*parlar; dire, digz*), singing ability (*cantar*), or musical self-accompaniment (*violar*). The most frequent judgment words are *be, bo, avinen, gen, nou,* and occasionally *mal*. A certain number of *vidas* express more significant style judgments by terms such as *subtil* (usually identifying a troubadour as an adherent of *trobar clus*) and *gai* (generally describing melodies). All such terms, whether applied to the musical or poetic side of the troubadours' art, show a climate conducive to critical consciousness.

Occasionally, the *vidas* mention a detail characteristic of a particular poet, usually concerning music, subject, or sometimes style. Thus the biographer comments on Peire Vidal's facility in composing, saying: "Plus leu li avenia trobars que a nuil home del mon." And we are told of the extensive use of comparisons by Rigaut de Berbezilh, who "se delectava molt en dire en sas cansos similitudines de bestias e d'ausels e d'omes, e del sol e de las estellas, per dire plus novellas rasos qu'autre non agues ditas." Arnaut Daniel is recognized as a proponent of the *trobar clus* school since he "pres una maniera de trobar en caras rimas, per que soas cansons no son leus ad entendre ni ad aprendre." Similarly, Raimbaut d'Aurenga "fo bons trobaires de vers e de chansons; mas mout s'entendeit en far caras rimas e clusas" (and here the *mas*, "but," seems to indicate the biographer's adverse opinion of the *clus* style).[2]

Some other *vidas* show a higher degree of judgment by passing a negative verdict on a troubadour's abilities, either musical or verbal. A few of these are of some stylistic interest. Thus Marcabru wrote "de caitivetz vers e de caitivetz sirventes," although it is unclear if style or subject is meant. Peire de Valeira "fez vers tals com hom fazia adoncs, de paubra valor," and "sei cantar non aguen gran valor, ni el." Jaufre Rudel wrote "bons sons" but "ab paubres motz" (probably, unimaginative and simple rimes and rime words).[3] Likewise, Albertet de Sestaro used "bons sons" but "motz de pauca valensa," and Uc de la Bacalaria "joglars fo de pauca valensa." Elias Cairel, although "ben escrivia motz e sons," "mal cantava e mal trobava e mal violava e peichs parlava."[4] These negative comments must reflect to some extent the canons of contemporary literary taste.

An interesting case is that of Guiraut de Calanso, who apparently received a "bad press" despite his recognized skills:

> Guirautz de Calanson si fo uns joglars de Gascoingna. Ben saup letras, e suptils fo de trobar; e fez cansos maestradas desplazenz e descortz d'aquella saison. Mal abellivols fo en Proenssa e sos ditz, e petit ac d'onor entre·ls cortes.[5]

And that is all we hear of him. The unfortunate troubadour — a bit pretentious about his knowledge of *letras*, perhaps, and overly *suptils* in his "artful but displeasing songs," apparently failed to get his share of kind words from the arbiters of taste at the various courts where he or his songs were known.

A further form of early literary criticism is the superlatives applied to a few troubadours. Gausbert Amiel, for example, "fetz los sieus

---

[2] Jean Boutière and Alexander H. Schutz, eds., *Biographies des troubadours*, 2d ed. (Paris, 1964), pp. 351, 150, 59 and 441, respectively. All our quotations from the *vidas* and *razos* are from this edition, hereafter *Biographies*.

[3] Alfred Jeanroy, in his edition *Les Chansons de Jaufré Rudel*, 2nd ed. (Paris, 1924), p. xiii, n. 3, seems to give a too general interpretation of *paubres motz*: "Il s'agit, à mon avis, de ce que nous appelons le style."

[4] *Biographies*, pp. 10, 14, 17, 508, 218, 252, respectively.

[5] *Biographies*, p. 217.

vers plus mesuratz de hom que anc mais trobes."[6] Whatever sort of "measure" or "moderation" is here indicated by *mesuratz,* the literary or possibly musical qualities of this troubadour are evidently being situated with reference to the biographer's conception of the Provençal poetic tradition. A still clearer attempt at comparative literary history occurs in two other *vidas,* possibly by a single author. We learn on one hand that Peire d'Alvernhe

> trobet ben e cantet ben, e fo lo premiers bons trobaire que fon outra mon et aquel que fez los meillors sons de vers que anc fosson faichs.... Mout fo onratz e grasitz per totz los valenz barons que adonc eran e per totas las valenz dompnas, e era tengutz per lo meillor trobador del mon, tro que venc Guirautz de Borneill.[7]

So Peire wrote the best melody ever, and "was held to be the best troubadour," until Guiraut de Bornelh, who

> fo meiller trobaire que negus d'aquels qu'eron estat denan ni foron apres lui; per que fo appellatz maestre dels trobadors, et es ancar per toz aquels que ben entendon subtils ditz ni ben pauzatz d'amor ni de sen. Fort fo honratz per los valenz homes e per los entendenz e per las dompnas qu'entendian los sieus maestrals ditz de las soas chansos.[8]

The idea of Guiraut, "called 'master of the troubadours,' "[9] succeeding Peire d'Alvernhe as the most appreciated troubadour, and remaining supreme down to the time of the biographer, shows the biographer's awareness of traditional poetic judgments dating back to the lifetimes of the great twelfth-century troubadours and perpetuated among what we would today call the "public."

---

[6] *Biographies,* p. 257.
[7] *Biographies,* p. 263.
[8] *Biographies,* p. 39.
[9] The use of this expression here may be inspired by Peire d'Alvernhe saying of himself in his literary satire: "Majestres es de totz" (P-C 323.11; XII, 82). Our practice will be, as here, to use the abbreviation "P-C" to introduce the conventional poem number in Alfred Pillet and Henry Carstens, *Bibliographie der Troubadours* (Halle/Saale, 1933); and the second set of numbers will, as here, represent the number and line number in the "standard" edition, if any, as identified in Bibliography B.

This public — composed of rich patrons, noble barons and, of course, beautiful ladies — obviously appreciated one troubadour's work more than another's; and some troubadours were better rewarded for their efforts than others. The existence of such public differentiation among troubadours implies certain criteria of judgment and ultimately what could be called "style consciousness." And after all, despite indubitable errors of judgment on both sides, thirteenth-century taste is not too far from our own: our century may perhaps prefer Bernart de Ventadorn or Arnaut Daniel, but Peire d'Alvernhe and Guiraut de Bornelh are still classified among the very best. Of their own standing, in terms of both poetic fame and material success, the troubadours were certainly aware; and indeed, it is only natural that they should have been highly conscious of the reactions and judgments of the audience upon whom their standing depended.

B. "Las Leys d'Amors"

The *vidas*' allusions to individual styles foreshadow the much more highly developed stylistic acuteness of Guilhem Molinier's slightly later *Leys d'Amors*, whose title is to be translated as "Rules of Poetry," *amors* having become synonymous with "love poetry." This fourteenth-century guide to poetic composition ranges in content from philological perceptions that rival Dante's [10] to detailed and well-documented discussions of genre, form, and style. In the original prose version, written between 1328 and 1337 and edited by A.-F. Gatien-Arnoult in 1841-43,[11] part I is devoted to phonetics, part II to form and genre, part III to morphology and grammar, part IV to stylistic

---

[10] Molinier is aware that Romance words derive from Latin (I, 338) or Greek (II, 24), while Dante considers Latin a learned and composite derivative of the vernacular dialects. Also, Molinier's treatment of accent (I, 64-92) in both Latin and *roman* is highly sophisticated; and his description of the two-case system in Provençal declension as derived from Latin cases with and without final *-s* is quite close to philological reality.

[11] On the date of the *Leys*, cf. Alfred Jeanroy, "Les Leys d'Amors," *Histoire littéraire de la France*, XXXVIII (Paris, 1949), 153. All our references to the *Leys*, unless otherwise indicated, are to the edition by Adolphe-Félix Gatien-Arnoult et al., eds., *Las Flors del Gay Saber, estiers dichas Las Leys d'Amors*, 3 vols. (Paris, 1841-43). In further references, volume and page number are given between parentheses in our text. All punctuation and italics in quotations and all translations into English from the *Leys* are mine.

"vices" and to figures and flowers of rhetoric, and part V to poetical precepts in the form of a series of textual analyses. Parts IV and V show a surprising awareness of the means of poetic expression, of their effects, and of stylistic errors to be avoided. In this, and in his patient cataloguing of poetic figures, Guilhem Molinier does justice to the troubadours' abiding concern with style.

Nor do the *Leys d'Amors* stand alone in the preceptive genre in Old Provençal. The *Leys* draw to some extent on the *Razos de trobar*, written in the neighborhood of 1200 by the Catalan Raimon Vidal de Besalù. The fertile tradition of works inspired by the *Razos de trobar* also includes the Sardinian Terramagnino da Pisa's *Doctrina d'acort*, Jofre de Foixà's *Regles de trobar* and, possibly by the same author, the *Doctrina de compondre dictats* — all three of the late thirteenth century — and also the two anonymous treatises of MS Ripoll 129, written between 1290 and 1310.[12] And a more immediate predecessor of the *Leys* is the troubadour Raimon de Cornet's *Doctrinal de trobar*, written as a manual for the first poetic contest of the Consistòri del Gay Saber in Toulouse in 1324. The *Leys d'amors* also constitute a direct continuation of the medieval grammatical tradition which went back to Latin authorities such as Priscian and Donatus, and which also received expression, rather successfully, in Uc Faidit's *Donatz Proensals*, written around 1240.[13]

Of all these works, the *Leys d'Amors* is the only one to treat extensively of rhetoric as well as of grammar and to pass judgment on examples of the troubadours' art. Further, the abridged prose *Leys* of 1355-56,[14] and the later *Glosari* and *Compendi* of the *Leys* by Joan de Castelnou, all omit the principles of rhetoric described in parts IV and V of the original *Leys* of 1328-1337 and, to a somewhat lesser extent, in part V of the versified version written by Guilhem Molinier himself in 1337-1343.[15] The description of the "vices" and "colors" of rhetoric in Berenguer de Noya's *Mirall de trobar* and in Lluis d'Aversó's *Torcimany*, though of interest, is not very complete.

---

[12] All of these have been edited by J. H. Marshall, *The "Razos de Trobar" and Associated Texts* (London, 1972). Hereafter *"Razos de Trobar."*

[13] J. H. Marshall, ed., *The "Donatz Proensals" of Uc Faidit* (London, 1972).

[14] Joseph Anglade, ed., *Las Leys d'Amors*, 4 vols. (Toulouse, 1919-20).

[15] Joseph Anglade, ed., *Las Flors del Gay Saber* (Barcelona, 1926).

So the original *Leys d'amors*, still available only in Gatien-Arnoult's antiquated edition, stand out as the Old Provençal treatise best dealing with poetics as well as with grammar. The *Leys* can even today be used and esteemed as what they were intended to be: a summary not only of the troubadours' language but of their poetic art and practice as well.

In the original prose *Leys*, Guilhem Molinier ingeniously represents stylistic elements by the presumably original allegory which explains how apparent linguistic vices can become poetic virtues and which forms the structure of his part IV, the most important part for our purposes.[16] Three kings, Barbarismes, Soloecismes, and Allebolus, make war on three queens, Diction, Oratio, and Sentensa, but through Dame Rhetoric's peace-loving intervention are married to the three queens' sisters, Metaplasmus, Scema, and Tropus, respectively. These unlikely couples correspond to the three levels of language distinguished by the *Leys*: pronunciation (*dictio*), word (*oratio*), and idea (*sentensa*).[17] On these three levels, the "vices" represented by the warlike kings, suitably tempered by their fortunate marriages, give rise to a progeny of corresponding *figuras* and *flors*. This idea — that grammatical or stylistic errors can become rhetorical figures when used with purpose and regularity — is one of Molinier's guiding principles.

Molinier's figures of "idea" center on metaphor and its varieties and also include periphrasis, hyperbole, irony, exclamation, and the

---

[16] Cf. Anglade, *Las Leys d'Amors*, IV, 80. Although Molinier's kings and queens seem not to be found before the *Leys*, the creation of such allegorical figures goes back at least as far as Martianus Capella and Boethius. Likewise, the idea of barbarisms, solecisms, and improper meanings being transformed by the genius of the best writers into metaplasms, schemata, and tropes, is prominent for example in John of Salisbury; cf. Daniel D. McGarry, trans., *The Metalogicon of John of Salisbury* (Berkeley, Cal., 1955, reprinted Gloucester, Mass., 1971), pp. 52-56 (chapters 18-19). Cf. also, in McGarry's notes to these pages, further references to Isidore, Donatus, and others.

[17] This scheme corresponds roughly to the usual medieval classification. Heinrich Lausberg, *Handbuch der literarischen Rhetorik*, 2 vols. (Munich, 1960), hereafter *Handbuch*, gives *tropi* (§ 552-598), *figurae elocutionis* (§ 604-754) or *verborum* (§ 602) and *figurae sententiae* (§ 755-910) or *sententiarum* (§ 602). This is the scheme of Geoffrey of Vinsauf, for a clear outline of which cf. the Appendix to Roger P. Parr, ed., *Geoffrey of Vinsauf, Documentum de Arte Dictandi et Versificandi* (Milwaukee, 1968), especially pp. 99-105. Molinier has assimilated tropes to figures of idea (like many other medieval authors) and has given equal prominence to the fifth and last part of rhetoric, *pronuntiatio* (cf. Lausberg, *Handbuch*, § 1091; § 1244, art. *pronuntiatio*).

like. His figures of "word" center on effects of repetition and contrast. His figures of "pronunciation" include phonetic phenomena like syncope, metathesis, etc. (but not the different forms of alliteration, which are considered figures of word).

Molinier distinguishes sensibly and sensitively between vice and figure. As the gardener first weeds out unwanted growth before planting the desired flowers, so the poet must learn to eliminate vices of style before making use of the corresponding figures and flowers of rhetoric. A vice can become tolerated or even praiseworthy when used *scienmen per (dreg) compas* ("intentionally and in consistent pattern"):

> Encaras devetz saber que nos havem alcus vicis los quals havem digz, *li qual son escuzat cant hom los pauza scienmen continuan son dictat*; et adonx d'aytals vicis podon penre nom alcunas coblas, coma de replicatio pot hom far cobla replicativa, et enayssi de lor semblans (I, 336).

> Et aytal dictat replicatiu, fayt *scienmen e per compas*, reputam per subtil e de gran maestria (III, 62).

Thus for Molinier it is the particular use, the application of a verbal phenomenon, that counts. This recognition of the unity of expression and meaning — the former producing the latter, the latter justifying the former — underlies the troubadours' art as well as Molinier's appreciation of it.

The Provençal consciousness of style is again attested by part V of the *Leys*. There, Molinier considers nineteen different ways of expressing a single idea in similar phraseology; he rejects one after the other for various violations of his doctrines, often for flaws which would not, on first examination, disconcert the perhaps less attentive twentieth-century reader; and he arrives finally at what is for him (though not necessarily for us) the ideal version. To emphasize his lesson that only a painstaking search can find the best expression of an idea, Molinier summarizes his principles as follows:

> Et enayssi hom que dicta deu tantas vetz trasmudar las dictios, e una metre per autra, e virar so denan detras e pel contrari, e sercar tantas rimas, entro que vengua en aquel cas en lo qual li dara veiayres que miels es dig e miels pauzat (III, 376).

Molinier is a true perfectionist in matters of style; and it is surprising how many of his remarks correspond to modern taste, notably as regards rhythms and verse structures. There is no doubt that this fourteenth-century critic perceived deeply the principles of lyric poetry.

Molinier introduces his work as having three motives: 1) to unite previously scattered materials; 2) to set forth clearly the troubadours' art; 3) to teach the proper sort of love (I, 2-4). The third topic is hardly Molinier's greatest concern, since he mentions it only sporadically and fails to fulfill his promise to treat it in Part V.[18] Furthermore, it may be assumed that for the Toulousain school which Molinier represents, as for the troubadours of the second half of the thirteenth century, the treatment of love as a moral virtue represents more a necessity imposed by the Albigensian Crusade and the Inquisition than an enthusiastic indigenous development.

It is, then, Molinier's first two stated motives which dominate the *Leys*. He does in fact unite previously scattered materials, both by expressing the consensus of the "School of Toulouse" and by drawing on other Provençal treatises mentioned above, most notably the *Razos de trobar*, which he cites several times.[19] And, most importantly, he does succeed in setting forth with clarity and detail the nature and principles of the troubadours' art.

It is interesting to examine for a moment Molinier's attitude toward the "classical" troubadours who will furnish our chief primary sources. He quotes verses by Peire Vidal (the *Leys*, III, 286), Raimbaut de Vaqueiras (I, 334), and Rigaut de Berbezilh (III, 286), identifying only the second (as "En Riambaut"). But Molinier quotes or alludes fully eighteen times to N'Ath de Mons (a poet of the second half of the thirteenth century)[20] in the abridged prose version, and twelve or thirteen times in the original version.[21] Most of Moli-

---

[18] This leads Jeanroy to conclude that: "L'ouvrage est très évidemment resté inachevé," in *Histoire Littéraire de la France* (cited in note 11), XXXVIII, 213. But it seems just as probable that Molinier merely had no particular interest in the art of loving.
[19] See Anglade, *Las Leys d'Amors*, IV, 92.
[20] See Jeanroy, *Poésie lyrique*, I, 339.
[21] These figures according to the index of Anglade, *Las Leys d'Amors*, IV; and to Anglade's index to Gatien-Arnoult, *Las Flors del Gay Saber*, entitled "Onomastique des Leys d'Amors," *Revue des Langues Romanes*, LXIII (1925), 69-82.

nier's examples, however, are quoted with no attribution and with no known author, and are presumably his own creations for purposes of illustration. We must assume either that Molinier found it less convenient to cite suitable examples from the classical troubadours or, more plausibly, that he partook of a natural tendency for a critic to downplay the poets of a century and a half before.

In general, Molinier seems to feel that the older troubadours allowed too many "vices" into their style. The truth of the matter is doubtless, on the contrary, that Molinier has an overly rigorous conception of poetry, demanding for example that figures of speech be used with regularity in consecutive verses or stanzas. In using the *Leys* as evidence for the troubadours' stylistics, we must thus make allowance for the greater strictness with which Molinier apparently construed the twelfth century's already significant trend toward formalism. We should not be surprised, then, that the best troubadours continually violate Molinier's precepts in advance. Certainly, attitudes toward style, as toward subject matter, evolved considerably in the century and a half separating Molinier from the time of the greatest troubadours.

But this does not mean that Molinier has no respect for the older troubadours. First, in linguistic matters, he occasionally allows the use of forms which no longer exist in his time and dialect, but whose authenticity is vouched for by the *anticz trobadors* (II, 196, 210, 402) or by *anticz dictatz* (III, 144).[22] His general rule about disputed pronunciation of words is this:

> cant es doptos si·s podon dir en una maniera o en doas, adonx deu hom recorre als *dictatz dels anticz* (II, 210).

Notably, he holds that certain forms are not French but legitimately Provençal since

> longz uzatges o requier, et enaissi los han pauzatz mant *antic trobador*, en tan que no·y podem contradire que no sian de nostre lengatge (II, 402).

Similarly, in illustrating a certain type of cobla, he advises the aspiring poet whose knowledge of *letras* is deficient to learn *lo bon lengatge*

---

[22] The same is true of Jofre de Foixà's *Regles de trobar*; see Marshall, *The "Razos de Trobar"* (cited in n. 12), p. xci.

by studying the *bos dictatz antig*[s] (I, 322). Similarly, in the domain of style, Molinier realizes that evolution of poetic taste should not obscure the older troubadours' merit, and that what he blames in contemporary works should not be held a vice in earlier ones.

One particularly revealing passage explains that the supposed vice of *replicatio* (alliteration) must not be held against the earlier troubadours:

> Jaciaysso que replicatios sia vicis ... pero d'aquesta e de quays replicatio en cant que pot esser vicis ne son exceptat li antic dictat, li qual en tot cas podon esser dezencuzat per una figura appelada Paranomeon, e majormen quar greu cauza es los anticz blasmar, li qual eran ignoscen d'aquestz vicis e d'autres (III, 62).

By stating the "gravity" of blaming the ancient troubadours, Molinier expresses his respect for the founders of the art, whose poetry can only have been a profound influence, whether direct or indirect, on Molinier and his time.

As some critics have recognized,[23] the *Leys* are hence a key the troubadours' work. The *Leys* can serve us as a projection into the future of the troubadours' methods and poetical taste. We can extrapolate backwards in time by "deformalizing" Molinier's precepts. For example, where he "excuses" alliteration when generalized through a stanza, we can assume that the troubadours appreciated alliteration not only there but also in less methodical uses. Molinier evidently inherited, albeit in a more rigorous form, the literary attitudes of the troubadours as well as of the rhetoricians. His emphasis on what Antoine Albalat calls "le travail du style,"[24] that is, the conscious manipulation of words until a desired effect is achieved, bears out our belief that the troubadours' art was a highly conscious one to which careful stylistic analysis can profitably be applied.

---

[23] Among others: Diez, *Poesie* (cited in Intro., n. 15); Karl Bartsch, "Die Reimkunst der Troubadours," *Jahrbuch für Romanische und Englische Literatur*, I (1859), 171-197 (hereafter "Reimkunst"); and Warner F. Patterson, *Three Centuries of French Poetic Theory* (Ann Arbor, 1935), vol. I, ch. I.

[24] Antoine Albalat, *Le travail du style enseigné par les corrections manuscrites des grands écrivains*, 3d ed. (Paris, 1905).

C. Manuscripts, Popularity and Style

Further proof of stylistic awareness in the Provençal literary culture is furnished by the very manuscripts of the troubadours' works. The number of manuscripts containing a given troubadour or poem varies astonishingly. Bernart de Ventadorn's universally acclaimed *Can vei la lauzeta mover* (XXXI) is represented in full or in part in twenty-eight different manuscripts of the thirty-eight containing portions of his work; but his certainly inferior numbers XIV, XXXVII and XLII are given by only one manuscript each.[25] Bernart's average of 11.5 manuscripts representing each poem, on the other hand, is not even approached by poets of lesser merit. We may assume at least a loose correlation between the fame of a poet and the number of manuscripts of his poems.

The same correlation can be found, in some cases, in the number of *vidas* and *razos* devoted to different troubadours. For example, the important poets Marcabru and Bernart de Ventadorn have two different *vidas* each; Bertran de Born has nineteen different *razos*, Guiraut de Bornelh six, and most lesser-known troubadours only one or even none. This principle has of course exceptions, due notably to the antiquity of different poets, to their susceptibility to romanticization (Jaufre Rudel, for example, having inspired the legend of the *princesse lointaine*), and, further, to the individual biographers' powers of imagination and to the completeness of their information.[26] But in general, the number of *vidas* and especially of *razos* does reflect to some degree the popularity of a poet. The more popular a poet, the more often his *vida* was probably recited by jongleurs, and the more poems of his were supplied with explanatory *razos*, on the whole.

The same principle applies to the number of manuscripts of the *vidas* and *razos*. Peire Vidal's *vida* is preserved in thirteen manuscripts, Bertran de Born's and the Monk of Montaudon's in seven, but those

---

[25] See Moshé Lazar, ed., *Bernard de Ventadour, troubadour du XIIe siècle: chansons d'amour* (Paris, 1966), table p. 48.

[26] Boutière and Schutz prefer to stress those cases I have described as exceptions: "... très souvent, l'étendue d'une *vida* n'est nullement proportionnée à l'importance du troubadour auquel elle est consacrée.... Le nombre et la longueur des *razos* ne sont pas non plus en rapport avec la notoriété des poètes ..." (*Biographies*, p. vii).

of many lesser poets in only one or two. Again we find exceptions: the *vida* of the not very inspired poet Guilhem de Cabestanh has four different versions in a total of nine manuscripts, thanks to its amalgamation with the folk-story of the eaten heart. But in general, the more famous a troubadour, the more manuscripts there are which contain biographical material on him. Further, all the best troubadours have *vidas* and most of them *razos*, while of the 460 troubadours known by name,[27] only 101 have either *vidas* or *razos*, and the remainder — generally the artistically least significant — have neither.

Similarly, the quotations of poems in the Old Provençal preceptive treatises also give a rough idea of contemporary popularity. Taking Marshall's "index of verse quotations" in the *Razos de trobar* and associated texts, we find Bernart de Ventadorn leading with eight different poems quoted from, then Peire Vidal and Gaucelm Faidit with seven, Folquet de Marselha with five, Guiraut de Bornelh with four, Raimbaut de Vaqueiras with three, and so on.[28] All these are certainly among the greatest troubadours; and the compilers must therefore have used some sort of esthetic criteria — hence having to do with what we call style — in choosing their examples.

Another thing we can learn, now from the false attributions made by the compilers of the manuscript anthologies, is those features that were held to be the individual characteristics of different poets. The medieval compiler, like the modern editor, had to decide to whom to attribute a text of unknown or disputed authorship, or whether to consider it anonymous. This explains the large number of isolated false attributions. The medieval criteria for making attributions may differ from ours but doubtless relied on the same basic principle of noticing resemblances between an unattributed poem and the work of known troubadours in terms of subject, form, references to people, and style.

Misattribution by compilers can be stylistically meaningful. Thus Rigaut de Berbezilh, as his *vida* shows, was known for his unusual *similitudines* (comparisons). Four of his nine poems generally accepted as authentic begin with comparisons involving the lion, the elephant, sunlight, and the hero Perceval; and others were attracted into his orbit in some manuscripts. Thus of the manuscripts of the poem *Si*

---

[27] The number of those having entries in P-C (cf. n. 9, above).
[28] Marshall, "*Razos de Trobar*" (see n. 12), pp. 180-181.

co·l soleilhs per sa nobla clardat (P-C 337.1), only one attributes it to Rigaut: the lone compiler was probably misled by the initial comparison. Another manuscript wrongly gives Rigaut the poem *Atressi co·l cignes fai* (P-C 366.2) and *Atressi com la candela* (P-C 355.5); and a third, the poem *Si com li peis an en l'aiga lor vida* (P-C 30.22). The same criterion — symbolic of the continuity of literary criticism! — is used by Anglade in assigning to Rigaut the poem *Eissamen com la pantera* (P-C 461.102), which the sole manuscript leaves anonymous and which Varvaro prudently considers "di dubbia attribuzione."[29]

The question of false attributions, if studied in full detail, could lead to important conclusions on the impressions various troubadours made on contemporary and later anthologists. But for our present purposes, it suffices to have shown that the attributions, as well as the space given to different poets and poems in the manuscripts, imply recognition and evaluation of individual characteristics.

D. The Troubadours, Rhetoric, and Literary Tradition

Traditional rhetoric will play an important role in the following chapters. Though the troubadours' art can also be described in modern terms, it is both convenient and logical to treat a medieval literature more in terms of medieval literary theory, as expressed in the rhetoricians who perpetuated the literary analysis and terminology of their classical predecessors. It certainly seems plausible that the troubadours — close as they were to the origins of Romance vernacular poetry, yet among the most learned and art-conscious of poets — should have been acquainted with the traditional poetic arts of their time.

Indeed, the troubadours' own outlook on poetry seems to be derived from that of the rhetoricians. It is well known that the height of the Provençal lyric is characterized by open debate between opposing schools called *trobar clus* and *trobar leu*, "closed style" and "easy style." The troubadours themselves frequently oppose the terms *leu, levet, leugier, vil, clar, descubert, non-clus,* and *plan* on one side to *clus, escur, greu, sotil, serrat, car, echartat, prim* and *ric* on the other,

---

[29] For discussion of all these poems, see Alberto Varvaro, ed., *Rigaut de Berbezilh: liriche* (Bari, 1960), pp. 217, 263, 268, etc.

while some recent critics have preferred to consider the last two terms, *trobar prim* and *trobar ric*, as designating a third, separate school, more or less intermediate between *trobar clus* and *trobar leu*.[30]

The stylistic debate among troubadours is best represented by a famous *tenso*, *Era·m platz*, *Giraut de Bornelh* (P-C 389.10a), written about 1170, in which Raimbaut d'Aurenga under the name Linhaure denounces Guiraut de Bornelh for abandoning *trobar clus*, while Guiraut upholds the merits of the *chan levet e venansal*, a style which he had apparently adopted recently. Others of the same series of terms are used by Lanfranc Cigala (fl. ca. 1235-70) in declaring that though he is capable of writing in the *clus* style, he prefers clarity ("technical" literary terms are here italicized):

> *Escur prim* chantar e *sotil*
> Sabria far, si·m volia,
> Mas no·s taing c'om son chant afil
> Ab tan *prima* maestria
> Que no sia *clars* com dia.
> (P-C 282.5; XII, 1-5)

And through the whole poem runs the contrast between *clar(s)* (lines 5, 10, 14, 20, 30, 43) or *clardat(z)* (7, 9, 19) and *escur(s)* (1, 15, 29).

Another series of critical terms, harder to interpret, opposes *vers entier* to *vers frag* and to *mot borrel, romput* or *peceiat*, particularly in the early troubadours Bernart Marti and Peire d'Alvernhe.[31] The latter alludes unmistakably but cryptically to this opposition in his very style-conscious poem beginning

> Sobre·l vielh trobar e·l novel
> Vuelh mostrar mon sen als sabens.
> (P-C 323.24; III, 1-2)

However, the relation of this "old way of composing and the new" to the schools of *trobar clus* and *trobar leu* remains obscure.

It is highly tempting, at any rate, to connect the troubadours' dualistic concept of poetry to the rhetorical categories of *ornatus*

---

[30] See Mölk, *Trobar clus - Trobar leu*, especially pp. 128-137, and Aston, "The Troubadours and the Concept of Style" (both cited in Intro., n. 3).

[31] See Mölk, *Trobar clus - Trobar leu*, pp. 110-114.

difficilis and *ornatus facilis*, "difficult" and "easy ornamentation." [32] Admittedly, the troubadours' and the rhetoricians' pairs are not identical. The two kinds of *trobar* are distinguished, at least initially, by difficulty of comprehension, while the two kinds of *ornatus* depend on the difficulty, or perhaps more precisely the prestige, of two different sets of figures, *ornatus difficilis* employing tropes (what we call loosely "figures of speech") and *ornatus facilis* employing all other figures.

Still, the parallels between these two sets of criteria for classifying poetical style according to its difficulty — of understanding or of creation — remain striking. These two categories are largely overlapping. It is true that the terms *ornatus difficilis* and *facilis* do not appear in surviving works before the early thirteenth century, [33] while the pairs *leu* and *clus*, *plan* and *escur*, *clar* and *sotil*, etc., are used commonly in Provençal throughout the twelfth century. But close interrelation of medieval Latin and Provençal terminology is shown by the great thirteenth-century rhetoricians' regular application of derivatives of *planus* and *levis* to the concepts represented by both *trobar leu* and *ornatus facilis*. Thus, according to Faral, *l'ornement facile* is designated by the following array of terms: *sermo levis* (Geoffrey of Vinsauf, Poetria nova, line 1094), *ornata facilitas* (Geoffrey of Vinsauf, Documentum de Arte Versificandi, II, 34), *via plana* (Eberhard the German, Laborintus, line 431), *materia levis* and *ornatus facilis* (both terms used by John of Garland, Poetria). [34]

Furthermore, it is not unlikely that both the troubadours' and the rhetoricians' classifications are derived from a simplified medieval version of the three classical sorts of style: *stilus* (or *sermo*) *gravis*, *mediocris* and *humilis*. This possibility receives support from the fact that the Provençal term *greu*, in the *trobar clus* series of epithets, is derived from Latin *gravis* (by way of Vulgar Latin *grevis*). There are good reasons, then, for equating the classical measurement of style (*modus*) and the medieval measure of ornament (*ornatus*), as does Roger Dragonetti in his discussion of the *trouvères*. [35]

---

[32] For discussion see Mölk, pp. 177-199; and Edmond Faral, Les arts poétiques du XIIe et du XIIIe siècle (Paris, 1924), pp. 86-98, hereafter Arts poétiques.

[33] Leo Pollmann, "*Trobar Clus*" (cited in Intro., n. 3), p. 46.

[34] Faral, Arts poétiques, p. 51.

[35] Dragonetti, Technique poétique (see Intro., n. 6), pp. 32, 59.

Both the concepts and the terminology we have discussed place the troubadours directly in the classical tradition of poetic criticism; and the troubadours have in common with the medieval rhetoricians an analysis of style according to levels of difficulty, and a manner of looking at poetry which is both descriptive and prescriptive. Often, in fact, a troubadour will sound almost school-masterly in announcing in advance both the genre and the stylistic level of his poem. Sordel, for example, begins a poem by saying:

> Bel m'es ab *motz leugiers* a far
> Chanson plazen et *ab guay so*;
> (P-C 437.7; IV, 1-2)

and Raimbaut d'Aurenga shares his intentions with us, saying:

> Apres mon vers vueilh sempr' ordre
> Una *chanson leu* per bordre
> En aital *rima sotil*.
> (P-C 389.10; IV, 1-3)

Additional evidence of the learned character of the troubadours, presumably derived from rhetorical influence, is their penchant for literary satires, the unmistakable sign of a highly developed and self-conscious literary culture. In these satirical poems, personal attacks and "character assassination" predominate, but stylistic critiques of fellow troubadours are not rare. Peire d'Alvernhe's famous poem *Chantarai d'aquestz trobadors* criticizes the appearance, personality, musical talents, and singing abilities of his poetic rivals, ending with a self-satirizing reference to his own adherence to the school of *trobar clus*:

> Peire d'Alvernhe a tal votz
> Que canta desobre e desotz
> E sei so son dous e plazen;
> Pero majestres es de totz,
> Ab qu'un pauc esclarzis sos mots,
> Qu'a penas nulhs om los enten.
> (P-C 323.11; XII, 79-84)

The Monk of Montaudon deliberately announces his debt to his model Peire d'Alvernhe in a similar satire beginning:

> Pois Peire d'Alverne a chantat
> Dels trobadors qui son passat,
> Cantarai al mieu escien
> D'aquels que pois se son levat.
>
> (P-C 305.16, 1-4)

Though dealing, like Peire, mostly with externals, the Monk makes use of the contemporary language of literary criticism in the expression *sonez levez e plas* ("simple and smooth tunes") in line 50.

In the same tradition, Uc de Lescura begins a poem (P-C 452.1) by proclaiming his own superiority to eight different troubadours on the basis of eight different criteria, including the use of *motz ricos* and the ability to *greu sonet bastir*.[36] Another troubadour, Uc de Saint Circ, almost seems to specialize in attacking his peers in acerbic *coblas* and *tensos*. Notably his *cobla Guillelms Fabres nos fai en brau lengage* (P-C 457.17; XXVIII) satirizes Guilhem Fabre's use of alliteration, assonance, root repetition, rare rimes and unusual vocabulary; and in other poems, Uc uses the technical terms *prim* (P-C 457.32; XXIX, 1), *leu* (P-C 457.8; XX, 1), *silaba* and *escritz* (P-C 457.27; XXVII, 6-7). In their literary and analytical aspect, the satires by these poets — Peire d'Alvernhe, the Monk of Montaudon, Uc de Lescura and Uc de Saint Circ — show that the attitudes and in all probability some form of the theory and terminology of rhetoric were known not only to these authors but also to their satirized peers and to the audiences for whom the satires were ultimately intended.

The same conclusions can be drawn from the troubadours' occasional parodies. For example, Raimbaut d'Aurenga humorously exaggerates the technique of the unrimed refrain by insisting playfully on the roots *mal-* and *astr-* in every line of his poem *Ar no sui ges mals et astrucs* (P-C 389.14; XXXVI). Peire Cardenal apparently mocks the alliterative excesses of some of his predecessors (and perhaps of himself as well) in his poem *Ar me puesc ieu lauzar d'Amor* (P-C 335.7; I, 41-52). Further, one of the three Provençal imitations of Arnaut Daniel's famous sestina, Guilhem de Saint Gregori's *Ben grans avoleza intra* (P-C 233.2) is apparently a parody. And Bernart de Ventadorn's beautiful song *Can la freid' aura venta* (P-C 70.37;

---

[36] In Alfred Jeanroy, "Poésies provençales inédites d'après les manuscrits de Paris," *Annales du Midi*, XVII (1905), 477.

XXVI) was obscenely parodied by an anonymous strophe beginning *Quand lo pels del cul venta* (P-C 461.202).[37]

An impressive case for the troubadours' familiarity with rhetoric is made by Dimitri Scheludko's "Beiträge zur Entstehungsgeschichte der provenzalischen Lyrik."[38] Part of his argument is based on a conjectured link between the traditional rhetorical term *inventio* ("the finding of thoughts fitting to the subject")[39] and the Provençal term *trobar* ("to find; to compose poetry"; and as a noun, "the art of making verses" or simply "poetry"). Scheludko holds that *trobar*, in its two senses, is a calque of *invenire*, quoting for example the definition "e son inventores dig tug li trobador."[40] It is, indeed, not unreasonable to suppose that the semantic broadening of *tropus* and *tropare* — from the domain of rhetorical figures and then of musical composition to the more general meanings of "inventing," "finding," and "composing" — may have undergone the semantic influence of *invenire* and *inventio* during the very period that the latter root was declining in the Romance languages.[41]

---

[37] See Carl Appel, ed., *Bernart von Ventadorn: seine Lieder* (Halle/Saale, 1915), p. cviii.

[38] Scheludko's lengthy article of this title appeared in four installments, of which we refer in notes only to the fourth, appearing in *Archivum Romanicum*, XV (1931), 137-206. Hereafter "Entstehungsgeschichte."

[39] Heinrich Lausberg, *Elemente der Literarischen Rhetorik*, 3rd ed. (Munich, 1967), § 40. Hereafter *Elemente*.

[40] Scheludko, "Entstehungsgeschichte," pp. 137-139; the quote is from Guiraut Riquier, *Declaratio*, in C. A. F. Mahn, *Die Werke der Troubadours in provenzalischer Sprache*, IV (Berlin, 1853), 185.

[41] This semantic evolution, including the influence of *invenire*, is according to Walther von Wartburg, ed., *Französisches Etymologisches Wörterbuch* (Basel, 1928-; hereafter FEW), vol. XIII, part 2 (Basel, 1967), art. *tropare*. Even if it be accepted that the true derivation is from *turbare*, "to disturb," whence "to drive and catch fish by troubling the water," becoming "to find fish" and then simply "to find" (for discussion see Ernst Gamillscheg, *Etymologisches Wörterbuch der französischen Sprache*, 2nd ed. (Heidelberg, 1969), art. "trouver"), the influence of the double meaning of *invenire* could still be retained. Wilhelm Meyer-Lübke, *Romanisches Etymologisches Wörterbuch*, 3rd ed. (Heidelberg, 1935; hereafter REW), arts. *tŭrbāre* and *trŏpāre*, distinguishes two identical Old Provençal words *trobar*, one meaning "to find," from *turbare*, and one meaning "to write poetry," from *tropare*; in this case, the influence of *invenire* could still be felt, perhaps even encouraging this convergent phonetic evolution.

Scheludko also cites several allusions by the troubadours to the traditional "colors of rhetoric." The comparison of these colors of rhetoric to flowers, which is frequent in the *Leys d'amors*, dates back at least to the eleventh century. As early as Cicero, the word *color* can refer to "*ornatus*, linguistically beautiful presentation";[42] it apparently means *ornatus* in Matthew of Vendôme and Geoffrey of Vinsauf.[43] Among the troubadours, William IX already seems to connect "colors" and "flowers" of rhetoric:

> Ben vuelh que sapchon li pluzor
> D'est vers si's de bona *color*,
> Qu'ieu ai trag de mon obrador:
> Qu'ieu port d'ayselh mestier la *flor*,
>   Et es vertaz,
> E puesc ne traire·l vers auctor
> Quant es lassatz.
>   (P-C 183.2; VI, 1-7)

Similarly, Arnaut Daniel claims that the variegated colors of nature (*Er vei vermeills, vertz, blaus, blancs, gruocs*) inspire a colorful and flowery song:

> So·m met en cor qu'ieu *colore* mon chan
> D'un aital *flor* don lo fruitz si' amors,
> E jois lo grans, e l'olors d'enoi gandres.
>   (P-C 29.4; XIII, 5-7)

Scheludko gives a number of other examples of the type *colorar un chan*, both in rhetorical treatises and in the troubadours, of which the most remarkable case is in the *ensenhamen* by Amanieu des Escas beginning *El temps*:

> ... Om deu gen *colorar*
> Sos faitz et al *parlar*
> Deu gen metre *color*;
> Si com li *penhidor*
> *Coloro* so que fan,
> Deu hom *colorar* tan
> *Paraulas* ab *parlar*

---

[42] Lausberg, *Handbuch*, § 1061: "ornatus, sprachlich schöne Darbietung."
[43] Faral, *Arts poétiques*, pp. 167, 220; cf. Lausberg, *Elemente*, § 167.

C'om no·l puesca reptar
Per razo ni mal dir.
(P-C 21a.—, 23-31)⁴⁴

Here, the juxtaposition of the repeated roots *parl-* and *color* again suggests the "colors of rhetoric." And to such examples might be added others of the similar type *daurar un chan*, which imply the poet's desire to give a very special "color" to his style.

Another revealing traditional metaphor is that of "polishing verse" (*polire carmen, motz polir,* etc.). Scheludko furnishes examples from the *Rhetorica ad Herennium* and Ekkehard IV and from the troubadours Guiraut de Bornelh and Arnaut Daniel,⁴⁵ to whom can be added others such as Cercamon with his reference to *motz politz* (P-C 112.1c; III, 34). As Lausberg shows, this metaphor stretches from Cicero and Quintilian to Boileau,⁴⁶ so that the troubadours are situated in the midst of a most distinguished rhetorical tradition.

The opinion that the troubadours owed much to rhetoric is shared by Kurt Lewent. Under the heading of "A rhetorical figure," Lewent describes a "figure which... giv[es] the attributes of different things strictly in the same order in which the latter are enumerated." He cites an example from Lessing, and adds: "In this, there is no doubt a smack of the pedant and schoolmaster, and it is not astonishing that we should find some examples of it in the troubadours, who had received their rhetorical schooling too." ⁴⁷

Since there is little direct evidence as to what sort of education the troubadours may have had, we must resort to piecing together isolated bits of information in order to determine the probable sources of the troubadours' acquaintance with rhetoric. Scheludko remarks that the passage from William IX's poem VI quoted above uses the

---

⁴⁴ Scheludko, "Entstehungsgeschichte," p. 142; this quote from Karl Bartsch, ed., *Denkmäler der provenzalischen Literatur* (Stuttgart, 1856), hereafter *Denkmäler,* p. 103.

⁴⁵ Scheludko, p. 142.

⁴⁶ Lausberg, *Handbuch,* § 1244, art. *polire;* § 1246, art. *polir.* Boileau, *L'art poétique,* I, 172:
Polissez-le sans cesse et le repolissez.

⁴⁷ Kurt Lewent, "Observations on Old Provençal Style and Vocabulary," *Modern Language Quarterly,* II (1941), pp. 203-4.

school words *auctor* ("witness, authority") and *obrador* (presumably designating the "study-room" in which the poet composed or read).[48]

We also learn from the *vidas* that various troubadours were knowledgeable in *letras* or were *ben letratz*: Arnaut Daniel, Guiraut de Calanso, Daude de Pradas, Peire d'Alvernhe.[49] And besides having their *letras*, others are credited with a clerical education: Arnaut de Maruelh "fo clergues de paubra generacion," and because he could not make a living from his *letras*, he went forth into the world; Uc Brunet was also a *clerges*, and Uc de Saint Circ was raised to be a *clerc*; Gausbert de Poicibot was raised and educated in the orders; Peire Cardenal was raised by the canonry of Le Puy; and Peire Rogier was the canon of Clermont till he became a jongleur.[50]

The *vidas* also tell us that Guiraut de Bornelh spent his summers traveling but that "tot l'invern estava en escola e aprendia letras" (probably "taught" rather than "learned" *letras*).[51] Though the reference may be to an ordinary grammar school, it is also possible that we have to do here with the same sort of school for poets as is known to have flourished in Austria, and which may be alluded to when Bernart de Ventadorn declares:

> Ja mai non serai chantaire
> Ni de l'*escola* N'Eblo.
> (P-C 70.30; XLIV, 22-23)[52]

The existence of such schools receives further support from Bruno Panvini's belief that Guiraut de Bornelh's title of "maestre dels trobadors" was wrongly interpreted by his biographer as referring to the excellence of his poems; rather, Panvini says, "Io ritengo... più probabile che quel titolo gli provenisse dal mestiere di maestre di

---

[48] Scheludko, p. 141. Cf. also the use of *auctor* by Uc Catola in his *tenso* with Marcabru, P-C 451.1, 17.

[49] *Biographies*, pp. 59, 217, 233, 263.

[50] *Biographies*, pp. 32, 199, 239, 233, 335, 267.

[51] *Biographies*, p. 39.

[52] On Reinmar von Hagenau's poetic school at Vienna, cf. Helmut de Boor and Richard Newald, *Geschichte der deutschen Literatur* (Munich, 1953), II, 283. On the expression "en l'escolh Linhaure," apparently meaning "in the manner of Linhaure" in Guiraut de Bornelh XXIX, P-C 242.37, 56, cf. Pattison, *Raimbaut d'Orange*, p. 23.

arte poetica che il trovatore effettivamente esercitava." [53] Guiraut could thus be seen as a sort of professor of poetry in a "school for troubadours." And according to Scheludko, Guiraut not only studied in Latin books the doctrine of the two sorts of *ornatus* but may also have instructed his own students in the techniques of *ornatus difficilis* and *ornatus facilis*. [54]

Another particularly revealing biography, that of the late thirteenth and early fourteenth-century Italian troubadour Ferrari de Ferrara, shows the continuing importance of bookish learning in the Italian offshoot of the Provençal tradition:

> Maistre Ferari fo da Feirara. E fo giullar et intendez meill de trobar proensal che negus om che fos mais en Lombardia e meill entendet la lenga proensal. E sap molt be letras, e scrivet meil ch'om del mond e feis de molt bos libres e de beills.... E qan venia qe le marches feanon festa e cort, e li giullar li vinian che s'entendean de la lenga proensal, anavan tuit ab lui e·l clamavan lor maistre; e s'alcus li·n venia che s'entendes meil che i altri e che fes questios de son trobar o d'autrui, e maistre Ferari li respondea ades.... E fes un estrat de tutas las canços des bos trobadors del mon.... [55]

Thus Ferrari was, and with reason, respected as a learned authority; and his *estrat* of "all the songs of the good troubadours of the world" is known to comprise a part of song manuscript D, [56] one of the manuscript anthologies which are our major primary source on the troubadours.

Whether the schools in which Ferrari de Ferrara, Guiraut de Bornelh and others may have studied were primarily for clerics or for poets, and whether the language of instruction was chiefly Latin or Provençal, the *letras* which they learned there no doubt included parts of the trivium. What role rhetoric itself may have played within the trivium, in twelfth-century southern France, is, however, unclear. As regards university instruction, James J. Murphy points out that "the subject of rhetoric is conspicuously absent from university cur-

---

[53] Bruno Panvini, *Le biografie provenzali: valore e attendibilità* (Florence, 1952), p. 108, n. 4. Cf. also Panvini's *Giraldo di Bornelh, trovatore del secolo XII* (Catania, 1949), pp. 100-102.

[54] Scheludko, p. 148.

[55] *Biographies*, p. 581.

[56] *Biographies*, p. 583, n. 4.

ricula until very near the end of the Middle Ages." [57] But of course this time scale takes us beyond the period of our subject; and at any rate the only university in southern France at the height of the troubadours' art, Montpellier, gave chief attention to medicine and law. It is known, though, that "solid rhetorical instruction was given at the University of Paris around 1170." [58]

Presumably, instruction in rhetoric would have taken place at a level lower than the universities, and we have no reason to believe that the troubadours could have learned rhetoric only at established universities. The trivium, including rhetoric, was widely taught elsewhere. For example, John of Salisbury (d. 1180) informs us of Bernard of Chartres (d. ca. 1130) that "in lecturing on the authors he showed what was simple and in accordance with the rules: the grammatical figures, the rhetorical colors, the subtleties of sophistry...." [59] And, about the same time, Bernard's brother Thierry of Chartres "had at his disposal most of the major writings on rhetoric that had been produced up to his own times — Cicero, Quintilian, Grillius, Victorinus, Boethius — and was prepared to use them in explicating what he thought to be one of the most significant of them all: Cicero's *De Inventione*." [60]

---

[57] James J. Murphy, "The Scholastic Condemnation of Rhetoric in the Commentary of Giles of Rome on the *Rhetoric* of Aristotle," in *Arts libéraux et philosophie au moyen-âge: Actes du Quatrième Congrès International de Philosophie Médiévale* (Paris, 1969), p. 833. Similarly, Charles Faulhaber in his thorough study *Latin Rhetorical Study in Thirteenth and Fourteenth Century Castile* (Berkeley, Cal., 1972), has found "nothing ... to indicate the teaching of rhetoric in Spain at either the elementary or the university level before the beginning of the fifteenth century" (p. 140). The classical rhetorical tradition seems to have survived in Spain chiefly through Isidore's *Etimologiae* (cf. Faulhaber, p. 36) until a multiplication of classical, French and then Italian rhetorical influences in the thirteenth century (cf. pp. 29, 48, 50-51, 140, etc.). "Hard" information on medieval curricula and availability of rhetorical works, such as Faulhaber amasses for Castile, remains to be collected and analyzed for the South of France.

[58] Louis J. Paetow, *The Arts Course at Medieval Universities with Special Reference to Grammar and Rhetoric* (Champaign, Ill., 1910), pp. 67-68. Hereafter *The Arts Course*.

[59] Quoted in Helene Wieruszowski, *The Medieval University* (Princeton, 1966), p. 126.

[60] James J. Murphy, "Cicero's Rhetoric in the Middle Ages," *The Quarterly Journal of Speech*, LIII (1967), 340. For more on schools and the troubadours, cf. Pattison, *Raimbaut d'Orange*, p. 22: "In my estimation there can be no doubt about the reality of the influence of the schools on the

The study of rhetorical techniques existed under other names as well: "Rhetoric lost much of its individuality. Its doctrines were often merged with those of grammar; thus, in the *Graecismus* of Eberhard, there is a chapter on the *colores rhetorici*. Frequently it is difficult to draw the line between grammatical and rhetorical instruction." [61] Also, the *ars dictaminis* which came to supplement and, especially in Italy, almost to supplant, the study of rhetoric, in fact owed much to the rhetorical tradition, from the time of Alberic of Monte Cassino's *Flores rhetorici* (ca. 1087) on. [62]

Certainly, then, the troubadours had ample opportunity to assimilate the teachings of rhetoric, just as they clearly had the necessary background and the interest to be capable of doing so. And furthermore, the troubadours' knowledge of rhetoric no doubt derived as much from a few well-worn and widely circulated Latin or vernacular treatises and from a prestigious word-of-mouth tradition as from formal scholastic training.

As good a summary as any of the respect for learning in the Old Provençal culture is furnished by the thirteenth-century romance *Flamenca*. The heroine, depicted as an avid reader, refers at one point to the skills of *dialectica, arismetiqa, astronomia, musica,* and *fesica* (lines 5443-48). And her lover William, raised in Paris, "learned so much of the seven arts that he could teach school anywhere, if he wished" (lines 1622-26). Flamenca's maid states that "Negus hom ses letras non val" (line 4810), and Flamenca agrees readily that all should learn *letras*, for a man without them is as dead (lines 4824-38). The most recent editors of the romance conclude, of the author Bernadet, that "one would not be surprised to discover that he, like William..., had studied with the great doctors who during the thirteenth century were making the University of Paris famous throughout the known world." [63] Although the above-mentioned passages may in fact reflect as much the ideal as the reality of this courtly and refined society, they certainly show at least that a high

---

troubadours; the only questions open to debate are its extent and its exact form," etc.

[61] Paetow, *The Arts Course,* p. 67.
[62] Paetow, pp. 72ff.
[63] Merton J. Hubert and Marion E. Porter, ed. and trans., *The Romance of Flamenca, A Provençal Poem of the 13th Century* (Princeton, 1962), p. 7. All our quotes from this edition, hereafter *Flamenca*.

esteem for *letras* on the part of the troubadours is entirely to be expected in the Old Provençal cultural context.

In addition to their background of formal or informal education, the troubadours were also well acquainted with the work of their predecessors and contemporaries, as is implied by the literary satires we have discussed, by the widespread popularity of the *tenso* and *joc partit* (which required two poets to be in relation with each other either at one court or by "correspondence"), by the troubadours' continually progressing mastery of a formally difficult mode of expression, and by the occasional borrowing of forms and of music, particularly in the *sirventes*, but also in the *canso* and other genres.

A famous poem could inspire more than one imitator, Arnaut Daniel's sestina having for example three: Bertoleme Zorzi (P-C 74.4), Guilhem de Saint Gregori (P-C 233.2), both with the same end words as Arnaut, and Pons Fabre d'Uzes (P-C 376.2), to say nothing of Dante and Petrarch. Further, Arnaut Daniel's poem *Si·m fos Amors de joi donar tan larga* (P-C 29.17; XVII) was imitated, with the same form and rimes, by Bertran de Born twice, by Guilhem de Durfort, and by Uc de Saint Circ; and at least four other poems show reminiscences of Arnaut.[64] But he is by no means the most imitated troubadour. At least ten poems of various troubadours definitely borrow the structures, and often even some of the rimes, of poems of Bernart de Ventadorn, and others show his possible influence.[65] For many other examples of borrowing, one has only to look through the listings in Frank's *Répertoire métrique*.

Occasionally we find what must have been open debates among the troubadours reflected in their works. Sordel, for example, began his famous *planh* on the death of Lord Blacatz with the line:

Plaigner voill en Blacatz en aquest leugier so.
(P-C 437.24; XXVI, 1)

Rising to the challenge, and carrying forward the metaphor of the noble heart to be eaten — but by worthy ladies rather than lords in need of courage — Bertran d'Alamanon somewhat discourteously re-

---

[64] These figures from István Frank, *Répertoire métrique de la poésie des troubadours*, 2 vols. (Paris, 1953, 1957; hereafter *Répertoire métrique*), I, 178; and U. A. Canello, *La vita e le opere del trovatore Arnaldo Daniello* (Halle/Saale, 1883), pp. 41-42.

[65] Appel, *Bernart von Ventadorn*, pp. cviii-cxii.

plies, with the same form and with two of the same rimes, in his *planh* beginning:

> Mout m'es greu d'en Sordel, car l'es faillitz sos sens.
> (P-C 76.12, 1)

And the last word is had by Peire Bremon Ricas Novas, who, again with the same form, starts out:

> Pos partit an lo cor en Sordels e'n Bertrans.
> (P-C 330.14, 1)

Similarly, a whole group of poems, in the genre known in French as *tournoiement des dames*, was composed by various troubadours in the early 1200's. Raimbaut de Vaqueiras' *Carros* (P-C 392.32) was the first; then a lost poem by a N'Aimeric (de Peguilhan?); then Guilhem de la Tor's *Treva* replies, starting:

> Pos n'Aimerics a fag far mesclans' e batailla;
> (P-C 236.5a, 1)

then Albertet de Sestaro (P-C 16.13), rejecting love altogether; and finally Aimeric de Belenoi (P-C 9.21), taking Albertet's form and rimes, makes himself the ladies' champion.

And there are other sorts of literary relationships among troubadours. For example, the several exordia in which Arnaut Daniel uses intensive alliteration probably influenced Guilhem Ademar's poem *Al prim pres dels breus jorns braus* (P-C 9.5). Apparent references to Jaufre Rudel's *amor de lonh* and *alberc de lonh* (P-C 262.2; V, 4, etc.; 16) and his *amors de terra lonhdana* (P-C 262.5) occur in Peire Vidal:

> E s'*alberga*·l seu
> Per *amor* de Deu
> Tener me pot *lonjamen*;
> (P-C 364.29; XVII, 91-93)

> Quar tan m'es *lonh* la *terr*' e·l dous pais
> On es cela vas cui eu sui aclis.
> (P-C 364.33; XLI, 8-9)

Also, two literary references are found in a *tenso* (P-C 10.6; Aimeric de Peguilhan VI) in which Albertet de Sestaro alludes in line 10 to

William IX's song of *dreg nien* (P-C 183.7; IV),[66] while Aimeric de Peguilhan refers in line 32 to Raimbaut d'Aurenga's *No sai que s'es* (P-C 389.28; XXIV).

We also know that jongleurs were expected to be acquainted with both contemporary and earlier troubadours. Thus the *ensenhamen* of Guiraut de Cabreira, who probably flourished in the third quarter of the twelfth century, takes to task the inexcusable ignorance of a certain "Cabra joglar," in these terms:

> Ja vers novel
> Bon d'En Rudel
> Non cug que·t pas sotz lo guingnon,
> De Markabrun
> Ni de negun
> Ni d'En Anfos ni d'En Eblon.
> (P-C 242a.1, 25-30)[67]

A wider sort of literary experiences is suggested by the general influence of Ovid[68] and Vergil, whether direct or through French translations (no Old Provençal translations are known of these two authors); by the troubadours' use of figures from classical mythology, legend or history (Tantalus, Narcissus, Dedalus, Atalanta, Peleus, Helen, Paris, Alexander, and many others); and by the frequent references to medieval literature (Tristan and Isolde, Perceval and Gawain, Floire and Blancheflour, etc.).[69]

---

[66] Another allusion to the same song of William IX may occur in Folquet de Marselha: "Be sai que tot quan faz es dreiz niens" (P-C 155.22; II, 9).

[67] From Bartsch, *Denkmäler*, p. 89; the line *Ni de negun* seems corrupt. Jeanroy identifies the author of the *ensenhamen* with a viscount of Cabrera, "probablement Guiraut III, connu de 1145 à 1179" (*Poésie lyrique*, I, 384). Dates of activity of the cited poets are: Marcabru, ca. 1130-48 (*Ibid.*, I, 384); Alphonse II of Aragon, 1162-96 (*Ibid.*, I, 336); Eble II of Ventadorn, "dès les premières années du XIIe siècle" and at least till 1137 (*Ibid.*, II, 16). So the poems our jongleur should know are certainly not all contemporaneous, but rather belong to two or three different generations.

[68] On Arnaut Daniel's and others' knowledge of Ovid, see Canello, *Arnaldo Daniello*, p. 14. Also: Raymond Gay-Crosier, *Religious Elements in the Secular Lyrics of the Troubadours* (Chapel Hill, 1971), pp. 27-28, and his bibliography.

[69] On classical and medieval figures and references, see Frank M. Chambers, *Proper Names in the Lyrics of the Troubadours* (Chapel Hill, 1971); Christian Stössel, *Die Bilder und Vergleiche der altprovenzalischen Lyrik* (diss. Marburg, 1886), hereafter *Bilder und Vergleiche*; Adolf Birch-Hirschfeld, *Über die den provenzalischen Troubadours des XII. und XIII. Jahrhunderts bekannten epischen Stoffe* (diss. Leipzig, 1878).

Instructions to jongleurs in the *ensenhamens* of Bertran de Paris de Rouergue (P-C 85-1) and Guiraut de Calanso (P-C 243.7a), as well as of Guiraut de Cabreira, have vast lists of literary subjects that every good jongleur was presumably expected to be familiar with, ranging from the stories of Troy and the founding of Rome to "la gran jesta de Carlon" and the Arthurian romances.[70] One example of a well-versed person is Arnaut de Maruelh, who, according to his *vida*, composed poetry, sang well, and also *lesia romans*,[71] which apparently means that he recited or read aloud to his lady from non-lyrical works, most likely *romans courtois* of the antique and Arthurian cycles. And there is no reason to suppose that Arnaut was the only troubadour to possess this very desirable talent.

A different sort of literary culture is exemplified by Uc de Saint Circ, "Maistre" Miquel de la Tor, and their fellow authors of the *vidas* and *razos*. These men of the thirteenth and early fourteenth centuries evidently had the background and the ambition necessary to undertake their biographical form of literary criticism. Specifically, Uc de Saint Circ's own *vida* tells us:

> Aquest N'Ucs si ac gran ren de fraires majors de se. E volgron lo far clerc, e manderon lo a la scola a Monpeslier. E quant ill cuideront qu'el ampares letras, el amparet cansos e vers e sirventes e tensos e coblas, e·ls faich e·ls dich dels valens homes e de las valens domnas que eron al mon, ni eron estat; et ab aquel saber el s'ajoglari.... Gran ren anparet de l'autrui saber e voluntiers l'enseingnet ad autrui....[72]

Even if Uc may not have taken full advantage of the *letras* taught at Montpellier, surely much of the *scola* rubbed off on his vaunted *saber;* he was undoubtedly an educated person. A similar education must be assumed for Raimon Vidal de Besalù and Uc Faidit who around 1200 and 1240 respectively already had the means to study and codify the language and usage of the troubadours. The analytical tradition which they helped to perpetuate, reaching to the various "editions" and successors of the *Leys d'amors*, again makes it hard to believe that the troubadours themselves did not also look at their own works in the manner taught by the schools.

---

[70] All three of these *ensenhamens* are printed in Bartsch, *Denkmäler*, pp. 85-101.
[71] *Biographies*, p. 32.
[72] *Biographies*, pp. 239-240.

In order to believe the troubadours deeply influenced by rhetoric, one need not contend that they spent their spare hours reading the *Rhetorica ad Herennium* or Matthew of Vendôme (though this is certainly possible in some cases). On the other hand, it is not necessary to hold with S. C. Aston that the Latin *Artes versificatoriae* guided only the scholastic and the clerk and not the vernacular poet, nor that the importance of medieval poetic treatises has been generally overestimated.[73] From the varied sorts of evidence we have adduced it does seem that both through direct and indirect channels, the influence of Latinity and its accumulated literary and linguistic knowledge — in the form of rhetoric — cannot be denied with regard to the troubadours: "Ces poètes étaient nourris de rhétorique classique."[74]

E. The Troubadours' Attitudes Toward Their "Craft"

The troubadours' work itself suggests a certain self-image. We have already mentioned their use of two metaphors, *polir un chan* and *daurar un chan*, describing the making or perfecting of poetry. Many similar metaphors place their poetry in the realm of arts and crafts, a concept dating back to the Greek term *poietés*, literally "maker, inventor, workman," whence "composer, poet, author." The troubadours shared the workmanlike attitude toward poetic creation that was held by many of their classical and medieval predecessors and later by the *grands rhétoriqueurs* and by Boileau, who said:

> Hâtez-vous lentement, et sans perdre courage,
> Vingt fois sur le métier remettez votre ouvrage;
> Polissez-le sans cesse et le repolissez....[75]

First of all, *obra* and its derivatives frequently designate the literary work, as do Latin *opus* and French *œuvre*. Among many examples is Aimeric de Peguilhan's boast:

---

[73] S. C. Aston, "The Troubadours and the Concept of Style" (see Intro., n. 3), p. 142.
[74] Albert Henry, oral communication, May, 1969.
[75] Boileau, *L'art poétique*, I, 170-172, in P. V. Delaporte, *L'art poétique de Boileau commenté par Boileau et ses contemporains* (Lille, 1888), I, 355-359.

> Car ieu non veich d'*obra* sotil e prima
> De nuilla leich plus sotil ni plus prim,
> Ni plus adreich *obrier* en cara rima.
> (P-C 10.47; XLVII, 3-5)

Similarly, Lanfranc Cigala refers to poetry with the words *fil* (here "handiwork," literally "thread") and *labor* (P-C 282.5; XII, 33 and 36); and William IX describes poetry as a *mestier* ("craft"):

> Qu'ieu port d'ayselh mestier la flor;
> (P-C 183.2; VI, 4)

(And this association may make the translation of *obrador* in the preceding line more likely "atelier," with Jeanroy,[76] than "study-room," which is Scheludko's interpretation, already mentioned.) Further, the genius of the poet is often compared to that of the *maestre* (a master craftsman or specialized workman). We have seen that Guiraut de Bornelh was known as "maestre dels trobadors"; Other troubadours speak of *maestria* or technical "mastery" of poetry;[77] and the poet Guilhalmi addresses the famed and respected Cercamon as *Maistre* in their *tenso* (P-C 112.1; Cercamon VII).

Other artisan metaphors for poetry refer to specific skills. Thus Cercamon applies the term *bastitz*, "built," to his *vers* (III, 32). Derivatives of Latin *faber* in the sense of "blacksmith" often designate poetry, as when Dante's Guido Guinizelli refers to Arnaut Daniel, the champion of *trobar clus*, as "miglor fabbro del parlar materno."[78] Thus among the troubadours, Peire Raimon de Tolosa uses *fabregar*, "to forge," of poetry:

> Bo·s tanh qu'un novel chan *fabrec*.
> (P-C 355.14; XII, 5)[79]

Other metallurgical metaphors occur in a variety of roots. Thus *afilar*, "to file, sharpen," in Lanfranc Cigala:

---

[76] Alfred Jeanroy, ed., *Les chansons de Guillaume IX, duc d'Aquitaine*, 2d ed. (Paris, 1927), p. 13.
[77] See Bernart Marti, P-C 63.6, V, 74; Lanfranc Cigala, P-C 282.5, XII, 4; etc.
[78] Dante Alighieri, *Purgatorio*, XXVI, 117.
[79] Peire Raimon, at least according to one reading, also compares his verses to tin, *eram*, in P-C 355.4, III, 10; cf. Alfredo Cavaliere, ed., *Le poesie di Peire Raimon de Tolosa* (Florence, 1935), p. 16.

> Mas no·s taing c'om chant *afil*
> Ab tan prima maestria;
> (P-C 282.5; XII, 3-4)

polir, "to polish," and *forbir,* "to burnish," in Guiraut de Bornelh:

> Polira,
> *Forbira*
> Mo chan;
> (P-C 242.16; XXV, 10-12)

limar, "to file," in Arnaut Daniel:

> Obre e *lim*
> Motz de valor;
> (P-C 29.6; II, 12-13)

> Que serant verai e cert
> Qan n'aurai passat la *lima.*
> (P-C 29.10; X, 4)

This *labor limae* metaphor was also commonly used in rhetoric before and after the time of the troubadours.[80]

Another frequent metaphor compares poetry to the weaver's trade by the verbs *lassar* ("to lace, tie, intertwine") and *liar* ("to bind, link, tie up"). Examples are William IX's

> E puesc ne traire·l vers auctor
> Quant er *lassatz*
> (P-C 183.2; VI, 6-7)

and Bernart Marti's

> E qui belhs motz *lass' e lia*
> De belh' art s'es entremes.
> (P-C 63.6; V, 75-76)

The rather mysterious word *entrebescar,* "to intertwine, entangle," is also applied to poetry, as in Raimbaut d'Aurenga's line

---

[80] On these metaphors, see Lausberg, *Handbuch,* § 1244, art. *limare,* with references among others to Horace, *Ars poetica,* line 291, "limae labor et mora"; *ibid.,* § 1244, art. *polire;* also *verba polita* in Matthew of Vendôme, *Ars versificatoria,* § 9, in Faral, *Arts poétiques,* p. 153; and the lines quoted above from Boileau, with further references to these and related metaphors in the ed. cited in our note 75, pp. 355-362.

> Cars bruns e tenhs motz *entrebesc*.
> (P-C 389.22; I, 19)

In general these weaving metaphors seem to designate the dense and artful word-weaving techniques of *trobar clus*.

Another series of metaphors juxtaposes poetry and carpentry. We find for example *planar*, "to plane, smooth, polish," as well as *entalhar*, "to sculpt," and other terms of the trades, in Cerverí de Gerona:

> *Obra sobtil, prim'e trasforia*
> Volgra *polir* si agues prim engeyn,
> Mas tot ades *entayll* e *plan* e lim
> Homils motz clars e un leuger sonet.
> (P-C 434a.43; LXXXVII, 1-4)

Perhaps the most famous example of such words is Arnaut Daniel's use of *capuzar* and *dolar*, both meaning "to plane":

> En cest sonet coind' e leri
> Fauc mots e *capuig* e *doli*.
> (P-C 29.10; X, 1-2)

The image of the poet as an *obrier* in wood and metal is expressed also by Aimeric de Pegulhan:

> Ses mon *apleich*   non vau ni ses ma *lima,*
>   Ab que *fabreich*   motz et *aplan* e *lim,*
> Car ieu non veich   d'*obra* sotil e prima
>   De nuilla leich   plus sotil ni plus prim,
> Ni plus adreich   *obrier* en cara rima
>   Ni plus *pesseich*   sos digz ni mieills los rim.
> (P-C 10.47; XLVII, 1-6)

These comparisons and many others show the healthy pride which the troubadours took in their work. This pride, leading to self-praise and to the disparaging of their fellows through satires and parodies, suggests that there existed certain established criteria according to which a troubadour could consider, or at least claim, his own creations to be superior. In a typical example, Guiraut de Bornelh immodestly announces that his audience is about to hear a "perfect song":

> Ar auziretz
> Encabalitz chantars.
> (P-C 242.17; XXX, 1-2)

Bernart de Ventadorn is particularly confident of his own excellence; he begins one poem by proclaiming:

> Non es meravelha s'eu chan
> Melhs de nul autre chantador,
> Que plus me tra·l cors vas amor
> E melhs sui faihz a so coman;
> (P-C 70.31; I, 1-4)

and his opinion that his own sincerity in love is the reason for his superiority is shared by many of his modern readers.

A troubadour's own editorial comments can also come at the end of a poem. Jaufre Rudel, for example, ends a poem by anticipating its successful performance:

> Bos es lo vers, qu'anc no·i falhi,
> Et tot so que·i es ben esta;
> E sel que de mi l'apenra
> Gart se no·l franha ni·l pessi;
> Car si l'auran en Caersi
> En Bertrans e·l coms en Tolza, a, a.
>
> Bos es lo vers, e faran hi
> Calque re don hom chantara, a, a.
> (P-C 262.3; VI, 31-38)

Instructing the jongleur not to "break" or "smash" the poet's work is frequent; and well-established troubadours apparently employed one or two jongleurs to broadcast their poems. Albertet de Sestaro, for example, instructs his jongleur by name:

> Peirol, violatz e chantaz cointamen
> De ma chanzon los mots e·l so leugier.
> (P-C 16.8; VII, 43-44)

And Jaufre Rudel looks forward to his work being learned, by more than one "singer," and heard, by courtly audiences of course:

> Adoncs vuelh mos chans si'auzitz,
> Et aprendetz lo, chantador!
> (P-C 262.1; IV, 52-53)

The kind of self-conscious climate in which the troubadours composed is illustrated by a *razo* in which Arnaut Daniel is challenged by another troubadour in the art of wielding *caras rimas*. The contestants, each having wagered his horse, are enclosed in separate, adjoining chambers by order of Richard the Lion-Hearted, and are allotted for their compositions "only" ten days; and the fact that the biographer considers this to be a brief time period for composing one poem shows the literary perfectionism of that culture. Arnaut, being in an uninspired frame of mind, learns by heart his rival's song, which he overhears, and boldly claims it as his own when the contest is to be judged. But all is set aright: Richard accepts the joke against the sanctity of individual creation, and rewards both poets handsomely.[81]

A more regular sort of contest was that held periodically at Le Puy (Haute-Loire), beginning in the mid or late twelfth century. A golden sparrow-hawk was awarded to the best knight, and poems were also judged according to criteria which it would be fascinating to know.[82] And it is reasonable to suppose that similar contests were held elsewhere, perhaps indeed at whatever court several troubadours happened to come together at the same time.

To insure that he would receive due credit, whether in public contest or in private performance, the troubadour occasionally wrote his own name into his work, usually in a tornada. Two of Cercamon's poems (P-C 112.4 and 3a; I and V) have tornadas beginning with the expression "Cercamon says"; and Cercamon also names himself in the final stanza of his *planh* on William X (P-C 112.2a; VI). Similarly, Arnaut Daniel proudly names himself at the end of all but three of his surviving poems, notably in the famous first-person self-characterization known to Petrarch:

> Ieu sui Arnautz q'amas l'aura,
> E chatz la lebre ab lo bou
> E nadi contra suberna.
> (P-C 29.10; X, 43-45)

Two tornadas of Bernart combine such self-identification with the self-satisfaction we have commented on:

---

[81] *Biographies*, pp. 62-63.
[82] See Reto R. Bezzola, *Les origines et la formation de la littérature courtoise en Occident*, part III, vol. II (Paris, 1963), 329.

> Lo vers es fis e naturaus
> E bos celui qui be l'enten;
> E melher es, qui·l joi aten.
>
> Bernartz de Ventadorn l'enten,
> E·l di e·l fai, e·l joi n'aten.
> (P-C 70.15; II, 50-54)

In a similar statement of his own skill, Marcabru cannot even wait till the end of his crusade song to inform us:

> Fetz Marcabrus los motz e·l so;
> (P-C 293.35, 2)

and in the middle of one poem Bernart Marti identifies himself, somewhat mysteriously, as "Bernart Martin lo Pintor" (P-C 63.5; IV, 38).

All that this section has discussed implies a conscious originality on the troubadours' part. A quest for an original subject (*razo*) for a song is revealed by Uc de Saint Circ:

> Longamen ai atenduda
> Una razon avinen
> Don fezes chansson plazen,
> Mas ancar no m'es venguda.
> (P-C 457.18; X, 1-4)

More frequently, a poet begins by announcing an original melody, a *so novel*, as when Bernart Marti says:

> Farai un vers ab son novelh;
> (P-C 63.7; VI, 1)

and, more pretentiously, Peire de Blai announces:

> En est son faz chansoneta *novelha*;
> *Novelha* es quar ieu chan de *novelh*.
> (P-C 328.1, 1-2)

The same may already be suggested by William IX's lines

> Farai chansoneta nueva
> Ans que vent ni gel ni plueva.
> (P-C 183.6; VIII, 1-2)

If so, it is testimony to the early quest in the Provençal lyric for formal originality, whose prestige is amply testified by the great variety of metrical patterns in Frank's *Répertoire métrique*.

A corollary to this esteem for original melody and form is that borrowing, when it does take place, is often acknowledged. For example, Uc de Saint Circ identifies two of his melodies as borrowed from En Arnaut Plagues (P-C 457.21 and 42; XXII and XXIII). Or, Bertran de Born announces:

Conselh vuolh dar el so de n'Alamanda,
(P-C 80.13, 25)

acknowledging his debt to Guiraut de Bornelh's poem beginning:

Si·us quer conselh, bel' ami' Alamanda.
(P-C 242.69; LXIX, 1)

Such concern for literary property is quite exceptional in the Middle Ages, which generally admitted the most extensive sort of unacknowledged borrowing, which we would call plagiarism or even literary theft. But respect for literary property is to be expected where the different factors we have described combine to make originality and recognition not only artistically but also socially and even economically important. The ultimate reward of a troubadour's skill can be, according to his ambitions, self-satisfaction, his lady's favors, public acclaim, or a gift from his patron, but in any case he is engaged in a competitive and skill-demanding craft whose technical practices we will investigate in the following chapters.

To sum up what we have seen of the ways in which the troubadours learned their art, composed, and sang: varied sorts of contemporary and slightly posterior evidence — their biographers, their anthologists, scholars like Guilhem Molinier, their own satires, metaphors, self-praise, signatures, and numerous references to the poetic art — all demonstrate a continuous esthetic attitude and an unbroken literary tradition which interpreted poetry as a highly conscious, careful, well-planned, and technically artful means of successful self-expression and ultimately of self-advancement in a society which to a large degree recognized, appreciated, and rewarded musical and poetic skills.

CHAPTER II

FIGURES OF REPETITION

A. Classification of Old Provençal Means of Expressions

Now that we have shown the importance of style to the troubadours and their contemporaries, we can begin to penetrate the essential nature of their collective and individual styles.

Long ago Diez wrote that "the possession of a literary history without that of a literature is a pitiful thing."[1] Diez was actually lamenting the lesser advancement of grammar, lexicology and textual criticism than of literary history. Yet in a different sense, we still possess a literary history and no literature. Until stylistic synthesis is undertaken, we cannot claim complete "possession" of the Provençal lyric. Although we cannot here inventory and analyze all the stylistic techniques at the troubadours' disposal, we can at least establish criteria for choosing a small number of related stylistic means, a "bouquet" which it will be within our grasp to study in meaningful depth.

Stylistic means have, as we have seen, traditionally been classified as figures of word (*figurae verborum* or *elocutionis*) and figures of idea (*figurae sententiarum* or *sententiae*), the latter often including tropes (*tropi*). Tropes (i.e., metaphor, including personification; metonymy; synechdoche; hyperbole; litotes; periphrasis; irony; emphasis; autonomasia) and figures of idea (i.e., apostrophe, "rhetorical question," antithesis, oxymoron, exclamation, comparison, allegory, etc.) actually describe more the finding and arranging of ideas, the "invention" of a poem, than the actual poetic execution. As Lausberg tells us,

---

[1] Diez, *Poesie*, p. x: "... Der besitz einer Literaturgeschichte ohne den einer Litteratur ein ärmliches Ding ist."

Figurae elocutionis concern... linguistic concretization itself, *figurae sententiae* on the other hand go beyond the domain of *elocutio* and concern the conception of thoughts. Consequently, *figurae elocutionis* actually belong under the heading of *elocutio*, while *figurae sententiae* should properly be treated under the heading of *inventio*.[2]

Our concern with style leads us to choose as our subject this "linguistic concretization" over "the conception of thoughts," hence *elocutio* over *inventio* and figures of word over figures of idea. It is true that some of the most beautiful and characteristic Provençal passages and poems rely on metaphor and comparison for their effect. Still, these and other figures of idea are often expressed with the aid of figures of word, so that we will not be entirely ignoring a whole aspect of the troubadours' work.

The same must be said of music. Music comprises half the troubadours' art, and it is regrettable to separate word from music. Yet we are concerned with literary style, and musical style is a wholly different thing although the two can cooperate for common effect. In this respect, music will enter our discussion occasionally as a reinforcer of verbal patterns.

Within our *figurae elocutionis*, we must again make a choice. One can here discern different stylistic levels: phonetic, lexical, syntactical and formal. The formal level is really a conventionalized outgrowth of the other three. A poet's choice of form — of syllabification, rime scheme, stanza pattern, etc. — certainly replies to stylistic criteria. Yet because form, like music, remains constant through a troubadour poem while the thought and sentiment vary, the link between the poet's emotions and his expression of them becomes less direct on the formal level, hence more difficult to analyze. Form will therefore figure in our study only to the extent that, in repeated or morphological rimes, for example, it represents a regularization or a codification of the other stylistic impulses which are to be examined.

---

[2] Lausberg, *Handbuch*, § 603: "Die *figurae elocutionis* betreffen die... sprachliche Konkretisierung selbst, die *figurae sententiae* dagegen überschreiten den Bereich der *elocutio* und betreffen die Konzipierung der Gedanken. Somit gehören die *figurae elocutionis* genuin zum Kapitel der *elocutio*, während die *figurae sententiae* eigentlich im Kapitel der *inventio*... zu behandeln wären."

Likewise, the syntactical level of style will be set aside, except as syntax serves to join figures of word together. The structural relations within sound or word patterns certainly depend on syntactical features such as grammatical constructions and word order; but these must in themselves be considered subsidiary to stylistic means, which actually create the poetic effects that make poetry what it is.

We are therefore left with word figures on the phonetic and lexical levels. Now, such figures can hardly consist of a single sound or word in itself, except as a sound may have some inherent suggestivity or as a word may belong to some special register of speech or technical vocabulary. Yet when sounds or words combine into patterns of the poet's conscious or unconscious choice, we have style. And such patterns must be described in terms of repetition and differentiation. If in a common context two or more features differ, this is hardly a subject of comment; but if they are the same, then they produce a stylistic structure in Zumthor's definition:

> *Structure*: ensemble d'éléments ayant un rapport mutuel autre que de simple addition ou successivité, et tel qu'il possède une valeur propre, une unité supérieure à celle de chacun de ses composants.[3]

Thus, a structure based on the repetitive principle will have a greater stylistic impact than the sum of its individual components, whether this structure consists of repeated words, roots or sounds or two of these or all together. After all,

> Repetition of a sound, syllable, word, phrase, line, stanza or metrical pattern is a basic unifying device in all poetry.[4]

And this is especially true of the troubadours' poetry.

B. Figures of Repetition and the Troubadours

We therefore choose to discuss those figures of word which are also figures of repetition. Different literatures may well prefer dif-

---

[3] Zumthor, *Langue et techniques*, p. 5.
[4] Alex Preminger, ed., *Princeton Encyclopedia of Poetry and Poetics* (Princeton, 1965), art. "Repetition," p. 699. Hereafter *Encyclopedia*.

ferent figures of repetition, but in Provençal, observation shows that repetition is most important on the level of words (repetition proper), of roots (morphemic repetition) and of sounds (alliteration, assonance, etc.). It would seem hard to confuse these different stylistic levels; each has its own purposes, structures and effects. Nevertheless, confusion has been frequent ever since traditional rhetoric applied such terms as *paronomasia, annominatio* and *repetitio* to several of these devices at the same time. Similarly, it is often unclear exactly what many modern critics mean by "repetition." Definition is therefore in order.

We will use "repetition," when unqualified, to designate lexical or lexemic repetition, that is, repetition of a word or group of words without change of meaning or pronunciation. Such repetition is an essential means of expression which cannot be replaced by synonymy. Real synonyms do not exist; each word is unique, and as Pascal says,

> Quand dans un discours se trouvent des mots répétés, et qu'essayant de les corriger, on les trouve si propres qu'on gâterait le discours, il faut les laisser.[5]

Our use of the term "repetition" will also include morphologically different but phonetically identical forms of one word, such as *gais* or *cavals,* both being nominative singular or oblique plural. The reason for this is that words showing only variation of function, without variation of pronunciation, are physically and psychologically closer to simple word repetition than to our second category, morphemic repetition.

Morphemic repetition, in our definition, is word repetition varied by a change of morphological and phonetic elements. This variation can range from a difference of one phoneme (*gais-gai*) to a difference of one syllable (*caval-cavaliers*) or more (*trob-atrobaire*). Morphemic repetition and its subtypes — morphological figure, etymological figure and composition — will be described in chapter IV.

Sound effects, the subject of our chapter V, are due to any repetition of phonemes that has an identifiable poetic value. This category will include homophonous words, whether they are etymologically

---

[5] Pascal, *Pensées,* quoted in William K. Wimsatt, Jr., *The Verbal Icon: Studies in the Meaning of Poetry* (Lexington, Ky., 1967), p. 186.

related (e.g., *vent*, "wind" and "that it blow") or unrelated (e.g., *cors*, "heart" and "body"). The reason for this classification is that homophony, the most complete form of phonetic similarity between words, is far rarer and more striking than any morphemic repetition that may happen to be involved.

And with this, the *Leys d'amors* appear to agree, condemning the riming of homophonous forms of a single root as *mot pezan* (i.e., words repeated without justification):

> ...Diversitatz de cas, de temps, ni de persona, can la votz rema una meteysha en la fi, no escuza mot pezan... (III, 92).

On the other hand, homophonous words of *different* roots (*motz equivocz*) and simple repeated words are carefully distinguished by the *Leys*, both in the rime and not:

> Li equivoc coma *fi* e *fi*... no fan vici de mot tornat, ans aytals acordansas equivocas reputam per mot belas e subtils (III, 96).

> ...Li veray equivoc no fan mot pezan (III, 92).

And further, homophonous words are distinguished from words having morphemic repetition either through composition or through different endings:

> ...Li compost no fan vici de mot pezan, coma *tener-retener-mantener, meni-ameni-desmeni-remeni* (III, 90).

> ...Si la fi de la dictio era diversa, adonx no faria vici de mot pezan, coma *coms-comte, clercz-clerc-clergues, ama-ame* et enayssi de lors semblans (III, 92).

This care for distinguishing different figures of repetition leads Guilhem Molinier to compare and contrast various sorts of word repetition and root repetition — *conduplicatio, epizeuzi, traductio, complexio, agnominatio,* and *poliptoton* — according in part to whether they show *variamen de cazes* or employ *una meteyssha dictio* in *un meteysh cas* (III, 180).

It is less easy, since the two often coincide, to distinguish sound repetition from root repetition. Some confusion of terms has arisen over cases like Guilhem de Montanhagol's poem beginning

A Lunel lutz una luna luzens
Qe dona lum sobre totas lugors.
(P-C 225.1; II, 1-2)

In this stanza, for further discussion of which see p. 172, below, Franco Branciforti says we have *replicatio* (alliteration), which "come si sa, costituisce gran parte della tecnica dei trovatori." [6]

But is this example really most accurately labeled "alliteration"? It would be convenient to be able to ask the poet whether his primary impulse in writing these lines was concerned with sounds or with roots — though even a modern poet would probably be unable to reply. So we are left to suppositions. Noting that all the words in *lu-* in this stanza except the place-name are etymologically related, and belong to the semantic field of light, [7] we can conclude that the dominant figure of repetition is here morphemic repetition and that alliteration is more an incidental or supportive factor. After all, repetition of a word or root is a "heavier" device than repetition of one or two phonemes. Thus, perhaps more properly than Branciforti, Coulet describes the case at hand as one of "répétitions de mots de même racine"; and Ricketts notes with Jeanroy that Montanhagol's alliteration derives chiefly from cognate words. [8]

In the preceding example, we can speak of "convergence" of alliteration with morphemic repetition; and of this, Guilhem Molinier provides another fine example in his *cobla refrancha*:

Corta, yest cortz de tota cortezia;
Quar de cortes descortes fas tot dia,
Menten, meten, prenden am desmezura,
Perden, penden, soen ses forfachura,

---

[6] Franco Branciforti, "Note al testo di Guilhem de Montanhagol," *Filologia e Letteratura*, XIV (1968), 349. Branciforti refers us to two passages in the *Leys d'Amors*, one on *replicatio*, the other on *derivatio* (in Anglade, *Las Leys d'Amors*, II, 129 and III, 19-22). But the two figures must be carefully distinguished.

[7] Antoine Meillet and Alfred Ernout, *Dictionnaire étymologique de la langue latine*, 2d ed. (Paris, 1939), art. *lūc-luc*. Although the place name Lunel is probably derived from a Gaulish proper name, Montanhagol no doubt believed it related to *luna* nonetheless.

[8] Jules Coulet, ed., *Le troubadour Guilhem Montanhagol* (Toulouse, 1898), p. 65, n. 1; Peter T. Ricketts, ed., *Les poésies de Guilhem Montanhagol, troubadour provençal du XIII⁰ siècle* (Toronto, 1964), p. 37; Jeanroy, *Poésie lyrique*, II, 92.

> Donan tal dan, dampnan et absolven,
> En tan que·s fan paubres li ric manen.
> A son gran greu de si meteys se pleia
> Qui longamen, cortz, vostre cors corteia (III, 170-172).

And Molinier is conscious of the importance of this "convergence," for he writes of *paronomazia* (our morphemic repetition):

> Et acorda se esta figura am replicatio ... en aysso que motas dictios comenso per una meteyssha letra o per una meteyssha sillaba, segon que par per l'isshample ayssi pauzat, et am rim faysshuc ... en aysso que atyals dictios son semblans o quaysh semblans en la fi (III, 172).

That is, morphemic repetition, alliteration, and non-methodical internal rime can coincide in the same words. Obviously, word repetition and to a large degree root repetition inevitably produce sound repetition. When this occurs in reasonable proximity, then we have "automatic convergence" of figures of repetition.

In a wider sense, chapter VI will define convergence also as the cooperation of different figures for common effect not only in the same words but also in the same passage, whether in an enumerative relation or not. It is evident that each poetic means is part of a whole and must not be viewed in isolation. Therefore, even while discussing the individual figures, we will use this poetic and stylistic whole as a point of reference.

C. Methods

Ideally, the whole troubadour corpus should be examined for figures of repetition. However, reasonable conclusions can be drawn from any justifiable sample. Different troubadours may have different habits and preferences, but their basic stock of poetic means remained constant. The troubadours selected among extant means without creating new ones; and no basically new structural principles enter the Old Provençal lyric after William IX. So we may select a few troubadours to represent all.

Our immediate corpus will include the works of three early troubadours, William IX, Cercamon, and Jaufre Rudel, and the more extensive production of three "classical" troubadours, Bernart de Ventadorn, Peire Vidal, and Arnaut Daniel. All of these flourished in the twelfth century, the *Blütezeit* of the Provençal lyric. One of these troubadours, Arnaut Daniel, represents the school of *trobar clus,* the others *trobar leu*; yet it will be seen that all six use figures of repetition in almost the same way. It would be profitable to include other troubadours, especially Marcabru, the most obscure troubadour, and Bertran de Born and Guiraut de Bornelh, two of the most prolific. But enough reference will be made to these and many others, when the occasion warrants, to provide an adequate survey of the range of Old Provençal style.

With respect to genre, the *canso* or song will inevitably dominate our study as it does the lyric output. Yet the *sirventes, alba, planh,* and so forth partake of the same stylistic principles and will be included in our discussions and statistics. *Tensos,* however, will not be considered, because the nature of dialogue may alter the "mix" of stylistic means, and because their dual authorship makes them awkward to use for statistical purposes.

The importance of statistics must not be exaggerated, yet they can confirm findings reached by other means. It is for example a fact that rime word repetition is more frequent than derivative rime in Peire Vidal's work. This statistic is subject to evaluation and interpretation, but not to contradiction. Or when we compute, in different poets, the average number of members belonging to groups in alliteration or assonance, this contributes a useful quantitative comparison. (Computing the number of members rather than of groups seems more significant because the size of groups varies greatly, while it can be held that two alliterating groups of two members each have approximately the impact of one group of four members, and so on.)

A distinction we will be making frequently is that between "major" and "minor" words or parts of speech. In our definition, "major" parts of speech are those which carry a substantial semantic value: verbs, substantives, adjectives, and adverbs. Of these, the first three permit variation by inflection (conjugation or declension), and hence are very conducive to morphological figure; and all four are capable of building on roots which occur in one or more of the other categories (e.g., *amar, amor, amoros, amorozamen*). "Minor" parts of speech, on the other hand, are those which carry only a limited semantic burden: prepositions, conjunctions, interjections, articles, and pronouns. Of these, the first three are invariable, while the last two are capable of some variation; members of all five categories are very often monosyllabic. In general, we will find the major parts of speech forming the most "weighty" figures of repetition, while the minor parts of speech contribute subsidiary, "supportive" figures which are often quantitatively more numerous, especially in simple word repetition.

Finally, we must emphasize that "un procédé stylistique ne vient jamais seul — ou presque." [9] Many of our examples will therefore illustrate more than one figure of repetition or more than one type of a single figure of repetition. Such cases will be considered under the figure which seems the most significant or powerful in the immediate context, and other figures will be seen as "supportive," "accessory," or "auxiliary." This system will allow us to discuss the inner workings of each figure of repetition, hence of each factor contributing to the convergence of figures of repetition; then, our final chapter will put these poetic "parts" back together to show how they cooperate and reinforce each other in expressing the poet's message.

---

[9] Riffaterre, *"Pléiades"* (cf. Intro., n. 13), p. 144.

CHAPTER III

WORD REPETITION

Although all the stylistic means treated in this study are variations on the theme of repetition, the unqualified term "repetition" will designate any expressive repetition of words or word groups whose proximity, common context or similar structural position produces a reinforced effect greater than the sum of its parts. In Riffaterre's words, *"le fait que le mot est répété traduit l'intensité du concept et le besoin d'expressivité qui en résulte."* [1]

Our purpose is to demonstrate the importance, varieties, and potentialities of repetition in the troubadours' art. The subject must first be discussed, briefly, in terms of modern criticism and medieval rhetoric. Then the troubadours' practice will be examined first according to position in the line, then according to position in the stanzaic and melodic structure, and finally in the context of the whole poem. The size of repetitive groups will be referred to throughout, and their grammatical nature will be discussed in a last section. However, the technical side must never be allowed to dominate the poetic.

Throughout, Leo Spitzer's warning must be borne in mind: "The mere repetition of words, no more than any other stylistic device, is not anything formulable in the abstract, but must always be felt and tested against the background of the particular psychic climate." [2] That is, repetition should be discussed in terms less of numbers than

---

[1] Riffaterre, *Pléiades*, p. 122.
[2] Leo Spitzer, "Speech and Language in *Inferno* XIII," in John Freccero, ed., *Dante* (Englewood Cliffs, N.J., 1965), p. 95. Hereafter *"Inferno XIII."*

of effect in particular poetic contexts; and this will be our guiding principle.

A. The Modern View

The modern view of word repetition has been unnecessarily negative. The classical French ideal of "purity" has propagated the opinion that repetition — especially, but not only, in the rime — betrays incompetence, negligence, or at best bad taste on the part of the writer. The condemnation of repetition in Pierre Larousse's classic *Cours de style*,[3] quoted from such an authority as d'Alembert, represents the influences to which many a generation of school children has been subjected. Thus Riffaterre pictures Gobineau feeling obliged to "correct" his spontaneous repetitions due to a "désir de varier, sans doute, mais plus probablement encore influence de l'enseignement où la tradition fleurit, encore aujourd'hui, de considérer la répétition comme la plus grave des gaucheries."[4]

Modern French style manuals still tend to ignore the artistic potentialities of repetition. Typically, Marouzeau pictures repetition as hovering between carelessness and monotony, and he enthusiastically denounces selected cases of excessive repetition as "tout près de l'insupportable et du ridicule" or worse.[5] Unwilling to admit that repetition can be a unique, hence irreplaceable, mode of intensification, he implies that *variation* (by synonyms) or *reprise approximative* (by morphemic repetition) will do just as well in stressing any given concept.

Some critics, however, have appreciated the stylistic importance of repetition on both conscious and unconscious levels.[6] Thus Riffaterre distinguishes the *tic* (repetition of obsessive words betraying "une

---

[3] Pierre Larousse, *Cours de style: Livre de l'élève* (52nd ed.; Paris, n.d.), p. 5.

[4] Riffaterre, *Pléiades*, p. 123.

[5] Jules Marouzeau, *Précis de stylistique française* (Paris, 1946), pp. 164-167.

[6] For the psychology of intensification by word and root repetition, cf. Leo Spitzer, "Paronomasie im Spanischen", *Stilstudien* (Munich, 1928), I, 101-108, with examples like It. *andar paese paese*, Sp. *de solo a solo*, Fr. *vis-à-vis*, etc.

intensité subconsciente") from *répétition voulue*.[7] These *tics*, identified by their abnormal frequency, are none other than the *Lieblingswörter* discussed by Spitzer[8] and the *mots-thèmes* and *mots-clés*, determined by frequency and impact, found in Valéry's work by Pierre Guiraud.[9] But this distinction *tic-répétition voulue* can hardly be made for the troubadours. Both lyric brevity and careful workmanship imply an awareness of repetition on their part and justify seeking its presumable purposes and corresponding results in concrete contexts.

However, troubadour editors have rarely commented on repetition in this light. Not only simple internal repetition but even anaphora and rime word repetition have been generally ignored. At best, scholars will mention repetition only as a methodical principle of stanza construction. Thus Bartsch treats well though briefly the linking of lines or stanzas through rime word repetition,[10] and Frank gives a useful list of all troubadour poems using refrains, *coblas capfinidas* and refrain words.[11] However, a negative tone prevails concerning the troubadours' supposed excesses in this direction. Thus Diez denounces as useless *Tändeleien* the use of one word twice in any line or once in each line of a stanza, and other *ähnliche Spitzfindigkeiten*.[12] But one must not give undue attention to the mechanical side of the troubadours' art, nor neglect the contemporary esthetic context in which their taste and works took form.

It must be realized that structural repetition is a far more basic tool of expression in medieval than in modern literatures. For example, medieval Latin metrical love poetry uses the refrain frequently.[13] The *chanson de geste* exploits simple "direct repetition" of words, and further extends the principle in "transformed parallelism."[14] This

---

[7] Riffaterre, *Pléiades*, pp. 117, 122-133. Riffaterre's reviewer H. Hatzfeld, however, protests in *Romanic Review*, XLVIII (1957), 219-222, against this distinction.
[8] Leo Spitzer, *Stilstudien*, II (2nd ed.; Munich, 1961), notably in Proust, Péguy and especially Boileau (p. 4 ff.).
[9] Pierre Guiraud, *Langue et versification d'après l'œuvre de Paul Valéry* (Paris, 1953).
[10] Karl Bartsch, "Reimkunst," pp. 178-182.
[11] Frank, *Répertoire métrique*, II, pp. 58-67.
[12] F. Diez, *Poesie*, pp. 86-88 (i.e., "triflings; similar subtleties").
[13] Peter Dronke, *Medieval Latin*, I, pp. 257-263.
[14] On these terms, cf. F. M. Warren, "Some Features of Style in Early French Narrative Poetry (1150-1170)," parts I-II, *Modern Philology*, III (1905-06), no. 2, pp. 1-31 and no. 4, pp. 1-27; and Jean Rychner, *La*

approximate repetition of a phrase or line using different rime words, when in the first lines of successive or otherwise related stanzas, produces the *laisses similaires* which are so characteristic of the *Chanson de Roland*, for example those beginning in haunting geographical descriptions such as

> Halt sunt li pui et li val tenebrús (814);
> Halt sunt li pui et tenebrus et grant (1830).

Also, both the Middle High German novel and lyric often use word repetition (like morphemic repetition) to stress thematic key ideas (*Leitbegriffe*) and words (*Leitwörter*).[15] In medieval Latin, French, and German literatures, then, word repetition serves thematic emphasis and architectural structure; if anything, the device has still greater importance in the Provençal lyric.

B. The Medieval Context

B 1. *Traditional Rhetoric*

The troubadours' familiarity with the stylistic device of repetition is made likely by evidence from contemporary rhetoric and from its later, specifically Provençal offspring, the *Leys d'amors*. Medieval rhetoric, ever attentive to subtle distinctions, groups several different forms of word repetition under the general heading of *conduplicatio* or *repetitio*.[16] The following chart summarizes the types of *Wiederholung* described in Lausberg's *Handbuch* (§ 612-632) and *Elemente* (§ 242-274). Each category often bears several synonymous titles; terms having two or more meanings in rhetoric are italicized to warn of the danger of ambiguity. The position of repeated words or ex-

---

chanson de geste (Geneva, 1955), especially his remarks on epic formulae in chapter 5. Zumthor (*Langue et techniques*, pp. 112-114) gives a series of verses spoken by Roland beginning in *(Jo)l'en cunquis* plus geographical names; and he notes variations on *esperons* modified by different adjectives and adjectival locutions like *d'or fin, burniz*, etc.

[15] Cf. Karl-Heinz Schirmer, *Stil- und Motivuntersuchungen zur mittelhochdeutschen Versnovelle* (Tübingen, 1969), pp. 48-55; and Vickie Ziegler, "Reinmar von Hagenau and His School: A Study in Leitword Technique" (Diss., Yale German Department, 1970).

[16] *Repetitio* is ambiguous and can also refer to two different subtypes of word repetition and to alliteration.

pressions in metrical or syntactic groups is represented schematically by these symbols:

/.../	a metrical or syntactic group
x	a repeated word or expression
y	a second repeated word or expression
( )	an optional element

Chart 1:

Figures of Word Repetition in Medieval Rhetoric

position of repeated words or expressions in metrical or synctactic groups	name in classical and medieval rhetoric
1. general	conduplicatio, *repetitio*
2. /x..x/	redditio, inclusio, epanadiplosis, k y k l o s, prosapodosis
3A. /(..)xx(x)(..)/	iteratio, pallillogia, epizeuxis ⎫
3B. /(..)x..x(..)/	separatio, interiectio, diakote, diastole ⎬ geminatio
3C. /(..)xyxy(..)/	repetitio, epanalepsis ⎭
4. /x../x../	anaphora, *repetitio*
5. /..x/..x/	epistrophe, conversio, epiphora
6. /..x/x../	reduplicatio, a n a d i p l o s i s, *epanadiplosis*, epanastrophe
7. /x..y/x..y/	complexio
8. /..x/x..y/y../	gradatio, climax, ascensus, conexio, catena, epiploke

These distinctions according to position are not mere technicalities; different categories, as we shall see for the troubadours, have their own characteristic uses and effects, both structural and poetic. The place of repetition in traditional rhetoric both introduces and justifies the detail of our discussion of the troubadours, who were certainly capable of exploiting the resources of rhetoric at suitable times and places. Within the rhetorical system, these different sorts of word repetition, like all figures of words (*figurae elocutionis*) and colors of rhetoric (*colores rhetorici*) contribute to *ornatus facilis* ("easy adornment" of style) and to *amplificatio* ("development" of ideas).[17] And *amplificatio* on the theme of love is the prime purpose of the troubadours' art.

B 2. *The "Leys d'amors"*

The *Leys d'amors'* treatment of repetition is largely derived from medieval rhetoric, as the following chart shows. The same categories

---

[17] Cf. Faral, *Arts poétiques*, p. 61.

and symbols are used as before, except that repetition at the cesura, here indicated by italicized *x*, has been added as category 9; and different sorts of *geminatio* are not distinguished. Uninterrupted italicization indicates that the same term designates the same category in the preceding chart; non-continuous italicization, that the same words designates a different category above. The four columns show the *Leys'* classification of repetition according to function: unjustified repetition is a *vice;* repetition with intent and regularity is a *figure of speech* or *flower of rhetoric;* [18] a figure or flower extended throughout stanzas produces different sorts of repetitive *coblas*.

Chart 2:

Figures of Word Repetition in the "Leys d'amors"

position of repeated words or expressions in metrical groups (i.e., verses)	name according to the Leys d'amors			
	VICE	FIGURE	FLOWER	COBLAS
1. general	mot pesan		conduplicatio	deffrenadas
2. /x..x/		epinalensi		recordativas
3. /(..)xx(..)/	"	epizeuzi epymone [19]		affectuosas
4. /x../x../	"	anafora	repeticio	capdenals
5. /..x/..x/	mot tornat bordo tornat		conversio	retronchadas
6. /..x/x../		anadyplozi		
7. /x..y/x..y/			complexio	duplicativas
8. /..x/x..y/y..z/		anadyplozi		capfinidas
9A. /..x..x/	pauza tornada		conversio	
9B. /..x../..x../				

From this largely self-explanatory chart, it will be seen that the dichotomy vice-virtue extends through most categories. The basic vice of repetition is *mot pesan* (III, 88-94, 370), literally "heavy words." In special positions this "vice" becomes *mot tornat* (repeated rime words), *bordo tornat* (repetition of a whole line) or *pauza tornada*

---

[18] Technically, "der *ornatus* mit dem Akzent auf der *varietas* ... heißt *flos*" (Lansberg, *Handbuch*, § 540, 8); but Molinier seems to consider Greek terms as *flores* and Latin ones as *figurae*.

[19] In the *Leys, epymone* designates not only *epizeuzi* but also a sort of morphological figure (III, 310; cf. section IV. B). In rhetoric, *epymone* describes only paraphrase varying a thoughtin several coordinated sentences. (cf. Lausberg, *Handbuch*, § 838, 1).

(repetition at the cesura). Yet any form of these "vices" can, if justified by intent and effect, become corresponding figures, flowers and *coblas*, according to the compiler of the *Leys*.

These figures and flowers will be discussed in the following sections of this chapter. It should be mentioned here that their extension in the corresponding *coblas* can occur either at stanza level or at poem level. Thus *coblas capdenals* repeat one or more rime words or verses at the beginning of successive verses or stanzas (I, 282-284); *coblas retronchadas* repeat rime words or verses at fixed intervals, not necessarily in succession (I, 286-288); *coblas capfinidas* repeat the last word or verse of one verse or stanza as the first of the next (I, 280); and so on. But these complex forms are less indicative for stylistic purposes than is the *Leys*' presentation of basic and simple word repetition having no fixed relation to metrics and thus giving free rein to the poet's spontaneous instinct for word-association.

This non-formalistic repetition of words regardless of position is *conduplicatio* (III, 168-170), in the *Leys*' examples

> Lauzor donem, lauzor a Dieu,
> Donem lauzor al filh de Dieu...

or more simply *Tu metes mal sobre mal*. Guilhem Molinier is admittedly less enthusiastic about such non-formalistic repetition than about multiple repetition with structural value; this is due to his stress on eliminating the undesirable and to the codifier's natural interest in form. His priorities are however reversed by the troubadours, whose repetition is "structural" less often than not. Still, Molinier's terminology will be useful to us; and the troubadours certainly shared his appreciation of the stylistic value of repetition. Speaking of *conduplicatio*, Molinier says:

> Item, deu hom saber que·l retornamen qu'om fay de dictios, per las manieras sobre dichas, en aquesta figura et en las autras, fay hom per miels mostrar la affectio gran quez ha aquel que ditz las paraulas, e per movre et excitar los coratges dels auzens, d'aquels a cuy hom ditz aytals paraulas soen tornadas (III, 170).

C. The Troubadours' Practice: Anaphora

C 1. *Minimal Anaphora*

Anaphora — repetition initial in the syntactical or metrical group, here the verse — is not rare, and is often effective, in the troubadours. A minimal though common form is repetition of the basic linking word *que*. Whether careless, inevitable, conscious, or intentional (it would be foolish to debate such a thorny question for such a little word), anaphora of *que* has the stylistic value of organizing and clarifying a correspondence of thought to verse. This is true even where *que* has the different functions of relative pronoun and conjunction, as in William IX:

> Qu'eu non ai soing d'estraing lati
> Que·m parta de mon Bon Vezi,
> Qu'eu sai de paraulas com van (X, 25-27).

Here, anaphora of *que(e)* is reinforced by the following first-person pronoun *eu* or *m(e)*.

Anaphora of other conjunctions like *e* and *ni* contributes to simple effects of accumulation, already in William IX:

> A manjar mi deron capos,
> E sapchatz *ac i* mais de dos
> E no·*i ac* cog ni cogastros,
>   Mas sol nos tres,
> E·l pans *fo* blancs e·l vins *fo* bos
>   E·l pebr' espes (V, 43-48).

This loose conjunctive repetition, introducing propositions of varying size and structure, is simply the most natural method of joining several details in *descriptio* of any scene. But details are not thrown together indiscriminately, and the stanza has a real structure molded by repetition. The first anaphoric group, in lines 2 and 3, is unified by common eight-syllable length and by internal repetition of the verb *ac*, first followed then preceded by the adverb *i*. The second anaphoric group, lines 5-6,[20] has an even denser repetitive unity: both

---

[20] Frank (*Répertoire métrique*, I, xxx) would consider this poem as having stanzas of 5 and not 6 lines, running Jeanroy's lines 5 and 6 together into

initial *e*'s and the supportive internal *e* are followed by the definite article ·*l*; and the verb *fo* is repeated within line 5 and understood in line 6; thus this group falls into three rhythmic segments, each of four syllables, each introduced by *e·l* plus noun. It is this context dominated by the linking conjunction *e* that gives prominence to the introduction in line 4, by the conjunction *mas*, of the stanza's most essential detail: "but only we three (were there)." An so the scene is set!

Elsewhere, William IX uses anaphoric *e* with a more oratorical intent demonstrated by repetition at absolutely regular intervals and by painstaking parallelism of elements:

>Per son joy pot malautz sanar,
>*E* per sa ira sas morir
>*E* savis hom enfolezir
>*E* belhs hom sa beutat mudar
>*E·*l plus cortes vilanejar
>*E* totz vilas encortezir (IX, 25-30).

William has found an effective way of juxtaposing the complementary contradictions of love by this anaphorically linked succession of antonymic expressions.

Another stanza of the same poem uses sustained anaphora again, this time to accumulate various details representing the poet's willingness to do anything his lady desires:

>Si·m vol mi dons s'amor donar,
>Pres suy *del* penr' e *del* grazir
>*E del* celar e *del* blandir
>*E de sos* plazers dir *e* far
>*E de sos* pretz tener en car
>*E de son* laus enavantir (IX, 37-42).

Here again, anaphora is the chief element of a repetitive structure that includes internal repetition of *e*, of *de sos* or *son*, and of *del*, the whole being dominated by parallel infinitives, used first as substantives, then as verbs. In such examples, conjunctive anaphora

---

a 12-syllable line, since the fifth is generally rimeless. But in this and the next stanza (thus stanzas VIII and IX), the fifth line does rime with lines 1-3, so that at least in this stanza VIII at least I have no hesitation at keeping Jeanroy's typography.

— of which countless other examples can be found in the troubadours — is thus a structural principle around which are organized other perhaps more important effects of enumeration, antonymy, etymological figures, etc.

C 2. *Independent Anaphora*

As the repeated word becomes semantically more important, anaphora begins to establish a stylistic context, for example one of negativity dominating time in another example from the "first troubadour," William IX:

> Farai un vers de dreyt nien:
> *Non* er de mi *ni* d'autra gen,
> *Non* er d'amor *ni* de joven,
>   *Ni* de ren au,
> Qu'enans fo trobatz en durmen
>   Sobre chevau.
>
> *No* sai en qual hora·m fuy natz:
> *No suy* a!egres *ni* iratz,
> *No suy* estrayns *ni sui* privatz,
>   *Ni no*·n puesc au... (IV, 1-10).

These insistent initial negations — their repetitive effect reinforced by the two verb groups *er* and *suy* and their negative effect by internal repetition of *ni* — help create the unreal and riddle-like mood which is the background for anaphoric characterization of William's own version of *amor de lonh*:

> *Anc non* la vi et am la fort,
> *Anc no*·n aic dreyt ni no·m fes tort (IV, 31-32).

An example where grouped monosyllables include a word of stronger semantic force is from Peire Vidal:

> Ab bona domna m'acompanh
> *E platz me* jovens e beutatz
> *E platz me* cors gen fassonatz
> Mas no *mi platz* bars que·m reganh... (XLIII, 33-36).

Here the same three-word group begins successive octosyllables. This repetition of the verb *platz*, also internally in the fourth verse, is related to the genre known as *plazer*, in which the poet lists his likes and denounces his dislikes. Similarly, the Monk of Montaudon's poem of this genre (P-C 305.15) uses the thematic verb *platz* or *plazon* an average of twice per stanza, including each first line, typically in the same expression as in Peire Vidal, *E platz mi*. So anaphora, reinforced by internal repetition, becomes the mark of a particular genre.

C 3. Architectural Anaphora

We thus arrive at multiple anaphora having structural functions within one or several stanzas. Each stanza of an entire poem can even be built on the anaphoric principle. Thus in Peire Vidal XXVII, the six stanzas enunciate anaphorically as many themes central both to the poet's immediate concerns and to the Provençal love tradition. The key elements of these themes are *agradar, amor, bel m'es, Deus sal, domna,* and *gaug,* all of which represent either the poet's joy or its causes.

In this poem intensity and regularity of anaphora vary from stanza to stanza. Stanza I establishes the poem's general tone with the line

Be m'agrada la covinens sazos (XXVII, 1),

then has five lines beginning in *E m'agrada* or *E m'agradon,* but in its last two lines enunciates the *agradar*-theme only by the noun *grat* repeated at the fourth syllable. Stanza III, on the other hand, shows exact alternation of two syntactically complementary expressions built around *bel* and followed (directly except in one line) by the conjunction *quar* or *quan,* thus producing four different combinations of the two juxtaposed pairs:

Bel m'es, bela domna, quan pens de vos,
E bel quar sui en vostre senhoriu,
Bel m'es quan n'aug bon pretz nominatiu,
E bel quan vei vostras belas faissos.
Bel m'es quan gart vostras finas beutatz
E bel quar sui tot vostr' endomenjatz,
Bel m'es quar ai en vos mon pensamen
E bel quar am vos sola solamen (XXVII, 17-24).

Anaphora remains at much lower density in stanza V, where each line begins in the word *domn(a)* (once varied as *Bona domna*). And stanza VI has no anaphora at all but internal repetition (with morphological figure) of *gaug(z)* at the second or fourth syllable of each line. Such rather artificial variations cannot, however, offset the somewhat mechanical effect produced by the frequency and length of the repeated elements, up to four syllables of a ten-syllable line. It seems that the poet has achieved an insufficient degree of variety or "asymmetry" and that he has surrendered too much of his liberty of expression to preconceived patterns. At any rate, the poem's architectural anaphora, especially in stanza III, can be cited as positive evidence for the usually rejected manuscript attribution to Peire of another poem, P-C 364.12, where five lines in each stanza begin with the expression *Ben aja ieu*.[21]

Bertran de Born exploits a similar anaphoric structure more imaginatively in the justly famous *sirventes Bel m'es quan vei*. The first stanza and the tornada state a general contrast between age and youth and thus frame the other four stanzas' chiastic treatment of this theme marked by the key words *vielh* and *jove*. This alternation stands out against treatment in two stanzas of ladies, then of men in two, so that stanzas II-V treat in order *vielha domna, joves domna, joves hom,* and *vielhs hom*. A further alternation, within each stanza, involves lines beginning in two different repeated expressions. As in Peire Vidal's poem discussed above, anaphoric regularity is relieved by variation. The most nearly regular stanza is the second:

> Per vielha tenh domna, puois qu'a pelatge,
> Et es vielha, quan chavalier non a;
> Vielha la tenh, si de dos drutz s'apatge
> Et es vielha, si avols hom lo-lh fa;
> Vielha la tenh, si ama dintz son chastel,
> Et es vielha, quan l'a ops de fachel;
> Vielha la tenh, puois l'enoian joglar,
> Et es vielha, quan trop vuolha parlar (P-C 80.7, 9-16).

---

[21] Cf. D'Arco Silvio Avalle, ed., *Peire Vidal: poesie*, 2 vols. (Milan and Naples, 1960), II, 438-439. As Avalle says, the use of architectural anaphora in P-C 364.12 recalls Peire's poem XXVII (Anglade's numbering); Avalle classifies the former poem as *di dubbio attribuzione* and leans against Peire's authorship on other stylistic grounds (cf. also our p. 101). Questions must thus be raised concerning the relative weight of various stylistic traits, and the importance of stylistic differences and similarities within the work of one poet.

Here the anaphoric structure extends far into the line by repetition of the varying elements *puois, si,* and *quan.* Thus, by skillful parallelism and variation of elements on the level of poem, stanza, and verse, Bertran has succeeded in expressing a series of witty remarks on human nature through the two all-inclusive contrasts of age and sex locked into an anaphoric framework.

C 4. *Melodic Identity*

With this example from Bertran de Born we arrive at interstanzaic anaphora, that is, initial repetition of the same word or expression in more than one stanza of a poem. One might well expect repetition within one stanza and especially in successive lines to be most effective. However, repetition between stanzas becomes not only noticeable but highly effective in the special case where it is reinforced by identity of musical context. Since all stanzas of any one poem (except of *descorts*) are performed to the same music, by both voice and instrument, all lines of equal position with relation to the stanzas have identical melody. In addition, since each tornada repeats the rimes and music of the last stanzaic segment of equal length, lines of a tornada and stanza are melodically identical if they occupy the same position measured from the end of the tornada or stanza. For example, in a given poem the sixth line of an eight-line stanza and the first line of a three-line tornada are melodically identical. If a given expression occurs at the beginning (or end) of these two lines, its force will greatly be increased by identical musical setting, conceivably for example a distinctive rhythm or remarkable melisma.

Such melodically reinforced anaphora occurs in varying density. For example, Peire Vidal XXIV begins two tornadas with the apostrophe *Coms de Peiteus.* Or, the *Chansoneta nueva* traditionally attributed to William IX repeats, at the beginning of two successive stanzas, an expression occupying half the verse:

> *Qual pro y auretz,* dompna conja,
> Si vostr' amors mi deslonja? (VIII, 19-20);
>
> *Qual pro y auretz,* s'ieu m'enclostre
> E no·m retenetz per vostre? (VIII, 25-26).

These two rhetorical questions, so emphatically stated and positioned, set the mood of the second half of the poem, where the poet reasons with his lady in an attempt to win her favors.

Melodically reinforced anaphora occurs more often throughout a poem than in just two stanzas. For example, Rigaut de Berbezilh cleverly extends the role of the *senhal*, usually restricted to the tornada, and contrives to name his lady, Miells-de-Domna, at the beginning of the eighth line of each stanza in his number III, *Atressi com Persavaus* (P-C 421.3), and at the beginning of the sixth line of each stanza in his number VI, *Lo nous mes d'abril comensa* (P-C 421.6). It is hard to imagine that his patroness should have remained unmoved by this flattering and original tribute.

A more usual position for such patterns is the first line of stanzas. For example, Guiraut de Bornelh's justly famous dawn-song *Reis glorios* (P-C 242.64) extends the refrain principle, obligatory in the *alba*, into initial position. In each stanza except the first, the repeated initial apostrophe *Bel companho,* addressed by the watchman to his friend fortunate in love, cooperates with the final refrain *Et ades sera l'alba!* to form a harmonious symmetry within and among stanzas. Guiraut here enriches the *alba* by recourse to a tradition of initial apostrophe seen also in the habitual repetition of the poetic adversaries' names at the beginning of alternate stanzas in *tensos*, and perhaps also in William IX's three poems addressed to his *Companho*.

As just one example of the frequency of anaphora, William IX's average poem contains 5.6 words that are initial in their line and belong to repetitive groups.[22] These consist almost entirely of minor parts of speech in enumeration, chiefly the conjunctions *e(t)* and *ni*. But what is more important than frequency is effect and effectiveness, as we have illustrated. The troubadours' use of anaphora, from the simplest initial repetition of conjunctions to the complex structure of masterpieces like Bertran de Born's *sirventes* and Guiraut de Bornelh's *alba*, can generally be said to conform to Henri Morier's dictum that "partout l'anaphore doit être le signe d'un sentiment dont la répétition seule réussit à épuiser l'expression."[23]

---

[22] This figure includes words only once initial but repeated in proximity within a line.

[23] Henri Morier, *Dictionnaire de poétique et de rhétorique* (Paris, 1961), p. 27. Hereafter *Dictionnaire*.

D. Internal Repetition

D 1. *Functional Repetition*

An intensifying function is also exercised by words repeated within the line, even when these serve chiefly to underline the parallelism of other elements, as in William IX's *devinalh*:

> No sai *quora·m* suy endurmitz
> Ni *quora·m* velh, s'om no m'o ditz (IV, 13-14).

In keeping with the poem's thematic use of antitheses, as in the preceding stanza the pair gay-angry and distant-intimate, the poet here exploits the complementary antonymic ideas of sleeping and waking to indicate that he *never* knows what he is doing. The length of the chosen expressions will not fit an eight-syllable line and thus obliges him to extend the contrast over two lines. So (as elsewhere in the poem) he repeats a conjunctive element which both stresses the two lines' parallelism and emphatically introduces the two antithetical terms:

> I don't know *at what time* I am asleep
> Nor *at what time* I wake, unless I'm told.

However, if the repeated element had less personality or bulk — say, simply *quan* instead of *quora(·m)* — it might be regarded as a mere grammatical tool without any significant stylistic function. Therefore we will reserve repetition of conjunctions, prepositions, and the like for a later section, III. J1, and also for our discussion of enumerative convergence in Chapter VI. In fact, almost all repeated "minor" parts of speech — conjunctions, pronouns, articles, prepositions — occur in enumeration, as the following statistics for internal repetition in a few troubadours show.

Chart 3:

Average frequency of Internal Repetition per Poem [24]

parts of speech: in enumeration?	major		minor		
	NO	YES	NO	YES	
poets					total
William IX	1.1	2.1	1.1	16.6	20.9
B. de Ventadorn	3.0	1.3	1.9	11.2	17.4
A. Daniel	0.6	2.1	0.3	9.4	12.4

This chart gives some idea of the relative importance of different grammatical types of repetition, especially by the predominance of the fourth column. But for the present we shall retain only repetition of major parts of speech, as an independent stylistic means, with elements of individual semantic value; coordinated repetition of minor as well as major words will be discussed in section J.

D 2. *Repetition with Semantic Importance*

Simple internal repetition is of greater frequency than anaphora but of lesser power and of subtler effect. It can, like anaphora, stress any chosen idea. An example of minimal lexical and semantic importance — a monosyllable expressing the idea of bigness — is found in Peire Vidal's lines

> Quant hom honratz torna en *gran* paubreira,
> Qu'a estat rics e de *gran* benanansa... (XIII, 1-2).

It is not mere chance that it is the poem's first lines that thus end in preposition plus *gran* plus substantive, expressing in successive rimes (the line's position of greatest stress) the antithesis between poverty and fortune. This careful parallelism announces the poem's major theme, that of the contrast between the joy which the poet's lady could give him and the misery into which she has cruelly plunged

---

[24] On "major" and "minor" parts of speech, cf. p. 69, above. Excluded from the present chart are words belonging to expressions that contribute to anaphora or to rime word repetition (for example, *vielha* in the anaphoric expression *Et es vielha* in Bertran de Born, P-C 80.7, quoted on p. 82). But words internal in their line and belonging to any other repetitive group are counted; thus an internal word repeated initially counts as one (1), etc. (this is rare, however, and hardly affects the overall count).

him. A certain variety derives from the expression of *paubreira*'s true antonym, *riqueza*, only by the different part of speech *rics*, while *paubreira* and *benanansa* form an incompletely antonymic pair. The emphatic effect of the adjective *gran* is heightened by its double occurrence on a tonic accent in the speech rhythm, both times after a preposition and before the pretonic initial of the substantive it modifies. These skilled effects justify repetition of the modifier *gran* at such a short interval.

The repetition of such a common word as *gran*, if at several lines' interval, would hardly be noticeable. But an increased interval can be compensated for by increased phonetic or semantic importance. Thus in the following example Peire Vidal repeats, with two intervening lines, the expression "I do not dare":

> Plus que·l paubres que jatz el ric ostal,
> Que noca·s planh, sitot s'a gran *dolor*,
> *Tan tem* que torn ad enoi al senhor,
> *No* m'*aus* planher de ma *dolor* mortal.
> Be·m dei doler, pos cela·m fai orgolh,
> Que nulha re tan no dezir ni volh:
> Sivals d'aitan *no*·lh *aus* clamar merce,
> *Tal paor ai* qu'ades s'enoi de me (XVIII, 1-8).

This stanza, an initial one, enunciates, like our previous example from Peire Vidal, the important theme of misery and joy of love in terms of poverty and wealth. Repetition of *dolor* in lines 2 and 4, varied by the progressively stronger modifiers *gran* and *mortal*, announces the correlative theme of pain. Through repetition and variation, the parallelism of the poem's two four-line segments becomes evident. Each half-stanza consists of one complex sentence which describes the poet's psychological condition, the first by a comparison, the second by a direct description. The conclusion in both half-stanzas is that fear, an idea reiterated synonymously by *tan tem* and *tal paor ai*, causes a lack of daring expressed both times by *no ... aus* followed by an infinitive describing the unperformed act: complaining or begging mercy. Of the three ideas involved, two are expressed by *variatio* and one, the central one, by word repetition varied by the different subsidiary elements *m* and *lh* placed between repeated *no* and *aus*. Thus one key to this whole technically intricate and poetically effective structure of symmetry and variation is the repetition of *no ... aus;*

ignoring this fact would hinder one's appreciation of the entire stanza, which is in turn the key to the poem!

So potent is such repetition that the sweeping effect we have described in this stanza is achieved by a basically simple pattern repeating one word in two lines and a two-word expression in two other lines. One direct recall of an idea suffices to make it thematic in a poetry of such verbal subtlety as the troubadours'. The effect can extend even to single occurrences in different poems: Arnaut's use (approaching Riffaterre's *tic*) of *ferm voler* six times in five different poems (IX, 45; XIV, 25; XV, 3; XVII, 26, 36; XVIII, 1) jumps to the eye (or ear) and justifies Toja's description of the term as "one of the key words of the famous sestina" (where it occurs only once!).[25] To have their effect, it is generally sufficient for major as well as minor parts of speech to be repeated in pairs, and not necessarily in larger groups.

D 3. *Multiple Repetition*

Multiple repetition — occurrence of a word or group more than twice in a coherent relationship — though rare even in anaphora and rime, can, if used sparingly and tastefully for a specific purpose, be highly effective. The complex repetitive pattern of Bertran de Born's famous *sirventes* in praise of battle, *Be·m platz lo gais temps de pascors* (P-C 80.8a), creates a masterful effect of excitement and drama. The poet's personal involvement in the action is expressed, as in the lines from Peire Vidal XLIII discussed above (p. 80), by the *plazer* leitmotif which occurs six times in the first two stanzas, chiefly in the anaphoric *E platz mi*, and then after a last occurrence in the third stanza gives way to other stylistic devices.

The first stanza skillfully introduces a contrast between sound and sight by presenting the motives of the poet's pleasure once by *quan auch* and twice by *quan vei*. The *heard* birdsong will soon be drowned out by the (to Bertran at least) more pleasing noise of battle, and the *seen* tents, horses and horsemen will soon be caught up in the more intense visual experience of battle expressed by repetition of these same verbs of perception, first in the use of *quan vei* twice in stanza II,

---

[25] Toja, *Arnaut Daniel*, p. 368.

supplemented once by *vei* alone, then later in the remarkable climactic stanza V with its far more complex pattern of repetition:

> Ie us dic que tan no m'a sabor
> Manjar *ni* beure *ni* dormir
> Com a, quan *auch cridar*: "A lor!"
> D'ambas las partz et *auch* ennir
>   Chavals vochs per l'ombratge,
> *Et auch cridar: "Aidatz! Aidatz!"*
> *E vei* chazer per los fossatz
>   Paucs e grans per l'erbatge,
> *E vei los* mortz que pe·ls costatz
> An los tronzos ab los cendatz (80.8a, 41-50).

The various repeated elements, underlined above, form a dynamic structure which draws our own imagined perceptions into the poet's game. In the first two lines, reference to pleasant but uninspiring everyday activities is punctuated by rather tame polysyndetic repetition of the conjunction *ni*. Then the pace picks up with four lines devoted to the sounds of the heat of battle. The first person *auch*, "I hear," twice reports by the infinitive *cridar* the shouts of warriors and once, by another infinitive, the whinnying of riderless horses. This "*auch*-section" culminates in the immediate repetition *Aidatz! Aidatz!*, which renders dramatically the moment when the outcome of battle hangs in the balance.

The following four-line section, devoted to visual images, describes the results of what we have just heard. This "*vei*-section," through repetition of the first person "I see," organizes the panorama of the wounded and dead strewn about the battlefield and intensifies our emotions at viewing the unhappy but exhilarating scene. Thus these two four-line sections, one of action and one of result, are differentiated by their thematic verb of perception. The verb of hearing is appropriate to the confusion of a mêlée from which the participant cannot emerge long enough to view what is going on; and the verb of seeing is appropriate to summation of the aftermath. The two sections are not disjointed but are united by a continuous enumeration of first-person propositions connected by the conjunction *e(t)*, thrice in the emphatic initial position, once interior. Certainly repetition — here both simple and multiple, anaphoric and internal — is a clue to appreciation of a beautiful stanza and poem.

D 4. *Structural Repetition*

Thus multiple repetition, well engineered, can effectively carry thematic weight. It can even become a structural device, when a given word is repeated several times through a poem or in successive lines. For example, reiterated negations set the tone of William IX's *Farai un vers de dreyt nien* and Jaufre Rudel's *No sap chantar qui so non di*. But this technique is rare, and is not often as successful as when Lanfranc Cigala states an idea dear to Bernart de Ventadorn, that of the link between the poet's inspiration and his song. In this case, Lanfranc studs his poem with thirteen words from the root *ioi-* and fourteen from *chant-*, within lines chiefly as the substantive *ioi*, and in the rime as the substantive or first-person verb *chan*. The two are combined by anaphoric *E* into a passage of unusually dense repetition:

> *E* qar am *ioi*, de *ioi chan*,
> *E* ab *ioi* voilh remaner,
> *E ioios* mon cor aver,
> *E* de *ioi* daurar mon *chan* (XXVI, 45-48).

However, such multiple repetition cannot long be sustained in isolation from other poetic means. Even this relatively pure example is reinforced by the etymological figures *ioi-ioios* and *chan* verb or substantive and by enumeration of parallel infinitive constructions. Were this not so, the result would probably be as lamentable as the example of *mot pezan* by which the *Leys d'amors* warn against the dangers of repetition:

> Ara segon *nostre* poder
> e segon *nostre* pauc saber,
> Dieu ajudan, *nostre* salvayre,
> Del Gay Saber *nostre* vejayre
> Nos platz ayssi mostrar a totz (III, 88).

This is careless multiple repetition, unjustified by any poetic or didactic effect, and as Molinier aptly comments, "here this word *nostre* is so often repeated that its pronunciation becomes harsh and annoying to the listeners, so that they are tired merely from hearing it." [26]

---

[26] III, 88-90: "Vet aquesta dictio *nostre* tan soen repetida que la pronunciatio e la votz red aspra et enuoiza als auzens, en tant que·ls esperitz d'aquels red fatigatz de sol l'auzir."

Multiple repetition of one word quickly loses any positive value when unvaried by other stylistic elements. Word repetition, which does not lend itself to semantic, lexical, or phonetic variation, therefore rarely stands alone to create its own stylistic atmosphere.

D 5. *"Epizeuzi"*

The last few examples have illustrated chiefly internal word repetition at varying intervals of separation and with varying density, but so far chiefly in different lines save in Lanfranc's

> E car am *ioi*, de *ioi* chan (XXVI, 45).

This line illustrates the especially potent, though also dangerous, technique of repetition at close quarters. Such repetition within one line expresses, here enumeratively, the length of Peire Vidal's waiting and patience:

> Tenria m'al us de l'enoios romeu
> Que *quier* e *quier* ... (XXIV, 21-22).

and, this time asyndetically, the scorn with which the saucy *pastorela* tells Marcabru (or his poetic surrogate):

> Per so n'auretz per soudada
> Al partir: *bada*, fols, *bada* (P-C 293.30, 54-55).

In these examples, the verse contains the same word twice in the same function and construction. However, the repeated element can function in two different contexts, as when Jaufre Rudel expresses the reluctance with which his lady announces (and he hears) unwelcome news:

> Mas *tart mi* ve e *tart mi* ditz (III, 44),

again with enumerative repetition. The repeated word can also have uncoordinated functions, such as modifying two different substantives. Thus a proverb cited by William IX:

> "A *bon* coratge *bon* poder,
> Qui's ben suffrens (VII, 23-24),

with supportive etymological figure of *ben*.

Such cases of close repetition are rare, and even rarer in the troubadours is immediate repetition, which Bertran de Born for example exploits to heighten the dramatic value of his battle description quoted above:

> Et auch cridar: *"Aidatz! Aidatz!"* (P-C 80.8a, 46).

This effective device is known to traditional rhetoric (cf. chart 1, above) as *geminatio,* here in the form of *epizeuxis,* and to the *Leys* (cf. chart 2, above) as *epizeuzi* (III, 170) or *epymone* (III, 310). The *Leys* explain that in cases like *veramen, veramen* or *senher, senher,* it is used "per mostrar major affectio o major affirmatio de so qu'om ditz" (III, 170) and otherwise would be mere foolishness (*nugatio*), as in

> Us bels *cavals, cavals* corria
> L'autrier fortmen per esta via (III, 310).

Thus Molinier, like the troubadours, recognizes both the dangers and potentialities of immediate repetition.

D 6. *Epistrophe*

Another special form of repetition is epistrophe, or repetition of words at the end of cola. This can occur at the cesura, as in the *Leys'* example of *conversio per clauzas*:

> Savis *es,* bels *es,* discretz *es*
> Le Reys, per que temegutz *es* (III, 166),

probably inspired less by the troubadours than by medieval rhetoric with its

> O *malum!* miserum *malum!* miserabile *malum.*[27]

Epistrophe — which is admittedly not very common in the troubadours — leads us logically on from internal word repetition to rime word repetition; since run-on lines are rare, rime word repetition is essentially the same thing as epistrophe final in the verse.

---

[27] G. de Vinsauf, *Poetria nova,* line 1099, in Faral, *Arts poétiques,* p. 231.

This concludes our discussion of internal word repetition. We have seen the varying effects it can have according to its semantic importance, its place in patterns of greater or lesser complexity, and the distance and grammatical linking between the repeated words. The frequency of internal word repetition is great even in isolation from other stylistic means. And when, as our chapter on convergence will show, internal repetition collaborates with other figures of repetition or with enumeration, the result is perhaps the most characteristic technique of the Provençal lyric.

E. Rime Word Repetition

E 1. *Importance of the Rime*

Like anaphora, rime word repetition inevitably occurs at an interval which is a function of verse length. An important difference, though, is that while anaphora generally occurs in successive or nearby lines, rime word repetition can be significant anywhere in the poem, since the rime is the privileged position par excellence. The interlocking pattern of rimes and the choice of suitable rime words were eternal subjects of interest to the poet and his audience. Rime, in fact, was apparently considered the most important single element of poetry.

Thus the *Leys d'amors* (III, 376-384) tell us — and aspiring fourteenth-century poets — to plan out our rimes first and to begin composing only when we have assembled enough rime words, by long and painful searching if necessary.[28] This recommendation implies that any repetition of rime words within one poem would be perceptible to both poet and audience. Such repetition must be condemned when in close succession and when unjustified by formal or expressive effect. The *Leys* properly denounce this example of *mot tornat*:

> Tostemps me fay gaug Tholoza,
> Quar yeu nasquiey en Tholoza (III, 100);

this repetition of a geographical name serves no poetic purpose.

---

[28] Molinier recommends this procedure when the poet has no given idea in mind (III, 376), i.e. (as the context shows), when neither translating from Latin nor expressing poetically a thought already stated in prose. Thus almost all *cansos* and *vers* (the genres Molinier cites here) fall under his prescription. Their subject is apparently supposed to emerge almost automatically from the rime words available, and from the *topoi* of *fin' amors*.

However, outside of such examples of gross negligence, Provençal does not have the later categorical prejudice against rime word repetition — a prejudice which has often blinded critics to the varied resources which this device affords the troubadours. One must after all adopt the troubadours' perspective: if they did not consider rime word repetition a fault in their poetry, why should we? They could have avoided it if they had desired; and in fact, it is not rare rime words or those participating in rare rimes that tend to be repeated, but rather the more common ones, ones for which substitutes could easily be found. The troubadours evidently felt that there was often good reason not to seek unrepeated rime words; or, to frame it more positively, that there was often a reason to repeat rime words.

E 2. *Minimal Effects*

There is of course a threshold below which poetic effect can hardly be discerned. Thus Peire Vidal's repetition in the rime of words like *dire* (XLI, 17, 30), *rete* (XX, 30, 101), or *sia* (XXII, 45, 71) is at such great distance as to be probably undetectable on oral performance, and is of little poetic significance, either positive or negative. One cannot really, in these cases, speak of themes of "telling," "retaining," or "being." Since these rimes -*ir(e)*, -*e(n)* and -*ia* are among the commonest, Peire could have replaced these rime words easily had his esthetic sense or contemporary taste so dictated; in fact, they clearly did not, and he did not bother.

E 3. *Thematic Rime Words*

On the other hand, rime words are often the semantically most important of the line and of the poem. It can be no accident that words like *amor* and *esperansa* are among those most often used in the rime by Peire Vidal. The thematic value of rimes can be quickly verified from an inventory of Bernart de Ventadorn's rime words.[29] The fourteen words he uses most frequently in the rime include the essential words for describing the poet's lady (*gen, be, re*), the poet's own psychology (*sen, me, ai, cor*) and the relation between poet and lady (*amor, talen, dire, merce, semblan*). These words occur from

---

[29] Lazar, *Bernard de Ventadour*, pp. 37-42.

nine to thirteen times in the rime except for the greater figure of twenty-two for the key word of the love lyric, *amor* (to which can be added no less than forty-two uses in the rime of words built on the root *am-*). Rime words occurring from five to eight times include almost all the thematic ones of Provençal love poetry: *dolor, afan, esperansa, plor, chan, dan, jauzimen, dezire, paor,* etc.

Lazar remarks that "les rimes semblent refléter la plupart des motifs et des idées développées dans les chansons, et les mots dont la fréquence est grande à la rime ont leur correspondance proportionnelle à l'intérieur des vers, sauf *joi*...."[30] So we can assume that, whether in the interior of the verse or in the rime, repetition of such words reflects the poet's desire to intensify one of these important themes.

The use of thematic rime words is not confined to the love poem. Thus Arnaut Daniel's salacious *sirventes* climaxes a colorful description of the horrible test to which a lover is put by stressing its "dangers" in the rime word of the last stanza's first verse and the only tornada's last verse:

> Ben es estortz de *perill* (I, 37).
> Puois poira cornar ses *perill* (49).

E 4. *The Distance Factor*

Thus even rime word repetition at some distance can be a conscious stylistic device producing a justifiable poetic effect. For example, three repetitive groups interlock to emphasize as many themes running through four stanzas of William IX's poem X:

> Ab la dolchor del temps *novel*
> Foillo li bosc, e li aucel
> Chanton chascus en lor *lati*
> Segon lo vers del *novel* chan (X, 1-4).

> Ni no m'aus traire adenan,
> Tro qe sacha ben de la *fi*
> S'el' es aissi com eu deman (10-12).

---

[30] Lazar, p. 33. *Joi* is virtually unrimable; cf. E. Erdmannsdörffer, *Reimwörterbuch der Trobadors* (Berlin, 1897; = *Romanische Studien*, II), p. 50. Cf. also *FEW*, art. *gaudium* (Basel, 1952), IV, 82: "Bei den troubadours ist *joi* das gebräuchlichste wort für 'freude,' doch findet es sich merkwürdigerweise nie im reim; während *jai* (s. *GAHI) oft im reim vorkommt."

> Enquer me membra d'un mati
> Que nos fezem de guerra *fi* (19-20).

> Qu'eu non ai soing d'estraing *lati*
> Que·m parta de mon Bon Vezi (25-26).

The *temps novel* of the first line is the cause of the bird's *novel chan*, and anticipates the second *novel*, interior in line 4. Use of *lati* twice in the rime suggests a parallel, frequent in the troubadours, between bird and man and also an ironic contrast between the joyous song of birds and the jealous rumors spread by *lauzenjors*. Finally, the repeated rime word *fi* (also repeated in line 28 and 32), by designating first the goal of the lover's efforts and then the cessation of conflict between lovers, suggests the desirability of the "ends" (to carry the pun into English) of love. Certainly, the themes whose key words are *novel*, *lati*, and *fi* figure among the poem's most important, and rime word repetition is a signal to this effect.

Or, the repeated element can occupy a good part of two lines. In Jaufre Rudel IV, a poem largely concerned with the theory of courtly love, the expression "I know full well" introduces two statements of the poet's confidence, first that patience in love is fitting:

> Qu'eras *say ben az escien*
> *Que* selh es savis qui aten
> E selh es fols qui trop s'irays (IV, 12-14),

then that true love never did any harm:

> Per qu'ieu *sai ben az escien*
> Qu'anc fin' amors home non trays (IV, 34-35).

This reiterated of confidence in *amor* is rather touching as a symbol of the troubadours' optimism, whether real or feigned, in their cult of love.

Ultimately, such key words or expressions can occur in more than two stanzas of a poem — more often in all stanzas than in a intermediate number. Thus Peire Vidal's exceptional poem XVII repeats in each of its eight stanzas a unique combination of twelve of the poem's sixteen different repeating rime words, including such significant ones as *auzel*, *amor*, *amador*, *Joven*. Their position changes according to a complex pattern governed by the principle of *coblas capfinidas* (cf. section G, below); this is typical of a number of other Provençal poems.[31] The most famous of these is Arnaut Daniel's sestina (XVIII), in which each stanza presents, in a new order, six repeating end words — not rime words, because unlike Peire Vidal's they lack rime among themselves. Their interlocking recurrences produce a suite of bizarre images: "enters, fingernail, soul, twig, uncle, room." The sestina's success flies in the face of the *Leys'* generally unexceptionable statement that "motz tornatz se fa vici ysshamens en rim estramp e dissolut" (III, 100; i.e., in lines unrimed in the poem or stanza).

E 5. Melodic Identity

Another peculiarity of rime word repetition is its frequent occurrence in melodically identical positions, hence (as explained above, p. 83) at the same distance from the end of different stanzas or tornadas. A statistical survey of Peire Vidal's work (in Anglade's edition)[32] will illustrate the troubadours' practice. The following chart shows the distribution of his 219 rime words belonging to repetitive groups. Included are forty-three *cansos* and *sirventes*; excluded are three *tensos* and also songs XVII and XXXI, whose word repetition is a thorough-going architectural principle and whose inclusion here would falsify the statistics for purposes of determining Peire's more usual techniques. Each member of a repetitive group is counted as one in this chart, thus a pair as two (often split between different categories), etc. Position within the poem is plotted horizontally, in terms of stanza or tornada. Plotted vertically is melodic position, according to whether a given repeated rime word has a mate in identical position or not.[33]

---

[31] Cf. Toja, *Arnaut Daniel*, pp. 50-51.

[32] Avalle's edition eliminates Anglade's no. XLVIII, which at any rate has no significant effect on our statistics; Avalle prints two other poems whose attribution is so doubtful that they cannot be included in statistics. One of these has far-reaching architectural anaphora and a refrain.

[33] Melodic position has been determined by referring in fact not to music, which is largely lost, but to position of rimes within stanzas and tornadas. Thus the slight possibility is ignored that repeated rime words may occur in verses having a different stanzaic position but the same melody. Since musical lines generally repeat only in the *pedes*, usually in the pattern *abab*, this possibility exists chiefly for lines 1 and 3 or 2 and 4 of a stanzaic pattern. But this relation exists among Peire Vidal's repeated rime words only in (by

Chart 4:

Melodic Identity in Peire Vidal's Repeated Rime Words

position in poem:	first	in stanza medial	last	in tornada	total	
melodic position:						
identical	11	60	12	41	124	} 219
different	11	42	8	34	95	
melodic identity as a per cent of the total	50	59	60	55	57	

These figures bring out that no matter what the individual repeated rime word's position in the poem, its chance of having a mate in identical melodic position elsewhere in the poem is half or greater, 57 per cent on the average. Random expectition of equal melodic position is somewhat less than half: 45 per cent on the average (a function of the average number of different rimes per stanza).[34] This high frequency of melodically reinforced repetition, 57 per cent compared to random expectation of 45 per cent, seems to reflect deliberateness on Peire's part.

It is no doubt safe to say that rime word repetition with melodic identity is frequent not only in Peire Vidal, but in the Provençal lyric in general. To represent other troubadours, it is fitting to choose a repetition of the key word and the most common rime word of the troubadours, *amor*, which occurs in the first line of the first and fourth stanzas of a poem of Guiraut de Bornelh, thus announcing and reiterating the central theme:

---

poem, stanza and line in stanza) nos. XIII, i, 3-iv, 1 and iv, 4-v, 2; and XLVIII (not recognized as Peire's by Avalle), iii, 1-vi, 3. The music of XLVIII is lost; that of XIII (in Friedrich Gennrich, *Der musikalische Nachlass der Troubadours*, I (Darmstadt, 1958), 74) in fact contains (like most of Peire's 12 surviving melodies), no musical repetition at all. We can conclude that at least for Peire Vidal, rime word repetition in equal melodic but different stanzaic position can hardly modify the results arrived at in our chart.

[34] The principle is this: if a given rime word is to recur in another stanza, it has as many possible positions as there are words that rime with it in that stanza. Thus if *amor* is to occur in the rime of a stanza having three rime words in *-or*, random expectation of occurrence in a given position is 1/3. To compute this random expectation for all Peire's work, we take the first stanza of each of his poems and divide the total number of different rime sets by the total number of verses. The result is 187/413 or .45.

Er' ai gran joi que·m remembra l'*amor*
Que·m te mo cor salf en sa fezeltat... (I, 1-2).

Ja no laissetz per me ni per *Amor,*
Fals lauzenger complit de malvestat... (29-30).

Here, as often, there is a progressive intensification, for the first use of the repeated word designates a specific love, while the second occurrence designates Love personified, as the editor indicates by using the capital letter.

E 6. *Refrain Words*

The last example illustrates simple repetition with two members, which is far more frequent in the rime than is multiple repetition. Triple repetition in identical stanzaic position is virtually non-existent. However, occurrence of words in a fixed position in every stanza (and occasionally even in the tornadas) of a poem is not uncommon. The repeated rime word is thus elevated to the formalistic status of refrain word, expression or line. The refrain word actually reflects the highest degree of poetic development, since it is a subtler form of repetition requiring a more attuned ear to pick it up than the bulkier refrain of the folk song, for example. It is all the more remarkable that while 64 of the 2,515 surviving troubadour poems of all genres [35] have a refrain of one or more lines, fully 166 have one or more refrains of one or more words recurring in fixed position in each stanza. The latter include 131 different refrain words, notably these, so significant in the Provençal lyric, occurring in more than two poems: *amor(s)*, in 13; *merce(s)*, 9; *cor*, 8; *alba*, 8; *ben*, 5; *mort(z)*, 3; *(de) vos*, 3.

The effect of a well-chosen refrain word is immense. A simple example is William's "chansoneta nueva" (No. VIII), which ends the fourth line of each stanza in *am* (once in *amam*), again stressing the ubiquitous theme of love.

Or one can cite, as a pendant to Rigaut de Berbezilh's anaphoric use of his lady's *senhal* in two different poems (cf. p. 84, above). Peire Vidal's repetition of his lady's *senhal* (or name, depending on

---

[35] The total number of poems is computed from the table of stanzas of different lengths in Frank, *Répertoire métrique*, II, 68; and the figures on word- and line-refrains from his lists in II, 58-67. Almost one troubadour poem in ten thus has some sort of refrain.

one's identification of her),[36] *Na Vierna,* in the rime of the last line of each stanza of his No. I. Given the usual progressive development of thought and imagery through the stanza, the final position is a fitting one for reiterated tribute to the *domna,* the *raison d'être* of the Provençal lyric.

A refrain word often summarizes the essence of a poem. Lanfranc Cigala XXVII, for example, expresses the unhappy side of love by repeating *marritz* ("sad") as the first rime word of each stanza; and his XXVI indicates his concern with the inspiration of poetry by repeating *chan,* alternatingly a verb and a noun, as the first and fourth rime word of each stanza. A poem can even derive its familiar title from an effective rime word. Thus Jaufre Rudel's "song of distant love" (V) is so called (by us, not by the Middle Ages, as far as is known) from the repetition, in lines 2 and 4 of each stanza, of *lonh,* "distant," chiefly in the expression *amor de lonh,*[37] subject of many a learned discussion, article, and book. Or, Marcabru's crusade song is usually known as the "song of the *lavador,*" "washing-place," from the characteristic, peculiar, and highly significant repetition of this term at the sixth rime of each stanza.

Though effective, use of refrain words can also be somewhat dangerous. As the number of refrain words in each stanza increases, their function tends to become more structural and less poetic. The poet sacrifices his liberty of choice to a preconceived pattern. His choice of this pattern, especially in his creation of the first-conceived stanza, is of course significant; but its every individual manifestation calls less for stylistic comment than does the context which is fashioned to fit it. This context does not always justify the refrain poetically. Thus in Peire Vidal XXXI (which we have excluded from our statistics because of its exceptional nature), Peire's choice of the two refrain words *guiza* and *gaia* certainly stresses the *manner* of his lady's behavior and her characteristic of being (or making him feel) *gay.* However, the six ocurrences of each often seem artificial and unrelated to the context of the poem's development in ideas and images.

---

[36] Cf. Avalle, pp. 18-21.

[37] The refrain word *lonh* is further strengthened by musical repetition, the melody of lines 2 and 4 of every stanza being identical in this poem; cf. Jean Maillard's transcription in *Anthologie de chants de troubadours* (Nice, 1967), pp. 24-25.

On the other hand, a perhaps greater poet wields more successfully the weight of three refrain words in the justly renowned *planh* on Young King Henry, usually attributed by scholars to Bertran de Born.[38] The refrain words (or expressions) *marrimen, jove rei engles,* and *ira* recur respectively in the first, fifth, and eighth line of each stanza and distill the mood, themes, and subject of the whole lament. Their effect has been beautifully kept in Ezra Pound's translation:

> If all the grief and woe and *bitterness,*
> All dolour, ill and every evil chance
> That ever came upon this grieving world
> Were set together they would seem but light
> Against the death of the *young English king.*
> Worth lieth riven and Youth dolorous,
> The world o'ershadowed, soiled and overcast,
> Void of all joy and full of ire and *sadness.*[39]

E 7. *Refrain Lines*

Multiplicity of refrain words verges on the refrain proper, i.e., repetition of one or more lines at the end of every stanza, which is typical of "popular" forms of poetry and of some poets and not of others. For example, the fact that Peire Vidal's known poems have no refrain lines may furnish evidence against attributing to him the poem *Ben aja ieu, qar sai cobrir* (P-C 364.12), where anaphoric *Ben aja ieu* is answered by the refrain ending each stanza, *E mal aja cui pesa.* This refrain technique becomes obligatory in certain genres. In the *alba,* the key word "dawn" must figure in the refrain, almost always as its last word; in the *balada* and *dansa,* the refrain indicates, at least originally, a change of singers and dancers.

F. REPETITION IN DIFFERENT POSITIONS RELATIVE TO THE VERSE

F 1. *Initial and Internal Repetition*

So far, we have discussed separately initial, medial and final repetition; but nothing prevents two of the three from combining in ef-

---

[38] Of 3 MSS, one assigns this *planh* to Bertran de Born, one to Peire Vidal, and one to Rigaut de Berbezilh. Another *planh* on Richard, known to be Bertran's, has the refrain word *planh.*

[39] Ezra Pound, "Planh for the Young English King," *Personae* (New York, 1926), pp. 36-37.

fects of various poetic and structural values. First, anaphora and internal repetition can work together. Thus in William IX's leavetaking poem, a repeated three-word group helps achieve the stanzaic solidarity which is all too rare in the Provençal lyric. Though the involved stanzas are not adjacent, their brevity and similar content make the link clearly perceptible:

> Qu'era m'en irai *en* eisil:
> *En gran* paor, *en gran* peril,
> *En* guerra laissarai mon fil,
> E *faran li mal* siei vezi (XI, 5-8).

> Si Folcos d'Angieus no·l socor,
> E·l reis de cui ieu tenc m'onor,
> *Faran li mal* tut li plusor,
> Felon Gascon et Angevi (XI, 13-16).

The impression of fatherly foreboding (created in part by repetition of *en (gran)* in the first stanza) is redoubled by *variatio* of the subject of the repeated verbal expression *faran li mal*. The first subject, "his neighbors," is both specified and enlarged in the second, "the majority (of his subject and vassals), wicked Gascons and Angevins" (from whom William had ample reason to fear vengeance). This progressive development of prospective enmities dramatizes the poet's increasing anxiety, as does the promotion of the repeated word group to the more expressive initial position in the line. Finally, this repetition creates a link within the four stanzas, II through V, whose theme is the uncertain future of the next William of Poitou. It is such concrete but imaginative techniques that organize the better Provençal poems, whether by repetition or other means.

In a more peculiar case, a four-word expression occurs first separated then rejoined. Deliberateness is made indubitable by melodic identity, by use in a tornada, and by the generally painstaking structure of this derivatively-rimed *vers* of Raimbaut d'Aurenga, where each rime word recalls several others by repetition or morphological figure (cf. p. 180, below). This framework allows repetition of one rime word to call attention to the recurrence of a particular word group, first initial in stanza V,

> *Mal grat dels* fals lauzengiers *croys* (XXXIX, 40),

then, ten lines later, internal in tornada I,

> Nos ten ensems *mal grat dels croys* (XXXIX, 50).

The strength of Raimbaut's poeticized love is here stressed by repetition describing the danger, conventional or real, which it must overcome in the person of the jealous *lauzengiers*. The resulting parallelism allows the second *croys* to take on the remembered impact of the preceding *fals lauzengiers croys*, so that the second line gains space for the extra thought *Nos ten ensems*. This progressive intensification is general in repetition-linked passages. But the separation of the four repeated words in their first occurrence and the repeated rime word's function as two different parts of speech (adjective then substantive) are evidence of Raimbaut's cult of originality and of his technical skill.

Often, such repetition is not simple but multiple, involving three or more word groups. Any anaphoric word group can be regarded as combining initial and internal repetition. We have already seen that, in Peire Vidal XLIII (cf. p. 80, above), the word *platz*, though never initial, belongs twice to an anaphoric group and recurs once within a different verse. Another stanza of the same poem further develops this technique:

> *Cen* cavaliers *ai* totz sols pres
> *E* d'autres *cent ai* tout l'arnes;
> *Cen* domnas *ai* faitas plorar
> *E* d'autras *cen* rire e jogar (XLIII, 45-48).

Peire is here vaunting his exploits in the manner of his "Boasting Poem" (*Vanto*, number XIV). He magnifies his own importance by repeating *cen(t)*, alternatingly initial and internal, in four successive lines. In addition, his triple internal repetition of the first person auxiliary *ai* stresses himself as the center of action; and anaphora of the conjunction *e*, reinforced by the attendant morphological figure *d'autres* (masculine)-*d'autras* (femenine), gives a effect of accumulation to his supposedly numerous feats of valor.

A denser combination of initial and internal repetition turns one stanza of the otherwise unremarkable poem *Ges per freg ni per calor* into an obsessive dissertation on how much the poet's lady is "better" or "best." If the author is not Rigaut de Berbezilh, it is a least someone aware of Rigaut's usual *senhal* for his lady *Miells-de-domna* ("Best-of-Ladies"? "Better-than-Lady"?) and of Rigaut's quadruple repetition of *miels* in his V, 33-35.[40] At any rate, the poem *Ges per freg* claims that everything about the lady is *miells*, a word that in one eleven-line stanza recurs seven times initially and as many internally. A short quotation,

> *Miells* de domna e *miells* d'amor,
> *Miells* de tot qan mais dir vueilh
> E *miells* d'autra qe·s despueilh (P-C 5.1, 34-36),

shows that, although the technique is dangerous, here at least the thematic importance of *miells*, the variation by morphological figure of alternating *de* and *d'*, and skillful parallelism of elements make this concentrated repetition more justified than that of *nostre* in the *Leys*' admonitory passage quoted above (p. 90).

F 2. *Internal and Final Repetition*

Internal and final repetition can also combine, especially by extension of a repeated rime expression far back into the verse. A revealing example is the fourth verse of successive stanzas of William IX's *Chansoneta nueva*:

> S'ieu *ma bona dompna am* (VIII, 10);
> Cum *ma bona dompna m'am* (VIII, 16).

Melodic identity makes this recall doubly forceful. The danger of monotony is countered by subtle variation: the rime word *am* (repeated in every fourth line except for *amam* in stanza V) here functions as a first-person then a third-person verb; the pronoun subject *ieu* is replaced by the object *m'*; and inversely, the internally repeated expression *ma bona dompna* functions as direct object then subject. This interlocking subject-object pattern aptly suggests the poet's and his lady's supposed inseparability in love.

Another combination of internal and final repetition, in which the same word functions in the rime and also internally, is suprisingly

---

[40] All MSS but one attribute the poem to Ademar de Rocaficha; the lone MS attributing it to Rigaut de Berbezilh is seen as insufficient evidence by Varvaro, *Rigaut de Berbezilh*, p. 223.

rare. On the whole, the rime word is repeated only in another final position or initially in another line.

F 3. *Initial and Final Repetition*

Repetition can also bind together the extremities of two successive lines. This technique magnifies the supposedly beneficial effect, on the Spanish king's peace of mind, of his donating a warhorse to the self-proclaimed war hero Peire Vidal:

> E s'eu agues caval adreit corsier,
> *Suau* s'estes lo reis part Balaguer
> E dormis se planamen e *suau* (XIV, 25-27).

By framing these lines with the word "gentle," repeated in the emphatic initial and final positions, Peire Vidal skillfully creates an appropriate impression of repose, reinforced by thematic sibilance and parallelism of propositions. Actually, we have here an example of *redditio* (cf. chart 1, above): the second and third lines form a syntactic unit, the result-clause of a condition, and this unit both begins and ends with the word *suau*.

This principle applied to the single verse, identified by the *Leys* as *epinalensi*, seems absent in the troubadours, as do the more complex forms defined as *complexio* and *conversio*. But *anadiplosis* does exist. Bartsch gives a few examples, though chiefly not with true anaphora but repetition merely near the beginning of lines, and chiefly not of word repetition but of morphemic repetition.[41] His most legitimate example (though even here morphological figure predominates in the poem as a whole) is from Uc Brunet or more probably Peire de Blai:

> En est son faz chansoneta *novelha*;
> *Novelha* es, quar ieu chant *de novelh*:
> *De novelh* ai chauzida la plus *belha*,
> *Belh'* en totz sens, e tot quan fay es *belh*... (P-C 328.1, 1-4).

This technique, which here emphasizes the *novelty* and *beauty* which the poet imputes to his own work, is actually not much used by the troubadours, even though Guilhem Molinier gives it a good deal of

---

[41] Bartsch, "Reimkunst," pp. 179-180.

attention. Rather, the troubadours prefer to use structural repetition more on the level of the stanza than of the verse.

G. Repetition with Relation to the Stanza

This last example shows *gradatio*, which is continuous *anadiplosis* (cf. chart 1, above). According to the *Leys* (I, 280) we have here *coblas capfinidas*; but the term, literally "head-finished stanzas," is usually applied only when this cooperating final and initial repetition is extended from verse level to stanza level. In such *coblas capfinidas*, the last word, word group, or entire verse of one stanza is also the first of the next. Again, Bartsch's few examples illustrate chiefly not word repetition but etymological figure, or else repetition not at but merely near stanzaic extremities.[42] The same can be said of István Frank's list of fifty-six poems in *coblas capfinidas*.[43] In fact no single Provençal poem respects the rigorous definition, which would require the last word of every stanza to be exactly repeated as the first of the next stanza.

What we do find is a certain number of examples where a word or group occurs somewhere in the last line of one stanza and again somewhere in the first line of the next stanza. This relaxed version of *coblas capfinidas*, allowed by Frank, involves chiefly repetition internal in the line; anaphora and rime word repetition are just too hard to fit into the same rigorous pattern. A typical example is Bernart de Ventadorn XXXIX, the first and last lines of whose five stanzas and one tornada are

> St. I Bel m'es can eu vei la brolha....
> Cella qu'*eu* dezir e *volh*.
>
> II *Eu* la *volh* can plus s'orgolha....
> So que totz jorns *s'amor colh*.
>
> III *S'amor colh*, qui m'en preizona....
> Que *tuih li mal* m'en *son bo*.
>
> IV *Bo son tuih li mal* que·m dona....
> Ilh me *chamja ma razo*.

---

[42] Bartsch, pp. 179-180.
[43] Frank, *Répertoire métrique*, II, 61; cf. I, xxxviii.

V   *Ma razo chamja* e vira....
    Can sa gran beutat *remir*.

(torn.) VI   Ma mort *remir*, que jauzir....
    C'atendre cuit per sofrir.

Here, what could be mere mechanical variation takes different forms in each stanza, as repeated elements recur in differing positions and constructions. At the end, the implied equivalence of *sa gran beutat* and *ma mort*, through their juxtaposition as objects of the repeated verb *remir*, summarizes both the poem's thought and a theme essential to the Provençal lyric: the equivalence of love and death.

Of *coblas capfinidas*, Jeanroy says: "ce procédé, qui eut en Italie un très grand succès, fut médiocrement goûté des troubadours: cette répétition mécanique de la pensée et du mot leur paraissait peut-être trop simple et quelque peu enfantin."[44] Admittedly, *coblas capfinidas* are rare and demand great talent to be successful; but one should surely not apply to the above example from Bernart the epithets "simple" and "childish."

Coblas capfinidas exemplify one particular fixed relation of repetition to the stanza: repetition at adjacent extremities of successive stanzas. When members of a repeated pair are separated by the exact length of a stanza, we have a new fixed relation. The *Leys* give no name for this relation, since their source, classical rhetoric, is unconcerned with stanza length. A relation operating at such distance is to be expected chiefly in emphatic positions, thus at the extremities of both line and stanza.

Let us consider Jaufre Rudel VI, where repetition at a stanzaic interval is initial in lines and in metrical divisions. The first line of the last stanza is this:

Bos es lo vers, qu'anc no i falhi (VI, 31)

and the sole tornada:

Bos es lo vers, e faran hi
Calque re don hom chantara, a, a (VI, 37-38).

---

[44] Jeanroy, *Poésie lyrique*, II, 80, n. 2.

This repetition is undeniably effective in stressing Jaufre's confidence — justified, as it happens — in his own powers of composition. The two occurrences of the repeated expression are separated by six verses, the length of a stanza. However, they are not melodically identical: within one poem, the first verse of a two-verse tornada is melodically identical not to a stanza's first verse but to its second-to-last verse.

H. Repetition with Relation to Melody

H 1. *Position in Different Stanzas*

Position within the stanza must therefore be defined according both to structure and to melody. Identical position on both these levels, shown by our sections C4 and E5 to be common enough at both extremities of the verse to prove some degree of deliberateness on the troubadours' part, helps the singer to recall the position of expressions and lines and the poet to stress certain ideas and words. However, this characteristic reinforcement of word by music has apparently so far escaped the usually watchful eye of Provençal scholars. Though our subject is primarily stylistic, it must be remembered that the Provençal lyric is half music.

Word and music can cooperate in any position within the verse, though generally in the emphatic positions. To take one example outside the rime, Cercamon's *planh* (VI) on William X, unlike Bertran de Born's on Young Henry, has no rimed refrain; but the same function is served by three repeated groups. Of these, two, of unusual length, show anaphora reaching through the verse right up to the rime word; and one shows internal repetition of a thematic expression. Their position in the poem is indicated here according to stanza and line within the stanza:

```
II,  3   Ai! com lo plagno li Barrau.
     4   Peza·m s'a longas sai estau.

III, 4   Peza·m s'a lonjas sai remaing.
     5   Segner, d'efern lo faitz estraing.

VI,  4   Lo defendetz del fel liam
     5   Del foc d'efern, que non l'aflam.

IX,  3   Ai! com lo plaigno li Gasco,
     4   Cil d'Espaign' e cil d'Arago.
```

Even the internal expression *d'efern*, comprising the third and fourth syllables of two fifth lines, recurs in identical stanzaic and melodic position. The clever step-by-step interlocking of the three repeated expressions in stanzas II-IV produces progressive development of the poem's essential themes — general lament, the poet's sense of personal loss, the prayed-for salvation of the deceased patron — all so fitting to a funereal lament.

The second theme is reiterated statically by the synonymous verbs *estau* and *remaing*, but the first and third themes show, more typically, development by *variatio*. Thus the expression *Ai! com lo plagno li* ... gains in force when the somewhat obscure Barrois are replaced as subject by more important Gascons and "*those* of Spain and *those* of Aragon" (with the supportive repetition of *cil d'*). Similarly, the second use of *d'efern* adds the concrete detail of hell's flames. Thus *conduplicatio* and *variatio* cooperate in melodically reinforced anaphora and internal repetition to play the role of refrain generally reserved for rime word repetition.

Here, repetition in melodically identical position occurs inside the stanza; however, it is often prominent in the stanza's first or last line. These emphatic stanzaic positions hardly affect internal repetition except under the relaxed definition of *coblas capfinidas* (cf. section G), where of course melodic identity is impossible. But sections C and E have suggested that emphatic position is very typical of both anaphora and rime word repetition, with or without melodic identity.

H 2. *Rime Word Repetition with Relation to Melody*

This point will now be borne out statistically, taking Peire Vidal as illustrative of the troubadours. Chart 4 has already shown that more than half of Peire Vidal's repeated rime words occur in a relation of melodic identity. The following chart will show that, in such a relation or not, his repeated rime words occur with above random frequency in the last verse of a stanza or tornada. In this chart the same general remarks apply as to chart 4. Position in the poem (in stanza or tornada) is plotted against position within stanza or tornada (in its first or last line or in neither). The slash (/) separates cases of melodic identity and non-identity. For example the first entry, 2/7, indicates that of Peire's nine repeated rime words occurring in the first verse of a stanza, only two (hence one pair) occur in a relation of melodic identity and the other seven do not.

Chart 5:

Position of Peire Vidal's Repeated Rime Words

position in poem:	any stanza		any tornada	
melodic identity:	yes/no	total	yes/no	total
position in stanza or tornada:				
first verse	2/7	9	11/6	17
medial verse	64/45	109	17/15	32
last verse	17/9	26	13/13	26
totals	83/61	144	41/34	75
per cent of last verses in totals	21%/15%	18%	32%/38%	35%
random expectancy of a line having any given position, in per cent		11%		28%

The figures in line 3 above, those for repetition in final verses, are exceptionally high, and are expressed in line 5 as a percentage of the total number of repeated rime words. Now, since Peire's average stanza has 9.2 lines,[45] any given line in a stanza has a random chance of 1/9.2 or 11 per cent of being last in its stanza. Thus even the figure of 15 per cent for repetition in last verses of stanzas without melodic identity is above random expectancy, and the 21 per cent with melodic identity is about twice it. Similarly, Peire's average tornada has 3.6 lines and each line of a tornada has a chance of 28 per cent of being last.[46] This figure is again exceeded by the 32 per cent and 38 per cent figures for rime word repetition in a tornada's last verse.

It can be concluded from this table that rime word repetition has a significantly high chance of ocurring in the last line of a structural unit. This chance is especially high with melodic identity in stanzas and without melodic identity in tornadas. This fact suggests that melodic identity was felt as a useful indicator of rime word repetition,

---

[45] The total number of lines in one stanza of each of Peire's 45 poems (excluding 3 *tensos*) is 413; 413/45 = 9.2.

[46] Peire's 52 tornadas have a total of 187 lines; thus a line known to be in a tornada has a chance of 52/187 of being final in its tornada, or .28.

as a signal that was less needed in the tornada, where the natural emphasis of special position often sufficed to call attention to repetition of words.

On the other hand, the totals of 9/144 and 17/75 for rime repetition in initial lines of stanzas and tornadas are well below random expectation of 11 per cent and 28 per cent. Clearly, the favored emphatic position is not the first but the last line of structural divisions. This is only natural: given the progressive development of verbal and musical rhythms within stanzas as well as lines, the stanza's last word is its most emphatic, especially followed as it was by a longer pause in performance than any other rime word of the stanza. This pause permits the extra time necessary for the full implications of coincident musical and verbal repetition to sink into the audience's ear and mind.

I. Repetition in the Context of the Entire Poem

I 1. *Repetition at Extremities of the Poem*

We have already seen the effect of position on repetition. Repetition has special force at either extremity of the poetic *verse* (i.e., in anaphora or rime word repetition; cf. sections C and E) or of the *stanza* (i.e., in its first or last line; cf. sections G and H). The same will now be shown of repetition at the extremities of the *poem* (i.e., in its tornada(s) or first stanza).

Each extremity of a poem has a character of its own. The first stanza often shows the most artistry and the closest cooperation between words and music, and furthermore is usually devoted to a special topic, nature description, typically in the form of lists of descriptive details linked by repeated conjunctions, whether internal or initial in the line. Such polysyndeton will be fully treated later in our chapter VI, on convergence. For now, let us give a fairly typical exordium of Cercamon containing anaphora of the conjunction:

> Quant l'aura doussa s'amarzis
> *E·l* fuelha chai de sul verjan
> *E l'*auzelh chanjan lor latis,
> *Et* ieu de sai sospir e chan ... (I, 1-4).

Anaphora, like any other poetic technique, has special force in the exordium, whose function is after all to set the poem's mood in both thought and melody.

One can give quantitative proof of the importance of repeated rime words in the poem's emphatic positions. A statistical survey of Peire Vidal's work will again illustrate the troubadours' practice. The following chart uses the same procedures as in charts 4 and 5. Position in stanzas or tornadas is plotted horizontally; position of stanzas or tornadas within the poem, vertically.

Chart 6:

Position of Repeated Rime Words Within Peire Vidal's Poems

position of stanzas or tornadas in poem:	in stanzas number	per cent	in tornadas number	per cent	total
initial	22	15	30	40	
medial	102	71	5	7	
final	20	14	27	36	
only			13	17	
subtotal	144		75		219
per cent of total		66%		34%	

(This total of 219 members of repetitive rime groups comprises the quite significant percentage of 8 per cent of Peire's roughly 2700 rime words.)

According to these figures, rime word repetition seems to have no special affinity for particular stanzas within a poem. The average occurrence of 15% and 14%, respectively, in first and last stanzas just about equals the 16 per cent of random expectation.[47] Similarly, the frequency of rime word repetition in either first or last tornadas only slightly exceeds random expectation in those poems that have two or more tornadas.[48]

On the level of the whole poem, however, the tornadas are affected by the preference for final emphasis that we have already seen on

---

[47] Peire Vidal's 45 poems (excluding 3 *tensos*) have a total of 277 stanzas, thus an average of 6.2 stanzas per poem. The chance of any given stanza being initial (or final) is 45/277 or 16 per cent.

[48] Of Peire's poems, 18 have 2, 3 or 4 tornadas for a total of 41 tornadas. The expectation that any of these tornadas will be initial (or final) is 18/41 or 44 per cent. According to our chart, 62 of Peire's repeated rime words occur in tornadas which are not single. Of these 62, 30 occur in initial tornadas and 27 in final tornadas, percentages of 48 per cent and 44 per cent compared to the random expectation of 44 per cent for each position.

the stanza level. Of Peire Vidal's repeated rime words, one third (75/219=34 per cent) occur in tornadas; yet tornadas comprise only 7 per cent of his poems' total lines.[49] Occurrence of repeated rime words in tornadas is therefore almost five times random expectancy. Though this conclusion could have been guessed at, statistical corroboration adds a new dimension of certitude.

This high frequency in tornadas is explained by their special function within the poem. They generally summarize the poem's themes, emphasize its key words and reformulate the poem's argument in the form of a request to the poet's protector or lady. And the *Leys d'amors* recognize the poetic justification of such repetition in the tornadas "Motz tornatz non es vicis en tornada" (III, 102). The very term "tornada" may reflect the fact that not only the metrical system and melody but also some of the previous rime words, return or may return in the post-stanzaic part of the poem.

I 2. *Rime Word Repetition in Tornadas*

Thematic summation is typified by Peire Vidal's tornadas repeating in the rime such words as *valors* (II), *temer* (IV), *fe* (XVIII), *greus* (XXXIII). Multiple repetition can even recapitulate preceding themes in more than one tornada; thus both tornadas of XXXIV repeat the rime word *amor* used already in stanza III. Or, more subtly, several different rime words can be paired with previous ones, as in the two tornadas of Peire Vidal XVI:

> I. Per Sant Jacme qu'om *apela*
> L'apostol de Compostela,
> En Luzi' a tal Miquel
> Que·m val mais que cel del *cel*.
>
> II. Francs reis, Proensa·us *apella*,
> Qu'en Sancho la·us desclavella,
> Qu'el en trai la cer' e·l *mel*
> E sai tramet vos lo *fel* (XVI, 71-78).

---

[49] Peire's average poem has 6.2 stanzas of 9.2 lines each, or 59 lines in its stanzas. But it has only 4.2 lines in tornadas (187 total lines in tornadas in 45 poems). The chance of any given line falling in a tornada is therefore 4.2/59 or only 7 per cent.

Here, the verb *apel(l)a* is repeated in equal melodic position; and the three other italicized rime words have already contributed, in lines 10, 19 and 40 respectively, to describing the poet's joy in love. That their repetition is conscious is suggested by melodic identity in all three pairs, by the final and hence equal position of both the *cel* and *fel* pairs in their structural divisions, and by the supportive homophony of *cel del cel*, "he from heaven." But the tornadas turn the previous amorous associations of the three words into political ones. Notably *mel* and *fel*, previously separated by twenty lines, now combine antithetically to dramatize with biblical aura the discord between the *franc rei* and *En Sancho*. So here the relation within repeated pairs is not so much reiterative as complementary, representing the two themes of love and politics that run through this *sirventes-canso*.

Summarizing repetition is even more common, especially where a poem's last two structural units work together, as in about half of William IX's surviving poems. Repetition can affect words, expressions or whole lines. An important rime word or expression can occur in two tornadas, as in William's poems VI and VII; or in the last stanza and in the tornada of what is apparently William's last known poem, *Pos de chantar*, which ends fittingly with an insistent finality:

> Que vengan tut e m'onren fort,
> Qu'eu ai avut *joi e deport*
> loing *e* pres *et* e mon aizi.
>
> Aissi guerpisc *joi e deport*
> *E* vair *e* gris *e* sembeli (XI, 37-42).

Here the expression *joi e deport* becomes thematic by its recurrence at two lines' interval and in equal melodic position. Each time developed by a triple enumeration with conjunctive repetition, it designates earthly pleasures, "joy and fun," first in the past context suggested by the perfect *ai avut* and by the real-life detail *e mon aizi*, "in my residence," then in the future context suggested by the present *guerpisc* describing the poet's intended abandonment of the world. Thus repetition and variation on the theme of now-unattainable *joy e deport* summarize the poem's preoccupation with the problem of life and death.

Or, a tornada can be virtually identical to the last segment of the last stanza, either in only one line (William's II and, if we accept

Jeanroy's suggested reconstruction, III) or in more (V). Thus in the "cat poem," lengthy amorous ventures are first summarized in the fourteenth and final stanza:

>Tant las fotei com auzirets:
>Cen e quatre vint et ueit vetz,
>Q'a pauc no·i rompei mos corretz
>   E mos arnes;
>E *no·us* puesc *dir lo malaveg,*
>   *Tan gran m'en pres* (V, 79-84),

and then further distilled in the sole tornada:

>Ges *no·us* sai *dir lo malaveg,*
>   *Tan gran m'en pres* (V, 85-86).[50]

This final reiteration not only summarizes the poem's ultimate result but also brings out a point of irony: after all, William's supposed *malaveg* has had its cheery side too.

William is only the first of many to use word and line repetition. Of Jaufre Rudel's two poems having tornadas, VI has anaphora of the self-praising expression *Bos es lo vers* in the last stanza and only tornada (cf. p. 58, above); and V ends with very effective repetition in three lines stressing the thematic contrast of desire and unattainability, of love and non-love:

>Ver ditz qui m'apella lechay
>Ni deziron d'amor de lonh,
>Car nulhs autres joys tan no·m play   45
>Cum jauzimens d'amor de lonh.
>*Mas so qu'ieu vuelh m'es atahis,*
>*Qu'enaissi·m fadet mos pairis*
>*Qu'ieu ames e non fos amatz.*
>
>*Mas so q'ieu vuoill m'es atahis.*   50
>Tota sia mauditz lo *pairis*
>Qe·m *fadet q'ieu non fos amatz!* (V, 43-52).

Cercamon and Peire Vidal use repetition only sparingly for the purpose of linking last stanzas to tornadas; but Bernart de Ventadorn

---

[50] The version having no tornada and having a final stanza concerning the cat is found only in MS *C*, printed in Jeanroy's notes, and is generally regarded as apocryphal.

does so in about one quarter of his poem, on a scale ranging from repetition of single rime words up to repetition of most of three lines. In Bernart's work, the most effective example is his lark poem, where a central theme of the last stanza's second four-line segment is taken up with almost identical words in the tornada, seconded by repetition and morphological figure of the preposition *d(e)* and of the pronoun *m(e)*:

> Aissi·m part *de* leis *e·m recre*;
> Mort *m*'a, per mort li respon,
> E *vau m'en*, pus ilh no·*m* rete,
> *Chaitius*, en issilh, *no sai on*.
>
> Tristans, ges no·n auretz de *me*,
> Qu'eu *m'en vau, chaitius, no sai on*.
> *De* chantar *me* gic *e·m recre*,
> E *de* joi e *d*'amor *m*'escon (XXXI, 53-60).

Here the remarkable effect of desolation results from recurrence of the expressions *e·m recre, vau m'en, chaitius,* and *no sai on*, which by often changing place relative to each other and to the line suggest the poet's mental disarray. These repetitions cooperate with parallel reflexive verbs expressing the idea of departure (·*m part,* ·*m recre, m'en vau, me gic, m'escon*) and emphasizing the first person pronoun *m(e)* and the preposition of separation *d(e)*. The means and effect recall those, simpler but equally skillful, used at the end of William's leave-taking poem (XI) for a similarly reinforced effect of despair and finality.

These are but a few examples from several early troubadours. It seems unnecessary to produce laborious statistics to demonstrate what can simply be observed by reading poems of different periods: that the importance of initial and especially of final repetition — whether on the scale of the line, stanza, or poem — remains great throughout the history of the Old Provençal lyric.

J. GRAMMATICAL NATURE OF REPETITIVE GROUPS

Whatever their relation to the line, stanza, or poem, two occurrences of a single word or expression always stand in an "indirect" grammatical relation. They cannot form the immediately linked groups characteristic of much morphemic repetition (*un can cantar*, etc.). The same word simply cannot have different functions, e.g. as noun and verb. But this does not mean that its two occurrences need be unco-ordinated. Very often, their semantic and phonetic effect is further reinforced, syntactically, by identical functions in parallel or enumerative structures.

J 1. *Coordinated Repetition: Minor Words*

Now, we distinguish repeated words according to their grammatical functions. Though as sections C through E have shown, any part of speech may be repeated, enumerative repetition generally affects minor parts of speech, whose numerical importance is graphically shown in the fourth column of chart 3. Minor words in enumeration comprise about three-quarters of all repeated words. As Riffaterre says, "l'efficacité de la répétition est telle, qu'elle *intensifie même les outils grammaticaux*: c'est-à-dire qu'elle parvient à transférer à des éléments, qui sont purement de structure, l'expressivité ou l'effectivité de la pensée qu'ils encadrent." [51]

Thus, among the minor parts of speech, a repeated article, almost always definite, very often introduces enumerated substantives or substantivized adjectives. This example, like all of those in this section, will be drawn from the work of Peire Vidal:

> Mout m'es bon *e* bel,
> Quan vei de novel
> *La* folh' el ramel
> *E la* fresca flor,
> *E* chanton *l'*auzel
> Sobre *la* verdor,
> *E·l* fin amador
> Son gai per amor (XVII, 1-8).

Here the repeated feminine article *la* introduces both members of the conventional alliterative pair *folha-flor*, to which can almost be added the expression *la verdor*, despite its different syntactic role, by reason of the common article, similar meaning and weak alliteration (*v-f*). Here, as often, a common article tends to group substantives. Similarly, the masculine plural article *·l* or *l*' (enclitic or proclitic) introduces the

---

[51] Riffaterre, *Pléiades*, pp. 128-129.

pair *auzel-amador* (for morphological figure between these two article groups, *la* and *l*, cf. sections D5 and F of chapter IV). In this example, density of repetition, continuous syntax and short lines permit the creation and appreciation of poetic effects.

As for the conjunction, its repetition occurs by definition in much enumeration, but its effect can be more or less dense. In the preceding passage, triply anaphoric *E* functions on two levels: on the word level, it unites the alliterative pairs *bon-bel* and *folh'-flor*; and on the clause-level, it structures the seven-line group introduced by *quan* into three clauses each describing spring from a different point of view and each built on its own declarative verb (*vei, chanton, son gai*).

Thus the repeated conjunction aligns parallel elements, either clauses:

> *Car* no·us vei lai e *car* midons no·m ve (XVIII, 58);

or else single words, often in dense succession:

> Ben amai d'amor
> Folh' *e* fruit *e* flor
> *E* ram *e* verdor... (XVII, 37-39).

This is especially frequent in *descriptio*:

> *E* l'olh *e*·l cil negre espes
> *E*·l nas.... (XXXV, 25-26).

Similarly, a preposition can hardly be repeated except governing parallel objects in enumeration:

> Anc no mori *per* amor ni *per* al (XXIV, 1);
> *Per* astre o *per* socors (II, 7);
> E *per* temps e *per* sazo (II, 39);
> *Ab* neu et *ab* gelada (VIII, 14);
> *Ves* domnas e *ves* amadors (VIII, 56);
> Car ges no·m fier *de* coutel ni *de* lansa (XII, 29);
> Mas *ab* bels ditz et *ab* plazen semblansa (XII, 30);
> *Ab* cortes ditz et *ab* bela semblansa (XIII, 30).

In these examples the preposition facilitates an accumulation of terms which are synonymous or complementary. The last two examples in particular show the excessive stylization which the device often attains, since the two linked expressions are virtually identical. In addition, this repetitive link is often strengthened by other elements like articles.

> Per *l'*enoi e *per l'*enjan (XXXVI, 4).

As for repeated pronouns, members of one pair generally serve the same function, whether reflexive:

> Mos cors *s'*alegr' e *s'*esjau (IX, 1);
> *M'en* rancur e *m'en* complanha (II, 20);

impersonal (e.g., *en* in the last example); or oblique (though almost never nominative):

> Dels olhs *vos* plor e del cor *vos* sospir (XXX, 6).

The same parallelism of function applies to the repeated possessive adjective:

> *Mon* cor e *mon* sen (XVII, 62);
> *Mos* maltraits ni *mos* dechazers (VIII, 21);
> Quar d'amor son *mei* fag e *mei* parven (XXVII, 16).

In such cases, the parallelism can be varied by a difference of function:

> Ab *l'*alen tir vas me *l'*aire (XIX, 1).

Here, the repeated article stresses the alliterating pair of similar meaning, *l'alen* and *l'aire*; the fact that one noun is a prepositional object and the other a verbal object gives a pleasing sort of *variatio*, as is often the case with repetition of what we have called minor parts of speech.

J 2. *Coordinated Repetition: Major Words*

Enumerative repetition of major words is comparatively rare. In an example from Jaufre Rudel, successive lines and clauses linked by the conjunction *e* have the common verb *es* surrounded by the pronouns *selh* and *qui*:

>   Que *selh es* savis *qui* aten
>   E *selh es* fols *qui* trop s'irays (IV, 13-14).

This common framework magnifies the stress obtained by expressing the same thought first positively then negatively, a variant of the figure of speech known as *expolitio*, here specifically *expolito eandem rem dicendo commutando verba*.[52] Again we see how repetition can be both a contributor and a clue to other figures of speech.

One grammatically major word frequent in enumeration is the adverb *tan*, of which Peire Vidal, among others, makes extensive and even excessive use:

>   C'anc en cambra non vitz *tan* plazentier
>   Ni ab armas *tan* mal ni *tan* sobrier (XIV, 22-23).

This repetition of *tan*, "so," modifying three adjectives linked by *ni*, makes Peire's self-praise sound somewhat insincere.

This same device might advantageously have been replaced by another means of intensification in the following homage to his lady's qualities:

>   Sabetz per que·lh port amor *tan* coral?
>   Car anc no vi *tan* bela *ni* gensor
>   Ni *tan* bona, don tenh qu'ai gran ricor,
>   Car sui amics de domna que *tan* val (XVIII, 41-44).

Still, Peire has at least held himself to one *tan* per verse by using *gensor* rather than *tan gen* in the second line, thus adding a bit of welcome asymmetry.

A similar case of enumerative repetition, but on a larger scale and involving not adverbs but verbs, occurs in two tornadas by Bertran de Born:

>   Mas si·l reis ve, ieu ai en Dieu fiansa,
>   Qu'ieu *serai vius* o *serai* per quartiers;
>
>   E *si* sui *vius, er mi grans* benananza,
>   E *si* ieu muoir, *er mi grans* deliuriers (80.25, 25-28).

---

[52] Lausberg, *Handbuch*, § 835-838.

Here the ideas of futurity and destiny are effectively introduced by the pair *serai . . . o serai*, which presents within one line the antonymic alternatives of survival and death. The linking of the two tornadas by repeated *vius*, "alive," helps indicate that the second tornada is in fact a typical enlargement of the first by *variatio*, to which contributes *expolitio* in the expression *ieu muoir*, a paraphrase of *serai per quartiers*. The second tornada, moreover, contains a pair of more extensive enumerated propositions, introduced by the words *E si* and joined by the shared expression *er mi grans* plus nouns of similar impact.

This well-structured context allows an effective repetition of the modifier *grans*. Bertran's subtlest twist here is that the contradictory conditions suggested by *si sui vius* and *si ieu muoir* produce a common effect in the poet's mind, one of happiness or deliverance, and that these two pairs, the antonymic one describing his fate and the synonymic one describing his reaction to it, are juxtaposed in the same repetitive framework — good evidence of the great potential of repetition as a grammatical tool and as a semantic catalyst.

The term "coordinated repetition" can also include repetition not in enumeration but in parallel structures whose elements have similar grammatical functions. For example, Arnaut Daniel expresses his sentiments by simply repeating the first person person verb "I love" with the pronoun object "her" at the end of one stanza and beginning of the next (a reduced form of *coblas capfinidas*):

> Mais *l'am* que qi·m des Luserna.
> Tan *l'am* de cor e la queri ... (X, 21-22).

In the rime, such parallelism often exists even at some distance. Thus, Peire Vidal uses one rime word three times as a past participle describing the lady as the object of an amorous quest:

> E s'aver puosc cella qu'ai tant *enquisa* (XXXVII, 29);
> Per la gensor *qu'anc fos d'amor enquisa* (32);
> Quar genser etz *qu'anc fos d'amor enquisa* (44).

Or, in a simpler example of major word repetition in parallel structures, Peire Vidal says:

> Pero *de bon* sen
> Am *de bon* talen (XVII, 13-14).

The effect is as if he had said *Pero am de bon sen e de bon talen.*

J 3. *Uncoordinated Repetition*

It must be emphasized that repetition of some minor and most major words occurs in neither enumerative nor parallel relations. A thematic word most often recurs in different grammatical functions, as in so many of the examples in preceding sections of this chapter. The epitome of this technique is the largely haphazard way in which a chosen word is worked into every line of a stanza built on the repetitive principle (cf. section D4) without any special syntactical structuring. This will again be illustrated in our analysis of Bernart de Ventadorn's skylark poem in section VI.E.

K. Conclusion

To sum up, the range of word repetition described by the *Leys d'amors* and inherited from traditional rhetoric corresponds at least qualitatively to the scope of repetition in the troubadours, from simple *conduplicatio* to the most complex architectural repetition. The Provençal terms for the "vices" in our chart have been most useful; the various sorts of *mot pesan, mot tornat,* and *pauza tornada* appear frequently in the best troubadours, not as vices but as effective stylistic devices.

Guilhem Molinier is also aware of the basic variable factors affecting word repetition, namely position in the line and relation among different groups. He distinguishes, in some detail, *anafora, mot tornat,* and *pauza tornada;* and he describes interlocking and sequential repeated pairs as *anadyplozi* and *complexio.*

But Molinier gives exaggerated importance to repetitive *coblas.* These do exist in the twelfth century, especially *coblas capfinidas,* generally with convergence of word repetition and morphemic repetition. But for each *cobla capfinida,* we find hundreds of examples of simple unrimed repetition of major or minor words, in enumeration or not. Also common are simple repeated rime pairs, often with thematic value, and word refrains, which one is surprised to find neglected by Molinier despite his usual concern for form. Perhaps his interest did not extend beyond the individual stanza to the poem as a poetic whole. But as has been seen especially in discussing thematic word repetition and its relation to melody and to the tornada, the context in which we must ultimately evaluate figures of repetition is the entire poem.

Chapter IV

MORPHEMIC REPETITION

A number of terms related to the subject of this chapter have often been used differently by various authors, both medieval and modern. It therefore seems best to start by defining our terms. "Morphemic repetition" will designate the repetition of morphemes, whether lexical (i.e., carrying a semantic value) or functional (i.e., carrying only a morphological value), under conditions producing mutual reinforcement. Morphemic repetition creates similar but more complex situations than word repetition. Morphemic repetition is more dynamic, since it permits parts of speech and inflections to vary. These variations will provide grounds for defining, in accordance with rhetoric and the *Leys d'amors*, three major subtypes of morphemic repetition: etymological figure (a common root in different words or parts of speech), composition (*compositio* being Molinier's term for etymological figure by prefixation), and morphological figure (different inflections of one word).

Morphemic repetition, a generally more fertile and more adaptable poetic means than word repetition, is more frequent in Old Provençal than in highly analytical languages like Modern English. Old Provençal retains enough of the synthetic character of Latin to have a large array of inflections, expecially verbal ones, which also receive in most cases the added distinctiveness of tonic stress (while in English, inflections are generally unaccented). Repetition of certain inflections can even constitute an independent figure under the name of *homoeoteleuton* or *homoeoptoton*. Since in these two figures, the repeated morpheme is often smaller than the variable element, they will be treated under the category of sound repetition, in section V.G3, as contributing chiefly to internal rime.

While word repetition is limited to producing an expressive "pattern" of identical elements, morphemic repetition has extremely varied potentialities. Perhaps because of this very adaptability, morphemic repetition does not share the special importance of word repetition at the beginning of verses, in identical positions of different stanzas, or in the tornada. Otherwise, the two figures have much in common in their poetic applications. Both figures, though occurring most often in pairs of words and in the interior of verses, take on special effect in larger groups and in the rime; and both can form the "architectural" basis of a stanza or of an entire poem. Both figures occur with differing impacts in contexts coordinated by conjunctions or uncoordinated, and have different strength and functions in major and minor parts of speech. And for both, average frequencies for different poets and for different situations within poems can be computed to complement qualitative evaluation of particular stylistic purposes and results.

The effects of morphemic repetition depend on some of the same factors as the effects of word repetition. The inherent importance of a particular root — its semantic character, its rarity, its phonetic individuality — helps determine its perceptibility when repeated. The effect of a repeated root also depends on the relation between its occurrences, in terms of frequency, distance, morphological kinship, grammatical linkage, and semantic relationship. And the place of the root in larger structures — in the verse (e.g., placed internally or in the rime), in the stanza (e.g., confined to one stanza or linking two or more), and in the poem (e.g., in the exordium, in the tornada, or thematic throughout) — also influences its ultimate poetic importance.

Before we discuss these and other aspects, first sections A through C will survey the treatment of morphemic repetition in traditional rhetoric, in the *Leys d'amors* and in modern scholarship. Sections D and E will discuss the various morphological and structural relations possible between occurrences of one root. And section F will deal with the "minor" roots, leaving major words and the questions of position in the verse and of frequency for sections G through J.

A. Rhetoric and Morphemic Repetition

The great range and variety of morphemic repetition explain why the terminology for it has never become standardized, even to this day. The most general term for morphemic repetition, as differentiated from word repetition, is *annominatio* in Latin and *paronomasia* in Greek. *Annominatio* is held to have an "unorganic" subtype which includes homophony and near-homophony; these will be discussed with other sound effects, in section V. H. "Organic" *annominatio*, the repetition of one root in two or more different words or in different forms, is the subject of the present chapter. It occurs, to use the rhetorical terminology, either *per adiectionem vel detractionem* (by the addition or elimination of letters or syllables), or *per immutationem* (by changing letters or syllables). Both types involve changing the beginning of a word (e.g., *erat-deerat, reprimi-comprimi*) or the ending (*supplicatio-supplicatione, maxime-maximo*).[1]

The most important subtype of *annominatio* is *polyptoton*,[2] which most rhetoricians reserve for anaphoric variation by declension of substantives or pronouns, but which can take on a wider meaning applying to any part of speech and to any position within metrical units. *Polyptoton* of nouns is also known as *declinatio* or *traductio*, as in the series *hominem-homo-hominis*,[3] or in Provençal the forms *om-ome-òmes*. Another sort of *annominatio*, more common in the troubadours, is variously called *derivatio* or *figura per pleonasmum*[4] or, in later terminology, *figura etymologica*. This figure associates two cognate words, very often a noun and a verb, as in *voce vocans* or *ire iter*.

It should be noted that *annominatio* belongs as a color of rhetoric to *ornatus facilis*:[5] and in most treatises it is the first-mentioned form of *interpretatio* or poetic development of a subject. There is nothing in rhetoric to support the contention that morphemic repetition is an unusual and difficult figure, or more to be expected in *trobar clus*

---

[1] Cf. Lausberg, *Handbuch*, § 647-648, and his *Elemente*, § 276-281.
[2] Lausberg, *Elemente*, § 280; *Handbuch*, § 640-648.
[3] *Rhetorica ad Herennium*, IV, xiv, 20, quoted in Lausberg, *Handbuch*, § 647.
[4] Lausberg, *Handbuch*, § 503, 648; *Elemente*, § 281.
[5] Cf. Faral, *Arts poétiques*, pp. 91-96.

than in *trobar leu*.[6] In fact, *annominatio* of all sorts is common in troubadours of the most varying personalities.

B. The "Leys d'Amors": "Paronomazia" and "Rim Derivatiu"

Like his Latin models, Guilhem Molinier analyzes morphemic repetition under the general heading of *paronomazia* (III, 170-172). He uses the term *compositio* (II, 100-102) to describe roots repeated with different prefixes. If prefixation does not change the meaning of a word, then we have *adjectio* (e.g., *trobayre-atrobayre*); but if the meaning changes, we have *dreyta compositio* (e.g., *cortes-descortes*). *Compositio* by suffixation produces *motz biaysshatz* ("diverted words," II, 204, e.g. *falha-falhensa* and *plazen-plazensa*).

These cases involve distinct words; in other figures, a single word varies by inflection. One of these, adapted from rhetorical *polyptoton* in the strict sense, is the orderly succession of different cases of one substantive, classed as one of the forms of *poliptoton* (III, 176-178), of *traductio* (III, 178) or of *agnominatio* (III, 172), thus *Dieus-de Dieu-a Dieu-Dieu*. But in the troubadours we will find only a less rigorous form of this figure, described by Molinier as a variety of *epymone*, occurring

> cant hom una meteyssha dictio no retorna, mas solamen lo comessamen de la dictio que haura dicha, si que la fis se variava d'aquesta dictio que retorna, coma
>
> > *Planhen planc* lo temps qu'es passatz
> > E *ploran plori* mos peccatz.
>
> Et aquest membre d'aquesta figura tenem per estranh e per vicios si donz no·s fazia scienmen e per compas continuan tot un dictat e tota una cobla (III, 310).

Here, then, as with other sorts of *paronomazia*, Molinier holds, against medieval rhetoric and against the troubadours' practice, that morphe-

---

[6] Thus Jean Bourciez in *Revue des Langues Romanes*, LXXI (1955), 115, reviewing Marco Boni's *Sordello*, writes erroneously:

> Sordel se rattachant à la tendance dite du *trobar leu*, c'est à peine s'il y a lieu de noter chez lui quelques séries dérivatives (fins de vers *guitz... guida*) ou quelques rimes 'équivoques' (*amar*-aimer et amer).

These features may well be rare in Sordel, but they are not rare in *trobar leu*.

mic repetition must be methodical and continuous to rise above the condition of vice.

The rime being so important for Provençal figures of repetition, Molinier adapts rhetoric's *annominatio* to describe different sorts of *paronomazia* in the rime (I, 184-186, etc.). His *rim derivatiu* (or *entretrach*) can occur by *mermamen* or *adjustamen* (or *creysshamen*) *d'una letra, d'una sillaba* or *de motas sillabas*, ranging from *mort-morta* to *humil-humilitat* and *trobayres-atroba*. And any of these sorts of derivative rime used through a whole stanza forms a *cobla derivativa, derivans,* or *entretracha* (I, 336). We will have frequent occasion to refer to the terms and examples used by Molinier, the very detail of whose discussion implies that morphemic repetition plays an important role in the poetry of the troubadours.

C. Scholarship

Modern critics have generally held the same attitudes toward morphemic repetition as toward word repetition. The two are actually not often distinguished. Thus the contributions of Diez, Frank, and Riffaterre mentioned in section III. A apply to both figures. When morphemic repetition is distinguished as an individual stylistic device, as by Bartsch,[7] the most attention is given to derivative rime and to derivative *coblas*, though as we shall see, non-rimed morphemic repetition is far more essential to the troubadours' art. In fact, our sections E through G especially will cover essentially new ground in Provençal scholarship.

Morphemic repetition was a major medieval literary device. M. B. Ogle shows that *polyptoton* and *homoeoteleuton* are typical of one of Walter Map's two usual styles.[8] The Middle High German novel and lyric use *Wortfiguren* combined with *Wortwiederholung* in the form of *Leitwörter* in order to stress *Leitbegriffe*.[9] Chaucer, influenced by the French tradition, uses *annominatio* and *traductio*.[10] Dragonetti

---

[7] Bartsch, "Reimkunst," pp. 192-193.
[8] Marbury Bladen Ogle, "Some Aspects of Medieval Latin Style," *Speculum*, I (1926), 170-189.
[9] Cf. ch. III, n. 15.
[10] Helge Kökeritz, "Rhetorical Word Play in Chaucer," *PMLA*, LXIX (1954), 937-952.

mentions *annominatio* as one of the *figures de répétition* belonging to *ornement facile* in the Old French courtly lyric.[11]

Perhaps most significant, the *Divine Comedy* uses clear-cut *annominatio* in about two hundred pairs or groups of words, including occasional paronomastic series like *orrevol-onori-onranza-onrate-onorate* (*Inferno*, IV, 72-80);[12] Curtius rightly indicates the troubadours as an influence on Dante in this respect.[13] Spitzer too comments on *annominatio*, among other "rhetorical artifices," in *Inferno*, XIII, notably in

> *Cred*'io ch'ei *credette* ch'io *credesse* (25);
>
> *Infiammò* contra me gli animi tutti,
>   E gl'*infiammati infiammar* si Augusto (67-68);
>
> *Ingiusto* fece me contra me *giusto* (72).

Stressing the Provençal influence on Dante, Spitzer here gives a fine example of contextual interpretation of stylistic phenomena.[14]

In non-medieval criticism, Joseph Fucilla mentions derivative rime alongside *parole identiche* in the fifteenth- and sixteenth-century sonnet.[15] Leo Spitzer discusses the Spanish types *al volver que volvió, en trayendo que trayese*, etc.[16] And, in the field of French stylistics, Marouzeau allows that

> La reprise approximative, destinée à souligner le rapport entre deux notions qu'on distingue, est un procédé plus délicat [than word repetition], qui peut avoir pour effet de prolonger comme par un écho une impression ou une évocation à laquelle on se complaît.[17]

---

[11] Dragonetti, *Technique poétique*, p. 40.

[12] E. R. Curtius, "Neue Dantestudien," *Gesammelte Aufsätze zur romanischen Philologie* (Bern, 1960), part IV: "Die *Commedia*," 333-338.

[13] Curtius, p. 335: "Für Dante ist wichtig, daß auch die Provenzalen die annominatio verwenden."

[14] Spitzer, "*Inferno* XIII."

[15] Joseph Fucilla, "*Parole identiche* in the Sonnet and Other Verse Forms," *PMLA*, L (1935), 372-402.

[16] Leo Spitzer, "Paronomasie im Spanischen," *Stilstudien* (Munich, 1928), I, 101-108. Another type which Spitzer might have mentioned is Modern Provençal *cantas que cantaras*, etc. For further remarks on *paronomasia*, cf. his index in vol. II, art. "Stammwiederholung."

[17] Marouzeau, *Précis de stylistique française*, p. 167.

These few examples give a background against which to assess the importance of morphemic repetition in Old Provençal. Many standard troubadour editions, unfortunately, refer to morphemic repetition only in the form of derivative rime, and this merely in passing. Joseph Linskill does comment on Raimbaut de Vaqueiras' use of "wordplay";[18] Branciforti refers to "ripetizioni di una voce in ogni strofe" and to "certe ripetizioni" of other sorts in Lanfranc Cigala, including two stanzas with architectural repetition of words and roots.[19] Avalle discerns some examples of *figura etimologica* in Peire Vidal;[20] and Mario Ruffini devotes two pages to *annominatio* as used by Aimeric de Belenoi,[21] while W. P. Shepard has written on "Two Derivative Songs by Aimeric de Peguilhan."[22]

Perhaps the most thorough treatment of morphemic repetition in the whole work of a single troubadour is Klara Fassbinder's study of *Wortspiele* in Raimbaut de Vaqueiras, including the types *am-amarai*, *soi-serai, ennuian-ennuios,* etc.[23] A similar section in each new troubadour edition or study would before long make possible broad conclusions on the troubadours' use of morphemic repetition and on the individual characteristic of different troubadours.

Although Friedrich Leiffholdt's *Etymologische Figuren im Romanischen*[24] is of occasional utility, there is no thorough inventory of Provençal morphemic repetition comparable to Martin Scholz's study of alliteration. And even Scholz, whom one would expect to find receptive toward other figures of repetition, is typical of most critics in considering "grammatical" and "etymological" figures as unworthy of "our purified taste"[25] (speaking sixty years ago, of course). Yet to

---

[18] Joseph Linskill, *The Poems of the Troubadour Raimbaut de Vaqueiras* (The Hague, 1964), p. 48.

[19] Branciforti, *Lanfranco Cigala*, pp. 101-103.

[20] Avalle, *Peire Vidal*, in his "Indice linguistico, metrico e rettorico," art. "Figura etimologica."

[21] Ruffini, *Il trovatore Aimeric de Belenoi* (cf. Intro, n. 9), pp. 81-82.

[22] William P. Shepard, "Two Derivative Songs by Aimeric de Peguilhan," *Speculum*, II (1927), 296-309.

[23] Fassbinder, "Raimbaut von Vaqueiras" (cf. Intro, n. 9), XLVII, 628-629.

[24] Friedrich Leiffholdt, *Etymologische Figuren im Romanischen* (diss. Göttingen; Hildesheim, 1883). Hereafter *Etymologische Figuren*.

[25] Martin Scholz, "Die Alliteration in der altprovenzalischen Lyrik," *ZfRP*, XXXVII (1913), 385-426; and XXXVIII (1917), 76-98, 193-210, 311-343. Hereafter "Alliteration," with reference to volume of *ZfRP* and

appreciate Provençal morphemic repetition, we need not even set aside our own taste and attempt to place ourselves in the situation of the contemporary audience; analyzing the troubadours' style in particular poetic contexts will permit us to understand and admire the great potential of this figure of repetition.

D. MORPHOLOGICAL RELATION AMONG OCCURRENCES OF ONE ROOT

Morphemic repetition takes on various morphological forms which remain basic whatever the surrounding syntactical or poetic structures, and whatever the frequency of position of the repeated roots. For the present, our main concern will be with roots carrying a definite semantic value, whose repetition intensifies our perception of a poem's message or imagery.

In the troubadours, the three categories mentioned earlier are all important. "Etymological figure" occurs in different parts of speech (e.g., *amor-amar*) or, more rarely, in words which, though of the same part of speech, are substantially different (e.g., *amor-amiga*). "Morphological figure" occurs in forms of one word which differ only by the inflection; these are hence of the same part of speech, and identical up to the ending (e.g., *am-amam-amarai*, all forms of *amar*). And "composition" indicates words of the same root and of the same part of speech, differentiated only by suffixes or prefixes (e.g., *astrucmalastruc*). Examples of these different categories will be given from various poets, and often enough from two in particular — Arnaut Daniel and Bernart de Ventadorn — to show that even two poets of such different poetic temperaments use in the same ways the same basic types of morphemic repetition.

D 1. *Etymological Figure*

In general, etymological figure, by its more "active" nature, produces a stronger effect than composition of morphological figure. The contrast between two different parts of speech (or substantially different words of the same part of speech) is not merely a contrast of inflection, prefixation or suffixation, but one of function and meaning. Any sort of word can participate in etymological figure, but certain

---

page. (This is an expanded version of his dissertation of the same title, Halle/Saale, 1913). Note 25 is to *ZfRP*, XXXVII, 425.

types predominate; the most common and perhaps most effective sort is the pairing of a verb and a noun, often in the "direct" relation of the type *cantar un can*.

Etymological figure can, when well handled, be just as effective without any direct grammatical relation between its components. One of the most beautiful verb-noun pairs — figuring in different clauses of a complex sentence and with two intervening lines but strikingly united by common imagery — is Bernart de Ventadorn's in

> Can la freid' aura *venta*
> Deves vostre païs,
> Veyaire m'es qu'eu senta
> Un *ven* de paradis (XXVI, 1-4).

These two winds, one from "your country" and one from paradise, occur in a parallelism reinforced by the alliterating rime words *païs* and *paradis*. Etymological figure on the root *cossir*- intensifies the idea of the poet's "cares" in Bernart's

> Ai las! com mor de *cossirar*!
> Que manhtas vetz en *cossir* tan (XX, 9-10).

And now within the confines of a single line, Bernat combines a cognate past participle and noun to stress the important theme relating love and death:

> *Mort* m'a, e per *mort* li respon (XXXI, 54).

Etymological figure between adjectives and substantives is also quite productive, not so often in the immediate succession and direct grammatical relation of Marcabru's *ses pareill paria*, "without similar company" (P-C 293.30, 19), as in the looser relation of William IX's lines:

> Qu'anc no cug qu'en nasques *semble*
> En *semblan* del gran linh n'Adam (VIII, 33-34);

Similarly, Guiraut de Bornelh says:

> *Pauc* d'ira·us notz e *paucs* jois vos aonda (LXIX, 19),

with the noun *pauc* and the adjective *paucs* used in two clauses whose antonymic elements (*ira-jois, notz-aonda*) are thereby juxtaposed at close quarters. Or, a self-pitying and despondent Bernart de Ventadorn writes:

> Per me·us o dic, que *mals* m'en es vengutz,
> Car traït m'a la bela de *mal* aire (IX, 34-35)

and, more indignantly:

> *Enoyos!* e que·us enansa,
> Si·m faitz *enoi* ni pesansa (III, 29-30).

Other morphological relations are possible, as of adverb and verb in Arnaut Daniel's expression "l'amors q'*inz* el cor m'*intra*" (XVIII, 23), "the love which enters into my heart." But the only other pairing of any importance between different parts of speech is that of adverb and adjective, especially of *be* and *bo*. Thus, in a line that curiously recalls to mind Keats' "Ode on First Looking into Chapman's Homer," Arnaut Daniel opens a stanza with

> *Ben* ai estat a maintas *bonas* cortz (XV, 15);

or Bernart de Ventadorn says, again as a stanza's first line,

> Mout ai *be* mes mo *bon* esper (II, 36)

and, in the same poem's first tornada:

> Lo vers es fis e naturaus
> E *bos* celui qui *be* l'enten;
> E melher es, qu·l joi aten (II, 50-52).

Positional emphasis within the stanza in these three examples fortifies their use of morphemic repetition on the theme *well/good*. On a higher semantic level, we find numerous pairs, like *coitozamen-coitos* ("eagerly-eager") in Peire Vidal XXV, 12-13.

Finally, etymological figure includes cognate words of the same parts of speech, varied by different elements. With verbs, examples such as *retinc-tenia* in William IX (I, 20-21) will be illustrated in sections E and G. Etymological figure with two nouns or adjectives is rare except in the many derivatives of *am-* (*amor, amic, amansa,* etc.), Peire Vidal's line

> E fa que pros per *amor* de s'*amia* (XI, 51).

On other roots, there are a few examples like Bernart de Ventadorn's complaint:

> Ni anc de nul *companho*
> *Companha* tan greus no·m fo (XXV, 7-8),

with direct succession of the pair "companion-companionship" linking two lines. But on the whole, etymological figure tends to involve different parts of speech, and this dynamic contrast is what sets it most apart from morphological figure.

D 2. *Compounds*

A special sort of etymological figure is composition, which to an independent base adds another lexical element, generally by prefixation. As will be shown in section I, composition has a noticeable effect chiefly in derivative rime, in the type *metre-entremetre* or in the different parts of speech of Arnaut XVIII's more imaginative *ongla-enongla*. For now, it is enough to give several representative examples.

In Bernart de Ventadorn's lines

> C'*astrucs* sojorn' e jai
> E *malastrucs* s'afana (XXVI, 49-50),

the antonymy of *sojorn' e jai* and *s'afana*, indicating pleasure and pain, hinges not on a contrastive conjunction like *mas* but on the negating prefix *mal-*. Also dominating two lines, a pair differentiated by another negating prefix occurs in Bertran de Born's lines

> Mas ses *mesura* non es res:
> Aissel que·s vol *desmesurar*
> No pot sos fachs en aut poiar (P-C 80.45, 14-16),

but this time in two different parts of speech. And Bernart de Ventadorn's

> Ja no *crezatz* qu'eu de joi me *recreya* (VII, 8)

contains both cognate words in a single line, again with one, the more important for the theme of abandoning love, stressed by position in the rime.

Etymological figure by composition, as later examples will show, involves more often verbs than adjectives and nouns. In general the language requires only one adjective and one noun formed from most roots, except for compounds with a negating prefix, while the larger number of verbal prefixes and other compositional elements provides more opportunity for using cognate compound verbs.

D 3. *Morphological Figure*

Morphological figure, according to our previous definition, repeats a single word and part of speech with differing inflections. Pronouns, possessives, and articles will be left to section F; prepositions and adverbs are invariable; this leaves us here with adjectives, nouns, and verbs, in that order of increasing importance. Adjectives have no more than four different forms (*bons-bon-bona-bonas*) and most substantives no more than two (*murs-mur*, exceptionally *trobaire-trobador-trobadors*). Differences in nominal inflection generally involve only added *a*, *s* or both, so that possibilities for variation are neither numerous nor exciting. Verbs, on the other hand, are subject to all the variations, often semantically and morphologically noteworthy, of tense, mood, person, and number.

Adjectival morphological figure is most noticeable with enumerated nouns of different genders or numbers. For example Bertran de Born complains that

> *Belas* personas, *bels* arnes
> Pot hom pro vezer e trobar,
> Mas no·i es Augiers lo Danes,
> Berartz ni Baudüis no·i par (P-C 80.45, 25-28).

The repeated root *bel-* effectively holds up its half of a contrast between the outward excellence and the inner worthlessness of present nobility.

The only other significant use of adjectives in morphological figure occurs in comparisons, when the positive grade is contrasted to the comparative or superlative. Thus Arnaut says (with one grade, as often, substantivized):

> Tant per es *genta*
> Selha que·m ten ioios
> Las *gensors* trenta
> Vens de belhas faisos (III, 49-52).

Arnaut's lady is so *gracious* that she surpasses the *most gracious;* the organic form *gensors* and contrasting stem consonants *t* and *s* make the element of variation more effective in Provençal than in English.

Substantival morphological figure can be illustrated from Bernart de Ventadorn I with its pairs *cors-cor* (3-5), *amor-Amors* (16-21) and *merces-merce*:

> Eu que·n posc mais, s'Amors me pren,
> E las charcers en que m'a mes,
> No pot claus obrir mas *merces*,
> E de *merce* no·i trop nien? (I, 21-24).

Here, in conjunction with the old but effective metaphor of the prison and the key, the progression of the word "mercy" from the subjective to the oblique case seems to symbolize the increasing separation of the poet from the mercy his lady refuses him.

These are the basic types of adjectival and substantival morphological figure; verbal morphological figure, on the other hand, is so common that it must be broken down into several subtypes according to structural criteria, which will be done in section E.

D 4. *Non-etymological Morphological Figure*

In the preceding section, an etymological relation perceived and utilized by the troubadours has been confirmed by modern philology. It is obvious that *merces* and *merce*, for example, are differently inflected forms of one word. This becomes less obvious when phonetic evolution has made related forms grow apart in sound. The stem's final consonant can be altered, as in the common pair *sai-saber*; and the thematic vowel can change as well, as in *dera* (third person singular, second conditional of *dar*) and *donatz* (second person plural, present indicative of *donar*, a derivative of classical *dare*).[26] A link was presumably felt between these last two words, because of their common initial *d*, and their identical meaning, both "to give"; hence, the parallelism in Guiraut de Bornelh's lines:

> Melhor conselh *dera* na Berengera
> Que vos no me *donatz* (LXIX, 39-40).

Similarly, identical meaning and the common initial *a* of *agues*, *agui*, and *ai* make all three felt as forms of one verb, *aver*, even though

---

[26] Oscar Bloch and Walther von Wartburg, *Dictionnaire étymologique de la langue française*, 2nd ed. (Paris, 1950), art. *donner*; Meillet and Ernout, *Dictionnaire étymologique* (cf. n. II, 7), p. 276.

the labial stem consonant has changed to *gu* or has fallen; we can speak of triple morphological figure in Bernart de Ventadorn's lines

> Tot' arma crestiana
> Volgra, *agues* tal jai
> Com eu *agui* et *ai* (XXVI, 57-59).

An even more common grouping of tenses of one paradigm involves the verb "to be." Bernart uses the present and future, *sui* and *serai*, to express the timelessness of love conditioned, in the future, only by the lady's will:

> Car eu *sui* seus plus qu'eu no dic,
> E *serai* tostems, si·lh platz (VI, 36-37).

Here common initial *s* makes an etymological relation evident;[27] and the same can be said of Arnaut Daniel's line

> Ans *er* plus vils aurs non *es* fers (XIV, 49).

But where the *s-* and *e-* forms mix, only the philologist can perceive the etymological connection; and when they are combined with the *f* forms of "to be," then we can speak properly of non-etymological morphological figure. Because of the importance of this verb, but also because of the intriguing fact of identical meaning and different sound, these different forms often join together for common effect, as in Bernart's

> E sol que bona *fos* la fis,
> Bos tenh qu'*er* lo comensamens (III, 3-4).

Such forms, combining the three times of past, present, and future, occur especially often in threes and even larger series, as will be seen in section H2.

The same tendency to juxtapose semantically similar but etymologically unrelated words applies to organic comparatives like *bo-melher*. Thus Bernart de Ventadorn's pair *bos-be* receives the third member *melher*, giving the poet's conclusion:

---

[27] Even though the closest common ancestor is the Indo-European root **es-*; cf. Meillet and Ernout, p. 1001.

> Lo vers es fis e naturaus
> E *bos* celui qui *be* l'enten;
> E *melher* es, qui·l joi aten (II, 50-52).

The same effect explains the choice of the *senhal* (Na) Mieills-be-ben by Arnaut Daniel (VII, 67; XVII, 33) and by Bertran de Born (P-C 80.12, 47). Similarly, when Bertran says of battle:

> Lo perdr' er *grans* e·l guazanhs er *sobriers* (80.25, 16),

his use of the derivative of Latin *superior* as the comparative of *grans* not only supplies a rime but also creates a greater differential between the losses and gains of battle than would the rather tame pair *grans-granhors*. The effect is enhanced by the properly superlative meaning of *sobrier* ("very big, superior," etc.), by the parallel structure, and by the emphatic position at the cesura and rime.

From non-cognate comparison it is only a step to complementary or contrasting terms in a group like "yesterday-today-tomorrow." Thus in Peire Vidal's pessimistic statement based on the synthetic comparison *mal-pejor*:

> Totz lo mons es en tal biais
> Qu'*ier* lo vim *mal* et *oi pejor* (XXXII, 25-26),

the pair *ier-oi* cooperates with the pair *mal-pejor* for a common effect. And here, we approach the troubadours' innumerable conventional antonymic pairs: *be-mal, sen-folor, ric-paubre, gran-pauc, mort-viu,* etc.[28]

Finally, non-etymological morphological figure may be considered to occur in personal pronouns and possessive adjectives of one person (*eu-meu, eu-me*) or perhaps, in a relation of contrast, of one grammatical function (*eu-tu-ilh*). These possibilities will be borne in mind in section F and chapter VI.

D 5. *Morphological Figure by Syntactical Phonetics*

We now turn to morphological figure arising not from significant or functional variations in one word but from variations due entirely

---

[28] A plausible influence on such antonymic pairs is the ecclesiastical type *in medio vitae morti sumus*.

to phonetic contexts. Such allomorphic variation can occur by elision of a final vowel or by euphonic preservation of a final consonant, in both cases whenever the following word begins with a vowel. Simple variants in spelling, however, like *vueil-vuelh-vuol-vol*, must be disregarded, since it can be supposed that each poet pronounced this first person of *voler* in a constant manner, however later manuscripts may represent it.

Syntactical doublets can produce morphological figure in major words, especially in third person verbs with elided final *-a* (*am'-ama*) or in feminine nouns (*domn'-domna*). Such effects are small, because of the lack of any semantic variation, and need no special comment. But in minor words the phenomenon is more significant, because of the relatively greater variable part in pairs like *de-d'* or *et-e*. For example, the variation *de-d'*, together with the repeated article *l*, helps to organize, contrast, and counterpoise the three rhythmical and syntactical parts of Arnaut's pleasing springtime line

Sai a*l* temps *de l'*intran *d'*abril (IV, 8).

This sort of morphological figure occurs more often in enumeration, where any functional element takes on added importance.

A simple example in enumeration is Jaufre Rudel's

E·l rossinholetz el ram
Volf *e* refranh *ez* aplana
Son dous chantar *et* afina (II, 4-6).

The verbal enumeration *volf-refranh-aplana-afina*, describing the nightingale's singing, is united by uses of the conjunction *e*, becoming *ez* or *et* (both pronounced with the voiced sibilant). The contrast *e-ez* (*et*) gives variety in the second line to the three verbs, while phonetic identity of the more distinctive form *ez* or *et* helps attach the next line's *afina* to the series.

Other functional elements, intervening between conjunctions and the terms of an enumeration, can also produce phonetic variation. Thus Marcabru puts two contiguous series into the mouth of a damsel lamenting her crusading lover's absence:

Ab vos s'en vai *lo* meus amicx,
Lo belhs e·*l* gens e·*l* pros e·*l* ricx;

> Sai m'en reman *lo* grans destricx,
> *Lo* deziriers soven e·*l* plors
> (P-C 293.1, 22-25).

The recurrent definite article organizes first a list of the lover's attributes, then a characterization of the damsel's psychological state; in both groups, the same movement from the full form *lo* to the reduced form *l* avoids any heaviness and accelerates the enumeration.

Variation of the preposition *de* is illustrated by Bertran de Born's enumeration of the relics of battle:

> En brieu veirem champs jonchatz *de* quartiers,
> *D*'elms e *d*'escutz e *de* brans e *d*'arzos
> E *de* fendutz per bustz tro als braiers.
> (P-C 80.25, 10-12)

The series *de-d'-d'-de-d'-de* has regular alternation save for consecutive *d'* and *d'* introducing the two vocalically alliterating terms *elms* and *escutz*. The second line's four groups of *d(e)* plus noun describing military equipment are framed by the two terms, introduced in the surrounding lines by the full prepositional form *de*, referring to human bodies. Further balance is provided by there being three occurrences of each form. The result of all this is to prevent any impression of monotony or of haphazardness.

Other such examples will be found in section F and chapter VI. Words subject to this sort of variation include the conjunctions *qu(e)* and *e(t)*; the prepositions *d(e)*, *a(d)* and *pe(r)* (as in *per la-pel*); the negations *no(n)* and *n(e)*; the possessives *m(a)*, *t(a)*, *s(a)*, *mo(n)*, etc.; the pronouns *m(e)*, *s(e)*, *t(e)*; the pronouns or articles *l(o)*, *l(a)*, etc.; and the adverb *tan(t)*, as in Peire Vidal's

> ... mais anc mais no menti
> Nulha domna *tant* azaut ni *tan* gen (XII, 20).

Such variation on one word is admittedly the least conspicuous, but certainly not the least common, of the different forms of morphological figure. The types discussed in sections D3 and D4, whether with cognate words or not, have semantically a greater effect, while etymological figure, whether by composition or not, is certainly the most dramatic form of morphemic repetition. Armed with these various concepts and terms, we can now turn from the morphological to the structural or syntactical relation between occurrences of repeated morphemes, always bearing in mind the poetic context which is their *raison d'être*.

E. Structural Relation Among Occurrences of One Root

Whatever the parts of speech involved, and whether in etymological figure, morphological figure, or any of their varieties, root repetition exercises poetic effect largely according to the degree in which a group's members are close to each other in both spatial distance and structural relation. In general, the tighter the structural link between repeated morphemes, the more perceptible is their relation and the closer they are in space.

At one extreme is morphemic repetition in successive words having a close structural link; at the other extreme, distant repetition in words belonging to different sentences or even stanzas. In the former case the effect is obvious; in the latter, thematic value, lexical rarity, or the like must compensate for distance if a poetic effect is to be perceived. In either case, this section will be concerned only with "major" words, leaving the others for section F.

E 1. *Morphemic Repetition in Enumeration*

Repeated morphemes receive a maximum of intensification in enumeration, simply because they are then easy to perceive as a group and generally very close in space. Such enumeration most often involves morphological figure in a relation either of declension or more often of conjugation.

Frequently, a verb occurs in temporally different uses. Thus Arnaut Daniel begins a poem by lamenting that

> Anc ieu non l'*aic*, mas ella m'*a*
> Totz temps en son poder Amors (VII, 1-2),

with the opposition *anc-totz temps* underlined by the conjunction *mas*.

Rather than both varying, the tense can remain constant while the person varies, as at the beginning of Peire d'Alvernhe's nightingale song:

> Rossinhol, el seu repaire
> M'iras ma domna vezer,
> E *digas* li·l meu afaire
> E ilh *diga*·t del seu ver (IXa, 1-4).

These two optatives, the second person referring to the bird and the third person to the lady, bring out the causal relation between the sent message and the expected reply.

Or, tense, person, and even number can all remain constant without preventing variation by morphological figure. Thus, in a contrast of active and passive, positive and negative, Jaufre Rudel ends the last stanza of his *amor de lonh* poem by fittingly developing the thematic root *am-*:

> Qu'enaissi·m fadet mos pairis
> Qu'ieu *ames* e no *fos amatz* (V, 48-49).

Both first person singular subjunctives, the active and the passive, are technically "imperfect" in tense but actually imperfective in aspect, so that the pair stresses the continuation, the atemporality, of the poet's state of loving without being loved. The same active-passive contrast, in the indicative and without negation, expresses Bernart de Ventadorn's more enviable condition:

> Car sai c'*am* e *sui amatz* (VI, 21).

Enumerative morphological figure of nouns and adjectives is not common, since these parts of speech do not share the verb's extensive variability. About the only adjective type is that of Bertran de Born's *belas personas, bels arnes* (PC 80.45, 25). More often, we do find enumerative cognate nouns differentiated by suffixation. For example William IX, not without humor, renders picturesquely the absence of any interloper between him and his two seductresses:

> E no·l 'ac *cog* ni *cogastros* (V, 45),

"There was neither cook nor chef." And Bertran de Born, as so often, accumulates related details in a battle scene:

> *Chavaliers* e *chavals* armatz (P-C 80.8a, 10).

Occurrence at close quarters within one line makes these pairs particularly effective in stressing and varying an idea. The first example is more typical in that variation operates progressively, the second term being weightier as well as emphasized by the rime.

E 2. *Morphemic Repetition in Direct Grammatical Relation*

Outside of enumerative structures, the closest relation between occurrences of one root is afforded by the "direct" linkage of subject and verb, verb and object, etc. This relation corresponds in part to rhetoric's *figura per pleonasmum*, one of whose types is *iter ire*. This illustrates the verb-object pairs which Friedrich Leiffholdt labels "etymologische Figuren im engern Sinne" [29] as opposed to the broader *adnominatio*.

Direct structural relation permits morphological figure only with auxiliaries in the type *ai avut*, "have had," as in Arnaut Daniel:

> C'aras sai ieu que mos cors e mos sens
> Mi *farant far*, lor grat, rica conquesta (XVII, 7-8).

But this intensification of the idea of making a "rich conquest" is admittedly slight.

Etymological figure demands more comment in direct grammatical relation. This relation is rare between preposition and pronoun or noun (*de dedinz*), between adverb and verb (*inz intrar*), or between adjective and noun (*bela beutat*). But it is frequent with verb and noun as direct object. The type *cantar un can* has received due critical attention. [30] Leiffholdt finds *doner, amer,* and *chanter* to be the most common Old French verbs occurring in this type, as "amer son ami," "chanter un chant (chansonete)" and "doner un don." [31]

In Provençal we find Bernart de Ventadorn commanding his jongleurs:

> Garsio, ara·m *chantat*
> Ma *chanso*, e la·m portat
> A mo Messager... (XXV, 61-63);

---

[29] I.e., "etymological figures in the narrower sense"; this is the title of the second part of Leiffholdt's *Etymologische Figuren*.
[30] For controversy on "lo joy jauzir," cf. p. 160.
[31] Leiffholdt, *Etymologische Figuren*, p. 37.

> Huguet, mos cortes messatgers,
> *Chantatz* ma *chanso* volenters
> A la reïna dels Normans (X, 43-45).

Or, on the root *don-*, William IX says of his lady:

> E que·m *donet* un *don* tan gran (X, 21).

And what better way to stress the idea of generosity than when Bertran de Born laments the disappearance of "those who used to give rich gifts"?

> E que solon *donar* rics *dos* (P-C 80.45, 37).

And the same type produces expressions like Peire Vidal's

> Ans quan cug *dir ditz* amoros (XXIX, 53)

and Peire d'Alvernhe's pair, corresponding to English "to *do* a *deed*," in

> E val mai
> Qui·ls *fagz fai* (IXa, 59),

again with verb and object in direct succession but in the less usual order.

Other roots yield different and perhaps more original effects. Thus in Marcabru's *pastorela*, a heavy pair occupying a whole line serves to impress the shepherdess with her tempter's learning and us with the humor of the situation:

> Toza, tota creatura
> Revertis a sa natura:
> *Pareillar pareilladura*
> Devem, ieu e vos, vilana,
> A l'abric lonc la pastura (P-C 293.30, 71-75).

And in a more complex example, Raimbaut de Vaqueiras combines this type with a third nearby word of the same root:

> Pero ben sai, si·m desesper,
> Qe·l *mieills* de pretz i desampar,
> C'amors fa·ls *mellors meillurar*
> E·ls plus malvatz pot far valer (VII, 11-14).

His lady is the best, and love betters the best (and even the worst).

Or, Peire Vidal combines a verb plus its object and a subject plus verb, all cognates:

> Per qu'al repropchier m'acort
> Qu'ai auzit dels ancessors,
> Qu'a temps *vens* om *vensedors*
> E per temps e per sazo
> *Vencut* fan gran *vensezo* (II, 36-40).

Peire's attribution of these lines to proverb suggests a possible popular influence on the troubadours' morphemic repetition; and whatever its source, this expatiation on the root *vens-* provides an effective lesson on the transience of glory in general and also an optimistic statement of Peire's hopes of eventually conquering his lady conqueror, whose effect on him is described at the beginning of this stanza by the same root in the preterite *venquet,* "conquered."

We also find the relation of subject to verb in Peire's claim of protecting his lord's domains:

> Que *raubador* ni malvatz rocinier
> No·l *rauberan* mais Autaves ni Crau (XIV, 29-30).

The subject and verb are separated only by a relative pronoun in Arnaut Daniel's

> Merces d'aitan, que·l mieils ai ad eslida
> Don part soleils duesc' al *jorn* quez *ajorna* (V, 20-21),

where the repeated root magnifies the expanse "from where the sun sets to the *day* that *dawns*" (i.e., "to where the day dawns"). And direct succession makes the stressed idea, that of foolishness, especially vivid when Bernart de Ventadorn illustrates the inevitability of acting according to one's character and destiny (as in the last quotation given from Marcabru), whether in folly or, by extension, in love:

> Mas costum' es tostems que *fols foleya* (VII, 29).

Direct grammatical relation, especially between verb and direct object, thus rivals enumeration in importance as a basis for morphemic repetition. Both bring two occurrences of one root into very close contact; however, neither is at all suited to multiple root repetition.

We now turn toward structural relations which, though "indirect" and often less evident, ultimately permit greater density of root repetition when used in conjunction with the two relations we have just discussed.

E 3. *Morphemic Repetition in Comparisons*

The next degree of structural closeness involves clauses set parallel by pronouns, or more often by conjunctions, in a relation of hypothesis, comparison, etc. The morphemic repetition associated with comparisons is almost always verbal. Thus Guiraut de Bornelh ends a ten-line description of a besieged castle and its defenders with the lines

> Sembla us ni us par
> Que lor ai' obs merce *clamar* (XII, 49-50),

then draws the conclusion of the comparison:

> Aissi us *clam* merce umilmens,
> Bona domna pros e valens (51-52).

The parallel between the besieged and the lover — built around the conjunction *aissi* already used to announce the allegory which occupies the entire stanza — is dramatized by verbal morphemic repetition and by substantival word repetition cooperating chiastically in the expressions *merce clamar* and *clam merce*.

Another comparison highlighted by verbal morphological figure is Bernart de Ventadorn's of the fish lured to the hook and of the lover lured toward love, with the verb *s'eslaissar*, "to hurl oneself," describing both actions:

> Aissi co·l peis qui s'*eslaiss*' el cadorn
> E no·n sap mot, tro que s'es pres en l'ama,
> M'*eslaissei* eu vas trop amar un jorn (IX, 8-10).

Variety in symmetry is provided by the apocopated inflection of the third person preterite as opposed to the tonic *-ei* ending of the first person, and by the different pronouns *s* and *m*.

A more complex example occurs in a typical exordium of Arnaut Daniel:

> Doutz brais e critz,
> Lais e cantars e voutas

> Aug dels auzels q'en lur latin *fant* precs
> Qecs ab sa par, atressi cum nos *fam*
> A las amigas en cui *entendem;*
> E doncas ieu q'en la gensor *entendi*
> Dei far chansson sobre totz de bell' obra (XII, 1-7).

The comparison between the sung prayers of birds and of lovers, united by the pair *fant-fam,* introduces another pair in etymological figure, this time the derivative rime *entendem-entendi.* These four terms in as many lines represent the logical progression of person and number from third person plural to first person plural to first person singular and of love's symptoms from birds to lovers to the poet — a good example of the dialectical morphemic repetition of which section G4 will describe another sort.

Morphemic repetition also functions in comparisons not of quality but of degree, typically with *plus,* "more." Thus Arnaut Daniel uses different forms of *aver* to underline a comparison of the poet's joy to that of Paris:

> Tals m'abelis
> Don ieu plus *ai* de ioia
> Non *ac* Paris
> D'Elena, sel de Troia (III, 45-48).

However simple, this pair *ac-ai* permits a much more effective statement than saying merely, "From whom I have more joy than Paris from Helen," without verbal reiteration. Similarly, with a weightier repeated root, Raimbaut d'Aurenga adds badly needed continuity to his otherwise hard-to-grasp comparison:

> Que nom *conquis* chans ni siscles
> Plus que folhs clercx *conquer* giscles (XXXIX, 37-38).

E 4. *Morphemic Repetition in Hypotheses and Other Complex Sentences*

Morphemic repetition, again chiefly by verbal morphological figure, can also link both parts of other complex sentences, often hypotheses with *si,* as in two examples from Arnaut Daniel:

> Maint bon chantar levet e pla
> N'agr' ieu plus *fait,* si·m *fes* socors
> Cella qe·m da ioi . . . (VII, 56-58);

> Liges soi sieus mieltz que de mieis:
> Si·m *for'* ieu si *fos* reis o ducs (XIV, 29-30).

In both examples, the repeated root recurs within one line, and in the first example the poet has overturned normal word order and used run-on lines to achieve this proximity.

Or take two successive conditions in Cercamon, separated by a stanza break:

> Qu'apres lo mal me *venra* bes
> Be leu, s'a lieys *ven* a plazer.
>
> S'elh no·m *vol, volgra* moris
> Lo dia que·m pres a coman (I, 41-44).

In the first condition, the contrast *venra-ven* corresponds to an initial enthusiastic statement, "good will come," qualified in the next line by the adverb "perhaps" and the *si*-clause "if it please her." In the second condition, the immediate succession "wish-would have wished" points out the lady's inconsistency in accepting the poet's homage without rewarding it. This passage and device are typical of the sophistic argumentation of courtly love.

A transition from hypotheses to other complex sentences using morphemic repetition in parallel clauses is provided by the following example from Guiraut de Bornelh's *alba*, with *si* meaning not "if" but "whether":

> Bel companho, si *dormetz* o velhatz,
> No *dormatz* plus, suau vos ressidatz (LIV, 6-7).

Here actuality and necessity are indicated respectively by the indicative and subjunctive of *dormir*. Or, William IX combines clauses of result and of hypothesis in this example:

> Pero si·m *retinc* ieu tan   de covenen
> Que s'el lo *teni'* un an   qu'ieu lo *tengues* mais de cen
> (I, 20-21).

Here *retinc* introduces a hypothesis which, by morphological figure on different tenses and persons of the verb *tenir*, tells how the lady's possessor is to be determined.

In another complex sentence, Bernart de Ventadorn expresses the superiority of ruse (*gens*) over boldness (*arditz*):

> Parlar degram ab cubertz entresens,
> E, pus no·ns *val* arditz, *valgues* nos gens! (XX, 47-48).

Again, asymmetry arises from the contrast of *val* without any ending to *valgues* with its unaccented root, from syncopated *ns* paralleling the full form *nos*, and from the chiastic sequence *ns-val-valgues-nos*.

E 5. *Morphemic Repetition in Unrelated Syntactical Structures*

As with word repetition and sound effects, many cases of morphemic repetition occur without grammatical interrelation, whether in one clause, one line, one sentence, one stanza, or at even greater distance. An important root can be held in mind through much of a poem, and any recurrence of it immediately becomes evident. One example gives its title to Bertran de Born's *escondich*, the only poem of its genre. This root meaning "excuse" occurs first in a first person singular verb, then in a noun. The intervening distance of twelve lines is compensated for by emphatic positioning in the poem's very first line and in the first line of stanza III, and by the occurrence of both words in equal syllabic position, so that they have an identical melodic setting:

> Ieu m'*escondisc*, domna, que mal no mier
> (P-C 80.15, 1);
> Autr' *escondich* vos farai plus sobrier
> (P-C 80.15, 13).

In an equally powerful case, the root "to abandon" reiterates William IX's abandonment of the world and its pleasures. The verb *guerpir* occurs in two different forms, in the first line of the second-to-last stanza and of the tornada (thus this time not in melodic identity), so that equal position again offsets the intervening lines:

> Tot ai *guerpit* cant amar sueill (XI, 33);
> Aissi *guerpisc* joi e deport (41).

At much closer, range, structurally unrelated occurrences of a single root often comprise the principal words of one line, as in Peire Vidal's

> *Bel'* es sobre tota *beutat* (XXXII, 53);

and again as the first and last words of a line in a poem that may be his:

> *Lau* segur sa *lauzor* (Avalle XLVII, 40).

The similar technique of these two examples might (like the architectural anaphora discussed in section III.C3) have encouraged Avalle to be less negative about the second poem's attribution to Peire.

Such root repetition occurs, within a single line, even more effectively because carrying a conventional but striking image, in Bernart de Ventadorn's

> *Miralhs,* pus me *mirei* in te,
> M'an mort li sospir de preon (XXXI, 21-22).

The use of *miralh* in the previous verse and the *m*-alliteration add further emphasis to this image which makes the transition from the lady's eyes to the legend of Narcissus.

F. Morphemic Repetition in Minor Parts of Speech

Sections D and E have shown that the function words which we call "minor" words are frequent in morphemic repetition, in various parts of speech and constructions, and especially in enumeration.

F 1. *Functional Monemes in Etymological Figure*

Occasionally, a preposition or adverb functioning as prefix can contribute to morphological figure. Thus Arnaut Daniel reinforces a verb by an etymologically related adverb:

> De mi pot far l'amors q'*inz* el cor m'*intra*
> Mieills a son vol c'om fortz de frevol verga (XVIII, 23-24).

The common idea and root shared by *inz* and *intra* magnify the supposed depth to which love has penetrated *into* the poet's heart. Similarly, two frequently paired adverbs are linked by identical first syllables in Cercamon's lines

> De leis m'es bel si m'escarnis
> O·m gaba *dereir'* o *denan* (I, 40)

(cf. French "*de*vant ou *der*rière").

Repeated minor morphemes can also be final in words. Repetition of the *-s* of declension will be treated as final consonance (section V.E6), since its chief effect is of sound. Repetition of verbal inflections is more prominent. Many easy rimes, for example, are sought in the infinitives *-ar* and *-ir* (cf. William IX's number IX, exclusively on these two rimes), the participles *-an* and *-at* (cf. the first part of Raimbaut de Vaquerias' "epic letter," with all forty-three verses rimed in *-at*), etc. Such endings repeated within one line, in the type *rir e bordir*, produce an effect either of structural parallelism or of internal rime (cf. sections V.G3-5). The type of parallel participles is especially noteworthy, in the types *rizen-jogan* and *jauzen-jauzitz* (cf. chapter V, note 109). Finally, etymological figure results from minor words used in different functions, for example *lo* pronoun and *los* article or *mo* adjective and *mieu* possessive pronoun. Several such examples will be observed later in this chapter.

F 2. *Non-cognate Morphemic Repetition of Minor Words*

Section D4 has discussed an extended definition of morphological figure including etymologically unrelated words of one paradigm or of one logical series. The effect of this technique should not be belittled as regards pronouns and possessives, since the idea of person — the first person singular designating the poet, the third person the lady, the first person plural their union — is central to the troubadours' conception of love and of poetry.

Such possibilities include the groups *eu-meu(mos)* and *il (ela)-seu (sos)*; these contrasts are thematic in many a verse and poem. The juxtaposition of different persons — like *ieu-ela*, or the pronominal contrast of *s'eslaiss'-m'eslaissei* in Bernart de Ventadorn (cf. p. 146, above) — would better be left to a study of complementary antonomy. One example of these techniques is Bernart's

> Pois *meus* no sui et *ilh m*'a en poder,
> Mais pert *ilh* qu'*eu* en lo *meu* dechazer;
> Per so *l*'er gen s'ab *son* ome plaideya (VII, 47-49).

The two interlocking series *meus-m'-eu-meu* and *ilh-ilh-l'-son* are an integral part of a typical argument designed to prove that the lady loses more by her aloofness than does her suitor.

Non-cognate pairs within one person — as in this example *eu-meu* and *ilh-son* — also contribute prettily to Jaufre Rudel's statement that when the *rossinholetz* produces *son dous chantar*, then

> Dreitz es qu'*ieu* lo *mieu* refranha (II, 7).

The parallel of the nightingale and the poet is borne out in a four-part equation, *rossinholetz/dous chantar=ieu/lo mieu*, with the proximity and internal rime of *ieu* and *mieu* adding to the effects of this implied comparison.

F 3. *Minor Words in Parallel Structures*

Obviously, such pronoun-possessive pairs can also be etymologically related, as in the common groups *tu-to(n)*, *se-so(n)*, *nos-nostre*, *vos-vostre*. The same applies to morphological figure in different forms of one possessive (*ma-mon*) or article (*la-lo*) and to allomorphs (cf. section D5) of one pronoun (*se-s'*), preposition (*de-d'*), negation (*no-non*), or conjunction (*e-et*). All these possibilities appear occasionally in other contexts throughout this study; here, we will consider them only at their most prominent: where they or associated major words form an enumerative relation.

In this egocentric poetry, the first person possessive is the most common in morphological figure. Thus Peire Vidal claims that:

> Ni anc mon cor des l'ora que la vi
> No·n poc partir, ni *m*'amor ni *mon* sen (XII, 11-12).

Masculine-feminine pairings seem especially sought after by the troubadours, and are especially fitting, given their usual subject. Peire Vidal says for example:

> ... Eu ai mes en vos ferm' esperansa
> E tot *mon* cor e tota *ma* fiansa,
> E fatz de vos *ma* domn' e *mon* senhor (X, 87-89).

Here cooperation with the morphological figure *tot-tota* reinforces the pair *mon-ma*; and the description of a single person by the pair *ma domn'* and *mon senhor* is especially piquant because morphological figure of the possessive brings out the troubadours' standard comparison of the lady to a lord.

Words designating the second person contribute, on a different and stronger tone, to Bernart de Ventadorn's denunciation of men of ill counsel:

> A! malvaza gens savaya,
> Qui *vos* ni *vostre* cosselh crei,
> Domnideu perd' e descreya (V, 22-24).

Third-person possessives, which are more common, often help to enumerate the fine qualities of the lady, as in Bernart's reference to

> *Sa* cortezi' e *sos* bels ditz (X, 17)

and in Peire Vidal's to

> *Son* dous esgart e *sos* bels olhs (X, 38).

Similarly, the definite article can help to create a simple effect of variation, as in Peire Vidal's lines

> *La* lauzet' e·*l* rossinhol
> Am mais que nulh autr' auzel (I, 1-2).

Surely this initial line would be less pleasing with not variation but repetition of the article, if the expression were, say, "*la* lauzet' e *la* colomba." In a different context, repetition and variation of the article can cooperate for different effects, in Guiraut de Bornelh's lines

> Can *la* peirer' abat *las* tors
> E·*ls* chalabres e·*ls* manganeus (XII, 42-43).

Here, the first two nouns, indicating a violent action, have variation of the article, while the second line, with its repeated syncopated articles ·*ls,* deprived of their vocalic element, focus our attention on a sound picture of these cumbersome sounding war machines, *chalabres* and *manganeus.*

Enumeration of more than two terms in a single line may allow triple morphological figure of the article, as in Guiraut de Bornelh's

> Can *lo* glatz e·*l* frechs e *la* neus
> S'en vai ... (XII, 1-2).

Note that morphological figure due to function (*lo-la*) and to allomorphic variation (*lo--l*) combine to produce welcome contrast in symmetry.

In a longer series, Peire Vidal's

> ... Segrai *los* mals e·*ls* bes
> E·*ls* tortz e·*ls* dreitz e·*ls* dans e·*ls* pros (XXXIX, 6-7),

the semantic variation provided by the three consecutive antonymic pairs, in six words, is perhaps insufficient to offset the monotonous effect of *e·ls*, conjunction plus article, repeated five times with monosyllabic nouns having final sibilance. Parallelism of organization and sound can be a virtue, but must not be overdone. On the other hand a very similar example of Peire's,

> Que sofrir tanh a senhor natural
> *Los* tortz e·*ls* dreitz e·*l* sen e *la* folor (XVIII, 25-26),

profits even more from quadruple variation of the article than from the relief of its monosyllabic rhythm by the final bisyllabic *folor*.

All these variation of function words will again be touched on later in discussing the generally weightier effects of more important repeated roots, both in and out of the rime.

G. Simple Internal Morphemic Repetition

Sections D and E have discussed the morphological and structural relation between manifestations of one root, and section F has dealt with the "minor" words. We reserve the questions of quantity and of position in the verse for sections H through J, so that for now we are left with simple internal morphemic repetition, the most important but most frequently underestimated sort of morphemic repetition in the troubadours.

G 1. *Cooperating Pairs*

Simple pairs, as chapter V will show for sound repetition, readily reinforce each other. For example, with skillful progression in concretization and in drama, Bertran de Born first makes us imagine what the onlooker sees as he approaches a beginning battle:

> Escutz tranchar a desguarnir
> Veirem a l'*entrar* de l'*estor* (P-C 80.8a, 32-33),

then describes the individual knight's entry into this battle:

> E quan er en l'*estorn entratz,*
>   Chascus hom de paratge
> No pens mas d'esclar chaps e bratz (P-C 80.8a, 37-38).

The interval of three intermediate lines is compensated for by the striking nature of the group *entrar-estor-estorn-entratz*, whose force is magnified by the presence of both roots in the rime, by their greater proximity in their second pairing, and by the consequent strengthening of their shared *e*-alliteration. Again common alliteration, this time consonantal, unites the two pairs of Peire Vidal's highly concentrated and apparently proverbial dictum:

> E *fols* quan *fai foudat* cuja *far* sen (X, 9).

A more complex example, also involving not a chiastic but an alternating relation, is Jaufre Rudel's

> Nuils hom no·s meravill de mi
> S'ieu *am* so que ja no·m *veira,*
> Que·l cor joi d'autr' *amor* non ha
> Mas de cela qu'ieu anc no *vi* (VI, 7-10).

The background of the repeated root "love" brings into relief the contrast afforded by morphological figure of the verb "see," which has as subject first the lady and then the poet, and as tense first the future and then the preterite. With both forms of *vezer*, the negation *no* reveals the paradoxality of *amor de lonh*, a theme expressed in others of Jaufre's poems and, with the same roots, in William IX's line

> Anc non la *vi* et *am* la fort (IV, 31).

The connection between seeing and loving is basic in the medieval idea that the arrow of love enters its victim's eye and, from there, his heart. So here, morphemic repetition expresses a major theme not only of one poet but of the medieval love lyric in general.

Not just two but three pairs cooperate in the first stanza of Peire Vidal XVIII, already discussed on p. 87 for its repetition of *no . . . aus* and of *dolor*. The repeated terms describing the poet's humility and anxiety are reinforced by morphemic repetition, once on the same root in *dolor-dolor,* once on a new root in *planh-planher,* and once in the homophonous noun-verb pair *enoi-enoi*. To these should be added variation produced on the idea of fear by the expressions *tant tem* and *tal paor ai*. The fact that all these pairs are divided between the two halves of the stanza and of the comparison bears out that figures of repetition are a clue to structure and idea.

Ultimately, several cooperating pairs can form a structural basis for successive lines or stanzas. The first case is illustrated by the *Leys d'amors* as one sort of *epymone*:

> Le razims en la vit *florish;*
> *Florit,* en gru se *convertish;*
> *Convertic* en gru, se *melhura;*
> *Milhurat,* enapres *madura;*
> *Madurat,* hom per temps lo *cuelh;*
> *Culit,* se desfay ins el *truelh;*
> *Trulhat,* se depura *colan;*
> *Colat,* hom ne beu trastot l'an (III, 312).

And on the stanza level, we have *coblas capfinidas* which, as seen in section III.G, occur in the examples referred to by Bartsch and Frank more by morphemic repetition than by word repetition. In a simple example, Cercamon ends one stanza with the line

> Q'*aqest segles* nos escharnis (VI, 24),

and begins the next by continuing the same thought with the same expression in a different case:

> *Aqest segle* teing per enic (VI, 25).

Also linking two stanzas, Arnaut uses the same principle to stress the safe escape of the lover forced to perform his odious task; one stanza of his *sirventes* ends with

> Lauzatz en Deu qe·us n'a *estort* (I, 36)

and the next begins with

>Ben es *estortz* de perill (I, 37).

The result is double: continuity of thought and vocabulary between two stanzas is assured; and an important root is emphasized.

These two examples embody the basic principle employed throughout poems entirely in *coblas capfinidas*. In perhaps the most intricate example of this technique, Arnaut Daniel ends each stanza with a rime word in *-uoilla* and repeats the same root to achieve an internal rime in *-uoill* in the first line of the next stanza:

>... E·il chan e·il braill
>Son a l'ombraill
>Dels auzels per la *bruoilla*. (II, 7-9)
>
>Pel *bruoill* aug lo chan e·l refrim... (II, 10);

and so on in succeeding stanzas. The structural importance and the artistic skill are undeniable here; and the choice of stressed roots (*bruoill-*, and in later stanzas *urguoill-*, *ianguoill-*, *accuoill-*, *duoill-*, and *capduoill-*) shows careful integration into the thematic development of the poem.

G 2. *Thematic Morphemic Repetition*

Cooperating pairs put us on the track of thematic morphemic repetition, which can reveal one or more of a poem's major themes. Thus in Jaufre Rudel's "song of distant love," morphemic repetition expresses the ideas of *seeing* and *loving*, which we have already discussed in the previous section, and also the ideas of *lodging* near his lady and of *joy* in love. All four ideas occur (one twice) in the poem's five pairs showing root repetition.

>Be·m parra joys quan li querray,
>Per amor Dieu, l'*alberc* de lonh:
>E, s'a lieys platz, *alberguarai*
>Pres de lieys, si be·m sui de lonh (V, 15-18);
>
>Iratz e gauzens m'en partray,
>S'ieu ja la *vey*, l'amor de lonh:
>Mas non sai quoras la *veyrai*,
>Car trop son nostras terras lonh (22-25);

> Ja mais d'amor no·m *jauziray*
> Si no·m *jau* d'est' amor de lonh (29-30);
>
> Car nulh autres *joys* tan no·m play
> Cum *jauzimens* d'amor de lonh (45-46);
>
> Qu'enaissi·m fadet mos pairis
> Qu'ieu *ames* e no fos *amatz* (48-49). [32]

Morphemic repetition here works closely with word repetition, which intensifies the ideas of love (as in lines 29-30) and of distance (as in the refrain expression *amor de lonh*). It is fitting that this poem should give double stress to two favorite Provençal themes: to that of *joy* by the two pairs in morphemic repetition, and to that of *love* by co-operation of morphemic repetition with word repetition.

Other genres than the *canso* also have certain conventional themes which can emerge from morphemic repetition. Thus the *alba* (aside from repetition of the word "dawn"; cf. section III.E6) generally refers to the *sleeping* lovers, the faithful *watchman*, and his warning *call*. In Guiraut de Bornelh's beautiful *Reis glorios*, these three themes are expressed by the repeated roots *dorm-*, *companh-*, and *chant-*. The first occurs in rapid succession:

> Bel companho, si *dormetz* o velhatz,
> No *dormatz* plus, suau vos ressidatz (LIV, 6-7),

with particularly effective passage from indicative to imperative. The group is reinforced by repetition of *no dormatz plus* in line 12 and is given a new twist later in

> Bel companho, pos me parti de vos
> Eu no·m *dormi* ni·m moc de genolhos (21-22),

and again in

> Bel companho, la foras als peiros
> Me preiavatz qu'eu no fos *dormilhos* (26-27),

in both cases with negation in a first-person context stressing the contrast between the sleeping lover and the sleepless watchman.

---

[32] I have corrected Jeanroy's *je* to *ja* (line 23) and *nos* to *no* (49).

The second of these themes represents the watchman as a "companion" by the roots of the apostrophe *Bel companho* which opens each stanza except the first, and by the words *companh* (3) and *companhia* (24). And the third theme occurs in the lines

> Bel companho, en *chantan* vos apel;
> No dormatz plus, qu'eu auch *chantar* l'auzel... (11-12),

later reinforced by *mos chans* in line 29. The connection between the song of the bird and of the watchman is a more than etymological one, since here the song of the bird is the cause of the watchman's song; and as one of the themes of his *alba*, Guiraut has adopted the frequent comparison of birds to man, not here to the poet, as is usual, but to the watchman.

G 3. *The Most Common Roots in Morphemic Repetition*

These two sections have, almost inevitably, enunciated the troubadours' favorite themes, those expressed by the roots *jauz-* (including *joy*), *chant-*, and *am-*. Of these the last, essential and ubiquitous, needs no special justification. To the above examples from Jaufre Rudel, one could add numerous examples with the most varied morphological and structural relations. Thus Bernart de Ventadorn uses etymological figure involving a verb and a dependent noun:

> Tan l'*am* de bon' *amor* (IV, 69);

a syntactically unrelated noun and verb:

> Be m'an perdut lai enves Ventadorn
> Tuih mei *amic*, pois ma domna no m'*ama* (IX, 1-2);

and a subject with a passive verb:

> Per so car no son gaire
> *Amat* li fin *aman* (XXVI, 23-24).

In a hypothesis, we find verbal morphological figure in Raimbaut de Vaqueiras'

> Eu sui tant de pretz enveios
> Que ben *amera* s'*amatz* fos (VII, 19-20),

which expresses the same opposition as Jaufre Rudel V, 49 (quoted on p. 157, above) between loving and not being loved.

The root *chant-*, also to be expected in sung love poetry, often occurs thematically through a poem as in Guiraut de Bornelh's *alba*, and especially frequently in the exordium exposing the poet's intentions, thus in Bernart de Ventadorn:

> Non es meravelha s'eu *chan*
> Melhs de nul autre *chantador* (I, 1-2).

Also noteworthy are the troubadours' elaborations on the Provençal derivatives of the Latin root *gaudium*.

Joy and *jauzimen*, whatever their precise connotations, figure among the dearest concepts in the troubadours' scheme of love. Charles Camproux would translate *joy* as an active "recherche de joie" and *jauzimen* as a passive "joie savourée."[33] The *FEW* similarly distinguishes *joi* and *gaug*, but *gaug* as "das allgemeine Wort für Freude" and *joi* as the more specialized *Minnedienst*: thus *joie d'amor* is frequent and *gaug d'amor* inexistant.[34] The semantic difference between *joie* and *jauzimen* or *gaug* helps explain why they are so often paired, since complementary near-synonymous pairs are such a common means of *variatio* and of *expolitio*. It is certainly frequent that "nos troubadours emploient, à peu de distance l'un de l'autre, le mot de 'joy' et l'une des formes qui continuent 'gaudium.'"[35]

Among other examples, already in William IX we find

> Ben deu quescus lo *joy jauzir*
> Don es *jauzens* (VII, 5-6);

> Mout *jauzens* me prenc en amar
> Un *joy* don plus me vuelh aizir (IX, 1-2);

in Jaufre Rudel a surprising number:

> E mou son chan *jauzent jòyos* (I, 3);

> Quar lai ay *joy* meravelhos,
> Per qu'ieu la *jau jauzitz jauzen* (I, 17-18);

---

[33] Camproux, "*Joy d'amor*," p. 130.
[34] *FEW*, IV (Basel, 1952), art. *gaudium*, p. 82, n. 4.
[35] Camproux, "*Joy d'amor*," p. 130.

Quar mais de *joy* m'i es cobitz,
E quant hom ve son *jauzimen*... (IV, 4-5);

Er ai ieu *joy* e suy *jauzitz* (IV, 8);

Car nulhs autres *joys* tan no·m play
Cum *jauzimens* d'amor de lonh (V, 45-46);

In Arnaut Daniel;

Iauzirai ioi, en vergier o dinz cambra (XVIII, 6);

Que d'als *iauzir*
No·m val *iois* una poma (IX, 67-68);

In Peire d'Alvernhe:

Joc e *joi* e *gaug* e ris (IXb, 24);

in Raimbaut d'Aurenga:

Mas mi ten vert e *jauzen Joys* (XXXIX, 7).

In order to substantiate his active-passive semantic differentiation between *joy* and *jauz-*, Camproux would have us believe in an etymological differentiation as well. He holds that *joy* is not derived, as generally believed, from Latin *gaudium* (like *gaug*), but rather from *joculum* (literally "little joke, toy"), whose root *iocum* gives also *joglar* (*ioculator, jongleur*), and *joc*, "game." Thus in Peire d'Alvernhe IXb, 24, above, not *joi e gaug* but *joc e joi* would constitute morphemic repetition. However, Camproux's arguments to do away with the *l* of *joculum* are unconvincing, and the *FEW*, like other authorities, considers Provençal *joi* a Poitevin derivative of *gaudium* accepted by the troubadours' literary language presumably under the influence of William IX.[36]

These two stems *joy* and *jauz-* often occur in the same structural relationship that frequently unites two uses of the stem *jauz-* alone. Thus Jaufre Rudel says *jauzent joyos* (I, 3) as he says *jauzitz jauzen* (I, 18) or *jauzens jauzitz* (III, 12), in the same immediate enumeration of adjectives, chiefly participles. And the other uses, listed above, of

---

[36] *FEW*, art. *gaudium* (cf. n. 34).

joy and *jauz-* have their parallels in similar elaborations on the sole stem *jau(z)-* like Jaufre's

> Ja mais d'amor no·m *jauziray*
> Si no·m *jau* d'est amor de lonh (V, 29-30);
>
> Ben sai c'anc de lei no·m *jauzi*,
> Ni ja de mi no·s *jauzira* (VI, 25-26).

The effect of the two combinations — *joy* and *jauz-* or two *jau(z)-*words — is similar phonetically, lexically, and semantically, with only a slight variation in meaning.

We are dealing here with a noteworthy complex of related words whose frequent association has several explanations. Not only do they share a probably common etymology, but also their meaning centers on the "joy" or "enjoyment" of love which is the essential subject of the Provençal lyric. Their sounds permit a distinctive *j*-alliteration generally reinforced by internal *z*, so that in a combination like *jauzens jauzitz*, phonetically [*džauzens džauzits*], with its various dentals and sibilants, close grammatical relation adds to the already great inherent importance of this root. One can easily understand how the use of this lexical family could become with Jaufre Rudel an obsessive *tic*, in Riffaterre's sense of the word (cf. p. 72, above).

G 4. *Dialectical Morphemic Repetition*

Our previous topics of cooperating pairs and thematic morphemic repetition combine in what may be called dialectical morphemic repetition, in which successive pairs, generally antonymic or complementary, carry the poem's argument through most or all of a stanza.

A skillful example occurs in a stanza of William IX designed to summarize the violent and contradictory effects of his lady's love:

> Per son joy pot malautz *sanar*,
> E per sa ira *sas* morir
> E savis hom enfolezir
> E *belhs* hom sa *beutat* mudar
> E·l plus *cortes vilanejar*
> E totz *vilas encortezir* (IX, 25-30).

Here morphemic repetition increase progressively in intensity and density through a series of infinitive clauses that are organically bound together by anaphora of the conjunction *e*. The first pair, the infinitive *sanar* and the substantivized adjective *sas*, spreads over two lines, while surrounding roots contribute the antonymies *joy-ira, malautz-sanar, sas-morir, savis-enfolezir*. Then the fourth line juxtaposes an adjective and a substantive derived from *bellus*. The earlier grammatical relation returns in the last two lines with their paired infinitives and substantivized adjectives combining the principles of morphemic repetition, antonymy and chiasmus in the effective group *cortes-vilanejar-vilas-encortezir*. These and the stanza's other repeated roots sum up the effects of internal turmoil upon the lover's outer being, on his physical attributes and then on his social qualities — all of which are overturned by love.

Two of the same roots, *cortes-* and *vilan-*, plus *fol-* (occurring in the third line above) form a similar series in Marcabru's *pastorela*, this time with only nouns:

> Don, oc; mas segon dreitura
> Cerca *fols* sa *follatura*,
> *Cortes cortez*' aventura,
> E il *vilans* ab la *vilana* (293.30, 78-81).

But here morphemic repetition, with a different relation between members of cognate pairs, illustrates an entirely different idea from the previous example, not the irresistible effects of love but the propriety (according at least to the shepherdess who is speaking) of loving at one's own level. In two poems, then, morphemic repetition chiefly on the same roots reflects contrasting conceptions of love as courtly and as naturalistic.

A similar structure in Bertran de Born again forms a method of argument, this time the satirist's against a decadent nobility:

> *Reiesme* son, mas *reis no* ges,
> E *comtat*, mas *no coms* ni bar;
> Las *marchas* son, mas *no*·lh *marques*,
> E·lh ric *chastel* e·lh bel estar,
> Mas li *chastela non* i so,
> Et avers *es* plus qu'anc no·n fo (P-C 80.45, 17-22).

Again derivatives of one root form one-line grammatical pairs; but rather than antonymy, negation of the second member of each pair by repeated *no(n)* provides the element of opposition. Four semantically complementary roots, succeeding each other in descending order of feudal rank (*rei-, comt-, marc-, chast-*) effectively represent the totality of feudal nobility.[37] This descent in rank is reflected lexically as well as semantically, for the abstract derivatives *reiesme, comtat, marchas* yield to the concrete term and unadorned stem *chastel*. Following this series, the last line quoted here adds a new twist with its allegation, intensified by the non-etymological morphological figure *es-fo*, that not wealth but only nobility, in the inward sense, is lacking in the medieval world as seen by Bertran de Born.

On a larger scale, Bertran de Born bolsters his *sirventes* on age and youth (P-C 80.7, already discussed on p. 82, above) by morphological figure on three of an adjective's four possible forms. *Vielha* in one stanza contrasts, with a difference of gender corresponding to the female and male objects of Bertran's satire, to *vielhs* and *vielh* in another two stanzas having their own alternance of nominative and oblique cases. So repetition of words and repetition of roots cooperate in a common argument and a common structure.

H. Multiple Unrimed Morphemic Repetition

The principles enunciated in sections D through G hold true in general for the more specialized sorts of morphemic repetition which take on extra force from frequency and position. The unrimed pair is the basic type of morphemic repetition which contains all its potentialities in germ; now, in this section, we will show the effect of greater frequency on internal morphemic repetition, and in the text two sections discuss position in the rime as a means of intensifying both simple and multiple morphemic repetition.

H 1. *Triple Morphemic Repetition*

Though morphemic repetition mots often affects pairs, there is something distinctive about groups of three. A pair is built on a one-to-one relation, but three related words can stand in a relation of continuity, or as two grouped either by morphology or by position

---

[37] Cf., in the *Leys* (III, 172), the similar series *emperadors-rey-comte-duc-marques-senescalc*, illustrating a sort of *agnominatio* by which "de motas cauzas ... pot hom parlar."

against a third member. Two members can be closer in space, or two can represent morphological figure related to a third word in etymological figure, and so on.

Triple root repetition beings in the Provençal lyric with the first troubadour. William IX's number I — built on the old erotic comparison of the mistress to the saddle horse (in this case two of each) — uses the thematic root *caval-* in three different lines whose distance from each other, rather than reducing their combined force, in fact allows them to dominate the poem through a noteworthy pun in the third occurrence of the root:

> Dos *cavalhs* ai a ma selha   ben e gen (I, 7);
>
> Que miels for' *encavalguatz*   de nuill autr' ome viven (12);
>
> *Cavallier,* datz mi cosselh   d'un pessamen! (22).

This apostrophe *cavallier* is often taken as referring to William's drinking companions; but the context of thematic morphemic repetition shows that they are thought of first here as his fellow participants in the art of loving.

The same poem also uses triple morphemic repetition at closer quarters:

> Pero si'm *retinc* ieu tan   de covinen
> Que s'el lo *teni'* un an   qu'ieu lo *tengues* mais de cen
>   (I, 20-21).

Similarly, a group of William's already discussed is

> Ben deu quascus lo *joy jauzir*
> Don es *jauzens* (VII, 5-6).

In both these groups, a pair of words in morphological figure receive variation from a third term in a relation of etymological figure to both (*retinc* in I, 20; *joy* in VII, 5). Or, three terms in morphological figure take on more of a "sequential" relationship in a final stanza of William's serving as a tornada:

> Fag ai lo vers, no say de cuy;
> E *trametrai* lo a selhuy
> Que lo·m *trametra* per autruy

Lay vers Anjau,
Que·m *tramezes* del sieu estuy
La contraclau (IV, 37-42).

The three clauses, linked by *que* first as relative pronoun then as conjunction, graphically send off the poem to its destination; and the motion away from the poet is reflected by a shift of person from first to third and of tense from future indicative to imperfect subjunctive.

Minor words should not be ignored, though with them triple morphemic repetition seems to have no special appeal. One example is Bernart de Ventadorn's

Can eu remire *so* cors gai,
Com es be faihz a totz chauzitz,
Sa cortezi' e *sos* bels ditz,
Ja mos lauzars no m'er avans (X, 15-18).

The isolated *so cors* describes the lady's physical appearance while the paired *sa cortezi(a)* and *sos bels ditz* describe her inner quality and its manifestation in words.

There are countless other examples of minor or major roots triply repeated, like *chantarai-chantan-chantar* opening Peire d'Alvernhe's satiric poem (XII, 1, 2, 4); *valors-valer-valc* stressing the great worth of Arnaut Daniel's lady (XIII, 20-21); *fag-far-fazendas* in the final (prose) line of Raimbaut d'Aurenga's proudly fabricated *No-sai-que-s'es* (XXIV, 47-48); *folor-fols-foldat* in Bernart de Ventadorn XXV (25, 26, 30) discoursing on madness and love; *cosselladors-cosselhan-cosselhs* describing Jaufre Rudel's need for good counsel to win his lady (III, 19-20); *ergolh-ergolhs-s'ergolha* on the theme of pride in Bernart VII, 20-23 (cf. section I 1); or *agues-agui-ai* in Bernart XXVI, 58-59.

H 2. *Multiple Non-etymological Morphological Figure*

Section D4 has described the juxtaposition of different roots in the same paradigm. It is only natural that different forms of the essential verb "to be" occur often in threes, since the ideas of duration and of change are most dramatically expressed on the three mutually completing time levels of past, present, and future.

Thus Raimbaut de Vaqueiras typically holds that time has no power over love and its attributes:

> E non *es* ni *er* ni *fo*
> Gensser de neguna leig (XIII, 61-62).

The three tenses succeed each other perhaps a bit too rapidly to give us a feeling of eternity. But a slower pace, marked by longer lines and by repetition of consonantally dense monosyllables, gives a much more convincing effect to the same triple series in Marcabru, describing not love but divine wisdom:

> Que·l Seigner que sap tot quant *es*
> E sap tot quant *er* e c'anc *fo*.
> (P-C 293.35, 28-29).

The liturgical-sounding repetition of *sap tot quant*, a repetition totally unnecessary for meaning, gives an appropriately solemn air to this crusading appeal.

A more remarkable series, combined with the morphemic repetition *vostre-vostr'-vos*, occurs with much greater and almost excessive effect in Bernart de Ventadorn's stanza

> Domna, *vostre sui* e *serai*,
> Del *vostre* servizi garnitz.
> *Vostr'* om *sui* juratz e plevitz,
> E *vostre* m'*era* des abans.
> E *vos etz* lo meus jois primers,
> E si *seretz vos* lo derrers,
> Tan com la vida m'*er* duran (X, 29-35).

The verbal series begins with four first persons, again representing three time levels, arranged in two pairs, *sui-serai* and *sui-era*, the two pairs marking different syntactical constructions. Then the person changes from first to second, as the lady moves to the center in the pair *etz-seretz*. Finally the third person *er* generalizes a conclusion to the two previous groups: the poet's love for his lady will last as long as he lives.

H 3. *Roots Repeated More than Three Times*

So far we have had only hints of really intense morphemic repetition, as in the series *corta-cortz-cortezia-cortes-descortes-cortz-corteia* contained in the *Leys d'amors*' example of the *cobla refrancha* (cf. p. 67, above). Such multiple root repetition reflects, with greater density, the same intensifying impulse as the "thematic morphemic repetition" discussed in section G2. Often, multiple morphemic repetition affects those commonly repeated roots discussed in section G3. Arnaut Daniel for example gives a rather extraordinary dissertation on the root *am-*:

> *Amors* e iois e liocs e tems
> mi fan tornar lo sen e derc
> d'aqel noi c'avia l'autr'an
> can cassava·l lebr' ab lo bou;
> era·m vai mieltz d'*amor* e pieis,
> car ben *am*, d'aiso·m clam astrucs,
> ma non *amatz* ioi gau en cers,
> s'*Amors* no vens son dur cor e·l mieus precs (XIV, 1-8).

The stanza is framed, in its first and last lines, by *Amors*, which personifies the forces operating in space and time (*liocs e tems*) upon the lovers' *sen*; and within this frame, the active-passive and positive-negative contrast of *am* with *non amatz*, dominates the movement of ideas.

A similar but less personal expatiation on love by Bernart de Ventadorn (II, 15-24) gives us the series *amor-amors-amors-amors-ama-amon,* dominating one stanza and spilling over into the next. It is not necessary to quote the passage to note that the first person and also adjectives modifying it are lacking in this series devoted to generalization and to moralization, in contrast to the preceding example. Here, in fact, the abstract nominative singular noun *amors*, thrice repeated, forms the body of the series, not as in the preceding example merely its frame.

On another densely repeated root, Peire Vidal writes:

> Pero dels rius e de las gens
> Ai dig cinc cens laus avinens
>   Per leis que·m fai
> Al peitz que *pot*, per qu'eu dirai
> No re mas be, qu'eu no *poirai*.
> E s'eu li *pogues* mal voler,
> Si Deus m'ampar, de mon *poder*
> Li for'eu mals et orgolhos;
> Mas no·n *posc* esser *poderos*,
> Qu'ab un ris et ab un esgar
> Me fai mi mezeis oblidar (XXIX, 34-44).

The italicized series of six terms is introduced by the third person *pot* referring to the lady, who acts as cruelly as she is *able;* thereafter, the root *pod-* occurs in the first person or in expressions referring to the first person, designating the poet's *inability* either to withstand her charms or to conquer her.

An irresistible *tour de force* is a *cobla* of Uc de Saint Circ devoted, with tongue-in-cheek moralization, to the art of giving:

> Valor ni prez ni honor non atrai
> A nul home ni *dons* ni cortesia,
> Qui bel *don dona* lai o non s'escai,
> Anz es tengut per los pros a follia;
> Qui *don dona* taing qe·l *dos* aitals sia
> Con es aqel qe·l *don* receb e pren;
> Qi en croi home bel aut ric *don* despen,
> Non es grazit, anz s'en fai escharnir
> E·ls autres *dos* q'el *dona* menz grazir (XXVI, 1-9).

The frequent type *un don donar* is doubtless the impetus for the ten occurrences of this root here.

A final type of multiple morphemic repetition involves separate groups on one root and cooperating pairs on different roots. Cercamon's lament on William X, for example, contains the pair

> *Plagnen* lo Norman e Franceis
> E deu lo be *plagner* lo reis (VI, 37-38),

and in a later stanza

> Lo *plainz* es de bona razo
> Qe Cercamon tramet n'Eblo.
> Ai! com lo *plaigno* li Gasco (VI, 49-51).

The thematic value of this root "lament" — reinforced by the semantically close pair *dolen-dolor* in lines 2-3 — recalls much of the word repetition discussed in section III, D. and particularly the word-refrain *marrimen* in Bertran de Born's lament on Young King Henry (cf. p. 101, above).

A more complex example, an exordium of Bernart de Ventadorn, displays triple morphemic repetition on two important roots associated with spring, plus simple repetition of a third such root:

> Lancan *folhon* bosc e jarric,
> E·lh *flors* pareis e·lh *verdura*
> Pels *vergers* e pels pratz,
> E·lh auzel, c'an estat enic,
> Son gai desotz los *folhatz,*
> Austresi·m chant e m'esbaudei
> E *reflorisc* e *reverdei*
> E *folh* segon ma natura (VI, 1-8).

These roots, largely grouped in the stanza's first two and last two lines, draw as so often a parallel between the natural surroundings and the poet whom they inspire to sing. An original factor is the implicit comparison of the poet to a spring-time plant by the first person verbs "reflower," "turn green again" and "grow leaves," juxtaposing the three repeated roots which are the key to this stanza.

But even such multiple root repetition, either in nearby groups or in larger isolated series, still falls short of the extreme density found in our next examples.

H 4. *The Unrimed Refrain*

We now enter the domain of the "unrimed refrain word," so named by W. T. Pattison.[38] The unrimed refrain, which can be so characteristic as to permit identification of a poem from a short passage, involves a repeated root in every line of a poem or a different repeated root in each stanza. Raimbaut d'Aurenga XXXVI is the first known poem in this style, but the existence of a previous tradition is implied by Raimbaut's apparently satiric intent. The poem, according to Pattison,

> partakes of the nature of the *gap,* treating the serious theme of the poet's misfortune in humorous fashion and indulging in a literary satire against refrain words at the same time. Raimbaut carries the fashion of repeating fixed words to its ultimate absurdity by bringing *malastre* or a derivative into every line of the whole work.[39]

---

[38] Pattison, *Raimbaut d'Orange,* p. 50.
[39] Pattison, p. 189; cf. the etymological figure by composition *astrucs-malastrucs* in Bernart de Ventadorn XXVI, 49-50, quoted above.

The technique of the unrimed refrain is lucidly described in Margaret L. Switten's article "Raimon de Miraval's 'Be m'agrada' and the Unrhymed Refrain in Troubadour Poetry." [40] Switten takes as typical Raimon's poem P-C 406.13, which builds each stanza around one of the thematic repeated roots *agrad-, desir-, jauz-, vir-, dir-,* and *serv-*. The sequence of these roots and stanzas carries the poem forward, from the initial stages of amorous attraction marked by *pleasure* and *desire,* through a stage of *enjoyment* marred by the fear of the lady's *turning* away, finally to a mature relation characterized by affirmation (*saying*) and, in the troubadours' habitual metaphor, *service.*

About twenty other Provençal poems can be compared to this one in having unrimed structural morphemic repetition. As Switten remarks, it is "curious that the form is not treated by the *Leys d'amors,* nor for that matter by any modern critic" previous to herself. [41] It is not our purpose to summarize her excellent discussion, to which the reader is referred. But we will point out that unrimed refrains must be described according to two criteria: 1) the density of root repetition; and 2) the number of different roots repeated. No two troubadour poems are identical in both respects.

Relative to the first criterion, we have already given examples of unmethodical root repetition, not occupying all lines of a stanza, and not necessarily in consecutive lines; on the other hand, as in Raimon de Miraval's poem, every single verse of a stanza or of a whole poem can contribute to morphemic repetition. Such poems can be described, according to our second criterion, as having stanzas with only one methodically repeated root or with more, and the same on the poem level. The following chart represents these possibilities:

---

[40] In *Romance Philology,* XXII (1969), 432-448.
[41] Switten, p. 433. Raimon's latest editor, L. T. Topsfield, *Les poésies du troubadour Raimon de Miraval* (Paris, 1971), gives, with regard to Raimon's poem *Be m'agrada* and to "la répétition de mots radicaux comme procédé de style, assez commun chez les troubadours," three references to editions of other troubadours (p. 137), but does not mention Switten's article nor deal with Raimon's place in the unrimed refrain tradition as a whole.

Chart 7:

Categories of Morphemic Repetition According to Density and Quantity

number of roots	(a) two or more per stanza	(b) one per stanza	(c) one per poem
1) more than one per line in given passage	1a	1b	1c
2) one per line through given passage	2a	2b	2c
3) less than one per line in given passage	3a	3b	3c

We cannot illustrate all nine categories, though all exist in the troubadours' work. Rather, we will describe, in several noteworthy examples, the relation of root repetition to meaning, which is our prime consideration. For example, Guilhem de Montanhagol's poem *A Lunel lutz* (P-C 225.1), already shown (pp. 66-67) illustrative of morphemic repetition with alliteration as a side effect, belongs to our category 1b), having one root repeated on the average more than once per verse through a whole stanza. We shall not here discuss the form, density, or quantity of root repetition, but rather its quality, derived from the choice and application of the repeated root.

Montanhagol's choice of the root *lu-* is not arbitrary. The troubadours often apply the image of shining to their lady and her qualities, by figurative use of the root *clar-*, by *senhals* such as *Esclarmonda* used by Montanhagol, by images of sun, stars, and light,[42] etc. Thus an established traditional imagery explains Montanhagol's comparison of his lady to the moon and other sources of light in eight lines having no less than thirteen uses of the root *lu-* (all etymologically related except the proper name):[43]

> A *Lu*nel *lu*tz una *lu*na *lu*zens
> qe dona *lu*m sobre totas *lu*gors;
> d'aqui pren *lu*m jois, dompneis ez amors
> e gais solatz e beutatz e jovens.
> E qan le *lu*ms pres a *Lu*nel *lu*zensa,
> q'en*lu*mina daus Tolsa part Proensa,
> estavan jois e dompneis tenebros,
> mas ara·ls fai *Lu*nels *lu*zir amdos (II, 1-8).

---

[42] Stössel, *Bilder und Vergleiche*, pp. 48-50.
[43] Cf. ch. II, n. 7.

This particular comparison is motivated also by a traditional pun; as Coulet tells us, "l'idée du jeu de mots se retrouve dans les armoiries de Lunel." [44] Thus Montanhagol, in order to intensify his comparison of the lady to light, uses punning and phonetic repetition centering around emphatic root repetition. [45]

Our next and last example of multiple morphemic repetition belongs to our category 3c. Again morphemic repetition affects a single principal root, with less density than before but through a whole poem, stressing a subject less typical of the troubadours than is its technique. We have seen how certain roots like *am-* or *jauz-* can be thematic throughout a poem; in another example, Arnaut Daniel spreads through a poem twelve uses of the otherwise almost unheard-of root *corn-*, chiefly in the verb *cornar*, apparently "to blow," and in the noun *corn* designating a certain part of the lady's body by near-homophonous punning (cf. section V.H). The full series is *cornar* (I, 6), *corn* (7), *corns* (12), *corn* (18), *cornes* (27), *corn* (27), *cornavatz* (31), *Cornill* (39), *cornes* (41), *corn* (47), *cornar* (47), *cornar* (49).

Though it is generally improper to examine such series out of context, we can immediately notice the pun on the place name *Cornill*, the humorous interest in the rare forms *cornes* (imperfect subjunctive, used twice) and especially *cornavatz*, and the concentration of two forms of the root in two different lines, both with etymological figure of the type *cantar un can*:

> E no·is cove que domna bais
> Aquel qui *cornes corn* putnais (26-27);
>
> Dompna, ges Bernartz non s'estrill
> Del *corn cornar* ses gran dozill (46-47).

The proliferation of this rare root, together with other stylistic traits, gives Arnaut's *sirventes* a place of honor in the series of poems on the same question by Turc Malec and Raimon de Durfort. [46] The latter's two *sirventes* notably use the root *corn-* sixteen and eleven times, including the geographical puns *Cornilh* and *Cornes*. But

---

[44] The arms of Lunel are "d'azur au croissant d'argent, accompagné en chef d'une étoile d'or" (Coulet, *Guilhem Montanhagol*, p. 65).
[45] Cf. Martianus Capella's example of *lambdacismus*: "Sol et luna luce lucent alba leni lactea" (Lausberg, *Elemente*, § 458).
[46] Cf. Toja, *Arnaut Daniel*, pp. 187-191.

Arnaut's refutation of his two colleagues' views on the subject must be termed poetically more successful, given the greater art with which he integrates the repeated root into his argument against the procedure *del corn cornar*.

We have chosen these two examples precisely because they are on the whole livelier, more imaginative and less regular in their morphemic repetition than examples like that from Miraval. Multiple morphemic repetition, like multiple word repetition, is soon in danger of becoming too mechanical and of forcing itself upon its context rather than arising organically from it. From the examples we have given for multiple repetition of both words and roots, it is clear that the two most often function concurrently, as indeed in all of the more than twenty poems either rejected or accepted by Switten as illustrating the "unrimed refrain." Still, repetition of words and of morphemes do represent different balances between repetition and variation; on the level of multiple as of simple groups, these two figures produce different effects and impressions whose coalescence can be all the more instructive.

I. Simple Morphemic Repetition in the Rime

I 1. *Generalities*

Sections G and X have already suggested that internal and final repetition of a root can work together, as in two *coblas capcaudadas* of Bernart de Ventadorn:

> Can l'us amics vol l'autre vil tener,
> Pauc pot amors ab *ergolh* remaner,
> Qu'*ergolhs* dechai e fin' amors capdolha.
>
> Eu sec cela que plus vas me s'*ergolha*
> E cela fuih que·m fo de bel estatge (VII, 19-23).

Here we are told first that pride is incompatible with love but then, in an about-face corresponding to the stanzaic division, that Bernart loves her who acts the most proudly toward him. Thus the contradictions of love are stressed by morphemic repetition on the pride theme, both in and out of the rime.

This example forms a transition between discussion of unrimed and rimed root repetition. The latter, as section C has shown, is the sort of morphemic repetition most often mentioned by editors and critics. Thus Bartsch, like our section D, divides "grammatischer Reim" into different morphological types: 1) *bon-bona* (masculine and feminine adjectives); 2) *cim-cima* (masculine and feminine nouns); 3) *volh-volha* (verbs); 4) *orgolh-orgolha* (noun or adjective and verb); 5) *ferm-fermansa* ("entferntere Ableitungen"); 6) *amar-amars* (differentiation by *-s* of flexion); 7) *entremetre-trametre* (compounds).[47] But Bartsch's and other scholars' occasional lists of cognate rime words are no substitute for even a brief analysis of stylistic purposes and effects.

A simple classification of rimed morphemic repetition, suggested indirectly by the *Leys d'amors* (cf. section B), distinguishes 1) compound rime (*compositio*), where two words differ only by prefixation from 2) derivative or grammatical rime (*rim derivatiu*), where two words differ by inflection, suffixation, morphology, or a combination. Compound rime arises from much of the compound morphemic repetition discussed in section D2 and derivative rime from other etymological figure and from all morphological figure. All compound and some derivative rime words in a given group rime among themselves. For example, different stanzas of Arnaut's sestina have the riming pair *ongla-enongla* (the former being a noun, and the latter a verb and neologism).

I 2. *Derivative Rime*

Derivative rime, like most figures of intensification, has its place of predilection in the exordium, as in two famous songs discussing the nature of poetry, Jaufre Rudel's

> Pro ai del chan *essenhadors*
> Entorn mi et *ensenhairitz* (III, 1-2).

and Bernart de Ventadorn's

> Non es meravelha s'eu *chan*
> Melhs de nul autre *chantador* (I, 1-2).

---

[47] Bartsch, "Reimkunst," pp. 190-192.

The first illustrates substantival morphological figure based on a masculine-feminine distinction continued, in the following lines, by an enumeration of the natural phenomena which are the poet's schoolmasters and schoolmistresses. And the second example shows etymological figure with progressively greater weight in its second member. The different morphological possibilities (cf. section D) of derivative rime are certainly great.

Of course derivative rime occurs elsewhere than in the exordium. Thus in the middle of a poem, Bernart de Ventadorn states that

> Ben a mauvais cor e mendic
> Qui ama e no·s *melhura;*
> Qu'eu sui d'aitan *melhuratz*
> C'ome de me no vei plus ric (VI, 17-20).

Here, as often, a generality — the favorite theme of betterment by love — is first announced by the third-person verb *melhura* and then applied to the individual lover by the nominative past participle *melhuratz*.

The same pair occurs in successive lines, cooperating with a second repeated root in a chiastic relation, in Peire d'Alvernhe's nightingale song:

> E crezatz
> Qu'*amistatz*
> Cascun jorn *melhura,*
> *Melhuratz*
> Et *amatz*
> Es cui jois s'aüra (IXb, 45-50).

Each of these four interlocking manifestations of the roots *am-* and *melh-* dominates its line, again stressing the basic idea of moral betterment through love. The height of finesse is the absolute consecutiveness of *melhura* and *melhuratz* in the center of the chiasmus.

In the rime, morphemic repetition is less common, though perhaps more effective, than word repetition. In Peire Vidal we find 219 members of groups in the latter relation,[48] but in the former only

---

[48] Cf. our chart 4; it will be recalled that this count excludes two poems where rime word repetition is a thorough-going principle; these two poems would add 112 to our figure of 219.

84,[49] of which 46 are in derivative rime and 38 in compound rime. About one-third the members in derivative rime belong to groups riming within themselves, for example *amador-amor* in XVII, 35-36; at greater distance, *amors-amadors* in VIII, 8, 56; and two nouns on another common stem in

> De lai on creisso·l fau
> Mi ven us *jauzimens*,
> Don sui gais e *jauzens* (XXIII, 51-53).

Clearly, these words having the repeated root *jauz-* or *am-* are further grouped and stressed by their common ending *-ens* or *-or(s)*.

But of Peire Vidal's derivative rime words two-thirds do not rime with their mates. It is noteworthy that almost all such rimes in Peire are in closely knit pairs, often in successive lines. Here more than before, distance affects the impact, since the emphasis of common rime is absent, and melodic identity, which we have seen linking far-off repeated rime-words, cannot be a factor. Different grades of recall, as always, can be distinguished, from the one-letter differentiation of *malanans-malanansa* (II, 11-12), to different forms of one word like *aver* and *agues* (XXXIX, 28-29) and even words differentiated by prefixation, resembling in this compound rime, like *recaliu-calors* (XVI, 45-46). In every such case, given the general importance of the rime word, a repeated root can be said to create, or at least reveal, a theme.

For example, noting in the rime the verb-noun pair *donar-do* in Peire Vidal XLIV, 29-31, we find the whole stanza, like Uc de Saint Circ's quoted on p. 169, above, to be in fact an embroidering on this root:

> Tant m'avetz *dat* pois que m'agues conques
> Que autre *dons* per me no·us er queritz;
> Mas vostre cors part los meillors chauzitz
> Sap que conven gardar en totas res;
> Pero cel qui ses querre vol *donar*
> Ben fai lo *dons* mais mil tans a prezar;
> Qu'eu ai ben vist ses querre far ric *do*
> E *dons* queritz mermar lo miels del pro (XLIV, 25-32).

---

[49] Here a qualifying word is counted as one even when it is repeated (in unchanged form) elsewhere in the same poem.

Here, though, the repeated root is less important in the rime than internally. In a simpler example, the root *manen-*, "rich," twice occurs in the rime, dramatizing Peire's moralistic judgment of the avaricious king

> Cui sobra aurs et argens,
> E cuja, quar es *manens*,
> Qu'autre Dia no sia
> Mas sa *manentia* (XXII, 43-46).

The pair *manens-manentia* becomes thematic in this passage, and again shows derivative rime to be one of the finest arms in the skillful poet's arsenal of expression.

I 3. *Compound Rime*

We have said that Peire Vidal uses compound rimes slightly less than derivative rimes. One must not exaggerate the importance of the former, which occur generally in quite distant couples, like *plazer-desplazer* in XXXIX, 9-36. After all, the use of riming compounds facilitates the poet's search for rime words without necessarily reflecting a thematic idea. Thus in XLIII, the triplet *refranh* (11)-*franh* (17, 44)-*sofranh* (60) hardly indicates a theme of "breaking," nor in XX *perdo* (65)-*do* (67, 95) -*ado* (99) a theme of "giving," even though the latter two terms occur in the first line of successive tornadas.

A definite effect does however emerge when the compound rimes are close to each other. For example Peire Vidal XXXVII, with three lines (quoted on p. 121, above) ending in the feminine past participle *enquisa*, "searched," has *conquisa* (line 37) and *quisa* in the tornada, summarizing the theme of the amorous quest:

> E N'Alazais, tan vos ai ades *quisa*,
> Qu'ar l'uns en ten l'autre per enoios
> Eu remandrai tant quant er faitz lo dos,
> Quar genser etz qu'anc fos d'amor *enquisa* (XXXVII, 41-44).

Again in XXV, previous use of one of the members and situation in the tornada make a group in compound rime quite effective, here on the theme of (*h*)*onor* (lines 16 and 59) and *deshonor* (line 63). The two tornadas even present this antonymic pair in melodic identity:

> Senher coms de Peiteus, be·m platz,
> Car etz en l'aussor grat montatz,
> Que gens vos vei cobrar l'*onor*
> Que perderon vostr' ancessor.
>
> Sitot s'es mals Mos Castiatz,
> Dolors m'en pren e pietatz
> Quars es velhs e pren *deshonor*
> E·m tol Na Vierna e s'amor (XXV, 57-64).

The honorable Count of Poitiers and the dishonorable Barral de Baux are graphically contrasted.

In general, though, compound rime tends to greater passivity than derivative rime, if only because the former is restricted to one part of speech per derivative group, and is limited by the number of prefixes applicable to any one root. Morphemic repetition in the rime, then, can very effectively cooperate with internal morphemic repetition or with other figures of repetition like word repetition, and of course gains in strength from such convergence. It remains to see how derivative rime, and to a lesser extent compound rime, become architectural principles by the collaboration of different groups through a stanza or poem.

J. Multiple Rimed Morphemic Repetition

Multiple rimed repetition of roots — though less often than of words — can attain architectural status. The troubadour corpus contains 230 poems using refrains of a word or a line, but only forty-five poems built partly or entirely on derivative rimes,[50] ranging from Marcabru (P-C 293.4) on up to the latest troubadours. Of these forty-five, most have derivative rime in every line, while almost no poems except the four sestinas have rime word repetition in every line unless combined with derivative rime. It is therefore surprising that structural derivative rime receives less attention in Diez's *Poesie* and Bartsch's "Reimkunst" than do *coblas capfinidas*.

"Architectural" morphemic repetition in the rime can occur on a small scale in several verses, or on a larger scale in either pairs or

---

[50] Frank, *Répertoire métrique*, II, 61-62: "Pièces à rimes dérivées." On Marcabru's influence, cf. Pattison, *Raimbaut d'Orange*, p. 50.

larger groups. The first case is illustrated by a stanza like Bernart de Ventadorn's

> Ab *joi* mou lo vers e·l *comens*
> Et ab *joi* reman e *fenis*;
> E sol que bona fos la *fis*,
> Bos tenh qu'er lo *comensamens*.
> Per la bona *comensansa*
> Me ve *jois* et alegransa;
> E per so dei la bona *fi* grazir,
> Car totz bos faihz vei lauzar al *fenir* (III, 1-8).

Here, in the context of triply enunciated *joi(s)*, two antonymic rimed groups, *comens-comensamens-comensansa* and *finis-fis-fenir* (plus *fi* within line 7), together fortify the poet's contention that "well *begun* is half *done*," in the art of achieving his lady's favors. This morphemic repetition is effective but isolated; nothing like it appears in the rest of the poem.

On a larger scale, each stanza of a poem can be built of derivative pairs, generally with alternating masculine and feminine rimes. Thus in Aimeric de Peguilhan XLVII, each stanza contains four pairs, in the first stanza *lima-lim, prima-prim, rima-rim*, and, with a change of order, *escrim-escrima*. Guilhem Ademar XIII has a first stanza of the same type, with the somewhat more imaginative pairs *braus-brava, nut-desnuda, cor-coratge, cortes-corteza, ferm-fermansa;* but subsequent stanzas, rather than contributing new rime words in the same pattern, invoke the principle of rime word repetition, giving new positions to the same rime words (with some change: *nuda, aferm, desnut* in different stanzas).

Bernart de Ventadorn V uses the same pair-principle but not sequentially; the first stanza has the rime words *solelh, rai, esmai, solelha, raya, esmaya, sordei, sordeya*, and the other stanzas fit new words into the same pattern. The distance separating members of one pair increases to stanza length in Raimbaut d'Aurenga XXXIX. The first stanza rimes on *enversa, tertres, conglapis, trenca, siscles, giscles, joys*, and *croys* and the second on cognate forms in the relation *-a/-e* or *-s/--*. The third stanza merely repeats the rime words of the first, etc., with the usual coinciding of structural morphemic repetition and word repetition.

Derivative rime has a perhaps more organic link to meaning in occasional than in thorough-going applications. Two or three derivative rime words in a stanza evidently express an idea important to the poem and poet, while the rime words of a whole derivative *cobla* or poem may be chosen for purely formal purposes and for the number of words cognate with them. W. P. Shepard's judgment is not entirely unfair:

> The poetical value of such *tours de force* is of course slight. Nevertheless, we cannot deny that in both songs Aimeic displays a certain mental nimbleness, which however often disappears in the translation. It is impossible, in English prose, to juggle with etymological jingles as the troubadour does in Provençal verse. He never quite attains absolute nonsense; and the second song especially is not unpleasing to the ear. Probably that is all that can be expected of such verbal acrobatics.[51]

K. Conclusion

The multiple and rimed varieties of morphemic repetition represent the culmination of the troubadours' penchant for this mode of intensification; but far more typical and frequent in the Provençal lyric are simple unrimed pairs. Their frequency seems quite similar among different troubadours. Counting the major parts of speech not in the rime, we find the following average number per poem of members of groups having morphemic repetition: Arnaut Daniel, 6.3; Peire Vidal, 6.4; Bernart de Ventadorn, 7.0. Almost all these groups consist of simple pairs, so that the average troubadour poem can be said to contain about three good examples of unrimed morphemic repetition. And derivative rime, judging from Peire Vidal's example, forms about one pair in the average poem (eighty-six derivative rimes in Peire Vidal's forty-five poems counted). To these figures must be added the much more extensive unrimed variation of function words, so that morphemic repetition has considerable quantitative importance in the troubadours.

In the quality and variety as well as in the quantity of their usage, the troubadours ably exploit the great potentialities of morphemic repetition, with its characteristic variation of repeated roots by different inflections, prefixes, suffixes, functions, and meanings. The

---

[51] Shepard (cf. n. 22, above), p. 297.

poems of the troubadours afford many a fine illustration of Lausberg's concise characterization of rhetorical *polyptoton*:

> The changing of the inflection in word repetition serves the purpose of *variatio*: from the contrast between the similarity of the word and the difference of the syntactical function, an enlivening effect is achieved. [52]

What is the importance of rhetoric and the *Leys d'amors* for the troubadours' morphemic repetition? Certainly all partake of the same originally classical inspiration. More specifically, the type known to rhetoric as *figura per pleonasmum* has considerable success in the troubadours (*un can cantar*). And Guilhem Molinier's *rims derivatius* are a well-known device in Provençal, ultimately in the rare but spectacular *cobla derivans* or *entretracha* (I, 336). It would seem that without the rhetorical tradition reflected in the medieval *artes poeticae*, simple morphemic repetition could hardly have expanded into such complex structures, nor an originally affective technique into a formal one.

---

[52] Lausberg, Handbuch, 640: "Die Lockerung der Flexionsform in der Wortwiederholung dient der *variatio*: aus dem Gegensatz zwischen der Gleichheit des Wortes und der Verschiedenheit der syntaktischen Funktion wird eine belebende Wirkung erreicht."

Chapter V

SOUND EFFECTS

The sound effects of poetry have been so irregularly studied that terminology is not firmly established. In the *Leys d'amors*, Molinier's excellent treatment of rime applies the term *consonansa* to identity of consonant sounds and *sonansa* to identity of vocalic sounds.[1] Since the *Leys* have at least the advantage of proximity to their subject, I propose to adopt these terms, to be translated as "consonance" and "vocalism,"[2] and to be united under the title of "sound repetition."

These three terms will thus designate repetition respectively of consonants, of vowels, and of both together. They have the advantage of implying no particular positions within words. Later, special cases such as initial consonance or tonic vocalism can be given their

---

[1] I, 144-160. The minimal forms of *consonansa* and *sonansa* are *consonansa borda*, "bastard consonance" (*fetge-metge*) and *sonansa borda*, "bastard vocalism" (*amors-vos*).

[2] "Consonance," according to the *Shorter Oxford English Dictionary* (ed. C. T. Onions, Oxford, 1933; hereafter *Shorter OED*), is "pleasing combination of sounds," a definition almost identical to that of Charles Duffy and Henry Pettit, *A Dictionary of Literary Terms* (Denver, 1953). But the term's etymological relation to the word "consonant" makes it less confusing to apply "consonance" to the repetition of consonant sounds only. Hence this definition in Sylvan Barnet, Morton Berman and William Burto, *The Study of Literature: A Handbook of Critical Essays and Terms* (Boston, 1960; hereafter *The Study of Literature*), p. 351: "Consonance: identical consonant-sounds and differing vowel-sounds in words in proximity (fail: feel; rough: roof; pitter: patter). Sometimes consonance is more loosely defined merely as the repetition of a consonant (fai*l*: pee*l*)." The usual meanings of "vocalism" are less close to that which I propose; but the term can mean "A system of vowels; the use of vowels" (*Shorter OED*), with perhaps some suggestion of the idea of recurrence.

own names, summarized in chart 8, below. Sections B through H will treat the various sorts of consonance and vocalism, then section I will deal with those sound effects which illustrate meaning not by repetition but by concentration of sounds.

A. Scholarship and Sources

A 1. *Scholarship*

A discussion of sound effects can be auspiciously launched by a quotation from Edith Rickert's *Study of Literature*:

> Although the continual use of tone color by all writers of artistic intent needs no demonstration, the extent to which stylistic effects are dependent upon mere arrangement of sounds is not realized by most persons today. Yet quotations might easily be assembled to show that very early writers were fully aware of the effects produced solely by the play of sound. Perhaps the following passage from Dante will suffice:
>
> "We must choose our words not only for elegance, but for sound — to perform which a mastery of the language is required. The poet must have a store of words, and must have the art to manage his vowels to the best advantage, that they may go the further. He must also know the nature of the vowels — which are more sonorous, and which more soft and sweet — and so dispose them as his present occasions require."
>
> And all good literature — both prose and poetry — is full of striking examples of tone color, used not only for producing general impressions of the most varied kinds, but also for suggesting very special and momentary effects....
>
> The search for the many devices of tone color in good writing is one of the most fruitful means of getting at the secrets of style. [3]

The particular sort of "tone color" that concerns us most here is sound repetition. As DeWitt Parker says:

---

[3] Edith Rickert, *New Methods for the Study of Literature* (Chicago, 1927), pp. 190-191. Cf. also David I. Masson's article "Sound in Poetry" in Preminger's *Encyclopedia*, pp. 784-790, for a sophisticated treatment of sound, especially alliteration, and a good bibliography.

> Every lover of poetry is aware of the large share which the mere sound of words contributes to its beauty. This is true even when we abstract from rhythm ... and think only of euphony, alliteration, assonance and rhyme. There is a joy truly surprising in the mere repetition of vowels and consonants.... If the repetition of the same color or line in painting, the same tone in music, can delight us, why not the repetition of the same word sound? In all cases a like feeling of harmony is produced.[4]

Yet Romance scholars have often failed to bear in mind the importance of sound repetition or tone color,[5] despite evidence like the passage from *De Vulgari Eloquentia* quoted by Rickert. Some scholars seem to impute to the Germanic scops and scalds some sort of monopoly on medieval alliteration and assonance. Others have occasionally commented on Romance sound effects. But their contributions, which will be discussed below in the appropriate sections, are generally restricted to the study of alliteration, often neglecting other types of sound effect and the general phonetic structure of the Provençal poem. For the troubadours, no synthesis on sound effects has been attempted.

The only hint at a general view of Provençal sounds is in Leo Spitzer's article on *Inferno* XIII. He notes that the "harsh-sounding, consonant-ridden words" of Dante's suicides have "much of the quality that is to be found in Provençal, with its tendency toward monosyllabism and its clusters of consonants."[6] But Spitzer has here generalized one aspect of Provençal from the two most "harsh-sounding, consonant-ridden" poems in the language, *Al prim pres* and *Guillems Fabres nos fai*, both of which will be discussed later. Dante, Spitzer says, uses such onomatopoeia or sound symbolism "with greater refinement and artistic economy"; and "while the Provençal poets were apt to resort to this procedure to excess, delighting in sound effects for their own sake, Dante was careful to limit it to cases where it was suitable to the context."[7]

---

[4] DeWitt H. Parker, *The Principles of Aesthetics* (Boston, 1920), p. 196.
[5] Even Riffaterre, *Pléiades*, ignores sound effects, which may be admittedly slight in Gobineau's prose.
[6] Leo Spitzer, "Speech and Language in *Inferno* XIII," p. 89. Spitzer's analysis of what he calls "consonant-ridden words" is perhaps influenced by Diez's "gehäufte Consonanten (*Poesie*, pp. 281-282).
[7] Spitzer, p. 90.

Even if certain troubadours had chosen to organize their poetry around sound rather than meaning, this would not justify automatic condemnation; some such poetry is rather successful.[8] But Spitzer's description simply does not fit the troubadours' poetry, concerned as it is with transmitting ideas, whether personal or political.[9] Their sound effects, like Dante's, are generally "suitable to the context" and are far more skilled and varied than Spitzer would have us believe. One can justifiably say that the troubadours just as well as Dante illustrated what Spitzer calls "the medieval (and ultimately ancient) ideas concerning the correspondence between meaning and sound."[10]

One of the passages that perhaps weighed too heavily on Spitzer's analysis also prompted others to appraise the sound factor in Old Provençal. This is Uc de Saint Circ's *cobla* XXVIII, directed against another poet's work:

> Guillems Fabres nos fai en *brau* lengage
> Manz *braus broncs brenx, bravan* de *brava* guia,
> E *rocs* e *brocs* qe met en son cantage,
> E *fils* e *pils* e motz d'algaravia,
> E *cornz* e *critz* e got - - - len,
> E *durs* e *mus* e *musas* e *musen*,
> E naus e mars e auras e freich ven
> E *pix* e *nix* qe trai d'astronomia.

Here, the vocabulary presumably parodies its victim's "harsh language" (*brau lengage*), by the six alliterating words in *br-* in the first two lines and by the alliterating groups of lines 5-6; by the morphological figures *brau-braus, bravan-brava, musas-musen;* by the heavy consonance of *broncs, brenx, cornz, critz;* by the assonances *durs-mus-musa* (including near-homophony), *naus-mars-auras;* and by the rare and heavy rimes *rocs-brocs, fils-pils, pix-nix*.

Spitzer quite rightly says that this "interesting allusion to the 'brau lengage'... must refer to the deliberate device on the part of Provençal poets to exploit the harsh strength to which their word-material so easily lent itself."[11] But this "deliberate device" is far rarer and

---

[8] E.g., Vachel Lindsay, E. E. Cummings, some medieval *fatrasies*, etc.
[9] The genres, significantly, are defined more by content than by form, except for playful inventions like the *no-sai-que-s'es*.
[10] Spitzer, p. 90.
[11] Spitzer, p. 89.

less acceptable to the troubadours than he thinks, as is proven by the very fact that the well-known Uc (an author of the *vidas*) condemns it. Furthermore, Uc, who can be taken to represent at least a certain period of Provençal taste, shares precisely Spitzer's opinion that sense must not be sacrificed for sound, since he accuses Guillem Fabre of speaking "gibberish" (*algaravia*) [12] and of seeking exotic and irrelevant terms as far afield as in astronomy for the sake merely, in Spitzer's words, of "sound effects for their own sake."

Moreover, even the isolated poets who show an occasional penchant for this *brau lengage* are not always playing with sound without regard for meaning; whether in Arnaut Daniel's winter scenes or Dante's *rime pietrose*, "harsh language" can be symbolic of a state of mind. But related to meaning or not, *brau lengage* should not be generalized into a major tendency of the Provençal lyric, as is done by Spitzer. At any rate, Uc's *cobla* does represent one extreme in poetic language; and the mystery of Guilhem Fabre's true identity has prompted scholars to examine the work of several troubadours from a stylistic point of view, with special reference to sound effects and particularly consonant alliteration. [13]

Some valuable remarks have also been made by scholars like Bartsch, Zenker, Toja, Almqvist, and others, whose contributions will figure in subsequent sections. Yet among students of Romance poetry it is, quite indicatively, the "non-professional" Ezra Pound who has best appreciated the sounds of Provençal. In his essay "Arnaut

---

[12] The application of *algaravia* to astronomical terms is particularly appropriate since the word derives from *al arabia* and the Arabs were the medieval masters of astronomy.

[13] A late thirteenth-century troubadour named precisely Guilhem Fabre is disqualified, perhaps a bit hastily, by Uc's editors Alfred Jeanroy and J.-J. Salverda de Grave, *Poésies de Uc de Saint-Circ* (Toulouse, 1913), p. 205: "Il ne saurait être question ici du troubadour narbonnais Guillem Fabre, qui vivait à la fin du treizième siècle et dont les deux poésies conservées n'offrent rien qui ait le moindre rapport avec la présente cobla." But these two surviving poems have little weight against the presumably much larger number of this poet's lost works, which may well have justified Uc's satire. The work of two other troubadours, Guilhem Ademar and Peire Raimon de Tolosa, is examined by the former's editor Kurt Almqvist (pp. 46-47) and by the latter's editors (pp. 205-206) for details capable of provoking Uc's critique, e.g., Peire Raimon's word play of *fil* and *apil* and Guillem's rimes in *-ocs* (including precisely *rocs* and *brocs*). However, these stylistic analyses, though on the right track, have as yet produced no generally accepted conclusion as to Guilhem Fabre's identity.

Daniel," [14] he speaks of Arnaut's "blending and lengthening of the sounds," his "care for the words" and "ear for hearing their consonance," his "aesthetic of sound," clear and opaque, heavy and light. And inimitable is the sound of Pound's English rendering of Arnaut's "bass onomatopoeia of the wind rowting in the autumn branches":

> Briefly bursteth season brisk,
> Blasty north breeze racketh branch,
> Branches rasp each branch on each,
> Tearing twig and tearing leafage,
>   Chirms now no bird nor cries querulous.... [15]

In particular, Pound goes to great lengths to render Arnaut's birdlike effects. The lines

> Nuills auzels, anz brai' e chanta
>   Cadahus
> En son us (VIII, 4-6),

for example, become in his translation

> Auzel in each tune contrasted
>   Letteth loose
> Wriblis spruce. [16]

Pound aptly comments that Arnaut "was very cunning in his imitation of birds, as... where he stops in the middle of his singing, crying: 'Cadahus, en son us,' as a bird cries, rhyming on it cleverly, with no room to turn about on the words...." [17] Thus, though limiting his remarks to one troubadour, Pound points the way in justifying the relation of sound to meaning in the troubadours' poetry.

Other scholars' generally negative view toward sound repetition derives ultimately from both traditional rhetoric and the French classical esthetic. Rhetorical *homoeoprophoron* or *paromoion* (properly "proximity of similar sounds — be they vowels or consonants," [18] but

---

[14] In *Make It New* (New Haven, 1935), pp. 43-92.
[15] Pound, p. 75.
[16] Pound, p. 62.
[17] Pound, p. 43.
[18] Heinrich Lausberg, "Zur Stellung Malherbes in der Geschichte der französischen Schriftsprache," *Romanische Forschungen*, LXII (1950), 177: "Nebeneinanderstellung ähnlicher Laute — seien es nun Vokale oder Konsonanten."

generally applied to consonance) was usually considered a *vitium* until the humanists rehabilitated it as *alliteratio*.[19] Malherbe prefers the classical interdiction to the Renaissance tolerance, and "his fear of sound repetition is... an acquired Latinism."[20] Thus Malherbe condemns anything resembling alliteration in Desportes, even the inoffensive expressions *tout entretien* and *de même en mes douleurs* and the rather good line

Un trait de ses regards me transforme en rocher.[21]

Another notable case of such classical prejudice is Gustave Flaubert, who describes himself as "très satisfait quand j'ai écrit une phrase sans assonance ni répétition."[22]

Such intolerance seems to have hidden from many readers the beauties of the troubadours' sounds. It is not enough to reject the general rhetorical and classical prejudice against sound repetition. One must realize, as we shall see later with regard to alliteration, that on occasion the rhetorical esthetic not only permitted but admired sound repetition, and that the Provençal lyric used this license with very remarkable results.

A 2. *The Problem of Sources*

What can be the sources of the troubadours' undeniable inclination for using sound effects? One could attempt to demonstrate indigenous development through such emanations of popular speech as proverbs. Eugen Cnyrim, however, finds even "unintentional" alliteration in only twenty-three proverbs out of 1090 and "clearly demonstrable" alliteration in just one: "*Per plus pretz plus pretz es compratz*" (No. 145, from Peire Cardenal).[23] What is more, Cnyrim's proverbs are all ex-

---

[19] Lausberg, *Elemente*, § 458.
[20] Lausberg, "Zur Stellung Malherbes," p. 177: "Angelernter Latinismus ist auch seine Furcht vor dem Gleichklang."
[21] *Ibid.*, pp. 177-178.
[22] In letter by Flaubert to G. Sand, Dec., 1873, quoted in Charles Chassé, *Styles et physiologie* (Paris, 1928), p. 29, n. 1. Or, as Maxime Du·Camp wrote, "la moindre assonance l'effarouchait," quoted in A. Albalat, *Le travail du style* (cf. n. I, 24), p. 67.
[23] E. Cnyrim, *Sprichwörter, sprichwörtliche Redensarten und Sentenzen bei den provenzalischen Lyrikern. Ausgaben und Abhandlungen LXXI* (Marburg, 1888).

tracted from the work of the troubadours, who may be supposed more inclined to add alliteration to popular sayings than to suppress it. On the other hand, to his examples one could plausibly add many cases such as "*S*en de *S*alamo" and "*S*aber de *S*alamo" (Nos. 1023-24) or "*A*dam *c*ujon *c*ontrafar" (No. 1031). And one must here cite such ubiquitous, obviously popular and semi-proverbial groups as *aur-argen, bel-bon, gran-gros-gras, lonc-larc-lat, maior-meillor-menor, pauc-pro-plus, petit-paubre, san-sau* ("safe and sound"!), *tort-travers, tost-tart,* etc., most of which exist in other Romance languages. Furthermore, the *Leys* state that *replicatio* (alliteration) can be excused *en lo proverbi vulgar* (in common or vernacular proverbs) such as

> Haias mal, haias be,
> Am lo *t*ieus *te* cap*te* (III, 65)

(the *t*'s of the second line are presumably meant). Also, William IX's alliterating nonsense words could be cited as indicative of popular speech tendencies:

> Anc no li diz ni *b*at ni *b*ut,
> Ni *f*er ni *f*ust no ai mentaugut,
>   Mas sol aitan:
> "Babariol, babariol,
>   Babarian.   (V, 26-30)[24]

Although a tendency to alliteration appears to some extent in Provençal popular sayings, there is not enough evidence to postulate them as a source of the troubadours' much more frequent alliteration. In this microcosm of the question of literary origins, one must look farther than southern France.

Such is the opinion also of Scheludko, whose well-reasoned article of 1931 on the origins of the Provençal lyric supposes "foreign influence" not only on Provençal but on all Romance alliteration.[25] By "foreign influence," Scheludko means that of medieval Latin, from which he gives enough examples of alliteration to render a Latin

---

[24] The case for reading in lines 28-30 one manuscript's supposedly Arabic words is worse than feeble according to István Frank, "*Babariol-Babarian* dans Guillaume IX," *Romania*, LXXIII (1952), 227-234.

[25] Scheludko, "Entstehungsgeschichte," p. 159: "... müssen wir fremden Einfluss annehmen."

origin of Provençal alliteration certainly more plausible than an indigenous, "popular" one.

Other critics go farther afield. Earlier Sachse, noticing in his study of William IX (1882) a far greater concentration of alliteration in two of the first troubadour's *Companho*-poems than in the rest of his work, ingeniously proposes that their archaic metric form, "derived (according to Bartsch) from an ancient Celtic meter, demanded alliteration, of which traces still emerge in William." [26] But despite Bartsch's authority, this supposed *uraltes keltisches Metrum* has long since passed from Provençal scholarship.

Furthermore, despite Jeanroy's statement that "the farther one comes from the origins, the rarer becomes the search for alliteration," [27] it seems rather that alliteration by no means declines during the twelfth century, and may in fact reach its greatest intensity in the late troubadour Peire Cardenal. Ernest Hoepffner, who finds little alliteration in the earliest Provençal and French literary monuments save in the *Chanson de sainte Foy*, is of the opinion that the use of alliteration actually increases during the literary period:

> ... Voulue ou non, acte réfléchi ou spontané, l'allitération a été pour notre auteur une forme de l'expression poétique, comme elle le sera avec plus d'ampleur pour les troubadours. Ici encore, le poète de la Chanson de sainte Foy se révèle comme un prédécesseur lointain de ces poètes-artistes qui, hantés par le souci de la forme et le poussant jusqu'à ses dernières limites, finiront par devenir les virtuoses du vers et les jongleurs de la rime que l'on connaît. [28]

A Germanic origin has also long been proposed for Romance alliteration. Scholz discusses the arguments in favor of this theory and refutes them primarily on the ground that the troubadours generally loaned to the North rather than borrowing from it. [29]

---

[26] Max Sachse, *Über das Leben und die Lieder des Troubadours Wilhelm IX., Graf von Poitou* (diss. Leipzig, 1882), p. 52: "... als auf ein uraltes keltisches Metrum zurückgehend (nach Bartsch), Alliteration erforderte, wovon bei Wilhelm noch Spuren zu Tage treten."

[27] Jeanroy, *Poésie lyrique*, II, 92: "A mesure que l'on s'éloigne des origines, la recherche de l'allitération devient plus rare."

[28] Ernest Hoepffner and Prosper Alfaric, ed., *La chanson de sainte Foy* (Paris, 1926), I, 225. Hereafter *Sainte Foy*.

[29] Scholz, "Alliteration" (cf. ch. IV, n. 25), XXXVII, 390-391. One can though, without inconsistency, concede to Gustav Gröber, in his review of

But Jeanroy's remark that Germanic and Romance alliteration are of different natures — the former excluding rime and the latter co-operating with it — is a telling point against the Germanic theory.[30] Ezra Pound's concoction of a *joglar engles,* "a possible hrim-hram-hruffer," from whom "Arnaut may have caught his alliteration," must be accounted, however clever, contrary to all evidence.[31]

Certainly no one who writes on the subject denies the frequency of alliteration in Latin, from archaic Latin on, nor the plausibility of a continued Latin-Romance alliterative tradition. The only question is one of degree. Scholz, after minimizing the influence of Germanic, Celtic, and Arabic, concludes that though medieval Latin and Provençal influence each other mutually, "very probably we must however assume independent introduction of alliteration in Old Provençal poetry as a real poetic means";[32] but for this last he is attacked by Scheludko, who in turn exaggerates in supposing *all* Provençal alliteration to be of foreign (i.e., Latin) importation.[33] The truth doubtless lies in between.

A common Romance tradition is amply proven both by Scheludko's examples from medieval Latin and by Scholz's table of alliterating groups, complete with literary references, in different Romance languages. Each group occurs with a certain frequency in two or more Romance languages and consists of members, most often two, bound by a common initial phoneme and by related or contrasting meaning.

E. Wölfflin, "Über die allitterirenden Verbindungen der lateinischen Sprache," *ZfRP,* VI (1882), 467-469, that the alliteration of proper names in the Old French epic (Gerin-Gerer, Basin-Basilie, etc.) may well, like most of the names themselves, be of Germanic origin. Alliteration of words other than names is also not rare in the French epic. Of the examples of "synonymous iteration" in the *Chanson de Roland* cited by Silvio Pellegrini, "Iterazioni sinonimiche nella Canzone di Rolando," *Studi Mediolatini e Volgari,* I (1953), 155-165, about one sixth have pairs showing consonantal or vocalic alliteration; full evaluation of this figure must await comparison with other epics and genres, however.

[30] Jeanroy, *Poésie lyrique,* II, 92.
[31] Pound, *Make It New,* p. 52; cf. also p. 43. Pound would read *joglars engles* for *joglars escomes* in the first sentence of the only surviving *razo* to a poem of Arnaut's (Boutière and Schutz, *Biographies des troubadours,* p. 62); but this reading seems impossible to justify.
[32] Scholz, "Alliteration," XXXVII, 392: "Sehr wahrscheinlich haben wir aber selbständige Einführung der Alliteration als eigentliches poetisches Kunstmittel in die altprovensalische Dichtung anzunehmen."
[33] Scheludko, "Entstehungsgeschichte" (cf. ch. I, n. 38), p. 159.

For example, the Latin pair *planctus-ploratus* passes into the vernacular as Provençal *planher-plorar*, Italian *piangere-plorare* and French *plur-plaigne;* and Latin *fructus-flores* gives Provençal *frug-flor*, Italian *frutto-fiore*, French *fruit-flor*.³⁴ Groups shared by different languages may be assumed to derive from Romance tradition; groups particular to one language, more from popular inventiveness or the individual poet.

The origins of vocalic repetition must be assumed similar to those of consonance. Germanic or Arabic influence seems quite dubious. A certain native element is evidenced by the incomplete replacement of assonance by rime in the early literary monument *Boeci*;³⁵ sporadic assonance for rime is also to be found in three poems identified in Frank's *Répertoire métrique*.³⁶ And vocalism, though more rarely than consonance, can also unite groups which, if not traditional in Romance languages, at least become more or less conventional in Provençal: this category includes both vocalic alliteration (*aire-ale*) and assonance (*dreit-lei*). Whatever the original inspiration of consonance and vocalism, their greatest importance lies in their varying application to literary expression by the individual troubadours that both shaped and perpetuated the Provençal lyric tradition.

B. Medieval Authority

Traditional rhetoric is not very concerned with distinguishing independent sound effects from those attendant on *annominatio* and on word repetition. Assonance goes completely unmentioned.³⁷ Initial sound repetition, however, is recognized in successive brief grammatical divisions, e.g., in this series: "invidia, iniuriis, potentia, perfidia."³⁸ And *homoeoprophoron* is described as a figure involving

---

³⁴ Scholz, "Alliteration," XXXVIII, 92 and 85.

³⁵ Assonance plays a smaller role in Provençal metrics than in Old French; cf. Hoepffner and Alfaric, *Sainte Foy*, I, 220.

³⁶ I, xxx, n. 2. To Frank's examples should be added cases like *alberguem* side by side with two rimes in *-en* in William IX's poem V, 31-33, where assonance is reinforced by homotypic consonants (both *m* and *n* being nasals).

³⁷ Lausberg, *Handbuch*, § 725-734. Yet it may be said that in rhetoric, accented or unaccented rime is considered under the heading of *homoeoteleuton* (cf. p. 124, below).

³⁸ Lausberg, § 939a, from the *Rhetorica ad Herennium*.

frequent repetition of the same consonant within several successive words, particularly at the beginning of these words.[39] Although these particular figures seem to have inspired little enthusiasm among medieval rhetoricians, or later among the French classical theorists, neither French nor Provençal has been insensible to sound effects. Racine, Victor Hugo, Rimbaud, Louis Aragon, and many others furnish ample evidence for Henri Morier's statement that "la langue française n'est pas qu'une langue abstraite: elle est une langue finement, délicieusement expressive."[40]

The *Leys d'amors* certainly say enough to encourage detection of sound effects, intentional or not, in the troubadours. Guilhem Molinier treats more readily of consonance than of vocalism, though generally considering the two together. His great failing doubtless is to demand too great regularity before recommending sound repetition for effect; and, as throughout his treatise, he considers avoidance of stylistic "vices" as far more vital than cultivation of stylistic virtues. After all, Molinier is writing for an audience of amateur poets competing in poetic contests in which, by nature, faults are easier to judge than genius. Yet what is important is that on occasion he recognizes the legitimacy and the beauty of the sounds of poetry.

Molinier's study of sound can conveniently be divided into the categories of imitation, concentration and repetition. The former, of course, is none other than *onomothopeia* (III, 228), classified as a daughter of Allebolus and Sentensa (i.e. as a figure of idea), presumably because an imitative sound can be considered subservient to the idea it represents. Like medieval rhetoric, Molinier treats onomatopoeia as a mode of word formation (technically *fictio*),[41] for instance *corp, cogul, belar, miular* ("crow, cuckoo, bleat, meow") derived from the sounds *croac, cocuc, be, miau*. Molinier's second category, concentration of sound, receives a remarkable treatment under the name of *collizio* (see section I, below).

In treating the third category, repetition of sounds, Molinier considers vowels and consonants together. The supposed vice of the same sound ending one word and beginning the next (III, 50-52) includes

---

[39] Lausberg, § 975.
[40] Morier, *Dictionnaire* (cf. ch. III, n. 23), p. 108; cf. also his articles "Consonne," "Voyelle," "Onomatopée," etc.
[41] Lausberg, *Handbuch*, § 547-548; Latin *fictio*, "word creation," in fact renders the Greek term *onomatopoeia*.

various forms of *cacosyntheton*. These are, with vowel repetition, *hyat* ("vocals denan vocals ... e divers mot"), [42] *iothacisme* (with -*ii*- or -*ii*, possible only in Latin), and *methacisme* (final -*m* before a following initial vowel, causing hiatus in Latin verse); and, with consonant repetition, *fre* (-*r r*-, -*s r*-) and *laudacisme* (-*l l*- and by extension -*n n*-, -*s s*-, -*x x*-, etc.). [43] Molinier actually disapproves of such repetition of sounds at contiguous extremities of different words, in keeping with his rhetorical sources. But he wisely adds that these "vices" are not so grave as to demand suppression of an idea that cannot be expressed otherwise (I, 30). Molinier hence opens the way to justifying sound repetition by the desirable effects produced.

The *Leys d'amors* also treat sound repetition at verse ends (I, 140ff), not only in rime but also in what might be called sub-rime, in the form of either *sonansa borda* (literally "bastard vocalism") — whether simple (*amọrs-vọs, tẹmps-fẹrms*) or double (*grAndA-FrAnsA, escazUtA-pergUdA*) — or *consonansa borda* (*fẹTGe-mẹTGe, m'abranDatuDa*). These forms of assonance and consonance are condemned as fit only for lower forms of poetry, specifically *viandelas*, but permitted in *rims estramps* (cf. section D 2 below). The *Leys* also treat repetition of initial consonants as the different forms of *replicatio* (cf. section E 1); and irregular internal rime receives attention as *rim fayshuc* (cf. sections G 3-G 5). Though his attitude toward all of these forms of sound repetition is generally negative, Guilhem Molinier invariably approves them when used for the special effects and purposes which will be discussed later.

C. VALUES OF SOUNDS

C 1. *Inherent Values*

This medieval familiarity with sound repetition — in both traditional rhetoric and the *Leys d'amors* — suggests that the troubadours were capable of using it for structural patterns. But more can be said: that they use sound with semantic undertones, whether to suggest,

---

[42] Anglade, *Las Flors del Gay Saber* (cf. ch. I, n. 15), lines 4644-45.
[43] These last three terms are apparently adopted from Martianus Capella's categories of *iotacismus, mytacismus* and *lambdacismus* (for which see Lausberg, *Handbuch*, § 975).

enlarge, illustrate, or complement lexical meanings. But whence come the semantic undertones of sound? Do certain sounds carry inherent meanings? This is of course an age-old question.

Many of the troubadours' autumn descriptions seem to profit from a certain "harshness" of initial *p, pr, b, br* and *ch*. If this is plausible, we must then ask if other sounds are appropriate to some meanings more than to others, for example do the *f*'s and *fl*'s common in spring exordia symbolize their subject in sound? Such sound symbolism is accepted by Henri Morier, who associates French nasals with desire, *f* with sudden bright light or cold, *l* and *m* with humidity and liquidity, *p* with weight, *fl* with breath, *r* with "circular or alternating movement," etc.[44]

Similarly, Valter Tauli holds that

> *Sound symbolism* (SS) is not merely a subjective feeling. Repeated observations have proved that people link certain speech sounds with certain meanings, that there is wide agreement in some cases among the speakers of several languages, and this reveals obviously more than random frequency.[45]

Tauli then brings out, in words both onomatopoeic and not, the "synesthetic and metaphorical associations" peculiar to different categories of vowels (front and "bright" vs. back and "dark") and consonants (voiceless stops often indicating momentary noise, nasals resonance, *l* flowing movement, *r* "articulate noises" or unpleasant things, labials facial expressivity, *ng* and *nk* "constriction," and so on). Also, he says, phonological quantity, reduplication and word length can be symbolic of meaning.

Similarly, particular vowels have sometimes been held to imply, or at least to illustrate, meaning. For example, Morier considers *a* to be a vowel of strong sonority and great intensity, especially apt for expressing largeness, flatness, horizontality, and directness;[46] and Tauli believes *a* and *i* to be near opposite ends of scales of suggestivity ranging from large to small, thick to thin, and dull to sharp.[47]

---

[44] Morier, *Dictionnaire*, art. "Consonne."
[45] Valter Tauli, *Introduction to a Theory of Language Planning* (Uppsala, 1968), p. 91, in chapter IX, "Phonemic Shape." Hereafter *Language Planning*.
[46] Morier, *Dictionnaire*, art. "Voyelle."
[47] Tauli, pp. 92-95.

In the troubadours, one good example of such semantically significant vocalic contrasts is the first line of Cercamon's perhaps most successful song:

> Quant l'aura doussa s'amarzis (I, 1)

To the dichotomy of seasons represented by the gentle and the harsh winds corresponds a contrast between the vowels *a* and *i*. The *a* dominates the line until it is suddenly evicted in the last syllable by the shrill vowel *i*, the highest of all in harmonic resonance according to Morier. This *i*, reinforced by the double sibilance of the surrounding *z* and *s*, sets the bitter autumnal mood of the remainder of the stanza. There is also a simultaneous thickening of the phonetic structure at the end of the line; only nine of the first eighteen phonemes are consonantal, while four of the last five are consonantal: [kant lawra dousa samar*dzis*]. So both vocalic contrast and consonantal density reinforce the ideas expressed by the line.

Still, it would be going too far to maintain that the meaning of the line could be deduced from the sounds alone. Tennyson's often-cited use of sound symbolism,

> The moan of doves in immemorial elms
> And murmuring of innumerable bees,

has inspired John Crowe Ransom's invention of a line,

> And murdering of innumerable beeves,

to show that almost identical sound can accompany a totally different meaning.[48] One must then admit that a given sound or pattern can illustrate different meanings; but in good poetry, sound rarely contradicts meaning. Thus sound symbolism can be sought in the troubadours with the realization that there is no tight correspondence between sound and meaning, but also with the supposition that sound frequently cooperates with other poetic tools — syntactic, rhythmic, lexical, and even musical to express or illustrate meaning or to call attention to it.

---

[48] Barnet *et al.*, *The Study of Literature* (cf. n. 2, above), p. 352.

For example the multiple active, open *a* sounds of a line of Bertran de Born, unrestrained by any heavy consonant group, seem particularly suitable for describing royal conflict:

> M*a*s *a*r*a*s *a*n t*a*l b*a*r*a*lh*a* (P-C 80.44, 12)

And Jaufre Rudel uses the same phonetic undertone to illustrate another conflict, that caused by his jealous rivals who

> *A*n comens*a*t t*a*l b*a*test*a*u (III, 44).

Yet the same vowel also has an open and untrammeled quality which often seems appropriate to a description of love, as in Cercamon's

> *A*nz don*a* joy *a*ls *a*rditz *a*moros (V, 56)

and Bertran de Ventadorn's

> Qu'en t*a*n *a*ut loc *a*uzei m'*a*mor *a*ssire (XXI, 27).

The same repeated vowel has a largely structural function in phonetically uniting Arnaut Daniel's name to his supposed characteristic:

> Ieu sui *A*rn*a*utz q'*a*m*a*s l'*a*ur*a* (X, 43),

thus contributing to the line's haunting fame. It will be conceded that, since the number of sounds in a language is limited, each sound may correspond to a variety of meanings. Particularly rich in possibilities is the vowel *a*, by far the most common in vocalic alliteration and in assonance.[49] The idea of meaning inherent in sound certainly needs more investigation before becoming anything but an hypothesis; but this is an hypothesis to which, with due caution and with due regard for the poetic context, we will find it profitable to refer in our analyses of sound.

C 2. *Value by Association*

Beside sound symbolism, Valter Tauli indicates another possible sound-sense relationship, "relational symbolism," which influences our

---

[49] Scholz, "Alliteration," XXXVIII, 311-314, gives numerous examples of alliteration in *a*.

interpretation of a word by the meaning of phonetically similar words. It is only natural to relate or confuse words of similar sound, at any rate to associate them, as we shall see under the heading of homophony. According to Tauli, sound can even be a factor in non-onomatopoeic word formation; thus, the frequency of Old English words in *fl-* indicating flight or flow encouraged creation of more such words in later times.[50] On this basis, it can be argued that the very size of Old Provençal groups like *folha-flor-frug* or *pensar-plazer-prezar-parlar* encouraged if not creation at least frequent grouping of terms from related semantic and phonetic categories.

Some Provençal sounds are in fact remarkably frequent in alliterating groups, as can readily be deduced from Scholz's tables. Counting all alliterating pairs occurring in three or more different poems (thus the omnipresent *bon-bel* as well as the only thrice-attested *blanc-brun*), one finds maximums of eighteen such pairs in *p*, ten in *f*, seven in *c* (or *q*), *s* (or soft *c*), and *d*. Another measure of these relative frequencies is the number of pages Scholz devotes to each, respectively 4 2/3, 3 1/3, 3, 2 2/3, 2 1/3. Again, now taking alliterating groups of three or more members (e.g. *folha-flor-frug*), we find that of the thirty-seven roots figuring in two or more such groups, fully twenty-one begin in *f*, *p*, or *s*.

Here, it would be more than risky to speak of sound symbolism, given the semantic field of most of these words. Of the twenty-one roots beginning in *f*, *p* and *s* belonging to two or more multiple alliterative groups, almost all (*fals, felo, fi, fizel, fol, franc, parlar, pensar, planher, plazer, plorar, prezar, saber, sen, sofrir, sospirar*) refer to human psychology. One can speak of onomatopoeia only for *sospirar*; and sound symbolism, though of course dependent on the poetic context, seems unlikely with abstract terms.

But here Tauli's "relational symbolism" can be applied. The ideas of infidelity or intelligence, for example, may almost automatically suggest to the troubadour essentially synonymous alliterating groups

---

[50] Tauli, *Language Planning*, p. 98. Cf. also, in Preminger's *Encyclopedia*, David I. Masson's article "Tone-color": "It is clear that every sound (-collocation) has multiple affinities. The whole picture is distorted by lexical associations. Thus one word (or set) may attract others *in the language* (*swing, sway, swirl, swill swish, swash, swoop, swat, switch*) and/or *in verse*..." (p. 857).

like *fals e felo* or *sen e saber*. Such association of terms helps not only to intensify the expression of important ideas but also to fill out the unused spaces that require filling as any metrical composition is being created.

The same relational symbolism may encourage grouping of alliterating words describing nature. Concepts like mountain (*mon*) and leopard (*leupart*) might not figure at all in the Provençal lyric if it were not for their fortuitous alliterative relation to terms like those denoting the sea (*mar*) or the lion (*leo*). In such cases, both terms might even be lacking in the lyric without their convenient interrelation. Thus, needing a comparison or detail from the world of nature, the troubadour would resort to one of these stereotyped groups as much for sound as for meaning.

As Scholz's lists show, almost as many common alliterative pairs derive from nature as from human psychology. Terms used in the troubadour corpus three or more times in alliterating groups include those describing earth (*flum-fon, mar-mon-montanha, aur-argen*), plants (*bosc-boysso, folha-flor-frug, ram-razitz*), fire (*foc-fer-flama-fust-fum*), animals (*cap-cor-cors-carn*, referring particularly to humans; *leon-leupart*), color (*blanc-brun-blond-bloi, vert-var-vermelh*), and size (*gran-gros-gras, lonc-larc-lat*). These terms describing colors have an especially privileged role, since they can be freely combined in various circumstances for desired effects of sound and length. All these typify the stock of words on which the troubadours could and did draw more for their associational value and sound than for their concrete meaning.

C 3. *Strength of Repeated Sounds*

The poetic value of repeated sounds depends not only on their semantic implications, whether inherent or associational, but also on the quantity and quality of repeated elements. It is evident that the impact of repetition increases with the size of the repeated element. The minimal repetition is that of sound as opposed to silence — a contrast that accounts for much of the rhythm of prose as well as of poetry. Increasing degrees of repetition involve consonants versus vowels; consonants or vowels of different articulations (occlusives, fricatives; open, close; etc.); identical consonants or vowels; identical combinations of phonemes; and ultimately words of identical sound, with or without identical meaning (i.e., word repetition and homophony).

We cannot here consider all these different "strengths" of sound repetition to the troubadours. It seems, however, especially useful to define three particular degrees of sound repetition. There seems no reason to differentiate, on this score, consonance from vocalism. The two may operate on different scales of intensity as well as of articulation;[51] the intensity of an expression like *abans* et *apres* may profit less from alliteration than *tost* e *tart*. But vocalism and consonance share the same capacity for gradation of effect according to the phonetic mass of repetition. Therefore we shall extend to vocalism the convenient terminology which Scholz inherited from earlier critics and applied in his study of alliteration.[52]

"Weak" sound repetition will include sounds whose pronunciation is similar but not identical,[53] i.e., different qualities of one vowel (e.g., close ẹ and open ę, close ọ and open ǫ),[54] and consonants of the same articulation but different voicing (e.g., *f-v*, *p-b*, *t-d*, *k-g*, etc.). It would seem, however, that "weak" alliteration, for example, should be discerned only when in association with stronger forms of alliteration. Scholz prudently forgoes the analogy of Germanic oral poetry (which permits alliteration of any two initial vowels), and concludes that in Old Provençal we must insist on identity of vowels in normal vocalic alliteration.[55] Hence, like Scholz, we shall consider "weak" sound repetition as at most a reinforcement of normal sound repetition.

Normal sound repetition will include repetition of single phonemes or of allophones.[56] The phonetic context of these sounds cannot much

---

[51] Cf. Ulrich K. Goldsmith, art. "Alliteration," in Preminger's *Encyclopedia*: "Alliteration of initial vowels is less frequent since they do not have the same acoustic impact as consonants" (p. 15).

[52] Cf. Scholz, "Alliteration," XXXVII, 387.

[53] Cf. Raymond Alden, *An Introduction to Poetry* (New York, 1909), pp. 210-211: "A characteristic effect is also produced by the use of vowels or consonants of like but not identical character"; the name "phonetic syzygy" has been proposed for this, Alden says.

[54] Close ạ (before nasals or *n mobile*) and open ạ (in other positions) will here be considered as sufficiently similar to constitute normal vocalism. These two sounds are the two composing *a utrissonan* in the *Leys d'amors* (I, 50-52).

[55] Scholz, "Alliteration," XXXVII, 387-388.

[56] The *Leys* (I, 38) distinguish two different pronunciations of *r* (apparently according to position) and of *l* (apparently according to etymological

influence their effect, and there is no reason to interdict, as in Germanic alliterating poetry, a linking of *s purum* and *s impurum*. Similarly, the accented vowel of a diphthong can perfectly well assonate or alliterate with the simple vowel: whether *a* or any other tonic vowel be followed by a consonant or a semivowel, it remains the vocalic dominant of its syllable, for example in the common expression *aur e argen* or in Cercamon's line

Ni mal no·m sent e si l'*ai* gr*an* (I, 32).

Or, a perhaps marginal case of *i*-assonance with and without the semivowel *u* is Jaufre Rudel's

Belhs m'es l'est*i*us e·l temps flor*i*tz (IV, 1).

Finally, "rich" sound repetition involves two or more consecutive repeated elements, whether a consonant group like *pl* and *br* or a vowel group (diphthong or triphthong) like *ai* and *ieu*. It is obvious that a repeated group brings greater intensification that a single repeated phoneme. Though higher grades of group repetition short of homophony could be distinguished — by sheer quantity, by duration, or by percentage of a whole — they are rare enough to be conveniently lumped together, in section H 1, under the title of "near-homophony." Thus the semantic value of sound repetition, whether inherent or by association, can be measured on a scale of intensity ranging from weak, normal and rich, up to near-homophony and ultimately true homophony.

D. The Position of Sound Repetition

D 1. *Position with Relation to the Word*

The "strength" of phonetic intensification depends not only on the semantic or phonetic value of repeated sounds, but also on their position relative to each other, to lexical units and to larger poetic

---

origin). But we shall consider any recurrence of *r* or *l*, whether single or geminated, as contributing to sound repetition, since such differences seem insufficient to warrant "demoting" such recurrences to the status of "weak" sound repetition.

rhythms. Position relative to words will be taken up first, since the word is, at least to the medieval listener, the unitary bearer of idea and image.

The position of sounds in a word determines their susceptibility to phonetic development and erosion. Intervocalic consonants and post-tonic vowels are relatively weak, initial consonants [57] and vowels relatively resistant, and so on. These relative strengths depend on the force of expiration and the care of articulation at different phases of the pronouncing of a word. The situation is far more complex than the simple contrast between accented and unaccented syllables, not only in the formative period of the Romance languages but also in their literary period. The typical Provençal word contains momentary segments of greater or lesser strength and hence perceptibility. The recurrence of sounds at identical positions in nearby words will therefore increase their mutual "strength." Furthermore, given the importance of the single word, sounds in identical position relative to the limits of words, as well as to their accents, tend to have a certain rapport. This supposition, borne out by familiarity with living languages, justifies paying special attention to initial sound repetition and to tonic vocalism, as these seem to be especially important in the troubadours. Repetition of sounds within single words, though lacking the power of drawing different concepts and different words together, will also be treated where it supplements inter-word sound effects.

Phonetic elements recurring with the same relation to the general shape or expiratory pattern of words thus have special significance, especially in the emphatic initial or tonic positions. Yet phonetic elements in different positions can also contribute to a common, though perhaps generally weaker, effect. Critics who have realized this have long debated whether initial and internal consonants can "alliterate."

Scholz maintains that alliteration can "jump over" non-alliterating atonic initial syllables, whether prefixal (*par-companh*) or organic (*setmanas-mes, amor-merce*). [58] However, these pairs are undeniably less strong than if both consonants were initial. Scholz adds that in

---

[57] Old Provençal initial consonants remain unchanged compared to Vulgar Latin, and all but *c* and *g* before *e* and *i* remain unchanged compared to Classical Latin (except for some consonants combined with semivowels).

[58] Scholz, "Alliteration," XXXVII, 393.

such cases, both alliterating consonants must begin tonic syllables; thus he disqualifies such *Anlaut-Inlaut* pairs as *pérdas-dans* and *dezir-badalh*.[59] Yet such effects, though lesser than those in tonic syllables, should not be entirely disregarded over a question of terminology. Scholz himself implies that position within words is a more important factor than accent in defining alliteration when he admits that in internal tonic syllables the presence or absence of alliteration must be decided on basically subjective grounds.[60]

The importance of such subjective, hence often arbitrary, judgments can be reduced by a broader view regarding any proximate repetition of sounds as potentially significant. Even a weak repetition at least reinforce stronger effects. We have established that position with relation to a word's limits and to its tonic accent influences the effect of sound repetition. Certainly, internal sound repetition (except assonance) has less force than initial sound repetition; and tonic vocalism has greater force than atonic vocalism (except perhaps vocalic alliteration). But such phonetic effects in different positions can and do cooperate.

There remains only the problem of definition according to the two interplaying criteria of accent and position. For example "alliteration" will designate initial sound repetition regardless of accent; "assonance," tonic vocalism regardless of position. It will be understood that either can work together with its own kind or with other sound repetitions. The various categories, and our terms for them, are indicated schematically in the following chart, with position in words plotted against the type of sound repeated:

---

[59] Scholz, XXXVII, 395.
[60] *Ibid.*

Chart 8:

Categories of Sound Repetition

type of sound repeated:	only consonants	only vowels	both consonant and vowel
position in word: initial phoneme	alliteration	vocalic alliteration	reinforced alliterating groups
internal syllable	consonant harmony	vocalic harmony	internal sound repetition
tonic syllable		assonance	reinforced assonance
tonic syllable and final, if any	*consonansa borda*	*sonansa borda*	*rim fayshuc* and end rime
non-tonic final syllable	final consonance	post-tonic vocalism	*homoeoteleuton*
combination of any of above	reinforced consonance	reinforced vocalism	multiple sound repetition

A different problem is that of compounds. Scholz is quite right to dismiss as "kaum Alliteration" [61] pairs like *aprendre-prendre* or *conferma-ferma*, which illustrate properly etymological figure in the form of composition, with incidental sound repetition in different positions in the words. What is important is to know which factor is more of a by-product of the other, the phonetic or the lexical.

Another problem in defining the relation of sound repetition to the word is that of vowelless words phonetically attached to other words. Scholz maintains that repetition of the proclitic particles *d'*, *l'*, *m'*, *n'*, *s'*, and *qu'* can either produce alliteration (*d'ivern e d'estiu, s'abais ni s'umil*) or be "jumped over" (*m'esdui e m'empenh*, vocalic alliteration).[62] But this problem is a false one, because these are properly examples of word repetition in enumeration; the only true alliterative pair here is *esdui-empenh*. It is true that the effect of vocalic alliteration after particles, especially different ones, is weaker; thus *e*-alliteration in *m'esdui e t'empenh* would be of minimal force. But this interference factor is lesser when not all members of a group are preceded by proclitics. The latter may then be ignored and the first sound of any major word considered as initial, as in William IX:

---

[61] Scholz, XXXVII, 394.
[62] Scholz, XXXVII, 393-394.

>   Companho, tant *ai* *a*gutz d'*a*vols conres (III, 1);
>   Tal paor *ay* qu'*a*des s'*a*zir (IX, 44);
>   No l'*a*us m'*a*mor fort *a*ssemblar (IX, 46).

The important concepts of these lines are *aver, avol, ades, azir, auzar, amor, assemblar*; the fact that many are preceded by a preposition, pronoun or conjunction does not significantly affect their phonetic interrelations. From other familiar contexts, the vowel *a* is felt as initial in all these "lexical words." Thus we return to the basic principle justifying the special effect of initial sound repetition: the first phoneme of the lexical unit, or word, enjoys privileged position, force, and effect.

D 2. *Position with Relation to the Verse: in Different Verses*

Sound repetition is most noticeable within the confines of single lines; the recurrence of a rime and of a pause in the melody at the end of each line makes the creation of any larger unities in sound repetition difficult, at least where lines are of normal length. Exceptionally, short lines and syntactical continuity allow us to speak of two-line alliterating groups, as in Arnaut Daniel's lines

>   Anz vos *d*esir
>   Plus que *D*ieu cill de *D*oma (IX, 84-85),

which rhythmically may as well be one decasyllable with triple alliteration.

Similarly, Jaufre Rudel reinforces one alliterating pair by related sounds in the following line:

>   Las *p*im*p*as sian als *p*astors
>   Et als en*f*ans *b*urdens *p*etitz (III, 9-10)

The recurrent labials — triply alliterating *p*, supported by the first line's internal *p* and the second line's internal *f* and initial *b* — imitate the flute sound produced by the instruments called *pimpas*. The parallelism signaled by repeated *als* and by alliteration of successive rime words reinforces the phonetic linkage of these two lines.

More rarely, alliteration can join two lines without forming a pair within either line. Thus a double correspondence links the first and last important words of two lines of Cercamon:

Ni *m*uer ni viu ni no *g*uaris,
Ni *m*al no·m sent e si l'ai *g*ran (I, 31-32).

Here again, parallelism, represented by repeated *ni* in enumeration, justifies our perception of this phonetic relation whose effect is to tie together the four concepts of death, cure, pain, and magnitude.

Or, the non-riming syllables of successive rime words can be joined by repeated elements. A certain number of examples will be found in Scholz's inventory: *a*BeLL*ida*-*o*BL*ida*, *es*Qu*i*rols-c*ab*Irols, ES*mai*-ES*glai*, ES*mai*-ES*trai*, ES*maia*-ES*chaia*, F*ian*sa-F*er*m*an*sa, etc.[63] A good example is the first stanza of William IX's number V:

> Farai un vers, pos mi s*o*nelh
> E·m vauc e m'estauc al *so*lelh.
> Domnas i a de mal c*on*selh,
>   E sai dir *cal*s:
> Cellas c'amor de c*a*valier
>   Tornon a mals (V, 1-6).[64]

Such playful interlinear sound repetition is particularly suited to introducing this adventurous and mildly scatological poem.

The pioneer Karl Bartsch was no doubt the first to call attention to sound repetition linking the tonic and/or following syllables of two or more unrimed end words in an internally unrimed or only partially rimed stanza. Such *rims estramps* — which rime between but not within stanzas — often have consonance or vocalism among themselves. Bartsch cites from different troubadours the examples *a*NH-*o*NH, *i*U-*e*U, O*tz*-O*cs*, OS-ORS-OR*tz*, *a*R*d*A-*o*R*t*A.

Rims estramps can form an effective block in a partly rimed stanza, contrasting to the intrastanzaic rimes. Thus, in Bernart de Ventadorn VIII, common phonetic elements unite three *rims estramps* in *-ira, -ina,* and *-enha* against the four rime words in the phonetically unrelated ending *-ai*. Or, even earlier in the troubadour tradition, Cercamon I sets the isolated rimes *-ęs* and *-ęr* against the intrastanzaic rimes *-is* and *-an*.

The technique is best developed in the most consistent user of *rims estramps*, Arnaut Daniel. His editor Toja remarks among many

---

[63] Scholz, XXXVIII, 311-343.
[64] On the division of lines, cf. ch. III, n. 20.

of Arnaut's rimes the "assonanze delle vocali toniche... realizzate con sapiente gradazione di suoni chiari e cupi" and the "effetti fonici ottenuti con modulazioni di successioni consonantiche." [65] These two types — assonance and consonance — combine frequently, as in the successive *rims estramps* -*etz*, -*ecs*, and -*encs* (IX, 5-7), etc.), brought further together by the brevity of lines respectively of two, one and five syllables. The assonance and final consonance of the immediately adjacent rimes in -*etz* and -*ecs* receive extra force from a continuous and direct grammatical relation in all six stanzas: adjective plus noun (*e·ls letz/ becs*), verb and complement (*car etz/ decs*), etc.

The most famed conjunction of end word consonance and vocalism occurs in Arnaut's sestina with the multiple phonetic interrelations of its six repeated end words *intra, ongla, arma, verga, oncle, cambra*, especially the assonating pairs in *o* and *a*, the frequent nasals and liquids, and feminine -*a* in all but one word. The resulting impression of unity reinforces an already tight structure symbolic of love's infinite power and duration.

Sound repetition can also link non-isolated rimes. Thus William IX's number IX is built entirely on rimes in -*ir* and -*ar*, sharing the final -*r* typical of the infinitive. Or, Bernart de Ventadorn XXIX unites phonetically the isolated rimes -*olha*, -*onda*, and -*enda* to the intrastanzaic rimes -*anda* and -*ans*. Bernart has a special penchant for series of rimes in -*r*, as in -*aire*, -*ire*, and -*or* in varying interrelations (IV, 61-72).

Such phonetic linkage also results from etymological figure in the form called by Appel "related rime" (*verwandter Reim*), for example in *uelh* and *uelha*. [66] But phonetically related rime of the same outward form can occur without etymological figure; thus Zenker discerns in Peire d'Alvernha I, first stanza, an interplay of -*elhs* and -*elha* on different roots (*auzelhs, fuelha*, etc.). [67]

Finally, sound repetition can also link successive cesura words, as will be discussed below in section G5. For now, though, consonance and vocalism will be understood to occur, when unspecified, within the bounds of single verses, thus unaffected by the interposition of rime and attendant rhythmic pauses.

---

[65] Toja, *Arnaut Daniel*, pp. 46, 47.

[66] Carl Appel, ed., *Das Leben und die Lieder des Trobadors Peire Rogier* (diss. Berlin, 1882), p. 24.

[67] Zenker, *Peire von Auvergne*, p. 70.

D 3. *Position with Relation to Stanza, Poem and Music*

Except in the form of rime, sound repetition lacks the special propensity of word repetition for occurring at intervals separated by several lines. Quite exceptional is an example from Jaufre Rudel in which multiple sound repetition appears to be linking the first rime words of two successive stanzas:

>D'aquest amor suy *co*ss*iros* (I, 15);
>D'aquest' amor suy tan *cochos* (I, 22).

The lines are otherwise so similar that a conscious parallel must be assumed; and further, the two synonymous words *cossiros* and *cochos* occur at the same point in the melody, and their near-homophony draws attention to the development of the poet's frame of mind from being "anxious" in line 15 to being "desirous" in line 22.

Although in this example the initial lines of stanzas are involved, phonetically linked terms seem to have no special frequency in that or any other position of the stanza, nor in the tornada. The one place of predilection for sound repetition is the exordium. Of the examples cited below, a surprising number occur in the opening lines of poems. Of Arnaut Daniel's eighteen first lines, XIV has an enumerated assonating pair (*iois-liocs*), II a simple consonantally alliterating pair (Plan-Prim); VII and IX have coinciding vocalic alliteration and assonance (Aic-A; Aur' AmAra); V has triple enumerative alliteration (Fuoill'-Flor-Frug); and XI, XIII and XV have remarkably intense sound repetition, chiefly alliteration. Several of these and of his other first lines also have final consonance in enumeration.

The importance of sound repetition in the exordium is due in part to the special emphasis derived from emphatic position. As a repeated word displays its thematic value most prominently in the extremities of a stanza or poem, so the stylistic value of phonetic illustration of meaning increases with positional prominence.

But just as important here is the psychology of creation. Since the first stanza is in most cases the initial and most natural expression of a poet's original conception uniting music, words and rimes in a common purpose, it may be expected to fulfill the ideals of stanzaic unity and artistic excellence better than other stanzas which may have to sacrifice artistry or harmony for the sake of fitting the pre-established pattern. Perhaps also the first stanza received greater care from its composer in the expectation of favorably disposing his audience toward the remainder of the composition. Also the generally descriptive nature of the exordium leaves greater opportunity for embellishment than does the more declarative content of later stanzas.

These reasons explain the usually greater concentration of stylistic means, particularly sound repetition and enumeration, in initial stanzas. Furthermore, the first line has special prestige. Not only does it set the tone; it is in fact the identifying mark of a poem: Provençal poems are, and presumably were, referred to by their first line in the absence of any title. The *razos*, for example, always identify compositions by their first verse or stanza. It is by no means anachronistic to suppose that a colorful first line like Arnaut Daniel's *Sols sui qui sai lo sobrafan qe·m sortz* could catch the public's imagination, remain in its ear, and serve well the poet's fame.

We should also raise a question which for now is beyond the power of scholarship to answer: What is the relation between verbal sound effects and their musical setting? If we can find alliterating or assonating syllables coinciding with long notes in the music, then the two reinforce each other. But musical rhythms may well also distract the hearer's attention from verbal sound recurrences. The question will remain unsolved until we have a definitive rhythmical interpretation of the neumes of early secular monody. Then, statistics can be established for coincidence of musical and verbal style effects, as we have done above for rime word repetition.

Similarly, pitch may well reinforce sound effects; for example, both members of an alliterating pair could fall on particularly high notes or on notes identical in pitch. At least, we can with certitude interpret pitch notation, unlike rhythm. Also, pitch variations are perhaps more easily apprehended in the singing voice than are rhythmical variations, and voice and instrument apparently follow identical patterns in performance. However, research will be rendered difficult by the fact that only about one-tenth of extant troubadour poems still have their music. General conclusions will probably have to await a proliferation of specialized articles like M. L. Switten's on the relation of music to meaning in Peirol.[68]

---

[68] Margaret L. Switten, "Text and Melody in Peirol's *Cansos*," *PMLA*, LXXVI (1961), 320-325. But she concludes that music does not consistently

E. Consonance

E 1. Consonance and Medieval Authority

Traditional rhetoric makes little of consonant repetition, which is not considered a separate figure of speech but, in Lausberg's classification, a feature of *compositio* involving *iunctura* of word-parts, specifically of non-adjacent sounds, under the title of *homoeoprophoron*, or "frequent repetition of the same consonant in several successive words, particularly at the beginning of words."[69] Lausberg's examples include, from Ennius, "o Tite tute Tati tibi tanta tyranne Tulisti" and "de domo domini deus dominus," cited from the Bible by Bede as an example of this device; Martianus Capella seems to have perpetuated a prejudice against consonant repetition by labeling most instances of it as "cuiuslibet litterae assiduitas in odium repetita," in this respect ultimately influencing Malherbe as well as Guilhem Molinier.

Molinier treats consonance with great thoroughness. As with other devices, he considers it a vice unless used with justifiable intent and result. It comprises a category of *cacosyntheton* called *replicatio general*. In his words,

> Replicatios es continuatios de dictios de motas sillabas (e soen am multiplicable replicamen en cascuna) o d'una, pronunciadas amb una meteyssha letra de meteysh so o am diversa d'aytal meteysh so, en lo comensamen del mot o de la derriera sillaba de la dictio preceden (III, 52).

Molinier dutifully condemns *replicatio* of various sorts: *replicatio plana* (alliteration of successive polysyllables: PRestres PRezican PRovizetz), *replicatio multiplicada* (the same reinforced by internal consonant repetition: verGes verGiers verdeJans verGenals), and *replicatio rigoroza* (cor Ferms Fay Far Faytz Francz; hAs Aur Augier; boNas NoeLas Lauzaretz). He also mentions *quaysh-replicatio* ("quasi-alliter-

---

reinforce the mood or meaning of the text, and that there is very little "rapport de sentiment" between melody and words in Peirol's songs.

[69] Lausberg, *Handbuch*, § 975: "häufige Wiederholung des gleichen Konsonanten innerhalb merherer aufeinanderfolgender Wörter, vornehmlich im Wortanlaut." Other references in this paragraph: *ibid.*

ation") in its different manners: *enterpozitiva* (a consonant in a group and not: Patz-Platz), *mitigativa* (one phoneme with two pronunciations in complementary distribution: moLa Lima, caRa Rima; also hard and soft *s*, thus rejoining Scholz's "weak alliteration": cauSa Sancta), *percussiva* (ToT es fayt), and *lenta* (cLar Lum). Such *quaysh-replicatio* is however a vice only where combined with true *replicatio*, Molinier says.

After displaying his classificatory ability and finesse of ear, Molinier next considers various "excuses" for sound repetition: when in *antics dictats* (i.e., works by classical troubadours); by necessity; with names, articles, and prepositions; to express a "good idea"; in proverbs; in verses of substantial length; with separating cesura; but especially in rhetorical figures:

> Per la dita figura *paranomeon*, e per un' autra apelada *paronomazia*, son dezencusat li novel dictat can scienmen e per compas de coblas, d'una o mays, hom precezish pauzan replicatio, en loqual procezimen non es cauza necessaria gardar compas de dictios replicativas per la difficultat de dictat, jaciaysso que plus bela cauza sia e plus neta gardar la una e l'autre. Et aytal dictat replicatiu fayt scienmen e per compas reputam per subtil e de gran maestria (III, 62).

Molinier gives us an example of such *gran maestria* under the heading of "cobla replicativa estiers dicha entretincha." This is a stanza of his favorite N'Ath de Mons which deserves citation as a literary curiosity. We underline consonant repetition, whether due to intentional sound repetition, to word repetition, or to etymological figure:

> Reys ricz romieus, mas man milhors
> Faytz far de dous cor Dieu aman.
> So sen savi salva viran
> Per plus perprendre pretz a lhors
>
> Don Dieus deu dar do de dous dezirier,
> Tant quar conoysh qu'el cre canque conquier,
> Gardan de dan per planhas e per portz
> Que ferm coferm lo bon cor bos cofortz (I, 248).

Such alliterative density will be found in the troubadours only in isolated lines, with a few exceptions. But on a less methodical level the troubadours take full advantage of the licence to employ the figure of *paranomeon*. In fact they use every varity of *replicatio* mentioned by Molinier.

E 2. *Consonant Alliteration: Scholarship*

The type of sound repetition which is perhaps most easily identified, and hence least often neglected, is consonance. At least one variety of consonance, known since the Renaissance as "alliteration," has often struck the eye of the Provençal scholar as it once struck the ear of the Provençal audience. Brief mention of alliteration, though frequently misplaced under the heading of "versification" or of "metrics" rather than of "style," is not rare in troubadour editions, especially in the nineteenth century with its faith in successive small contributions to a general corpus leading to an eventual definitive synthesis.

The first "modern" troubadour edition, Bartsch's *Peire Vidal*, notes that although alliteration is less significant in Romance than in Germanic poetry, in Provençal it nevertheless "served the poetic artists as an excellent means to increase the harmony of their verses through the repetition of certain similar sounds at the beginning of words, and thus to paint with sounds."[70] This last felicitous expression, *mit Lauten malen*, has more than once served other critics in describing the sound effects created by the troubadours. Like Bartsch, Albert Stimming states that "a means of increasing the charm and harmony of single verses is alliteration, which is rather frequently employed by the Provençal poets."[71] Also in the nineteenth century, Max von Napolski cites alliteration "in numerous examples" from Pons de Capduolh,[72] as does Carl Appel in his edition of Peire Rogier.[73] Bertoni gives a few examples of alliteration from the Genoese troubadours,[74] as does Otto Hoby from Guiraut d'Espanha,[75] while

---

[70] Karl Bartsch, *Peire Vidal's Lieder* (Berlin, 1857), p. lxxxv.

[71] Albert Stimming, ed., *Der Troubadour Jaufre Rudel* (Kiel, 1873), p. 32: "Ein Mittel, den Reiz und den Wohllaut einselner Verse zu erhöhen, ist die Alliteration welche von den provenzalischen Dichtern ziemlich häufig angewandt wurde."

[72] Max von Napolski, ed., *Leben und Werke des Trobadors Ponz de Capduoill* (Halle/Saale, 1879), pp. 42-43 ("in zahlreichen Beispielen").

[73] Appel, *Peire Rogier*, pp. 22-23.

[74] Giulio Bertoni, ed., *I trovatori minori di Genova* (Dresden, 1903), pp. 63-64.

[75] Otto Hoby, ed., *Die Lieder des Trobadors Guiraut d'Espanha* (diss. Freibourg, Switz., 1915), pp. 107-108.

Diez, on a less positive note, dwells rather on "that meaningless sort of alliteration in which insofar as possible all words of a verse begin with the same letter, a well-known game of monastic poetry." [76]

The best treatment of alliteration as used by any single troubadour is Zenker's in his edition of Peire d'Alvernhe. "A very remarkable formal peculiarity of Peire's poems," Zenker says, "is his extensive and occasionally even prodigal use of alliteration as an artistic means"; Zenker finds alliteration less in the "well-known alliterative linking of coordinated concepts" (i.e., where alliterating terms are joined by conjunctions) than in the generally "freer" alliteration of uncoordinated members. [77] Zenker concludes that almost all Peire's poems use alliteration consciously, that no such extensive alliteration has been shown in any other troubadour, and that for the sake of comparison studies of alliteration in other troubadours would be very useful. [78] All three statements remain true today.

This chiefly German climate of pre-World War I alliteration study inspired Martin Scholz's dissertation and articles entitled *Die Alliteration in der altprovenzalischen Lyrik,* [79] still the most important investigation of any single Provençal stylistic trait. His corpus of examples is quite thorough, though his goals do not include the assessment of alliteration in its relation to meaning. Scholz's work is a convenient point of reference and departure; it is unfortunate only that no similar work exists treating non-initial phonetic effects.

More recently, doubts about the attribution of the poem beginning

> Al prim pres dels breus jorns braus,
> Quan branda·ls brueils l'aura brava,
> E·ill branc e·ill brondel son nut
> Pel brun tems sec que·ls desnuda ... (P-C 9.5, 1-4)

---

[76] Diez, *Poesie,* p. 87: ". . jene bedeutungslose Art der Allitteration, nach welcher wo möglich sämmtliche Worte eines Verses mit demselben Buchstaben anfangen, eine bekannte Tändelei der Klosterpoesie."

[77] Zenker, *Peire von Auvergne,* p. 70: "Eine sehr bemerkenswerte formale Eigentümlichkeit von Peires Gedichten ist der ausgedehnte, bisweilen geradezu verschwenderische Gebrauch, den er von dem Kunstmittel der Allitteration macht, und zwar handelt es sich weniger um die bekannte stabreimende Verknüpfung coordinierter Begriffe, als vielmehr um jene freiere Form der Allitteration, welche Worte der verschiedensten Art in einem oder mehreren Versen durch ähnlichen Anlaut bindet."

[78] Zenker, p. 77.

[79] Cf. ch. IV, n. 25.

have led scholars to look for similar sound effects (and etymological figures) in the work of two troubadours to each of whom one or more manuscripts assign the poem, namely Aimeric de Belenoi and Guilhem Ademar. The latter's editor Kurt Almqvist agrees with the former's editor Maria Dumitrescu that style, notably alliteration, militates for Guilhem's authorship despite the adverse weight of manuscript attributions. Almqvist comments as follows

> Nous avons déjà dit, à propos de l'attribution de la chanson n° XIII, que Guilhem Adémar se sert volontiers de l'allitération. Une de ses pièces est particulièrement remarquable à cet égard: le n° XIV, justement, *Comensamen comensarai*. Quant à *Al prim pres dels breus jorns braus* (XIII), ce qui contribue, dans une large mesure, à lui donner son caractère dur et austère, c'est la fréquence du son *r*, qui se répète dans tous les mots-rimes sauf deux, et aussi, à l'intérieur des vers, surtout — précédé de *p* ou de *b* — dans la première strophe. A part cela, dans cette pièce, il n'y a d'allitération qu'entre quelques mots de la fin de chacune des trois premières strophes et quelques mots du début de la suivante; cela établit un nouveau lien entre les strophes, que nous avons déjà vues liées par le système des *coblas capcaudadas*. [80]

Other remarkable consonant concentrations have not been entirely ignored. Peire Cardenal's poem *Ar me puesc ieu lauzar d'Amor* (I), for instance, has in its last stanza and its tornada extraordinarily dense alliteration in lines like

> Pauc pres prim prec de pregador (41);
> Leu l'er lo larcx laus lag loinhatz (46),

which have been amply commented on by several scholars (though not by Cardenal's editor René Lavaud). It cannot be denied that such an illustration of Guilhem Molinier's *cobla replicativa* proves a clear quest of sound effects — whether essentially expressive, or as Spitzer believes for their own sake, or (as some critics believe of this passage) parodic of conventional love poetry. [81]

---

[80] Almqvist, *Guilhem Adémar*, pp. 80-81; cf. his p. 45 and Maria Dumitrescu, *Poésies du troubadour Aimeric de Belenoi* (Paris 1935), pp. 32-33.
[81] Albert Stimming, ed., *Bertran de Born* (Halle/Saale, 1879), p. 236, n. to No. IV, 12; Zenker, *Peire von Auvergne*, p. 77.

Another troubadour generally credited with alliterative effects is Arnaut Daniel, whose editor G. Toja writes:

> Nel Daniel le allitterazioni sono molto frequenti, più di duecento, spesso ricercate per ottenere speciali effetti fonici, come nel serventese (I) il gioco fra *corn* e *cornar* (vv. 27, 47), *corn conduch* (18), o di altri incontri consonantici frequenti specialmente nella strofe V.
>
> Negli esordi delle canzoni, l'allitterazione amplifica fonicamente la *variatio*, come in V, 1: *vei fueill'e flor e frug;* XIII, 1: *vei vermeills, vertz, blaus, blancs, gruocs* (*vergiers*), o accentua una intonazione melodica triste con la successione della sibilante: XV, 1: *Sols sui qui sai lo sobrafan qe·m sortz*, o con la combinazione di labiale e dentale (*br*) suscita desolate immagini invernali: *L'aur'amara / fa·ls bruoills brancutz* (*clarzir*) e quasi la stessa sensazione fisica del freddo: XI, 1-2: *En breu brisara·l temps braus / e·ill bisa busin'els brancs.*
>
> Sono questi i più begli esempi arnaldiani, in cui l'alliterazione diviene strumento della tecnica musicale del trovatore.[82]

Through many such discussions runs the attempt to define alliteration and to subdivide it. As indicated in section D 1, we will here restrict "alliteration" to identity of initial phonemes in different words. And we will adopt Zenker's distinction of coordinated and uncoordinated alliteration as generally corresponding to two different degrees of linkage between juxtaposed ideas. Scholarship has distinguished different sorts of alliterating groups according to the positional relation among their members, and we shall refer to these where useful. It is fitting to begin by quoting the justly enthusiastic statement about the troubadours' alliteration which appears, not in any Provençal critic, but, oddly enough, in a non-specialized work, Preminger's *Encyclopedia*:

> All the troubadour poets of Old Provençal practiced alliteration (*replicatio*), aiming with great skill at achieving parallelisms between sound and meaning. They favored alliteration especially at the beginning and at the end of a poem.[83]

---

[82] Toja, *Arnaut Daniel*, pp. 49-50.
[83] P. 15, in Ulrich K. Goldsmith's art. "Alliteration."

SOUND EFFECTS 217

The latter point has been discussed in section D 3 (without, however, our finding any special frequency of alliteration at the end of poems); the former point will now be illustrated and proven.

E 3. *Coordinated Alliteration*

Coordinated alliteration, framed by enumeration, is the most easily recognized sort of alliteration, and the most clearly intentional on the poet's part. Its special force comes from accumulation of identical parts of speech, generally nouns or adjectives, in a recurrent grammatical structure marked by repetition of either conjunctions (polysyndeton) or significant pauses (asyndeton). As might be expected, the frequency and effect of coordinated repetition vary from poet to poet and poem to poem.

As one example, Bernart de Ventadorn's forty-one surviving poems (excluding three *tensos*) make relatively sparing use of enumerative alliteration, which occurs in up to seven words per poem with an average of 1.7 (as previously, all such statistics represent not the number of groups but the number of members in groups, thus a group of 2 counts as 2, of 3 as 3, etc.). Bernart's maximum is reached in *Lo tems vai e ven e vire* (XLIV, 1); triple repetition of this voiced continuant *v* seems especially appropriate to the expressed idea of temporal continuity, and illustrates the common principle of complementary antonymy ("goes and comes and turns" expressing the totality of possibilities) and the similar principle of enumeration of parts to express a whole (type: "the rich and the poor" to mean "all men"). In the same poem, the expressions *dol e dans* (line 9) and *saus ni sas* (line 44) illustrate the more usual virtual synonymy of enumerated pairs.

To this poem should be compared another of Bernart's having the same sounds similarly grouped:

E mainh genh se *v*olv e·s *v*ira
Mos talans, e *v*en e *v*ai (VIII, 1-2);

*V*iatz *v*en e *v*iatz *v*ai (VIII, 31).

These lines are linked together by the repetition of the sound *v*, by word repetition, and by an interplay of synonyms and antonyms. By their importance in the exordium and the tornada of this poem, the alliterating words sum up the main themes. Because of their very frequent use by the troubadours, Scholz renounces any attempt to list occurrences of the pairs *vai-ve* and *volver-virar*.[84]

As these examples show, alliterating groups can very as to number of members. The most usual is two, but Scholz's lists include ninety-seven different groups of three or more members, almost all enumerative, with some groups occurring in more than one poem. An extreme case, in the thirteenth-century, is Cerverí de Girona's enumeration of place names:

> Qu'entre Canet e Castelnau n'auria;
> E Cortzavi e Cabrens que·y comtava,
> E Carmanço... (XIV, 11-13).

Yet even groups having, like most, only two members can on occasion reinforce each other, as in Bernart's

> Cọr e cọrs e sabẹr e sẹn (I, 5),

whose two alliterating pairs — the first unified by near-homophony, the second by assonance, and both by the triply-repeated conjunction — ably sum up the extremes of the human entity.

Many of these examples, as well as Scholz's inventory,[85] show that alliterative enumeration is especially frequent in the exordium (often but not uniquely in nature descriptions). Another position of predilection is in *descriptio,* especially of the lady. In all these cases, the alliterative terms need not be adjacent in order to produce their effect; for example, again from Bernart:

> *F*rancha, doussa, *f*in' e leiaus (II, 39),

describing the lady's qualities with non-adjacent alliteration; and, using the same sound and pattern in a nature description:

> Can *v*ei la *f*lor, l'*er*ba *v*ert e la *f*olha (VII, 1),

with the weak assonance *ẹr-ẹr* plus identical following consonant uniting *erba* and *vert,* and with the pair of *v*'s supporting the *f*'s in weak alliteration.

---

[84] Cf. Scholz, "Alliteration," XXXVIII, 341-343.
[85] Scholz, XXXVII, 397-398.

The situation in many troubadours is much the same as in Bernart. Peire Vidal uses coordinated alliteration with almost the same average frequency: 1.8 members per poem. His maximum occurs in his exceptionally long XLV, with the expressions *conselh ni castics, Laroqu' e Lavaur, ·l melhs e·l mai, crebacor e compenha*. Here, as almost always in Peire, the alliterative terms are more or less synonymous, as one might expect of an "easy" poet. It is only natural that the association of ideas by meaning and sound in the poet's mind should give rise to synonymous alliterative pairs.

Yet the "harder" poet Arnaut Daniel does not disdain this form of alliteration. He uses it with the somewhat greater average frequency of 2.8, and with unusual concentration in two poems, for example in the exordium of his number V, two of whose lines are twinned by triply alliterating etymological figure:

> Lanquan vei *f*ueill'e *f*lor e *f*rug (1);
> Doncs mi *f*ueill' e·m *f*loris e·m *f*ruch Amors (5).

Similar alliterative technique binds together the first two lines of Arnaut XIII:

> Er *v*ei *v*ermeills, *v*ertz, *bl*aus, *bl*ancs, gruocs
> *V*ergiers, *pl*ans, *pl*ais, tertres e *v*aus (XIII, 1-2).

Here is Arnaut's personal touch at its best. Each line contains a richly alliterating adjacent pair (*bl-*, *pl-*); the lines contrast by the subject of their five terms (color vs. topography), but are united by the repetition of a pair in *v-* and of another in a labial stop plus *l*; the first line has the supportive alliteration of *vei* and the second has the chiastic (or "crossed," or "transverse") alliteration *v- pl- pl- v-*.

Arnaut often indulges this tendency to separate alliterating terms:

> Cum ieu vas lieis d'aver *f*in cor e *f*ranc (XVII, 2);
> *L*ausengier fals, *l*enga de colobra (XII, 23);
> Car en patz *p*renc l'afan e·l sofr' e·l *p*arc (XVII, 19);
> Cui encubic al *p*rim vezer e *p*uois (XV, 5).

Though he does not scorn such stereotyped pairs as *plan e prim* (II, 1), *pons ni planchas* (XVI, 29), or *fis e frems* (VIII, 16), he also creates original pairs on these models, such as *·l vais e·l vims* (III, 4) and *sofr' e sega* (IV, 40). The poet seeking originality must in fact use rare words and imaginative pairs, since the number of alliterating words of clearly related meaning is limited. It is thus more by quality than by quantity that Arnaut's alliterative enumeration distinguishes itself.

A slightly higher average frequency of 3.3 members of alliterating groups per poem is found in the earlier poet Cercamon, largely in the stereotyped pairs *sen-saber* (I, 18), *dereir'-denan* (I, 40), *fals-fis* (I, 52), *plass'-pes* (I, 55), *plaing-plor* (II, 13), *petit-pro* (III, 23), *moiller-marit* (IV, 27). Once, in Arnaut's manner, he separates alliterating terms in parallel construction:

Ni dorm ni *v*eil, ni aug ni *v*ei (III, 12);

but on the whole his practice, except from the point of view of frequency, entirely resembles Bernart's and Peire Vidal's.

Lesser use of alliterative enumeration is to be found in William IX's eleven surviving poems with their low average of about 1.5 members per poem. And in fact half of his examples occur in one poem, his rollicking number V, chiefly in its nonsense phrases; otherwise we find only the clichés *bon-bel* (V, 39; X, 7), *joy-joven* (I, 3), *plassa-pes* (IV, 27) and the beautiful convergence with word repetition:

En gran *p*aor, en gran *p*eril (XI, 6).

Jaufre Rudel's use of enumerative alliteration can easily be shown to be even sparser. Thus although this device was certainly known to the earlier troubadours, one cannot realistically hold with Jeanroy and Sachse (cf. section A 3) that it played a larger role in the early lyric than later. Certainly, the frequency of stock phrases which show enumerative alliteration, as in *bon e bel*, does not at all diminish during the classical period of the Provençal lyric; and there is ample evidence of the creation of new alliterating combinations by poets like Arnaut Daniel.

E 4. *Uncoordinated Alliteration*

Uncoordinated alliteration takes any grammatical form, other than that of enumeration, providing its members are brought into contact by spatial proximity or semantic similarity. The lack of parallelism can be compensated for by a high density of sound repetition, as in Bernart de Ventadorn's tornada

> Si d'aisso m'es certana
> Autra vetz, la·n *cr*eirai;
> O si que no, ja mai
> No *cr*eirai *cr*estiana (XXVI, 61-64).

This rich alliteration on *cr*- knits together two major words of the poem's last line. A further bond is provided by their assonance on *a*, by their immediate succession, and by the direct grammatical relation of verb and direct object. Moreover, they are tied to the rest of the poem by previous occurrence in the rime (lines 57 and 62), and summarize the theme of the poet's ambiguous feeling toward love.

Another means of strengthening the effect of uncoordinated alliterating pairs is mutual reinforcement, as in William IX's

> ... e li aucel
> *Ch*anton *ch*ascus en *l*or *l*ati (X, 2-3),

where double sound repetition creates a musical effect appropriate to birdsong. That these sounds belong to a conventional nature exordium stock is suggested by similar effects and words in an "autumn poem" of Cercamon's:

> E·l fuelha *ch*ai de sul verjan
> E l'auzelh *ch*anjan *l*or *l*atis,
> Et ieu de *s*ai *s*ospir e *ch*an (I, 2-4),

with its *l*'s, *ch*'s and also the group in *s*-. Similar pairing of two alliterating groups, here rich and bound by a common second element, has often been discerned in Guilhem Ademar's

> Al *p*rim *p*res dels *b*reus jorns *b*raus (XIII, 1).

A particularly convincing case, where alliterating pairs contribute to an impression of moral indignation, is Cercamon's line

> Drut, *m*oiller e *m*arit, *t*ug *t*res (IV, 27).

And even when spread over two lines, such pairs if syntactically interdependent can reinforce each other, as in Arnaut's

> Mas *p*er *p*aor
> Del *d*evinaill (II, 30-31).

Or again, such pairs can interlock, as when Bertran de Born says:

> Que *m*ais *v*al *m*ortz que *v*ius sobratz (P-C 80.8a, 40);

or, with still greater effect, Arnaut:

> Fals *l*ausengier, *f*uocs *l*as *l*engas vos arga (XVII, 41).

Finally (as in the last example if the definite article be considered) a line can consist chiefly or even entirely of interlocking or adjacent alliterative groups of varied size; thus Arnaut describes his sorrow both lexically and phonetically:

> *S*o *d*on *d*olens *s*i *s*oiorna (VII, 15).

Yet even when only one phoneme is involved there is no logical limit to the size of an alliterative group. Peire Cardenal's poem I (see p. 215, above) is not unique. Such *replicatio* need not, however, in the *Leys'* terminology, be *plana* (in successive polysyllables) or *rigoroza* (in successive monosyllables). Any extensive consonant repetition can correspond to an extreme of feeling, as when Bernart rejoices:

> Vai *m*i doncs *m*al d'amor?
> Ans *m*elhs que no fetz *m*ai! (XVIII, 7-8),[86]

or when Arnaut plays on the same sound:

> *M*as *m*estiers *m*'es qu'eu fassa *m*erceiar
> A *m*ans... (VI, 5-6);

or in his noteworthy first lines

> *S*ols *s*ui qui *s*ai lo *s*obrafan qe·m *s*ortz (XV, 1);
> En *b*reu *b*risara·l temps *b*raus (XI, 1),

---

[86] This reading is that of Appel and Lazar; but C. A. F. Mahn, *Die Werke der Troubadours in provenzalischer Sprache*, 4 vols. (Berlin, 1846-53), I, 40, reads:

> Vai *m*i del *m*al d'amor
> *M*out *m*iels qu'anc no fetz *m*ai,

which has about equal Ms authority and is preferable from the points of view of alliterative efficacity, of rhythm and of meaning.

of which the latter should be compared to the first seven lines of Guilhem Ademar's *Al prim pres* with their thirteen words beginning in *br-*. Perhaps the earliest such sound multiplication comes when William IX puts an effectives final touch to an erotic gaming metaphor in one of his characteristic summarizing tornadas (speaking of dice, *datz*):

> E *fi*·ls *f*ort *f*erir al taulier,
> E *f*on joguatz (VI, 61-62).

Relative position of alliterating terms varies according to linkage. We have already seen that enumerated terms are generally separated (and joined) by a conjunction, are occasionally adjacent in asyndeton, or are more rarely separated by other words in the same enumeration. Non-coordinated terms in direct grammatical relation are generally adjacent, for example in Arnaut Daniel II *son seignor, tal trebaill, mi muoilla, mal m'es, de doussor* or in Bertran de Born *de dos drutz* (P-C 80.7, 11), *serem sol* (P-C 80.15, 16), *per pechs* (P-C 80.25, 14) and the more colorful *valen vassalatge*[87] (P-C 80.8a, 25) or *peitavi pifart* (P-C 80.44, 46). Yet they can also be separated by a functional term such as article or negation, as when Bernart says

> Com *f*a la *f*olha contra·l ven (I, 44),

and Bertran *que mal non mier* (P-C 80.15, 1) or *metra a muois* (P-C 80.25, 5).

One peculiarity of non-coordinated alliteration is linkage of the two metrically important words of a verse, those at the cesura and rime. This is common in the Old French epic.[88] Among numerous Provençal examples, here are several from Bernart de Ventadorn:

> Las! e *v*iure que·m *v*al (XVII, 33);
> Com la *n*eus a *n*adal (XVII, 38);
> *D*e las *d*omnas me *d*ezesper (XXXI, 25).

---

[87] Cf. Raimbaut de Vaqueiras, poem VII, 15: *volpill vassal*.

[88] Alliteration between cesura words and rime words occurs, for example, in over 10 % of verses in a representative sample of *Le voyage de Charlemagne à Jérusalem* and *Gui de Bourgogne*, according to Moritz Koehler, *Ueber alliterierende Verbindungen in der altfranzösischen Literatur* (diss. Leipzig, Oppeln, 1890), p. 17.

In all three, sound effect adds to an already logical link: "worth" describes the value of "living"; "Christmas" intensifies the image of "snow"; "ladies" are the habitual cause of the troubadour's "despair." In all, then, sound and idea coalesce.

This sound-sense link is even clearer when the words involved belong to one construction, as in Marcabru's

> Quar li *m*ellor de tot est *m*on (P-C 293.1, 20),

where "world" magnifies the idea of "best," or in Bertran's

> E de fendutz per *b*ustz tro als *b*raiers (P-C 80.25, 12),

"from head to heel," as we would say, alliteratingly though less picturesquely.

Or, alliteration can strike words which are important in the line not so much by position as by meaning. Thus Bertran's

> E *p*latz mi, quan vei sobre·ls *p*ratz (P-C 80.8a, 6)

shows that distance, here compensated in part by irregular internal rime in -*atz*, need not lessen effect. On the contrary, alliteration between the two most important words of the line binds its two hemistichs into an effective whole. Or, in a single line three major words can be affected. In Cercamon's

> *D*omna c'aja *d*rut *d*esleiau (IV, 35),

the "lyric" cesura word *aja* is unaffected, but the first and last words participate in a triple bonding of the factors in the eternal story of love and infidelity: lady, lover, disloyalty.

We have already found that original groupings are rare in the often stereotyped manifestations of coordinated alliteration; this last example similarly brings into contact words that we are not surprised to find together. But non-coordination does leave the poet more room for inventiveness, since he need not respect the usually synonymous or at least complementary semantic relation of enumerated terms and their inevitable functional identity. Only a few uncoordinated expressions, generally adjective or preposition plus immediately following noun, occur with frequency, e.g. *gran gaug, mos mielhs, a per pauc,* or, with vocalic alliteration, *aquest' amor, autr' amor*. Otherwise, the troubadours' imagination supplies the various sorts of semantic juxtapositions, whether predictable or surprising, of which we have seen representative examples.

E 5. *Frequency and Effect of Alliteration*

So far we have noted differences of quality but not of quantity in different troubadours' use of alliteration; but now a brief survey of frequency is in order. The following chart divides alliterating groups into four classes according to grammatical criteria. Class 1) includes enumeration; 2) direct grammatical linkage (verb plus adverb or direct object, preposition or adjective plus noun, etc., generally adjacent); 3) indirect linkage between the major word of two hemistichs; 4) other generally less effective linkage. As in previous tables, each member of a group illustrating this stylistic device is counted as one.

Chart 9:

Frequency of Alliteration

classes:	1	2	3	4	total
poets:					
Peire Vidal	1.8	3.7	4.4	5.7	15.6
William IX	1.5	5	4.6	2.3	13.4
Bernart de Ventadorn	1.7	5	3	2.9	12.6
Arnaut Daniel	2.7	5.2	1.9	2.4	12.2
Cercamon	3.3	4.7	2.8	0.3	11.3
Jaufre Rudel	0.7	4	2.2	3	9.9

The distribution among classes 2 and 4 may be admittedly subjective, but for both class 1 and the totals some claim of objectivity may be made. Lengths of poems by different troubadours may reasonably be supposed to average out and not be a significant factor.[89] Length of line may be more of a factor, since a longer line has more room for alliteration; but on the other hand choice of a shorter line is partially motivated by priority given to rime and rhythm over sound, so that a poet who prefers shorter lines *ipso facto* may be said to

---

[89] Ideally one would compute the frequency of alliterating terms per 100 words; but again, the problem of how to count unaccented particles would arise; and one must not exaggerate the value of quantitative evaluation.

deemphasize alliteration with respect to quantity. This factor helps to explain the unexpectedly low total average of Arnaut Daniel.

The relative frequencies indicated by the above chart are corroborated by Scholz's findings, and thus his remarks on other troubadours can be cited with some confidence. The important poets who seem to him the most prolific in alliteration are, in chronological order, Raimbaut d'Aurenga, Peire d'Alvernhe, Guiraut de Bornelh, Bertran de Born, Arnaut Daniel, Raimbaut de Vaqueiras, Peire Cardenal, Guiraut Riquier and Guilhem de Montanhagol. Of these, he says, Bertran and Arnaut [90] have an average of about five alliterative groups (not, as in our computations, members of groups) per poem; the minor troubadour Guilhem Anelier de Tolosa's four surviving poems have an average of six, Marcabru of less than three; and Peire d'Alvernhe uses alliteration the most frequently. Thus certainly nothing in Scholz supports the contention that alliteration is a "primitive" element that declines from the origins on.

Another way of assessing alliteration quantitatively is in terms of multiple groups. From Scholz's inventory we can compute that thirty troubadours use from one to ten groups of three or more alliterating terms. Of these Peire Cardenal uses ten; Guiraut de Bornelh seven; Peire d'Alvernhe, Peire Vidal, and Bertran de Born six. These may owe their high totals in part to their large number of preserved works; but they also rate high in our previous figures based on average frequency per poem. Number of works is not all: Peire Vidal, with about the same number of surviving poems as Bernart de Ventadorn, uses twice as many multiple alliterative groups; Cerverí de Girona left more poems than any other troubadour but uses only two multiple groups; Sordel's forty-three poems include only one such group. So personal taste is clearly a factor.

For example, Peire Cardenal's extraordinary twelve-line exercise in multiple alliteration beginning

Pauc pres prim prec de pregador (I, 41)

may well be in part a parody but certainly also corresponds to a personal technique in which Peire is the troubadours' master (for

---

[90] Note that Scholz's figure for Arnaut of about 5 alliterating groups per poem corresponds almost perfectly to our figure of 12.2 members of alliterating groups, since the average group must contain about 2.5 members, in Arnaut at least.

some reason, probably because having no coordinated alliteration, this passage is neglected by Scholz's inventory; Peire's true total should be nearer twenty than ten). If troubadours such as he show a more marked preference for multiple alliteration than for simple alliteration, and others less, there is no doubt that alliteration is a feature of individual style measurable in part by quality, in part by frequency.

What, finally, is the range of possible meanings of alliteration? The examples given so far are fairly typical in this respect. The extremes of human sentiment hold the fore; description of nature or of the poet's lady often gain from alliteration; moral feelings can be made more intense. But actually the gamut is unlimited, even within the work of a single troubadour, from the martial effects of Bertran de Born's voiceless dental stops:

*T*rombas, *t*abors, senheras e penos (P-C 80.25, 17)

(cf. French *tambour et trompette*) to the funereal tones of the more subdued and muted voiced dentals of his great *planh*:

*D*on es *d*olors e *d*esconortz et ira (P-C 80.41, 32).

Other effects are as common. Witness the gaiety of Jaufre Rudel's

Las *p*impas sian als *p*astors (III, 9),

the harshness of Guilhem Ademar's

Quan la *b*runa *b*iza *b*randa
De la *f*orest *f*raysses e *f*aus (IX, 1-2),

and the effect of eternal recurrence of Bernart's

Lo tems *v*ai e *v*en e *v*ire (XLIV, 1).

These examples show probable sound symbolism; in some others, alliteration does not illustrate but only organizes meanings, especially in enumerations like Arnaut's

Er *v*ei *v*ermeills, *v*ertz, *b*laus, *b*lancs, gruocs (XIII, 1).

Whatever its effects, what is the relation of alliteration to different genres, periods, and schools of poetry? Scholz computes that alliteration occurs in the *cansos* of Guiraut de Bornelh, Bertran de Born, and Guiraut Riquer between one-third and one-half more often than in their other poems.[91] This is only natural: the slower pace and more stereotyped content of the *canso* leave it more space and time for artistic effects, and as the most esteemed genre it probably demanded greater attention and skill from its practitioners.

From a diachronic viewpoint, we have already shown that, rather than declining, alliteration in fact becomes more common through the Provençal literary period. With reference to literary schools, one can discern a certain tendency toward alliteration in *trobar clus*, in its leading representatives, Raimbaut d'Aurenga, Peire d'Alvernhe, Arnaut Daniel, though not Marcabru. This is to be expected, in that *trobar clus* carries Provençal art-consciousness to its greatest heights and generally adopts difficult and refined effects such as rare rime and unusual forms, a complex to which alliteration like etymological figure logically belongs.

E 6. *Final Consonance*

Emphatic position gives special value not only to repeated initial consonants, but also to repeated final consonants, although to a lesser degree because they anticlimactically follow the expiratory stress and hence the moment of greatest phonetic and psychological intensity. Such final consonant repetition has a variety of names; one style manual gives the following definition:

> Half-rhyme (or slant-rhyme, approximate-rhyme, near-rhyme, off-rhyme): only the final consonant-sounds of the rhyming words are identical; the stressed vowel-sounds as well as the initial consonant-sounds, if any, differ (soul:oil; firth:forth; trolley:bully).[92]

Since in the troubadours this sound correspondence occurs chiefly not in the rime but inside verses, we will adopt the name of "final consonance" as being the most descriptive and accurate.

In one example, William IX's line

                Mas sol nos tres (V, 46),

---

[91] Scholz, "Alliteration," XXXVII, 401.
[92] Barnet *et al.*, *The Study of Literature*, p. 351.

description of an intimate scene with two bold ladies profits from the "cosy" effect of these final -*s*'s as well as from monosyllabism, the line's brevity, a supportive initial *s*, and adjacent assonance. Similarly, the final -*n*'s of the same poem's

> Ta*n* gra*n* m'e*n* pres (V, 84, 86)

help produce an effect of lassitude and finality appropriately reiterated in two different lines at the end of herculean adventures in *amor*. Or, William's line

> E que·m do*n*et u*n* do*n* ta*n* gra*n* (X, 21)

uses the same final nasality, reinforced by irregular internal rime in -*an* and by the etymological figure *donet-don*, to link the lady's "gift" to its three monosyllabic qualifiers. And in

> E quam lo boc*x* e*s* taillat*z* nai*s* plu*s* espe*s* (III, 16),

concentration of final sibilants contributes to the image of a forest growing back thicker than before being cut.

Similarly, in Bernart de Ventadorn's

> Aut*z* e*s* lo pret*z* qu'e*s* cossenti*tz* (XLII, 49),

the three important words describing the boon granted the poet are linked by a common nominative singular ending -*s* combining with the dental stem consonants as -*tz*, the three being welded together by the repeated and also sigmatic copulative *es*. On a lesser scale, final consonance unifies rather prettily William IX's line

> Qu'eu non ai soi*ng* d'estrai*ng* lati (VII, 25);

and the same technique helps unify the common expression *li seu belh olh* with a delicate liquidity. To demonstrate the efficacy of such final consonance one need only read aloud one line of Racine's *Phèdre* (l. 1112) in which final consonance, in conjunction with other sound effects, reflects the beauty and harmony of the thought:

> Le jou*r* n'est pas plus pu*r* que le fond de mon cœu*r*.

Final consonance can furthermore be reinforced by a second similar group, as in Cercamon's

> Pe*r* s'amo*r*, durme*n* o velha*n* (I, 26),

which parallels by its symmetry and its repetition of final continuants the atemporality of this *amor*.

Despite these examples — and many others could be cited — final consonance seldom stands alone as an independent sound effect. Often it results from morphological figure in which the final -*s* of the masculine nominative singular or oblique plural is repeated. And generally, it combines with other forms of sound repetition, based either on the same or on complementary sounds.

E 7. *General Consonance*

Till now we have discussed effects of consonance only in initial or final position of different words. But the same effects can also occur 1) internally in one or more words, 2) between different positions in one word, and 3) between different positions in different words. In the first case, similar to rich alliteration's initial groups, internal consonance reinforces initial consonance in what the *Leys* call *replicatio multiplicada* (cf. p. 211, above: ver**G**es ver**G**iers, etc.). The second case is known to Molinier as *cacenphaton*, thus **B**o**B**ansa, **M**er**M**a**M**en, ba**D**a**D**a, etc., of which he says: "Ges per so no reputam a vici qui pauza aytals motz, jaciaysso que bo sia qui s'en sap gardar" (III, 26). The third case, which eludes Molinier's usually watchful eye, contributes to what we have called "general consonance," that is, any combination of initial, medial, or final consonants repeated for a joint effect.

For example, final consonance cooperates with alliteration in the parallel structure of Cercamon's line

> Mas, cui que *plass*' o cui que *pes* (I, 55).

This double consonance explains in part the great popularity of this convenient antonymic space-filler based on the pair *plass-pes*, "pleases-displeases." This is a fairly simple example, but on a larger scale, where multiple consonance occurs in varied positions, we can speak of an overall "consonant harmony." Thus it can be said that an obsessive sibilance contributes to the desired effect of strangeness produced when Raimbaut d'Aurenga introduces to the poetic world a new genre:

> E*s*cotat*z*, ma*s* no *s*ay que *s*'e*s*,
> *S*enhor, *s*o que vuelh comen*s*ar.
> Ver*s*, e*s*tribot[*z*] ni *s*irvente*s*
> Non e*s* ... (XXIV, 1-4).

The same sibilance, in a context of milder sounds and lesser density, reinforces the quite different effect of airiness and height in a group used twice by Arnaut to describe tree-tops:

> E l'au*ss*or *c*im
> *S*on de color (II, 3-4);
>
> Del*s* au*ss*ors entre*s*im*s* (III, 2).

Or, we have the melancholy sibilance of the love-crossed Rigaut de Berbezilh's line

> *S*ol*s*, *s*e*s* *s*olat*z* (qu'aital*s* e*s* mo*s* talen*z*) (II, 17),

with its average of one *s*-sound per syllable.

Perhaps the most beautiful example of this technique is a passage of William IX whose liquids and *b*'s in close conjunction, especially in the near-homophonous *sobre* and *arbre*, create precisely the feeling of tremulous delicacy that motivates the comparison of love to the trembling branch:

> La nost*r*' amo*r* vai enaissi
> Com *l*a *b*ranca de *l*'a*l*bespi
> Qu'esta so*b*re *l*'a*r*b*r*e *tr*em*bl*an (X, 13-15).

It is however infrequent that, as here, consonance gives its tone to a whole passage without the cooperation of vocalism. Therefore after studying the latter, we will return to their convergence for common effect in our section on "general sound repetition," below.

F. Vocalism

F 1. *Generalities*

As we have seen, critics have often appreciated the sounds of poetry, but more in consonants than in vowels, which are subtler in effect and less easily related to meaning. Vocalism, though having the quantitative importance of consonance, is generally less striking due to the less distinctive and less forceful nature of its sounds. Yet no technical difference separates vocalism from consonance in their structures or in their applications.

Vocalism and consonance have already been discussed in similar terms in our section C. Section C 1 has raised the question of the inherent meanings of sounds, notably in the contrasting vowels *a* and *i*. Section C 2 has treated value by association. Section C 3 has defined different strengths of vocalism as of consonance: weak ($ę$-$ę$, $ǫ$-$ǫ$), normal ($ę$-$ę$, $ę$-$ęi$), and rich ($ęi$-$ęi$). And section D 1 has shown that the effects of vocalism can extend to any tonic or initial vowel in a repeated group, with or without the interposition of consonants in the form of pretonic particles. It remains here to investigate the troubadours' use of vocalism, first initial, then tonic.

The problems in analyzing "vowel configuration" are presented in a recent article by Robert P. Newton.[93] Newton cites several critics who hold that "verbal music" derives not from the pitch, duration, or intensity of vowels but from their timbre. Repeated timbres form certain rhythmic sequences, such as we have already found in consonant repetition. In fact, vocalism resembles consonance with regard to grammatical linkage, group sizes, mutual cooperation of groups, position in poems, and ultimately the faculty of reinforcing meaning by sound.

With regard to position in the word, initial position confers emphasis on vowels as well as on consonants, and Scholz rightly puts vocalic and consonantal alliteration side by side in his discussions and inventories. Non-initial vocalism, like non-inital consonance, has less prominence in general; final and other atonic vocalism, as well as

---

[93] Robert P. Newton, "The First Voice. Vowel Configuration in the German Lyric," *Journal of English and Germanic Philology*, LXVIII (1969), 565-592.

repetition of vowels within single words, is usually perceptible only within a context of consonant repetition, and hence will be reserved for later discussion. However, one particular sort of non-initial vocalism stands alone; as we gave special attention to final consonance earlier, so must we here to tonic vocalism, or assonance. As will be shown, the initial and tonic vowels of major words, especially in enumeration or at the cesura and rime, dominate the verse's "verbal melody."

F 2. *Vocalic Alliteration*

It is well known that the initial vowel has a privileged status in the Romance languages. Whether absolutely initial or not, the vowel of the initial syllable resists phonetic erosion better than vowels in any other position except the tonic vowel, yet it rarely undergoes the tonic vowel's frequent deformation by diphthongization. Thus Latin pairs linked by vocalic alliteration, such as *aureum-argentum*, have as good a chance of remaining intact in the different Romance languages as do consonantal pairs, and are well represented in the multilingual groups reported by Scholz (cf. p. 193, above).

One such traditional group is twice used by Peire Vidal:

> Mas del ver tenc l'*a*ir e l'*a*le (VIII, 60);
>
> Ab l'*a*len tir vas me l'*a*ire
> Qu'eu sen venir de Proensa (XIX, 1-2).

Similarly, initial vocalism perhaps motivates William IX's selection, from his legendarily numerous paramours or from the large stock of female names, the N'*A*gnes and N'*A*rsen subjected to the steed and saddle metaphor of his number I.

The relative frequency of different vowels in such relationships can be roughly calculated on the basis of Scholz's inventory, which gives over three pages of alliterative groups in *a-*, one and one-half pages in *e-*, but only seven groups in *o-*, three in *i-*, and one in *u-* (*human-humil*, only once attested).[94] These relative frequencies are approximately those of words beginning in these vowels in the language as a whole: Levy's *Petit dictionnaire provençal-français* gives for *e-* forty-seven pages (almost all absolutely initial *e*'s are close and

---

[94] Scholz, "Alliteration," XXXVIII, 311-343.

therefore alliterate with each other), *a-* thirty-eight pages, *o-* nine, *i-* two, and *u-* one and one-half. That *a-* ranks higher in alliteration than in overall frequency is no coincidence, but due either to its greater expressivity or to the phenomenon of relational symbolism discussed in section C 2. For example the fact that the central root of the lyric vocabulary, *am-*, begins with *a* permits formation of no less than thirty-nine alliterative pairs such as *adreit-amoros, afar-amor, amar-azirar, amic-abric,* etc.).[95]

Frequency of vocalic alliteration seems fairly stable, and for a few exemplary troubadours can be computed as follows (classes 1 through 4 being defined as in chart 9).

Chart 10:

Frequency of Vocalic Alliteration

classes:	1	2	3	4	total
poets:					
William IX	0.4	2.1	0.8	0.3	3.6
Cercamon	0	3	0	1	4
J. Rudel	0	1.7	0.8	0.8	3.3
P. Vidal	0.3	0.9	0.8	0.4	2.4
A. Daniel	0.2	2.4	0.5	0.9	4

Clearly, vocalic alliteration does not have the quantitative importance of either consonant alliteration (notably in class 1) or assonance (notably in class 2). Its effects tends to be more organizational than illustrative; that is, it helps to group terms of similar meaning but rarely participates in sound symbolism, although it does share with consonantal alliteration the characteristics discussed in section F 1.

F 3. *Assonance in the Romance Tradition*

The poetic importance of initial sounds, whether consonantal or vocalic, has thus not been ignored by scholars. But the importance of the tonic syllable, and of the tonic vowel in particular, has often been overlooked in Romance poetry. Early Germanic poetry of course combines accent and alliteration as the organizing principles of verse, and modern Germanic poetry still bases its metrics on patterns of tonic and atonic syllables. Yet French and Provençal poetry among

---

[95] *Ibid.,* pp. 311-314.

others, medieval or modern, are often analyzed rhythmically and stylistically without regard for their tonic accent. This unfortunate practice goes back to classical poetic theory with its concern not with stress but with quantity, the basis of Classical Latin meter. Quantitative metrical theories were appropriate to the classical languages but failed to be superseded as quantity gave way to accent as the organizing principle of poetry. Thus medieval rhetoric is highly defective in its treatment of stress and of stressed vocalism, i.e., assonance. Even though Guilhem Molinier (I, 58) states that each word has a tonic accent, whose position can distinguish otherwise homonymic *motz accentuals* (*cózi-cozi*, etc.; cf. section H 1), he fails to mention equivalence of tonic vowels as either a vice or a virtue, except for *sonansa borda* (i.e., assonance used in place of rime; cf. p. 195, above). This lack of any clear Romance tradition regarding stress or assonance has often led both medieval and modern scholarship to neglect the multiple harmonies of tonic vowels.

It is, however, easy to show the importance of the Gallo-Roman tonic accent. As is well known, Latin vowels have developed differently according to whether they occur before, at or after the tonic accent. Poetical rhythms are determined by the coincidence of a tonic accent with a syntactical pause, not only in the rime but even within the typically French alexandrine, which almost invariably consists of four stressed and eight unstressed syllables in varying patterns. Assonance, of course, functioned alone in many early Romance works,[96] notably in the *chanson de geste*, until it came (earlier in Provençal than in French) to be regarded as merely a defective form of rime (the *Leys d'amors' sonansa borda*). And rime itself is nothing but assonance, either final in the word or reinforced by final consonance of other elements.[97]

One Romance scholar to come to grips with the problem of tonic accent is Pius Servien, who distinguishes a *rythmique tonique* from the conventional *rythmique arithmétique* based on mere syllable

---

[96] In Provençal, for traces of assonance in *Girart de Rossillon* and *Boeci*, cf. Vincenzo Crescini, *Manuale per l'avviamento agli studi provenzali*, 3d ed. (Milan, 1926), p. 140.

[97] For example of the thematic effect of cooperating rime and assonance, see Mallarmé's poem *Le vierge, le vivace et le bel aujourd'hui*, which has been labeled as his "sonnet en *i* majeur" because of its obsessive tonic *i*'s symbolizing cold, sterility, effort and despair.

count.⁹⁸ His study of rhythmic structures, "symmetries," "themes," and verses could usefully be extended to the troubadours. In their art one could describe a further chapter of repetition based on an esthetic of recurrent stress and non-stress in relation to verse, rime, and cesura. But here we can only draw the lesson that the tonic syllable must be specially studied in terms of sound repetition.

The form of vocalism involving tonic vowels is generally known as "assonance."⁹⁹ In the Romance languages we cannot describe it as Newton does for German assonance, by discerning patterns like *abab* or *abcb* in a typically four-beat line.¹⁰⁰ Rather, we must consider such patterns not so much in the abstract as in their relation to the poetic context and to the inherent or associational values of the repeated vowel.

F 4. *Assonance in the Troubadours*

We have seen that consonantal alliteration gives the greatest appearance of deliberateness when it occurs in enumeration; the same is true of vocalism in general and of assonance in particular. A pairing of words often appears not only deliberate but conventional and even semiproverbial when sound and semantics combine. Thus a song of William IX ends on the optimistic note that when it comes to love,

>   Nos n'avem la pęssa e·l coutęl (X, 30).

The assonating "piece of bread" and "knife" symbolize the different but complementary elements in the "feast" of love. William uses another such near-synonymous pair in

>   E diz que no volo prendre drẹit ni lẹi (II, 4),

as does Cercamon in denouncing the

>   Enganador f*a*ls e tru*a*n (IV, 31)

---

⁹⁸ Pius Servien, *Lyrisme et structures sonores* (Paris, 1930), p. 34, etc.

⁹⁹ Barnet *et al.*, *The Study of Literature*, p. 351: "Assonance: identical vowel-sounds preceded and followed by differing consonant-sounds, in words in proximity." *Shorter OED* (cf. n. 2, above), art. «Assonance," 2: "Rhyme by accented and following vowels but not consonants."

¹⁰⁰ Newton (cf. n. 93).

and Arnaut in the line

>   ... Anz brai' e chanta (VIII, 4).

Such pairs in two successive lines help leave us with a feeling of finality at the end of William's *comjat* (in all these examples, supportive assonance of other types will be indicated too):

>   Aissi guerpisc joi e deport
>   E vair e gris e sembeli (XI, 41-42).

The conventional nature of this technique is proven by the presence of one pair in different works, for example *trebalh-afan* in Cercamon:

>   Las! qu'ieu d'Amor non ai conquis
>   Mas cant lo trebalh e l'afan (I, 7-8)

and in Rigaut the Berbezilh (in a variant attested by several manuscripts):

>   E ma vida m'es trebaillz et affans (II, 18 var.).

The pairs *joi-deport* and *senhor-companhon* are particularly common, occurring for example almost side by side in Arnaut Daniel VI, 27 and 29; the antonymous pair *cIma-ra(z)Itz* also forms a stock expression, as in Jaufre Rudel III, 34.

In assonance as in alliteration, different pairs in the same enumeration can reinforce each other, as in Bernart's

>   La boch' e·ls olhs e·l fron e·ls mas e·ls bratz (XXI, 20);

though the symmetry is broken by a fifth term, *olhs*, resonating on open *o*, approximately intermediate between *o* and *a*, the five terms are united by quadruple repetition of the conjunction, by recurrence of the definite article and by a common function in *descriptio* of the lady.

Again, the number of assonating terms can be multiplied, though generally more discreetly than alliteration allows. Thus in a nature description, Bernart speaks of

>   Prat e deves a verger,
>   Landas e pla e boschatge (XXXIV, 15-16);

note that the four assonating terms of the six-term sequence are not consecutive but rather enfold chiastically the two weakly assonating terms *devęs* and *vergęr*.

A similar enumeration helps Jaufre Rudel to express the peace of mind that he finds in a new philosophy of love:

> M*as* a*ra*s vęy ę pęs e sęn
> Que pass*at* *ai* *a*quęlh turmęn,
> E non hi vuelh torn*ar* j*a* m*ay*s (IV, 19-21).

The three monosyllabic verbs — "see," "think" and "feel" — assonate not only with each other but also with the repeated conjunction *e* and with the expression *aquelh turmen* in the next line; and the unity of *vey, pes* and *sen,* expressing the totality of human perception, stands out in contrast to the three surrounding groups having each three assonating or alliterating *a*'s. The more common and open vowel *a* thus serves as background to the rarer and more intense close *e*.

When such a coordinated group reacts within its larger vocalic context, we find more subtle and more complex sorts of verbal music. For example, William gives assonating instructions to his jongleur:

> Dic e m*an* que ch*an* e no br*am* (VIII, 30).

We have here two enumerated pairs, *dic-man* and *chan-bram,* with internal rime in the interior members *man* and *chan* and assonance between them and the final *bram*. Final nasality unites the latter three verbs, while the position of two of them at the cesura and rime gives extra stress. One can compare to this example a rightly admired line of Racine's *Phèdre,* with very similar techniques, except that all four verbs assonate:

> Tout m'afflige et me nu*i*t et consp*i*re à me nu*i*re (161).

Some of our examples of enumerated assonance have already included supportive uncoordinated assonance. Uncoordinated assonance can also function, perhaps more subtly, by itself. Several examples from William IX's "courtly" number VIII will represent the various possibilities of this technique. Assonance often strengthens a direct grammatical link:

SOUND EFFECTS 239

> Ni de grans laus no·m sai formir (8);
> Et tota ricor obezir (20);
> Ren per autruy non l'aus mandar (43).

(Supportive vocalism is also indicated here.) A special case is

> E per la carn renovellar (35),

with an identical following consonant *r* and with the two terms comprising the major (or only) word of each hemistich. A looser grammatical and rhythmic link is found in

> Si·m vol mi dons s'amor donar (37),

with supportive weak assonance in *vol*.

One peculiarity, assonance at the cesura and rime, can be well illustrated from Cercamon I, where it occurs thirteen times (six times on *a*, one on *ę*, four on *ę*, two on *i*) in fifty-eight lines (the poem is octosyllabic, and the cesura almost invariably after the fourth syllable). Given that Provençal has seven different tonic vowels (or principal diphthong elements), this average frequency of one case of cesura-rime assonance per four and one-half lines greatly exceeds random expectation. An especially noteworthy case is two lines both assonating on *a*, with the same end rime, with riming words at the cesura, and with the end rime supported at the cesura of the intervening line:

> Quant l'aura doussa s'amarzis
> E·l fuelha chai de sul verjan
> E l'auzelh chanjan lor latis,
> Et ieu de sai sospir e chan... (I, 1-4),

thus producing the pattern

```
................. ai ............... an
............... an an .....................
................. ai ............... an.
```

In general, recurrence of a following phoneme, as here in the groups *ai* and *an*, strengthens the parallelism of assonating words (and cf. *rim fayshuc* in sections G 3-G 5, below).

Evidently, as with alliteration, two pairs can coexist within one line. As two examples again from Cercamon show, their position can be either consecutive:

> Vueil un novel chant comenzar (II, 3)

(the poet's "new song" being presented by a songlike and singsong vocalic pattern), or else interlocking:

> Non sai si ja l'aurai ni quan (I, 34)

(where quadruple assonance, varied by the alternating presence and absence of the following semivowel *i*, renders the theme, dear to the troubadours, of the seemingly endless duration of the lover's trials and sufferings). These very same sounds occur, but in consecutive pairs, and uniting three enumerated direct objects to their verb, in Bertran de Born:

> Que, s'ai fraire, germa ni quart (P-C 80.44, 4).

Although sound effects should be evaluated, as we have just done, more by effect than by frequency, more by quality than by quantity, it may nevertheless be useful to illustrate graphically the average frequency of members of assonating groups in several troubadours. The four classes plotted horizontally are the same as in charts 9 and 10, above.

Chart 11:

Average Frequency of Assonance per Poem

class:	1	2	3	4	total
poet:					
William IX	2.4	5.9	3.5	1.5	13.3
Cercamon	3.0	27.8	10.5	4.8	46.1
Jaufre Rudel	2.2	15.2	4.3	8.5	30.2
Arnaut Daniel	3.0	10.8	3.9	3.0	20.7

Cercamon's average of 46.1 members of assonating groups per poem seems so extraordinary that an illustrative stanza must be given, one in which persistent assonance helps render in the first five lines a dark and toneless autumn scene, and in the sixth, on a more rapid rhythm, the unintimidated joy of all good lovers:

SOUND EFFECTS

> Puois nostre temps comens' a brunezir
> E li verjan son de lor fuelhas blos,
> E del solelh vei tant bayssatz los rays,
> Per que·l jorn son escur e tenebros
> Et hom non *au* d'*au*zelhs ni chans ni lays,
> Per joy d'amor nos devem esbaudir (V, 1-6).

Vowels which participate in these effects either are italicized, or their quality is indicated in subscript. The poem continues with such expressions as *no·n doble·l gazardos, tAn verAys, vAY en biAYs, grAn blAsme, sOn encombrOs, bon' Amors,* etc. There is no doubt that if Peire d'Alvernhe is the master of the troubadours with respect to alliteration, the honor with respect to assonance is held by Cercamon.

Thus assonance must be accounted the chief sort of vocalism used by the troubadours, and one of their quantitatively most important poetic techniques; and with regard to quality, its gamut runs from ubiquitous and simple expressions like *totz jorns* to skillfully created pairs like Jaufre Rudel's haunting refrain *amor de lonh* (number V) and to cooperating groups like those of the same poet's beautifully sleepfilled line

> Et en dormen sotz cobertors (III, 35).

And ultimately, assonance dominates entire passages, like that quoted above from Cercamon, or contributes to the general effect of passages like Jaufre Rudel's quoted below.

G. GENERAL SOUND REPETITION

G 1. *Combined Vocalism and Consonance*

We have so far seen consonance and vocalism chiefly isolated from each other. But the two often reinforce each other in one passage, line or word. This occurs with or without convergence with other poetic means, and whether the individual consonantal or vocalic effects are capable of standing alone (as in our sections E and F) or not (as in "weak" sound repetition, in atonic internal or final vocalism, etc.).

It seems appropriate to begin this discussion with an example of the troubadours' verbal harmonics at their best, the first stanza of

Jaufre Rudel's famous "song of distant love" (and here various symbols identify the significant groupings of repeated vowels and consonants):

> LAnquAn li jorn son lonc en mAy
> M'es belhs dous chans d'auzelhs de lonh,
> E quAn mi suy partitz de lAy
> Remembra·m d'un' amor de lonh:
> VAu de tAlAn embroncx e clis
> Si que chAns ni flors d'Albespis
> No·m plAtz plus que l'yverns gelAtz (V, 1-7).

Sound and rhythm here cooperate with word meanings to express beautifully the languor of spring, the depth of the poet's melancholy, the strength of his distant love. Throughout, a thematic contrast between the lighter sound of the open vowel *a* and the gloomier sound of the *o*, both frequently followed by the slowing effect of diphthongs and nasals, is resolved in favor of the *o*, which notably dominates the refrain expression *amor de lonh*.[101] The first line in particular combines these sounds to make the days of May *sound* long: six of its eight syllables contain lengthening nasals; the repetition of vowel plus *n* in *lanquan* and *son lonc* gives a feeling of duration; and the line tapers slowly off on the falling diphthong *ai*.

Line 2 reproduces just as faithfully the poet's momentary joy at hearing birds sing. Final sibilance in five words and the internal rime *belhs-auzelhs* create a gayness and musicality which then give way to the sad and slow rhythms of lines 3 through 7. Notably line 3 is built around the paired diphthongs, at the cesura and rime, of *suy* and *lay*, and line 4 around an insistent nasality including four *m*'s. Line 5 expresses the poet's dejection by the harsh sounds and packed consonants of the synonymous pair *embroncs e clis*. Meanwhile, the only actions performed by the poet, his past departure and his present wanderings, have been intensified, in an otherwise immobile stanza, by the assonance of *suy partitz* and *vau de talan*.

Jaufre again exhibits his phonetic mastery in a springtime vision orchestrated on open *a*'s, intervocalic *n*'s and liquid *r*'s:

---

[101] Emil Levy, *Petit-Dictionnaire Provençal-Français*, 2d ed. (Heidelberg, 1923), gives the pronunciation *lonh* or *lonh*; but Carl Appel, *Provenzalische Chrestomathie*, 2d ed. (Leipzig, 1902), gives *lonh* in his glossary, p. 268. At any rate, in Jaufre Rudel's poem, the association with *lonc* (line 1) and with other close *o*'s make it reasonable to accept the pronunciation *lonh*.

Quan lo rius de la fontAna
S'esclArzis, si cum fAr sol,
E pAr la flors Aiglentina,
E·l rossinholetz el rAm
Volf e refrAnh ez aplAna
Son dous chantAr et Afina,
Dreitz es qu'ieu lo mieu refrAnha (II, 1-7).

This gayer vision has none of the concentrated consonants and somber sounds of the previously cited passage. Rather, vocalic effects (refrAnh-ApAnA-chAntAr; dreitz es; ieu-mieu) dominate occasional light consonance (s'esclArzis-sol; Rossinholetz-Ram). Further, five of the stanza's seven rime words have the gentle feminine ending -a (whereas none of the rimes of *Lanquan li jorn* is feminine!). These feminine rimes are further harmonized by a post-tonic nasal, so that -ina, -ana, and -anha reply to each other throughout the stanza and poem, the latter two with a-assonance reinforced by the masculine rime -am.

Another master of sound, Cercamon, complements the assonance pervading the beginning of his number I (quoted above, p. 239) with consonance of *ch* and *l* (cf. p. 221). These two early poets meet their match in Arnaut Daniel and his poem IX, with its expansive syntax interrupted by brief and jerky phonetic units, its peculiar reverberations of occasional one- and two-syllable lines, and its initial alliteration developing into paragrammatic word play (with words beginning in the letters a/a/b/b/c/d/e/f) and into multiple interlinear sound repetition:

L'Aur' AmAra
FA·ls bruoills brAncutz
ClArzir
Qe·l dous espeis' ab fuoills,
5. E·ls letz
Becs
Dels auzels ramencs
Ten balps e mutz,
Pars
10. E non pars (IX, 1-10).

An uneasy singsong is produced by alternance of *e*'s of contrasting quality in lines 5-8; and the hard-to-pronounce recurrent final consonances -tz, -cs, -ls, -rs (not to mention the isolated -*lps*) symbolize phonetically the "stuttering and silent" condition to which the "bitter breeze" reduces the birds.

These examples show sound repetition on a large scale, with several interacting sounds dominating large parts of stanzas and even, by the continuance of rimes, whole poems. But the scale can be lesser and groups smaller. Thus Cercamon unites a line's three major words by assonance and final consonance converging at the cesura in the central and thematic word *amor*:

> Cercamons ditz: greu er cortes
> Homs qui d'amor se desesper (I, 57-58).

This evenly balanced and somewhat singsong quality seems particularly appropriate to aphorism.

Large or small, such groups are most often grammatically uncoordinated. However, they can also render enumeration particularly effective. Thus Jaufre Rudel links four botanical categories by assonance on *a* in two of them and consonance of *r* and *s* in all four:

> PrAtz e vergiers, Albres e flors (III, 3).

Note also the two *l*'s, homotypical with the dominant liquid *r*'s. Similarly, he ties a verb to its three enumerated objects by alliteration, assonance and concentration of diphthongs:

> E *l*aus en *l*ieys e Dieu e *l*or (IV, 25).

Or, three verbs, paired by alliteration of *f* and assonance of *a*, help give to Cercamon's line

> Jovens s'en *f*uig, *f*rAing e dechAi (IV, 11)

a feeling of desolation reinforced by their abrupt masculine endings *-ig* and *-aing* and by the falling final diphthong *-ai*.

Or, coordinated sound repetition can express a given thought periphrastically by a series of contradictory or complementary pairs, as when Cercamon enlarges on the word *re*, "anything," by an extensive apposition:

> *P*etit ni *p*ro, ni tAn ni qAn,
> Ni mAl ni be, ni so ni qei (III, 23-24).

Among these varied phonetic correspondences note the first pair's alliteration; *rim fayshuc* in the second pair; assonance at the cesura and rime of the second verse; and alliteration of successive rime words. Thus sound repetition reflects the thought, frequent in the troubadours' dialectic, that a whole is the sum of contrasting but interrelated parts.

This technique in the hands of an imaginative craftsman produces the twinned enumerating lines of Arnaut Daniel already discussed in terms of alliteration. Their almost incredibly complex interplay of varied phonetic elements is indicated here graphically insofar as possible:

$$\text{Er vei vermeills, vertz, BLAus, BLAncs, gruocs}$$
$$\text{Vergiers, PLAns, PLAis, tertres e vAus (XIII, 1-2).}$$

Note the four words alliterating on v; the two richly alliterating pairs in bl- and pl- sharing a-assonance; final sibilance of all nine enumerated words; and the two consecutive terms in the bizarre final consonance -cs. This entire sound pattern fittingly complements the strangeness of a poetic vision, almost impressionistic, which breaks the green world of nature down into contrasting color groups.

Thus, in coordinated or uncoordinated groups, interplay of consonance and vocalism produces tone color and sound symbolism essential to the troubadours' art and to our appreciation of it. As described in section C, possible effects augmented by sound repetition include sadness and gaiety, autumn cold and spring rebirth, simplicity, force, etc. The relation of sound repetition to poetic space is generally a loose one; but, as in the last example, consonance and vocalism can cooperate within the same words to constitute the denser varieties of sound repetition.

G 2. *Multiple Phonetic Correspondences Among Words*

Sections E and F have shown how multiplication of either consonantal or vocalic elements increases the resulting intensification of ideas. Such multiple phonetic linkage is even more effective when consonance and vocalism combine. Thus in the last example from Arnaut, the group er occurs five times and er once; and the semantically and phonetically interrelated words *blaus-blancs-plans-plai* all contain central -la-, final -s and initial p- or b- variously combined with internal n or a diphthong (au, ai). These multiple correspondences tightly link parallel enumerations of colors and topographical terms as Arnaut demonstrates the continuity but peculiarity of the love-struck senses' vision of the physical world.

Such multiple sound repetition is typical particularly of Arnaut, as also in

> Ma·l cǫrs ferms fǫrtz
> Mi fai cobrir
> Mains vers (IX, 45-47).

Two of the first line's monosyllables share the consonantally reinforced assonance *ǫr*; and a common consonantal frame [*f-r-s*] links the two alliterating monosyllabic qualifiers. This consonantally as well as syntactically dense construction corresponds phonetically to the self-proclaimed "force" and "firmness" of the poet's amorous heart.

But the effect need not be so dense. Thus three repeated elements, less consonantal than vocalic, produce a light and musical motif symbolically uniting William IX's lady to her flattering epithets in the expressions *bǫNǫ dǫmpNǫ* (VIII, 10 and 16) and *dǫmpNǫ cǫNjǫ* (VIII, 19), all with tonic *ǫ* followed by *n* and feminine -*a*.

Effects again vary. Witness the bizarre and mocking suite of three repeated sounds in Peire d'Alvernhe's satire of Bernart de Ventadorn's parentage:

> E sa mair' *calfava·l forn* (P-C 323.11, 23).

The spreading of the second *alf* group over three different words, the intermediate supportive vocalism of *a* and the weak consonance of *v* further add to the ludicrousness of this sequence of sounds *alfavalf*. Or, denser sound repetition produces a slower and more melancholy sequence when Jaufre laments that only his lady can remedy his *sosPiRs* e *PloRs* (III, 51, where Scholz would see *p*-alliteration "jumping" the prefix *sos*-; cf. p. 203, above).

Several of these examples bring out one particular form of multiple sound repetition: contiguous vocalism and consonance, often in the tonic syllable. Pairs in *-ǫlh-* (spelled *olh*, *oill*, etc.) are especially frequent. This back vowel and palatal liquid seem to lend a melancholy allure to Arnaut Daniel's description of winter branches as *despoILLat de fuoILLa* (XVI, 2). Another pair, *olh-molhar*, is particularly prized, perhaps for its liquidity which seems appropriate to describing tears moistening the eye, as in Arnaut's line

Dont sovens l'u*oill*s mi mu*oill*a (II, 42)

and Bernart de Ventadorn's

L'aiga del cor, c'amdos los *olh*s me m*olh*a (VII, 43).

That the pair is stereotyped, thanks presumably to its sound as well as meaning, is proven by its frequent effective use in rimes such as Peire Vidal's

> Mas mi ten en tal lanha,
> De que ploron soven mei *olh*,
> Si que la car' e·l peitz m'en *molh* (VIII, 40-42).

Multiple sound repetition also includes non-adjacent consonance and vocalism; particularly effective is conjunction of alliteration and assonance, which explains the success of stereotyped pairs like s*e*n-s*abe*r and sA*n*-sA*u*. This relation is frequent at the cesura and rime, thus in William IX:

E silh qui no volran cr*e*ire   mos *c*ast*e*is (III, 13)

and in Cercamon:

Don er *p*arlAt tro en *P*eitAu (IV, 42),

in both cases linking the line's two rhythmically and semantically most important terms.

In other positions, coinciding alliteration and assonance are also quite perceptible (especially where two important words are concerned), and in William IX's line

*C*avalli*e*r, datz mi *c*oss*e*lh d'un pessamen (I, 22)

link together the initial word and cesura word, the subject and object of William's apostrophe (along with some help from the shared *l mouillé*). Or, Jaufre Rudel links a possible reaction, that of marveling, to a cause, himself:

Nuils hom no·s *m*eravIll de *m*I (VI, 7).

G 3. *"Homoeoteleuton," "Homoeoptoton" and "Rim Fayshuc"*

Multiple sound repetition in the form of side-by-side vocalism and final consonance produces rime, whether tonic or post-tonic. "Unaccented rime," like assonance an ancestor of tonic rime, was widely used in the Goliards' Latin love poetry, which can be regarded as ancestral to the Provençal lyric. For example, the anonymous "pre-courtly" tenth-century *invitatio amicae* beginning *Iam, dulcis amica, venito* has fifteen unaccented rime pairs like *venito-diligo* or *sparguntur-miscentur* and only seven accented rime pairs.[102] But such unaccented rime was not accepted by the Provençal lyric in place of true end rime. Moreover, identical post-tonic syllables are a rarity in a language like Provençal (or French) where the tonic accent tends to finality and where almost all suffixes are tonic. Thus the nature of the language permits fewer effects logically lying between final consonance and true rime than does Latin.

True rime, which has no place in classical Latin poetics, falls into two rhetorical categories describing similar final syllables in successive cola. Most authorities define *homoeoteleuton* as phonetic but not necessarily morphological identity of final syllables (*facere-dicere*; cf. Provençal *amor-flor*)[103] and *homoeoptoton* as morphological but not necessarily phonetic identity of final syllables (*criminanti-cohortanti-molienti*; Provençal *jogan rizen*).[104]

Some rhetoricians, however, distinguish these two categories according to accent or to parts of speech. The *Leys,* following the latter tradition, apply *omotheleuton* and its "flower" *similiter desinens* to verbs ending in the same syllable, and *omoptoton* and *similiter cadens* to such nouns (III, 176). Accent and etymology are no longer factors; and since these figures and flowers in fact describe non-methodical internal rime, they are discussed here rather than as morphemic repetition.

In the *Leys'* scheme, the figures *omotheleuton* and *omoptoton* legitimize the vice of *rim fayshuc* (literally "annoying, importunate rime"), which is excessive riming within one line, in from two to

---

[102] Text in Helen Waddell, *Medieval Latin Lyrics* (Baltimore, 1952), pp. 156-158.
[103] Lausberg, *Handbuch,* § 725-728.
[104] *Ibid.*, § 729-731.

four words according to the number of syllables per word and per line (III, 68-86), for example

> Lang*or*, trist*or*, dol*or* e pl*or* tot dia (III, 70),

or in a shorter line

> Dev*ers*, pod*ers* e sciensa (III, 74).

Traditional rhetoric also forbids the proximity of several words which have the same ending or are in the same case,[105] although identical inflections at the end of cola are considered a *virtus*. Molinier does exclude the end rime when counting up the number of riming syllables allowed in lines of various lengths; and he permits as many as three internal riming syllables in an eight-syllable line, for example:

> Gr*an* d*an* f*an* li clergue tru*an* (III, 74).

Furthermore, he excuses *rim fayshuc* "per affectio e per acordansa final no principal" (III, 70). In other terms,

> *Rims fayshucz*, can se fay scienmen per dreg compas per escuzatio d'alcunas figuras o per ornat d'alcunas flors de rethorica, es permes, et en tant escuzatz que so qu'era vicis torn en ornamen (III, 86).[106]

Molinier thus pushes tolerance to the point of circular reasoning: the vice of irregular internal rime is excused by the figure of irregular internal rime. At any rate, he certainly leaves an open door to artistic use of the device. He specifically states of these lines:

> Totz homs es dupt*atz* e prez*atz*
> Et hondr*atz* fort per sa riqueza,
> E s'il falh es f*atz* apel*atz* (I, 126)

---

[105] *Ibid.*, § 965.
[106] By speaking here of "regular, intentional" *rim fayshuc* (*scienmen per dreg compas*), Molinier does not mean to designate internal rime recurring regularly in identical positions of different lines or stanzas. He recognizes (I, 272-274) that such regular internal rime produces a form, *coblas refor-sadas*, which may as well be considered as longer stanzas of shorter lines, just as I. Frank (*Répertoire métrique*, I, 30) states that "il n'existe, pour nous, ni rime sans vers ni vers sans rime." Here, then, Molinier is merely following his general principle that a vice several times repeated for effect becomes a figure of speech.

that

> E jaciaysso que aquesta maniera de dictar sia dins los termes de rim fayshuc, pero trop no la trovam pezan ni fayshuga, per que soen la pauzam ses vici que no·y fam (I, 126).

Molinier is in good company in allowing irregular internal rime. Preminger's *Encyclopedia* tells us that

> One word may echo another anywhere in its immediate neighborhood and apart from the metrical scheme. The purpose of such inner, internal, or medial rhymes is then more rhetorical than metrical, as where... Swinburne suggests the darting flight of the bird in: —
>
> Sister, my sister, O *fleet sweet* swallow. [107]

The troubadours, as we shall see, were amply aware of such possibilities.

G 4. "Rim Fayshuc" in the Troubadours

Of the technique which Guilhem Molinier calls *rim fayshuc*, Carl Appel says: "Another tendency [than towards alliteration] is towards the combining of riming and assonating words inside the verse. Here too, many ready-made groupings are furnished by the language," such as *sai e lai, tan ni quan, gran afan, rir e bordir.* [108]

Such terms need not be grammatically coordinated. For example, the same consonance as in the pair *olh-molhar*, which we have encountered already, occurs, preceded by the "lighter" and "clearer" vowel *ę*, in two common and appropriately light-hearted rimed pairs. Both of these are found in Jaufre's "song of distant love":

> M'es bęlhs dous chans d'auzęlhs de lonh (V, 2);
>
> Fos pels sieus bęlhs huęlhs remiratz (V, 14).

---

[107] Preminger, *Encyclopedia*, art. "Rhyme," p. 706. A doubtless more famous example is Shakespeare's line

Hark! hark! the lark at heaven's gate sings.

[108] Appel, *Peire Rogier*, p. 23. "Ein anderes Streben geht auf Zusammenstellung reimender und assonirender Wörter innerhalb des Verses. Auch hier werden viele Verbindungen von der Sprache fertig geliefert."

The second of these rimed pairs, reinforced by final consonance on *s* and by *e*-assonance in other words, is particularly successful in reflecting in sound the beauty of the lady's gaze.

In another such example, Jaufre Rudel states that his song should be sung

> En pl*ana* lengu*a* rom*ana* (II, 31);

a simple and open allure, often achieved in Italian, is contributed by the three consecutive words ending in -*a*, of which two rime on the light sequence -*ana* with its two vowels and lone consonant. Or, in one of Arnaut's beautiful spring scenes, irregular internal rime symbolizes the music of birdsong in the line

> La flors e li chan e *il clar quil* (IV, 5).

These "clear cries" harmonize on the riming article *il* and the substantive *quil*, supported in their liquidity by the *l* and *r* of *clar*.

An example now with morphemic repetition is Cercamon's

> Si el visqu*es* ni Deu plagu*es* (VI, 45).

The third person singular imperfect subjunctive ending -*es*, strategically repeated at the cesura and rime, reinforces the effect of the contrary-to-fact condition which reminds us that William X, the subject of this *planh*, in fact did not live long enough to accomplish all the deeds of valor he would have liked. A similar case occurs in Rigaut de Berbezilh's poem *Si co·l soleilhs*:

> Se li plagu*es* que n'agu*es* piatat (P-C 337.1, 31).

In addition to this imperfect subjunctive ending -*es*, the -*an* of the present participle and the -*ar* and -*ir* of infinitives also contribute frequently to *rim fayshuc*, as they do to normal end rime. Thus Arnaut Daniel uses the common interplay of two present participles whose endings have both morphological and phonetic identity:

> C'am*an* prei*an* s'afranca cors ufecs (XIV, 40).

The riming asyndetic participles create a strong effect of present action, here of "loving" and "beseeching." *Rim fayshuc* of participles in *-en* is less common; but a good example is the tornada of Lanfranc Cigala's number VI, whose repeated roots are summed up at the end:

> Jauz*en,* plaz*en,* riz*en,* chant*an,* ioios
> Mi fai iois, chanz, ris, plazers, alegransa (VI, 41-42).

The proximity of *rizen* and *chantan* brings up the distinctive type *jogan-rizen,* which represents *homoeoptoton* in its usual definition of morphological but not phonetic identity (cf. p. 248, above); but since the type represents properly neither morphemic repetition nor *rim fayshuc,* but only final consonance, examples will be relegated to a footnote.[109]

The early importance of *rim fayshuc* is amply demonstrated by a number of cases in William IX, all typically with masculine endings and generally in a structure of enumeration or of direct grammatical linkage (adjective plus substantive, etc.):

> Dos cavalhs ai a ma selha b*en* e g*en;*
> Bon son per armas et adreg e val*en* (I, 7-8);
> De Gim*el* ai lo cast*el* e·l mandam*en* (I, 25)
> Ni·m *fes* que·m plassa ni que·m *pes* (IV, 27);

---

[109] The pair referred to in our text is found in Peire d'Alvernhe:
> Lo vers fo faitz als enflabotz
> A Puoich-vert tot jog*an* riz*en* (XII, 85-86)

and in Uc de Saint Circ:
> Una danseta voil far
> jog*an* ris*en* (XXIV, 1-2).

Arnaut especially enjoys the technique:
> Qe·l seu bel cors bais*an* riz*en* descobre (XII, 31);
> Q'el cor e·l sen tenc dorm*en* e veill*an* (XIII, 19).

The latter pair, antonymic and unlike the previous examples not asyndetic but with a conjunction, is also found in Cercamon:
> Totz trassalh e bran e fremis
> Per s'amor, durm*en* o velh*an* (I, 25-26);

and to this pair Jaufre Rudel adds a third participle:
> Vell*an* e pueys somnh*an* dorm*en* (I, 16).

Such *homoeoptoton* could also be cited with infinitives in *-ar, -er,* and *-ir;* past participles in *-atz, -itz,* and *-utz;* etc. We should note a final peculiarity, cooperation of a cognate present and past participle in Jaufre Rudel's line

> Per qu'ieu la jau jauz*itz* jauz*en* (I, 18).

In general, *homoeoptoton* of this sort is one of the troubadours' most distinctive forms of variation on the theme of morphemic and sound repetition.

SOUND EFFECTS

> E·m v*auc* e m'est*auc* al solelh (V, 2);
> Als gr*os* carb*os* (V, 42);
> ...m*on* B*on* Vezi (X, 26);
> Que tal se v*an* d'amor gab*an* (X, 29);
> ...fel*on* Gasc*on* (XI, 16).

And more than one troubadour has complained of love's *gran afan* or qualified his love as *tan gran*. These two examples, like most in this section, show the internally riming terms in close contact; and now another type, involving the position of greatest emphasis in the verse except for the rime, must be discussed.

G 5. "Rim Fayshuc" at the Cesura: "Vers Enpeutatz"

Rim fayshuc involving the cesura word produces, in the *Leys'* terminology, *vers enpeutatz* or "grafted verses," whether the interior rime occurs at the cesura of one verse:

> Mon c*or* se m*or* (I, 124);
> Am gran coss*ir* me faytz amors langu*ir* (III, 84);

or at the cesura of successive verses:

> Mant home v*eg* ques als autres defen
> So ques apl*eg* fay tot jorn e cossen (I, 126).

Though Molinier judges *vers enpeutatz* negatively, the troubadours use both sorts effectively. The first sort has already been illustrated in the preceding section; the second occurs for example in Jaufre Rudel's lines

> E non ir*ay* jam*ai* alhor
> Ni non querr*ai* altrui conquistz (IV, 10-11),

combining *vers enpeutatz* (*iray-querrai*) with normal *rim fayshuc* (*iray jamai*) and stressing the ideas of futurity, associated with the future first person ending *-ai*, and of negation, by means of repeated *non*.

The same poet uses *vers enpeutatz*, again with morphemic repetition but this time of the infinitive ending, at the beginning of his reflections on the nature of poetry:

> No sap chant*ar* qui so non di
> Ni vers trob*ar* qui motz no fa (VI, 1-2).

These two infinitives — parallel by form, function, position and sound — sum up the two qualities essential to the aspiring poet: singing and composing.

A more complex example from Arnaut Daniel, the master of the intricate in sound, weaves together the terms of a three-line comparison by a series of five words containing the combination *or*, including the riming pair *cor-flor* at successive cesuras:

> So·m met en c*or* qu'ieu col*or*e mon chan
> D'un aital fl*or* don lo fruitz si' am*ors*
> E iois lo grans, e l'ol*ors* d'enoi gandres (XIII, 5-7).

And, just to show that all is not to be taken straight-faced in such techniques, let us cite two lines from Arnaut's scatological *sirventes*:

> Que si corn*avatz* per dep*ort*
> Ben trob*avatz* f*ort* contraf*ort* (I, 31-32). [110]

The occurrence of the rare second person plural imperfect ending *-avatz* at the cesura of successive verses, and the fact that the cesura falls precisely between the tonic and the post-tonic syllable of this ending, correspond to the general air of satire and humor; furthermore, *rim fayshuc* by etymological figure occurs by *fort* riming with *contrafort*. [111]

The ultimate in *rim fayshuc* and *vers enpeutatz* is the curious *rim serpenti*, rhetoric's *paromoeosis*, [112] where each word and often each syllable has its rime in the next verse:

> B*os* D*ieus*, cl*arr* *atz* c*ara*;
> L*os* m*ieus* g*ardatz* *ara* (I, 172).

Molinier rightly condemns the device as having "mays de difficultat que d'utilitat" (I, 172). But at least regarding lesser sorts of *vers enpeutatz*, Molinier grants that they may often be used "ses vici que no·i fam," without vice (I, 126). Molinier, after all, can hardly con-

---

[110] A translation may be of use here: "For if you blew (on her anus or genitalia) for sport, / You surely encountered great resistance."

[111] This context makes it hard to resist seeing a pun by *enpost liamen de las dictios* (cf. p. 260, below), thus *con trafort*.

[112] Lausberg, *Handbuch*, § 732.

demn categorically the troubadours' application of his law of justification by effect, which transforms theoretical vice into stylistic device according to the skill of its application.

H. Homophony

Multiple sound repetition, or partial phonetic identity of words, leads logically toward homophony or total phonetic identity of words. The terms "homophone" is "applied to words having the same sound, but differing in meaning or derivation." [113] Between multiple sound repetition and homophony, we shall distinguish an intermediate stage, to be known as "near-homophony"; within homophony proper we shall distinguish the category of equivocal rime; and puns, marked by intentional ambiguity, will be shown to arise from either partial or complete homophony.

H 1. *Near-Homophony*

All these concepts are known to traditional rhetoric. *Annominatio* or *paronomasia* includes near-homophony of 1) successive words having identical syllables (*fortunatam natam*), [114] and 2) neighboring words differentiated only by a changed prefix (*reprimi-comprimi*), an added prefix (*erat-deerat*), one changed letter (*nobilem-mobilem*), one added letter (*leones-lenones*), a changed inflection (*maxime-maximo*), a changed quantity (*mălum-mālum*), or transposed letters (*navo-vano*). [115] Some of these cases illustrate morphemic repetition and have been treated in the relevant sections of chapter IV; the others have their proper place here.

The *Leys d'amors* do not show great interest in this topic. Molinier does identify words differing only by accent as *motz accentuals* (I, 56-58), which if rimed constitute *rim accentual* (I, 192, 196, 278), thus *botó-bóto* or with *motz trencatz* (split words) *tres só-trésso*. Similarly, words differing only by vowel quality are *motz utrissonans* (I, 16) or *motz enpost* (I, 52) — thus *vas-va(n)s*, [116] *pes-pes, col-col* — which

---

[113] *Shorter OED*, art. "Homophone."
[114] Lausberg, *Handbuch*, § 963.
[115] *Ibid.*, § 637-638.
[116] On open and close *a*, cf. n. 54, above, and Aurelio Roncaglia, *La lingua dei trovatori* (Rome, 1965), pp. 48-49.

in the rime produce *rim utrissonan* (I, 196, 278). These two sorts of near-homophony seem unappreciated by the troubadours, who however, do frequently use the sort of near-homophony consisting of phonetically identical syllables or nearly identical words in close proximity. This device, like those described by rhetoric, often calls attention to a logical relation between two words related by sound but not, at first sight, by meaning.

The troubadours' awareness of near-homophony has already been seen from Uc de Saint Circ's satire of Guilhem Fabre, which ridicules the neighboring use of words like *mus, musa,* and *musen* (cf. pp. 185-187). Of course Fabre is not alone in using this technique; the opposition *cor-cors* (describing, together with *sen* and *saber,* the essence of the human being) and the parallel *be-bo* are frequent, and probably of Latin origin. Another common pair of roots, brought into contact by the Isidorean type of etymologizing, is *don-* in the senses of "lady" (*domina*) and of "to give" (*donare*); the pair is used quite effectively as early as William IX:

Si·m vol mi *dons* s'amor *donar* (IX, 37).

The logical link is impeccable: the lady is, in the highest sense, a "giver." The lady's importance is similarly magnified, in a verse of Bernart de Ventadorn, by phonetic resemblance to another word which differs from it only by addition of one phoneme:

Vol me *doncs* mi*dons* aucire...? (XIX, 50).

The word *dons,* which here could just as well be separated from the possessive *mi,* differs by only one letter from *doncs*; and the etymological figure of *me* and *mi,* again with only one letter's difference, further adds to the effect of near-homophony.

Other examples of the rhetorical category of addition of one letter are Jaufre Rudel's line

Per so·m *sen* trop *soen* marrir (III, 15),

where words indicating feeling and frequency reinforce each other semantically and phonetically; and Bernart's immortal lines

Tout m'a mo cor, e *tout* m'a me,
E se mezeis e *tot* lo mon (XXXI, 13-14),

where insistence on the stem of *tolre* (by the diphthongized past participle *tout*, repeated in line 13, and by the preterite *tolc* in line 15) supports the phonetic link between *tout* and *tot*, demonstrating that what has been *taken* from the lover is indeed his *all*.

Not addition but changing of one phoneme is illustrated by the end of William IX's *comjat*:

> Qu'eu ai avut joi e deport
> loing e pres et e mon *aizi*.
>
> *Aissi* guerpisc joi e deport
> E vair e gris e sembeli (XI, 39-42),

whose successive *aizi* and *aissi* help link the poem's conclusion to its body; and Cercamon's line

> Ni·l *fis* so don *fos* irada (II, 28),

with near-homophony of two verbs stressing two past actions: doing and becoming.

Words differing by more than a single sound can also reinforce each other if their similar sounds form a sufficiently striking parallel. For example two words having one identical syllable and an identical following consonant magnify an oath of Peire Vidal's in conjunction with near homophony two lines later:

> Per Sant Jacme qu'om apela
> L'a*post*ol de Com*post*ela,
> En Luzi' a tal Miquel
> Que·m val mais que c*el* del c*el* (XVI, 71-74).

Or, a transposition of sounds adds to the attractiveness of Jaufre's imagined conversation with his far-off lady by rearranging the sounds of the root *parl-*:

> Adoncs *parra*·l *parla*mens fis (V, 19).

Nearly homophonous groups can also cooperate in a general atmosphere of sound repetition, as in Bernart's harmonious line

> *Lan*can v*e*i per m*e*i *la lan*da (XXIX, 1),

dominated by the syllables *lan-can-la-lan* and the riming pair *vei-mei*. Similarly, in an extraordinarily effective example, the last line of Bertran de Born's lament on Young Henry uses near-homophony in a context of slow rhythms dominated by vowels and liquids to describe the heavenly kingdom to which the Young King is hopefully destined:

> Lai on Anc dol non Ac ni Aura ira (P-C 80.41, 40),
> There where there is no grief nor shall be sadness. [117]

The pair *on-non* exploits the slow sounds of close *o* and the following lengthening nasal; *anc* and *ac*, with their unusual final consonance, intensify the idea of eternity; and the pair *aura-ira*, with their slow-moving vocalic concentration in the poem's final two words, creates an impression of repose and harmony. The latter two pairs are furthermore linked by triple assonance and by the morphological figure *acaura*.

A final example shows near-homophony applied for a comic purpose in Arnaut Daniel's scatological satire, especially in the rime. Most of the first stanza's rare rime words have more phonemes in common with each other than are different; these words include *secs, becs, pecs, plecs, precs,* and *grecs*. The next stanza makes the thematic images *pelutz* ("hairy") and *palutz* ("swamp") into near neighbors; and the poem ends, with obscenity and near-homophony in the rime, in this tornada:

> Dompna, ges Bernartz non s'estrill
> Del corn cornar ses gran dozill
> Ab que seire·l trauc del *penill*,
> Puois poira cornar ses *perill* (I, 46-49).

In connection with the play on *corn-* in this second line (cf. p. 173, above), one must note in stanza II the sequence of related sounds *corns* (12), *iorn* (13), *cor ne* (16), and *corn* (18). The whole is a

---

[117] Ezra Pound, *Personae* (New York, 1926), p. 37. Cf. Arnaut Daniel's line with some of the same phonetic elements:
> On anc non ac d'auzels agre (XI, 24),
describing the songless desert where the poet speaks of doing penance.

seldom-equalled display of sound for satiric ends, and one more example of the wide applications of phonetic similarity.[118]

H 2. *Homophony or "Motz Equivocz"*

Total phonetic identity is the ultimate in sound repetition on the word level.[119] It is known to rhetoric as *amphibolia* or *ambiguitas*, a category of *obscuritas* including accidental homophony (*cacemphaton, deformitas*) and intentional ambiguity.[120] To Guilhem Molinier, homophony is known as *equivocatio,* which "se fay en respieg du meteys vocable significan diversas causas o diverses faytz o cascu d'aquetz" (II, 34) and which produces *motz equivocz* (I, 54) such as *fe* ("makes; faith") or *fi* ("fine; end") or *do* ("gives; gift"). One of these very pairs given by the *Leys* occurs in William IX:

> Amigu' ai ieu, no sai qui s'es,
> Qu'anc non la vi, si m'ajut *fes*;
> Ni·m *fes* que·m plassa ni que·m pes (IV, 25-27).

The playful context of this "nonsense-poem" implies that the repetition of *fes* with two entirely different meanings in close succession is part of an over-all scheme aiming to break down normal paths of communication by intentional negations and contradictions and, here, homophony, interior rime (*fes-pes*), and the antonymous alliterating pair *plassa-pes*. It should, however, be noted that full homophony occurs more often, or at least is more perceptible and effective, when in the rime.

H 3. *Equivocal Rime*

The example given in the preceding section already includes one member at the verse end; often, the necessity of rime establishes a situation favorable to having both members in the rime, while metrical emphasis gives them extra prominence. Homophonous rime if of

---

[118] Cf. also Arnaut's line of superlative negativeness:
> Q'el *mon non* a *home* de negun *nom* (XVII, 29).

[119] As a linguistic curiosity, homophony is further extended to the verse level by the preposterous French couplet:
> Gal, amant de la reine, alla, tour magnanime,
> Galamment de l'arène à la Tour Magne à Nîmes.

[120] Lausberg, *Handbuch,* § 1068-70, 222-223, 658-659.

course unknown to traditional rhetoric, which did not deal with rimed verse. But the *Leys d'amors* define a flower of rhetoric called *traductio* [121] (III, 178), one of whose forms is illustrated by the rimes *fe-fe* ("faith; makes") and *cara-cara* ("dear; flesh"). Molinier enthusiastically states that "aytals acordansas equivocas reputam per mot belas e subtils" (III, 90); and these, used throughout a stanza, form the *cobla equivoca* (I, 278).

Not such *coblas equivocas* but at least isolated equivocal rimes are well attested in the troubadours, thanks both to the necessity of finding convenient rimes and to the admiration for this sort of ingenuity reflected in the *Leys*. Occasionally, equivocal rimes gain in effect from successive position, as in Cercamon:

> Plagnen lo Norman e Franceis,
> E deu lo be plagner lo reis
> Cui el laisset la terr' e·l *creis*;
> Pos aitan grans honors li *creis*... (VI, 37-40),

where two derivatives from one root, meaning "offspring" and "grows," stress the idea of growth apparently paradoxical but actually, in Christian ideology, quite appropriate in a funereal lament.

When, rarely, equivocation exceeds the bounds of single words, we have the rhetorical vice of *cacemphaton*, [122] denounced by Guilhem Molinier as *enpost liamen de las dictios*, "unskilful combination of words," as in *del monges*, which can be mistaken for *del mon ges* (III, 108-110). But this vice can also become an accepted form of equivocal rime occurring for example in one of Molinier's *coblas dubitativas* (I, 292) as *dece-de se* ("immediately; from her") and in Bernart de Ventadorn I, 14 and 31, as *mes-m'es* ("month; is to me") in a playful context of morphological figure and antonymy.

Equivocal rime, whether in such *motz trencatz* or in *motz entiers*, is less frequent than repeated rime words. Thus Peire Vidal's work contains 219 rime words belonging to repeated groups (cf. chart 4, above), but only 54 belonging to equivocal groups, thus only 27 pairs in 45 poems. Still, for both rime phenomena, melodic identity and position in the tornada are sought after.

---

[121] One meaning of *traductio* in rhetoric is homophony or near-homophony, generally with intentional ambiguity; cf. Lausberg, *Handbuch*, § 658; Faral, *Arts poétiques*, pp. 96-97.

[122] Lausberg, *Handbuch*, § 222, 964, 1070.

SOUND EFFECTS

Again Peire Vidal will be taken as illustrative of the troubadours. One-third of his equivocal pairs have one or more members in a tornada; and of his 54 equivocal rime words, 20 occur in tornadas, a ratio of 37 per cent compared to random expectation of only 7 per cent [123] repetition in the tornada, whether (as seen before) of identical words or (as now) of words having the same pronunciation but different meaning, seems to be felt as not only justifiable, but actually useful to development of previous motifs. And where both members of the equivocal rime pair fall in one tornada (as in Peire Vidal XXIV) or in successive tornadas (as in his XX and XXXIII), they together receive the added emphasis of finality in the poem.

Thus, one of Peire's songs ends with the effective tornada

> Coms de Peiteus, bels senher, vos et eu
> Avem lo pretz de tota l'autra *gen,*
> Vos de ben far et eu de dir lo *gen* (XXIV, 60-62),

where rimed occurrences of *gen*, "people" and then "beautiful," specifically describe the particular domains of the lord and the poet and receive the stress not only of successive occurrence but also of absolute finality.

Again as for repeated rime words, we find in equivocal rime word pairs a tendency to occur in melodic identity. Of Peire Vidal's twenty-seven pairs, sixteen, or 59 per cent, occur in melodic identity, as opposed to random expectation of 45 per cent. [124] This implies a feeling that the musical setting can help bring out the phonetic resemblances of words, whether for illustrative or playful effect. It is particularly significant that nine of these sixteen melodically identical pairs, thus over half, occur in successive metrical groups (stanzas and/or tornadas), so that the principles of melodic repetition, verbal repetition, finality in the verse and spatial proximity here coincide. In a particularly clever example, Peire Vidal situates in the first verse of successive tornadas a homophonous verb and place name:

> La Loba ditz que *seus so,*
> Et a·n be dreg e razo,
> Que, per ma fe, melhs sui seus
> Que no sui d'autrui ni meus.

---

[123] Cf. ch. III, n. 49.
[124] Cf. ch. III, n. 34.

> Bel*s* *S*embeli*s*, *S*aut et *S*o
> Am per vos et Alio;
> E quar la vista·m fo breus,
> En sui sai marritz e greus (XXXIII, 49-56).

Though the ideological link may require imagination to perceive, the playful intent, underlined by alliteration in both cases, is clear. In general, homophony attains its greatest importance in the rime, where it ranks with word repetition and morphemic repetition as a means of intensification and as a figure of repetition.

H 4. *Puns*

The pun, "a figure of speech depending upon a similarity of sound and a disparity of meaning," [125] has long been practiced on the basis of homophony and near-homophony. The pun is one sort of rhetorical *ambiguitas* and *annominatio* and of the *Leys'* *equivocatio*. Specific puns, like alliterative groups, passed occasionally from Latin into the Romance languages; thus *amari* ("to be loved; bitter") gives Old French *amer* and Provençal *amar* ("to love; bitter"), a group to which Béroul's *Tristan* adds *la mer*. [126]

Another such international pun (though not of Latin origin), based this time on imperfect homophony, is Old French and Provençal *marit-marrit* ("husband-sad"). Thus in a *tenso* debating whether it is better to be a lover or a husband, Elias d'Ussel concludes that

> Maritz a son ioi ses affan
> E·l drutz l'a mesclat ab dolor,
> Per qu'ieu am mais, cals q'en sia lo critz,
> Esser *maritz* gauzens que drutz *marritz*.
> (P-C 194.2, 45-48)

Similarly, the tempting pair *saber* (French *savoir*)-*sabor* (French *saveur*), ultimately related in Latin (*sapere-saporem*) is played on in immediate contact by Arnaut Daniel:

> Per so q'il es dels bos *sabers sabors* (XIII, 34).

---

[125] Preminger, *Encyclopedia*, p. 681.
[126] Cf. Faral, *Arts poétiques*, pp. 96-97.

Whether we translate *sabers* as "knowledge (about love?)" or with Toja [127] take *bos sabers* as "pleasure," the word game remains clever, and obviously complimentary to the lady who inspired it.

The puns given by Guilhem Molinier are also ingenious, as in

> Hom manja de ma *cozina*;
> Anticens es ma *cozina*;
> Donx hom manja d'Anticen;
> Solvetz aquest argumen (III, 108),

playing on the Provençal growing-together of Latin *coquina* and *consobrina*, "cousin" and "kitchen." Another example,

> Tota res que *corr* ha pes;
> Garonna *corr*, donx ha pes (III, 108),

uses one word in two senses ("to run" literally and figuratively), a device known to rhetoric as *antanaclasis*.[128] Similarly, Peire Vidal uses another *cor*, "heart," in its physical sense then in an idiomatic expression:

> E·us ren mon *cor* de bon *cor* e d'amor (X, 90),

and Bernart de Ventadorn gives to *via* the same contrasting uses, in "al*ways*" and "along the high*ways*," in successive rimes of his tornada

> Lo vers, aissi com om plus l'au,
> Vau melhuran tota *via*.
> E·i aprendon per la *via*
> Cil c'al Poi lo volran saber (XI, 57-60).

So far our examples have used pairs, whether of similar-sounding words or of the same word; but one occurrence of one word can stand for two different meanings. Thus the international pun *cors* (*corpus-cor* with analogical *-s*)[129] perhaps appears in Jaufre Rudel's line

---

[127] Toja, *Arnaut Daniel*, p. 323, n. 34.
[128] Lausberg, *Handbuch*, § 663; Preminger, *Encyclopedia*, p. 681.
[129] This near-homophonous pair *cors-cor* occurs in Bernart de Ventadorn's line
> Cor e cors e saber e sen (I, 5),

and also in the line just quoted from Peire Vidal X, 90, if we accept the reading of Avalle, *Peire Vidal* (his No. VIII, 90; "paronomasia," he comments):

> E·us ren mon *cors* de bon *cor* e d'amor;

Per vos totz lo *cors* mi dol (II, 9),

where the context can justify either meaning, the more spiritual or the more physical one. A clearer case, recalling the obscene tradition in Latin punning, occurs in the mouth of Marcabru's saucy and uncooperative shepherdess:

> Mas ieu per un pauc d'*intratge*
> Non vuoil ges mon piucellatge
> Camjar per nom de putana.
> (P-C 293.30, 68-70).

Intratge is defined as "entrance fee" or "act of entering," each giving its own very apt interpretation here.

Another type of pun involves rhetoric's *interpretatio per etymologiam* [130] in that a concrete meaning is developed from a proper name. This has been noted in geographical terms — Proensa, Valensa, Argensa, etc. — by Frank M. Chambers,[131] who concludes that Peire Vidal probably taught this device to the five other troubadours who use it.[132] A typical example from Peire Vidal contains the series

> Que fag e dig e parvensa
> A de *Monbel* e d'*Argensa*
> E de *Monrozier* color
> E sa cambra es de *Valflor* (XXXV, 37-40);

---

here the first term would be "body, self" and the second "heart." Confusion between the two words is sometimes eliminated in the nominative singular by the fact that cor, "heart," being a Latin neuter, often has no -s ending; cf. Oscar Schultz-Gora, *Altprovenzalisches Elementarbuch*, 4th ed. (Heidelberg, 1924), § 101, p. 68.

[130] Cf. Franco Branciforti, "Note al testo di Guilhem de Montanhagol," *Filologia e Letteratura*, XIV (1968), 351. The name Gauseranda, for example, is interpreted as *gai seran* in Montanhagol II, 11.

[131] Frank M. Chambers, "The Lady from Plazensa," in Urban T. Holmes, ed., *Essays Presented to Honor Alexander Herman Schutz* (Columbus, Ohio, 1964), pp. 196-209.

[132] These are Peire Guilhem de Luserna, Peire Bremon Ricas Novas, Torcafol, Peire Cardenal, and Aimeric de Pegulhan. To them should be added Raimon de Durfort and Arnaut Daniel for their use of the place name Cornilh, and Raimon's use of Cornes, in their two *sirventes* built on the root *corn-* (cf. p. 173, above). Also, Arnaut Daniel may be referring to the place name Agremon in his line

> Lai on doutz motz *mou* en *agre* (XI, 50);

cf. Toja's note to this line.

and his poem XLV contains the troubadours' most remarkable concentration, about twenty such names in all, some real, some probably not. The same poem further illustrates his penchant for punning on names [133] by sarcastically applying the epithet *Lans' agud'* (line 61), literally "sharp spear," to the unwarlike Marquis Manfred I Lancia. [134] Nothing daunted, Manfred counterattacks by inaugurating an abusive *tenso* whose first stanza includes the line

Res non es meins, mas que *peiras* non *lansa* (XXI, 7),

which seems, whatever its precise meaning, to derive from their respective names [135] a play on words strengthened in the same stanza by the equivocal rime *lansa*, "lance" (4) and "throws" (7).

An even clearer example of *interpretatio per etymologiam* occurs in Lanfranc Cigala's attack on Boniface II of Montferrat:

En *Bonifais* es clamatz falsamen,
Car anc *bon* faig non *fes* far a sa via (XXI, 15-16),

with the pun intensified by the etymological figure *faig-fes-far*. One could cite numerous examples to bear out Jules Coulet's conclusion that "les jeux de mots sur les noms propres sont un des procédés de développement les plus aimés des troubadours." [136]

Still, punning is not usually a serious poetic means in Old Provençal. Its purpose is generally humorous or satiric, even though "the pun was not looked on by classical, medieval, or Renaissance writers as primarily a vehicle for humor." [137] Perhaps then the troubadours were ahead of their time, since not till the seventeenth century did the pun lose its double capacity of being used as "a means of emphasis and an instrument of persuasion" as well as "for comic effect." [138]

In its generally comic purpose, the pun stands in contrast to the troubadours' use of near-homophony, homophony, and equivocal rime. These, though certainly often betraying a touch of playfulness, serve

---

[133] Cf. also the pun on *Fenics* and *m'amor fenirai* in lines 92-94.
[134] Cf. Avalle, *Peire Vidal*, p. 294, note to XXXV, 61.
[135] Cf. Avalle, pp. 419-420, note to XLIV, 7.
[136] Coulet, *Guilhem Montanhagol*, p. 65, giving examples.
[137] Preminger, *Encyclopedia*, p. 681.
[138] *Ibid.*

the same ends as other forms of sound repetition: to enhance the sound of verse, to juxtapose certain ideas by bringing out a hidden or already suggested logical link, and to summarize and recall a poem's major themes.

I. Density and Duration

Sections D-H have discussed *repetition* of various sounds and sound groups, which is the most important of the three categories — imitation, repetition and concentration — into which we earlier divided the *Leys'* treatment of sound effects. Of these categories, *imitation*, or neologism by onomatopoeia, seems not to be used by the troubadours, and at any rate does not legitimately belong to our chosen subject, intensification through recurrence.

I 1. *Concentration of Sound*

However, *concentration* of either consonant or vowel sounds may be described as repetition of sounds of a certain articulatory type. Individual poets and works, like different languages, are often characterized by a particular density of consonants or of vowels. German can thus be called a consonant-language and Italian a vowel-language; or Arnaut Daniel, perhaps, a consonant-poet and Bernart de Ventadorn a vowel-poet.

Naturally, these subjective evaluations would have to be verified statistically before general conclusions about different troubadours are drawn. But in our present discussion, it is important not to compare troubadours from this point of view, but to show their general awareness of sound concentration and of its poetic possibilities. Here, the *Leys d'amors* are particularly revealing, and seem to strike an original note in medieval poetics. The closest that traditional rhetoric comes to treating phonetic density is in describing cacophony, whether as *dysprophoron*, any hard-to-pronounce series of sounds, [139] or as *structura aspera*, the disagreeable conjunction of two of the "harsh" consonants *s, x, r* and *f* (for example, *ablata*s g*R*atis). [140]

---

[139] Lausberg, *Handbuch*, § 976.
[140] *Ibid.*, § 968.

The *Leys d'amors* describe such difficulties of articulation, when due to consonant repetition, as *cacenphaton* [141] (III, 26) and as different forms of *cacosyntheton* (cf. pp. 195, 211, above). But, for harsh sound sequences not arising from sound repetition, Molinier uses the term *collizio*, which he classifies as a subtype of *cacosyntheton*. [142]

Collizio, is a vice, according to Molinier, except when used intentionally in paired verses (III, 50). It results (I, 62-64; III, 50) from occurrence in one line of four or more *motz retardius* (or *dictios retardivas*), which are words that occupy unusual time per syllable. This "retardation" can be produced by a diphthong (*vay, joy*), by a diphthong plus one or two consonants (*quaysh*) or by a monophthong plus two or three consonants (*cars, fortz*). Molinier thus recognizes what too often is ignored: the interpenetration and interreaction of consonant and vowel patterns and rhythms in poetry. He states that syllables with diphthongs are longer than those with monophthongs, and that either sort of syllable increases in length as more consonants are added; also, syllables with open vowels (*plenisonans*) are longer than those with close vowels (*semisonans*) (I, 60-62).

Here is one example of Molinier's own application of his theory of duration. If two verses differ only by substitution of *tostemps* for *leumen*, then "each verse has as pleasant a cadence as the other, for the syllable *leu* and the syllable *temps* are about of the same proportions as to time, since the diphthong slows the pronunciation of *leu* and the plurality of consonants that of *temps*" (III, 370). [143] In both words, concentration affects duration.

Collizio, this "aspra e dezacordable contencios de sillabas" (I, 64), can occur alone:

> Philips es bels reys, blanx, frescz, nautz,
> Larcz, francz, justz, fortz, castz et asautz (I, 64),

or in contrast to verses of normal duration, producing thus "un autre [vici] per lo retardamen":

---

[141] However, rhetoric's *cacemphaton* corresponds to what Molinhier calls *enpost liamen de las dictios*.

[142] But in Lausberg, *Handbuch*, § 493, the term *conlisio* designates the contact of vowels in *synaloephe*.

[143] "Ayta bela cazensa haia la us rims coma l'autres, quar aquela sillaba *leu* et aquesta *temps* assatz son d'una proporcio cant al temps, quar le diptonges fay retardar *leu* e la molteza de las consonans *temps*...."

> Philips es bels reys, castz, francz, pros,
> am cor humil e piatos (I, 64).

Since diphthongs are not here a factor, this disconcerting time differential between these two octosyllables results entirely from different consonant-vowel ratios (speaking phonetically, not orthographically) of 22/8 and 8/8. By commenting on this time differential, Molinier implies that duration in time, like syllable count, must be about equal for rhythmic equivalence among verses.[144]

As a result, any variation in sound density may have stylistic consequences. We have already noted the progressive "thickening" of Cercamon's line

> Quant l'aura doussa s'amar*z*is (I, 1).

Similarly, we have mentioned the consonantal density — thirteen consonants for four vowels — of Arnaut's line

> Ma·l cors ferms fortz (IX, 45),

symbolizing the heart's "firmness." Consonantal *collizio* is in fact especially noteworthy in Arnaut, both in individual verses and, if one may thus extend the scope of *collizio*, in the hard rimes typical of his and others' *trobar clus*. This tendency to consonant accumulation, though not as Spitzer believed typical of the Provençal lyric in general (cf. p. 185, above), is characteristic of Arnaut and of *trobar clus* and is among the best evidence of Arnaut's influence on Dante's *rime pietrose*.

I 2. *The Time Factor*

Collizio is related to word length. Monosyllables, having only one vowel and usually several consonants, tend toward relatively high con-

---

[144] A similar realization, that an equal number of tonic syllables regardless of the number of atonic syllables can unite two lines rhythmically and temporally, is the basis of English "sprung rhythm" — from nursery rimes to G. M. Hopkins —, in which "a foot has one stressed syllable, which begins the foot, and any number of unstressed syllables" (Barnet *et al.*, *The Study of Literature*, p. 350). But in Provençal the importance of "quantity" derived from diphthongs or series of consonants is greater because the tonic accent is somewhat weaker.

sonant density. Thus, the *motz retardius* cited above among *Leys'* examples of *collizio* have often four or even five consonants for one vowel (*larcz, francz*, etc.), and the same is true of many of Arnaut Daniel's densest passages, like

> Er vei vermeills, vertz, blaus, blancs, gruocs
> Vergiers, plans, plais, tertres e vaus (XIII, 1-2).

Furthermore, monosyllables tend both to occupy more time and to produce a staccato effect by the fact that each monosyllable has, at least potentially, a tonic accent, whereas the atonic syllables of a polysyllable may be pronounced more rapidly and smoothly. Monosyllables thus weight and retard the flow of poetic expression, while phonetically lighter polysyllables permit freer and more varied rhythms. This factor may contribute to the condemnation of numerous successive monosyllables both by traditional rhetoric and by Malherbe.[145] For example, Quintilian (IX, 4, 42) notes the undesirable "jumpy" effect of accumulated monosyllables.[146]

It is also evident that monosyllables, by their individual density and brevity, are more suited than polysyllables to express certain brief actions or concise concepts.[147] Thus in the two lines just quoted from Arnaut Daniel, consonantal density and generally monosyllabic blocks produce an emphasis on details and slow staccato rhythms fitting to his peculiar poetic and amorous vision of nature.

I 3. *Vocalic Density*

Effects of density and duration are not confined to consonants. Carl Appel was perhaps the first to comment on the special effect of different diphthongs in close succession: "A certain effect is also

---

[145] Cf. Lausberg, "Zur Stellung Malherbes" (cf. n. 18, above), pp. 178-179.

[146] Lausberg, *Handbuch*, § 958: "etiam monosyllaba, si plura sunt, male continuabuntur, quia necesse est compositio multis clausulis concisa *subsultet*."

[147] Tauli, *Language Planning*, p. 97: The *length of the word*, too, has symbolic meaning. In some cases there is a feeling of harmony between the meaning and the word length." Thus duration symbolizes magnitude in Shakespeare's "multitudinous seas incarnadine."

produced by a similar sound of the vocalic element," [148] as in his examples *creys e nays, uey sai, lai ab lieys creys ioys, mais de lieys.* But Appel does not push his analysis to the point of defining this "gewisse Wirkung," which in fact depends on the *y-* or *w-* element shared by diphthongs and on their retarding effect.

Guilhem Molinier seems very sensitive to the duration of diphthongs and to the time differential between them and monophthongs. Thus of these problematic lines:

E p*au*bretat de l*eu* passar;
E l*eu*men sofracha passar,

the first, he says (III, 366), is inferior because of its two diphthongs. Similarly, he says, *leu* should be replaced by *tost* in this line:

Anta ve l*eu* e va s'en gr*eu* (III, 370),

because of its two *motz retardius* (*tost* is apparently less *retardiu* than *leu*, since Molinier considers *leu* and *temps* to have equal duration; and in this quotation *leu* has the further disadvantage, for Molinier, of producing unwanted internal rime (*rim fayshuc*).

Yet the best troubadours have no prejudice against multiplicity of diphthongs; the most famed Provençal poem of all, Bernart's skylark poem, has in its first stanza four lines with two diphthongs each; and the same poetic master concentrates diphthongs for an effect of amorous disorientation when he says:

Amors, *ai*ssi·m f*ai*tz tressalhir:
Del j*oi* qu'*eu ai*, no v*ei* ni *au*
Ni no s*ai* que·m dic ni que·m f*au* (XIII, 19-21)

(with five diphthongs in a single octosyllable). In general, then, not only syllabification but also the time effect of different sounds must be observed to permit appreciation of the troubadours' rhythms.

In general, the troubadours exploit repetition not only of specific sounds but also of articulatory types (expressed in density or sound texture) and of rhythms in time (expressed in duration or time effects). Every quality of sound is suited to produce different sorts of effect.

---

[148] Appel, *Peire Rogier*, p. 23: "Gewisse Wirkung wird auch schon durch ähnlichen Klang des vokalischen Elementes erzeugt."

The troubadours and Guilhem Molinier anticipate Alexander Pope's famous recommendations on symbolic duration,[149] often with surprising sophistication.

J. Conclusion

This chapter began by discussing modern scholarship, medieval rhetoric and the *Leys d'amors*; how relevant are these in fact to a study of Provençal sound effects? Scholars have very often picked out some of the most striking sorts of phonetic repetition, especially alliteration, for discussion, as we have indicated in the appropriate places. Yet assonance, final consonance, homophony, and other forms of sound repetition less adapted to the occasionally spectacular effects of dense alliteration, have not received due attention. In particular, no one seems to have previously tried to analyze and justify the varied effects of repeated vowels and consonants working together in the troubadours' poetry. And for our analysis of density and duration, we have had to draw almost entirely on medieval sources and on our reading of the troubadours.

Medieval rhetoric and the *Leys d'amors* often hit upon a useful analysis and terminology for sound effects. It was a mere matter of convenience for us to speak of vocalism and not of Guilhem Molinier's *sonansa*, of alliteration and not of his *replicatio*. In some cases, though, the *Leys* furnish terms which seemed indispensable, like *rim fayshuc* and *collizio*. Thus medieval rhetoricians not only demonstrate by their detailed analysis a consciousness of sound effects contemporary with the troubadours, but have also provided us with useful terms and ideas. One can criticize rhetoric and the *Leys* in particular for being too prompt to condemn as "vices" effects of repetition which seem to us, and apparently also to the troubadours, very acceptable means of poetic intensification; yet the medieval theorists at least recognized and defined the individuality of these techniques.

---

[149]   'Tis not enough no harshness gives offence,
   The sound must seem an echo to the sense....
   When Ajax strives some rock's vast weight to throw,
   The line too labors, and the words move slow;
   Not so, when swift Camilla scours the plain,
   Flies o'er th'unbending corn, and skims along the main.

This passage often serves the English prosodist; see the especially enlightening discussion of repetition and quality of sounds and rhythms in Northrup Frye, *Anatomy of Criticism* (Princeton, 1957), pp. 250-268.

In speaking of "intensification," we bring up a problem which we have perhaps, though of necessity, slighted. We could not, in a treatise on a definite body of poetry, discuss the general and difficult question of "effect" versus "harmony" in figures of sound. Does sound repetition merely produce a phonetic structure which is pretty or striking in itself, or does sound repetition relate to and intensify the meaning of words? The former case has occasionally seemed true, especially in vocalism with its somewhat less precise register of expressivity ("De la musique avant toute chose," as Verlaine recommended). But in general, we have supposed that in a poetry as conscious as that of the Middle Ages and of the troubadours, and in a genre as compact as the lyric love song, there should be a link between sound and meaning. Very often we have been able to identify such a link, by assuming a "sound symbolism" or at least a certain semantic value, either inherent or associational, to be implied in the sounds of poetry. We need not even suppose this relation of sound to meaning to be intentional on the poet's part (though surely it often is); sound and word, after all, and music as well, proceed from the same mind and inspiration at one moment of conception.

We have just referred to the love song; what about the problem of genre? Genre in Provençal depends more on subject than on form; and if our assumption about the general relevance of sound to meaning is correct, then different subjects call for different sounds and sound patterns. This has seemed the case in what we have seen of the martial sounds of Bertran de Born's several *sirventes* or the melancholy sounds of the *planh*. But the language has a limited number of sounds and of techniques. Alliteration, assonance and other forms of sound repetition must be adapted by the poet for the effect he consciously or subconsciously wills, whether of lightheartedness or melancholy, strife or harmony, whether in play or in earnest. We have concentrated on effects and techniques, although it would have been possible to make a detailed survey of different genres, periods, and poets, and to describe the particularities of each. We have at least shown the characteristic uses of sound by a few leading troubadours and the permanence of sound effects throughout the Provençal lyric, and developed a method and a background which could facilitate more specific investigations into the troubadours' admirable use of the sounds of their language.

Chapter VI

CONVERGENCE OF FIGURES OF REPETITION

A. Convergence: The Three Types

The convergence of poetic techniques or common effect has existed in literature and in criticism far longer than this particular name for it. Already the classics occasionally apply the verb *coniungo,* the noun *coniunctio* and the adverb *coniunctim* to the "combination of two figures."[1] The English term "conjunction," if it did not already have a specific grammatical meaning, would be a perfectly acceptable rendering of this idea. And perhaps Patrick Boyde has this classical background in mind when, speaking of repetition of letters, of words, of roots and of concepts, he writes: "Although each species may occur in isolation, it is more common for one to occur in conjunction with others, and, in particular, for conceptual repetitions and antitheses to be pointed and reinforced by verbal repetitions."[2]

We have seen (p. 68, above) that while Guilhem Molinier distinguishes carefully between different figures of repetition, he also has some idea of their conjunction when he writes that one figure "acorda se" with two others which occur in the same words (III, 172). If we were to retain Molinier's terminology here, we could speak of the "accordance" of different figures.

Dragonetti hints at the same idea when he describes rhetorical *expolitio* as "l'art d'accumuler les mots autour d'une idée ou d'en

---

[1] Lausberg, *Handbuch,* § 1244, arts. *coniunctum, coniunctio,* and *coniungere;* "von der Kombination zweier Figuren." Cf. § 633, 763.

[2] Patrick Boyde, *Dante's Style in his Lyric Poetry* (Oxford, 1971), p. 237.

varier la figure expressive par les mots, le ton de la voix ou le tour de la pensée." [3] Naturally variation "par les mots" is the most important four our purposes, as in Dragonetti's examples of "variations verbales." [4] So we well might adopt here his terms "accumulation" and "variation."

Other critics, especially Curtius, Spitzer, and Hatzfeld, [5] have described, though not always labeled, the phenomenon. A reference worth quoting is Alfredo Schiaffini's to a "group" of figures which combine to produce certain sound effects:

> ... un gruppo di procedimenti rettorici legati tra loro da nodi strettissimi e caratteristici per la loro estesa utilizzazione nella prosa isidoriana, alla quale avevano la virtù di conferire una preziosa "consonanza": l'alliterazione, la figura etimologica, il gioco di parole. [6]

This particular description recalls especially some of Arnaut Daniel's remarkable groupings of different figures.

Any of these terms — "conjunction," "accordance," "accumulation," or "grouping" of figures — could well describe our present subject. But another term has recently gained some prominence, that used by Machael Riffaterre throughout his *Pléiades* and notably in the title of his chapter V: "Convergences de procédés stylistiques."

Riffaterre is, as we have tried to be, always aware that "les procédés [de style]... sont rarement isolés; ils n'ont tout leur effet que si plusieurs convergent vers le même but." [7] Since "tous [les procédés d'intensification] se ramènent à l'accumulation de mots sur la même idée ou autour d'idées voisines," [8] his *convergence* is simply the accumulation of words comprising two or more different means of intensification around one idea or around related ideas. And convergences converge, so that Riffaterre's ultimate goal is to study "les synthèses de groupes convergents de procédés." [9] The study of these

---

[3] Dragonetti, *Techniques poétiques*, p. 288.
[4] Dragonetti, pp. 289-291.
[5] Ernst Robert Curtius, *Gesammelte Aufsätze* (Bern, 1960), especially pp. 69-74, on the Old French *Saint Alexis*. Leo Spitzer, "Inferno XIII." H. Hatzfeld, "Style 'roman.'"
[6] Alfredo Schiaffini, *Tradizione e poesia*, 2d ed. (Rome, 1943), pp. 59-60.
[7] Riffaterre, *Pléiades*, p. 190.
[8] Riffaterre, p. 162.
[9] Riffaterre, p. 22.

convergences and of their synthesis is, or should be, an important tool of stylistic criticism, and its eventual goal.

Another recent and interesting study, Yvette Louria's on *La convergence stylistique chez Proust*, gives the word a more specialized meaning: "La convergence est un ensemble d'éléments, composés chacun d'un morphème ou d'un syntagme, et exerçant tous la même fonction grammaticale par rapport à un 'pivot' commun, autre morphème ou syntagme."[10] Essentially, Louria means the enumeration of parallel elements, whether in conjunction with other stylistic techniques like word repetition and morphemic repetition or not. Indeed, enumerative convergence is essential in the Proustian world of eternal variation and adjustment of ideas.

The same is true of the troubadours' style. However, their lyric density also gives convergence in Riffaterre's wider definition great importance. Within the domain of our figures of repetition, we can therefore define convergence in the troubadours, on three different levels, as cooperation of different figures of repetition for common effect 1) in the same words; 2) in enumeration; and 3) in the same passage or poem. These will be called 1) automatic convergence; 2) enumerative convergence; and 3) free convergence.

Automatic convergence needs little attention here since it has been stressed throughout that one figure can give rise automatically to another. Notably, words and roots cannot be repeated without repeating the sounds that compose them. This is one characteristic setting figures of repetition apart from mere repetition of ideas. Even synonymous iteration is a rather pale device unless reinforced by root or word repetition, if only as repetition of conjunctions, with consequent sound repetition and typical tightening of the poetic structure.

Yet enumeration is unnecessary for convergence. We have seen (p. 67, above) an example of root repetition, Guilhem de Montanhagol's *A Lunel*, producing a very impressive concomitant effect of sound repetition in the numerous words beginning in *lu-*. This is automatic convergence of morphemic repetition and alliteration. On a lesser scale, one need only page through the examples given in section IV.G to see how even simple morphemic repetition adds to the phonic atmosphere of its context, particularly where the distinctive sounds

---

[10] Yvette Louria, *La convergence stylistique chez Proust* (Geneva, 1957), p. 93.

of a syllable like *jauz-* are involved. This first and evident, though effective, sort of convergence, must cede here to the more complex second type, enumerative convergence.

B. Enumeration in the Troubadours

In order to appreciate the second sort of convergence, we must first discuss its underlying structure, enumeration. Enumeration can be considered a figure of repetition to the extent that, especially in Provençal, it consists of synonymous iteration, or repetition of ideas with variation of words. Thus a typical list of natural phenomena or of feminine attributes merely express in several different manners the one idea of natural or feminine beauty.

Scholars have not been unaware of the importance of enumeration in Provençal. Thus Branciforti illustrates from Lanfranc Cigala the "accoppiamento di termini sinonimi," meaning essentially synonymous enumeration.[11] Ruffini gives examples of *enumerazione* in Aimeric de Belenoi.[12] And Klara Fassbinder discusses in some detail enumerative "Wortkoppelungen" in Raimbaut de Vaqueiras, especially in synonymous and antonymous pairs.[13]

Enumeration is certainly not peculiar to the troubadours, and it can be supposed that they drew largely on classical tradition. *Enumeratio* and *epitheton*, *asyndeton* and *polysyndeton* are well-known rhetorical concepts.[14] Still, like enumerated kennings in the Germanic epic and synonymous iteration in the *chanson de geste,* the troubadours' enumerations has some peculiarities. For example, asyndeton is extremely rare, whether in the simple pair of Jaufre Rudel's

Et als enfans *burdens petitz* (III, 10);

in the "interrupted" enumeration of Bertran de Born's *francha terra cortesa* (P-C 80.1, 1); in parallel participles of the types *aman preian*

---

[11] Branciforti, *Lanfranco Cigala*, p. 101.
[12] Ruffini, *Aimeric de Belenoi*, p. 75.
[13] Fassbinder, "Raimbaut de Vaqueiras," XLVII, 629-631.
[14] Cf. Lausberg, *Handbuch*, § 665-687 and, in the *Leys, polissintheton* (III, 182) and *dyaliton* (III, 182).

and *jogan rizen* (cf. p. 252, above, and note V, 109); or in the multiple enumeration of Arnaut Daniel's

> Er vei vermeills, vertz, blaus, blancs, gruocs (XIII, 1).

Although the Latin writers apparently preferred to list items by threes, the Romance languages tend to use what Boyde calls "binomials," both in poetry and in prose.[15] Certainly, the synonymous or antonymous pair is the basic and favorite form of enumeration in the troubadours. For example, three lines of Peire Vidal contain three quasi-synonymous enumerative pairs:

> Qu'*ab joi viu* et *ab sen renha:*
> Gen sap *donar* e *retener*
> E creis *s'onor* e *son poder* (XLV, 5-7);

and again in the next stanza:

> No volh sobras *d'argen* ni *d'aur,*
> Tant ai lo cor *gai* et *isnel.*
> E quan trob *tornei* ni *cembel* ... (XLV, 13-15).

The same poem also contains a number of antonymous pairs like *ven e ... vai* (11), *viu o mort* (19), and *mal mati ... e mal ser* (66). The basic desire seems to be to achieve a balance of complementary or opposite ideas forming a whole, dualistic like the troubadours' concept of love and non-love, joy and pain, body and soul. Hence (as is fitting in a poetry devoted chiefly to love) the great importance of the pair.

Such synonymous and antonymous pairs can combine with each other to form larger groups, as in Bertran de Born's line

> E gaug e plor e dol e alegranza (P-C 80.25, 14),

where the synonyms *gaug* and *alegranza* enfold their near-synonymous antonyms *plor* and *dol*. Or, here asyndetically, Arnaut Daniel claims of love:

> E fai·m irat, let, savi, fol (VII, 3),

---

[15] Boyde (cf. n. 2, above), p. 253.

again with chiasmus, the positive attributes *let* and *savi* being framed by the negative ones *irat* and *fol*. In both examples, the contradictory emotions of battle or love are well brought out by enumeration of pairs in one semantic field.

These examples form a logical transition from simple to multiple enumeration. Most multiple enumeration merely lists complementary or synonymous terms creating an effect of intensification and accumulation. Thus Bertran de Born gives a list of beneficial things:

> Que *jois* e *pretz* e *deportz* e *gajiesa*,
> *Cortesia* e *solatz* e *domneis*
> S'en ven a nos... (P-C 80.1, 3-5);

and Peire Vidal dramatizes his own amorous captivity:

> Qu'aissi m'a vostr' amors *conques*
> E *vencut* e *lassat* e *pres* (XXXIX, 45-46).

Even in such lengthy series, however, enumeration remains a passive element whose effect depends largely on the surrounding syntactic and stylistic context. Thus both our examples owe much of their effect to the polysyndetic linkage afforded by repetition of the conjunction *e*. Also, all the members of the first example profit from the final consonance -*s* (thrice -*tz*) or from the final vocalism -*a*; and our second example profits from *homoeoptoton* in that all terms are past participles, arranged, what is more, with chiastic final sound repetition -*es*/-*t*/-*t*/*es*. It is in fact rare to find an enumeration of any significance which does not represent a convergence with other figures of repetition, whether as here with repetition of conjunctions and sounds or, as in the first example of this section, with repetition of prepositions, possessives, and other function words.

Were enumeration to be treated in itself, it could profitably be regarded according to various criteria: the frequency of enumerated groups, their size, the parts of speech involved, etc. Different troubadours can also be compared, as in the following chart of members of enumerative groups in Peire Vidal and Arnaut Daniel:

Chart 12:

Average Frequency of Enumeration per Poem and Part of Speech

Term enumerated:	noun	adj.	verb	proper name	clause	adverb	total
Peire Vidal	4.3	2.7	1.7	0.8	0.6	0.2	10.3
Arnaut Daniel	5.9	3.7	4.6	0.5	2.9	0.1	17.7

The frequency of enumeration in general, and of verbs and clauses in particular, is significantly greater in Arnaut. Yet enumeration is not our chosen subject here, except as it serves as a catalyst for enumerative convergence.

C. Enumerative Convergence

Enumerative convergence — convergence which is neither automatic nor free — includes a large part of all Provençal enumerations and is one of the troubadours' essential resources. Many of our examples of different figures in chapters III through V, especially of consonance, vocalism, and general sound repetition, have actually occurred in enumerative convergence. Of the different sorts of enumerative convergence, the lowest level, that accepted by Yvette Louria (cf. p. 275, above) includes any single figure of repetition occurring in an enumeration.

On this level, we have seen that repetition of words, especially of function words, often gains strength from enumeration (sections III. J 1-J 2). Even more frequent is enumerative morphemic repetition in major words (section IV. E 1); and enumeration makes repetition of minor roots into an important element of variation (section IV. F 3). Finally, "coordinated" alliteration and assonance are perhaps the most forceful sorts of sound repetition (sections V. E 3 and F 4).

An interesting convergence, with enumerated inflectional repetition producing the rime words of four successive verses, is the refrain of a dance by Uc de Saint Circ:

> Ab dous chan
> En dansan
> Voil que s'anes conort*an*,
> Barat*an*
> E trich*an*
> Las domnas e gali*an* (XXIV, 7-12, etc.).

The occurrence of this syllable *-an* in all six lines of the refrain probably corresponds to a particular phase of the dance, and is quite successful also as poetry. Here the asyndetic link between *conortan* and *baratan* gives way to a polysyndetic linkage marked by repeated *e*, which serves to connect the last member *galian*, following its own direct object, to the series. So enumeration is the structural basis which allows these words to be juxtaposed for the desired effects.

As this example shows, polysyndeton contains an element of word repetition absent in asyndetic enumeration. Polysyndetic convergence is more common and easier to handle for the poet, especially when enumeration of clauses is involved. In addition, morphological figure of the two allomorphs of the conjunction *et* or *e* can add variety to an enumeration, as in the first four lines of this descriptive stanza by Uc de Saint Circ:

> Na Maria de Mons es plasentera,
> Francha *et* humil *e* d'avinen senblansa,
> *E* fa honor *et* acuoill volontera
> Los bos e lor mostra bell' acoindansa,
> *E* sos cors es joves *e* bels *e* bos,
> *E*·ill dich *e*·ill fach *e*·ill senblan amoros:
> Per que li voill de ben dir far honransa (XVIII, 1-7).

The polysyndetic linkages of the last three lines might have profited from the same variation *e-et*, had the phonetic context permitted.

Polysyndeton, however, is not necessarily the more forceful sort of enumeration. By its very rarity, asyndetic convergence can produce a more vivid effect, as at the beginning of Arnaut Daniel XIII, with its amazing phonetic correspondences (cf. p. 245, above):

> Er vei vermeills, vertz, blaus, blancs, gruocs
> Vergiers, plans, plais, tertres e vaus (XIII, 1-2).

Still, polysyndetic convergence is perhaps the most characteristic feature of the Provençal exordium, whose conventional nature description, here illustrated from Jaufre Rudel, proceeds either by enumeration of clauses and verbs:

> Quan lo rossinhols el folhos
> *Dona* d'amor e·n *quier* e·n *pren*
> E *mou* son chan jauzent joyos
> E *remira* sa par soven
> E·l riu *son* clar e·l prat *son* gen ... (I, 1-5);

or by enumerated nouns (producing in line 3 the general sound repetition already analyzed on p. 244):

> Pro ai del chan *essenhadors*
> Entorn mi et *ensenhairitz:*
> *Pratz* e *vergiers, albres* e *flors,*
> *Voutas* d'auzelhs e *lays* e *critz* (III, 1-4).

Very often the Provençal enumeration is not static but involves a definite development of idea, size, etc., just as Riffaterre observes that, in Gobineau's "polymer" enumerations, "presque toujours la gamme est ascendante."[16] Thus in the first of the above two quotations from Jaufre Rudel, four lines describing the nightingale's activities, with the bird as the subject of five different verbs, introduce a fifth more compact line describing the topographical surroundings by two clauses built on the shared repetitive frame *e·l ... son*. And in the second example, the progression moves the other way, toward three nouns, *voutas, lays,* and *critz,* governing the important prepositional locution *d'auzelhs*.

With some of these examples, we move into the higher levels of enumerative convergence, in which convergence of different figures would exist even without enumeration. As a simple example, not a typical but a symbolic one, we can take the nonsense words pronounced by William IX imitating a dumb-mute:

> Babariol, babariol,
> Babarian (V, 29-30).

Repetition of *babariol* is followed by variation of the last syllable in *babarian*. Of course, no syntax is implied; but we can perhaps imagine that the supposed deaf-mute would utter these three terms in asyndetic enumeration, the simplest way of combining words. The alliterative recurrence of these syllables *baba* (representative of meaningless speech) produces effective nonsense, yet does not forsake the principles of repetition and of variation so dear to the troubadours.

A more serious example is Jaufre Rudel's unusually dense passage

> Anc *tan* suau *no* m'adurmi
> *Mos* esperitz tost *no fos* la,

---

[16] Riffaterre, *Pléiades,* p. 146.

> Ni *tan* d'ira *non* ac de sa
> Mos cors ades *no fos* aqui (VI, 19-22).

Here the conjunction *ni* connects two result clauses, each built around *tan* with understood *que*, and each containing the repeated elements *tan* ... *no(n)* ... *mos* ... *no fos*. The allomorphic variation *no-non* gives a hint of the greater semantic variation produced between the two-line segments by the antonymous pairs *esperitz-cors*, *la-sa*, *sa-aqui*, and in a certain sense *tost-ades*. In effect Jaufre says the same thing twice: he is always thinking of his lady. But far from creating an impression of unnecessary repetition, the passage receives much of its force and charm from its parallelism of contrasting elements in a repetitive context.

There are passages of even denser enumerative convergence, like stanza II of Uc de Saint Circ XVII or the beginning of his *salut*, where virtually every word contributes to some figure of repetition, as several different enumerations of adjectives and nouns form a continuous coordinated structure, marked also by the allomorphic contrast *ses-senes* (lines 6-7) and the antonymous pair *bes-mals* (line 7).

> *Bella* donna gaja *e valentz*,
> Pros *e cortesza e* conoissentz,
> *Flors de* beltatz *e* flors d'onors,
> *Flors de* joven *e de* valors,
> 5 *Flors de* sen *e de* corteszia,
> *Flors de* presz *e ses* vilania,
> *Flors de* totz bes senes totz mals,
> Sobra *totas* fina *e* leials... (XLIV, 1-8).

The clear influence of rhetoric on Uc suggests that in its later phase the Provençal lyric becomes even more conscious of rhetorical effects than in the "classical" period we have concentrated on. But such an example is exceptional. The simple convergent enumerations (*de — e de —*; *la — e·l —*; *qui — o qui —*) illustrated in all phases of this study are more typical of the troubadours' manner of expressing the association of ideas which carries along the flow of their poetry.

D. Free Convergence

Our third type of convergence, free convergence, occurs wherever cooperation of different figures of repetition is neither automatic nor enumerative. On the simplest level, free convergence involves a pair in one relation standing in a different relation to a third term. Thus a pair in morphemic repetition alliterate and share their following vowel with a third, preceding term in Uc de Saint Circ's powerfully derogatory lines

> E sa fes
> Non es ferms ses fermansa (XIX, 11-12),
>
> And his word of honor
> Is not trustworthy without guarantee.

The literal English translation, which loses this convergence as well as the *rim fayshuc fes-es-ses*, shows how much less important in troubadour poetry is idea than expression.

Other such examples of free convergence among repetition of words, roots, and sounds have dotted our preceding pages. Now, we turn to convergence between word and root repetition with resulting automatic sound repetition. We have already seen that multiple unrimed word repetition and morphemic repetition generally mingle, either inside the verse (sections III. D 4 and IV. H 4, also IV. G 4) or in the rime (section IV. J, as in Raimbaut d'Aurenga XXXIX). Furthermore, successive stanzas can be linked in *coblas capfinidas* by either word repetition (section III. G) or morphemic repetition (section IV. G 1).

In such cases, morphemic repetition and word repetition collaborate according to their individual capacities. Morphemic repetition, the more variable figure, can produce larger groupings without monotony, and hence predominates in the unrimed refrain. And there are many more poems rimed entirely on repeated roots than on repeated words. Yet only word repetition permits the refrain (section III. E 6): placing different cognate words in a given line of each stanza would be almost impossible since they would have to rime together, and at any rate their force would be less, at such distance, because of their variable element. Thus the different characteristics of morphemic repetition and of word repetition complement but do not duplicate one another.

The first case to be discussed is convergence of the two figures around a single root (producing sound repetition automatically). For example, Bernart de Ventadorn announces the *joi*-theme in line 3 of an exordium, then uses *joi* and *jois* each three times, all in six lines linking the first and second stanzas:

> C'aisso es mos melher mesters,
> Que tostems ai *joi* volunters,
> Et ab *joi* comensa mos chans.
>
> Qui sabia lo *joi* qu'eu ai,
> Que *jois* fos vezutz ni auzitz,
> Totz autre *jois* fora petitz
> Vas qu'eu tenc, que·l meus *jois* es grans (X, 5-11).

This passage from three obliques to three nominatives can be held to correspond to progressive intensification of the concept. Here we have a single root in free convergence, which could, however, easily cooperate with a second root in a development of the technique of "dialectical" pairs (cf. section IV. G 4). We have, for example, discussed in Lanfranc Cigala XXVI the use of thirteen derivatives of *ioi-* and fourteen of *chan-* (p. 90, above).

A beautiful example of repetition of words and roots on a pair of themes is another of Bernart's exordia:

> *Chantars* no pot gaire valer,
> Si d'ins dal *cor* no *mou* lo *chans;*
> Ni *chans* no pot dal *cor mover*
> Si no·i es fin' *amors coraus.*
> Per so es mos *chantars* cabaus
> Qu'en joi d'*amor* ai et enten
> La boch' e·ls olhs e·l *cor* e·l sen (II, 1-7).

The series *chantars-cor-chans-chans-cor-coraus-chantars-cor* is complemented by the pairs *mou-mover* and *amors-amor*, since according to Bernart *love* must *move* from the *heart*, the seat of love, into *song*, the expression of love. The phonetic side is represented by the weak alliteration of the palatals *ch* and *c*, both in the two chief thematic roots and in the expression *chantar cabaus* (which also shows assonance, pretonic vocalism and final consonance). This is indeed *chantars cabaus*, "superlative song."

Again chiefly on two themes, concerning not love and the heart but good and bad or pain, Bernart repeats roots and words in an atmosphere of antonymy, alliteration, and dialectical argument:

> *B*en es *m*os *mals* de *b*el semblan,
> Que *m*ais val *m*os *mals* qu'autre *b*es;
> E pois *m*os *mals* aitan *b*os *m*'es,
> *B*os er lo *b*es apres l'afan (I, 29-32).

The alliterating expression *mos mals* contrasts first with *ben* and *bel*, then with *bes*, and finally with *bos* — all four being cognate,[17] alliterative, and partially homophonous. These three lines represent the basic contradictions within love, which the fourth line symbolically and optimistically resolves, in a future context, by repeating *bos* and *bes* in the absence of *mos mals*, whose synonym *afan* is implicitly negated in advance. The collaboration of opposing concepts and words is intensified by near-homophony not only within the group *ben-bel-bes-bos* but also in *mos-bos* and *val-mals*; and *m'es*, in the rime of line 30, is a sort of two-word composite of *mos*, *bes*, and *mais*. The poet is not just playing games here, but mingling different figures to convince somebody — us, his lady, or most likely himself — that a just reward awaits him.

A last example from Bernart again combines morphemic repetition, word repetition and alliteration, with the added factor of rime compensating for the greater distance between linked terms. At the end of the sixth of seven stanzas, Bernart claims that his lady's favors would visibly metamorphose him and cause public comment:

> Deus! s'er ja c'om me retraya
> — "A! *cal vos vi* e *cal vos vei!*"
> Per benanansa que·m *veya?* (V, 46-48).

Here already repetition of *cal vos* strengthens the enumerative tense opposition *vi-vei* (preterite-present); the rime reinforces the mood opposition *vei-veya*; and *v*-alliteration, twice in *vos* and thrice in forms of *vezer*, dominates and organizes the harmonies of the passage.

The end of the next and last stanza, on the same rimes and of course the same melody, gives us a foretaste of further convergence to come. In these three lines, internal *merce* introduces the opposition, in the rime, of the noun *mercei* and the verb *merceya*:

> Ai, domna, per *merce*·us playa
> C'ayatz de vostr' amic *mercei*,
> Pus aitan gen vos *merceya!* (V, 54-56).

---

[17] According to Meillet and Ernout, *Dictionnaire étymologique*, p. 114, *bellus* is a diminutive of *bonus*.

The same theme and words are immediately taken up by the first tornada, with a certain added personalization, *vostr' amic* becoming the poet's "signature" *Bernartz*:

> Bernartz clama sidons *mercei*,
> Vas cui tan gen se *merceya* (V, 57-58).

Now prepared for this sort of convergence, we return, in the second and last tornada, to the earlier *vezer*-theme:

> E si eu en breu no la *vei*,
> Non crei que lonjas la *veya* (V, 59-60).

With his characteristic note of sincerity and despondency, Bernart places the lover-poet persona in the central position by the cognate first persons *vei* and *veya*, repeated from stanza VI. Meanwhile, as in *sidons* and *cui* in the preceding tornada, the lady recedes into the more distant and less attainable third person of the repeated direct object *la*. Always revealed and expressed in convergence, the theme of seeing has won out, by its absolute finality, over the mercy-theme, in an atmosphere last marked by the repeated negation *no(n)* of the last tornada, indicating the poet's fear of *never* (*lonjas*, with litotes) seeing his lady again. The thematic and poetic value of such convergence of words, roots, and sounds is truly remarkable, whether perceived almost instinctively by an actual audience, or more consciously by the student of literature.

E. Convergence in an Illustrative Poem

It seems fitting to tie together the findings of this chapter and of this entire study by analyzing a complete poem from the point of view of figures of repetition, of their convergences, and of the "syntheses of convergences." For this purpose, we will choose probably the most famous Provençal poem, Bernart de Ventadorn's "skylark poem," so labeled for its striking initial image. Its haunting melody certainly deserves some of the credit, in whatever rhythmic interpretation we listen to it. Yet the poem's sheer beauty and unity in word and image are also hard to match. A number of thematic words and roots carry the poem's argument irresistably forward toward its conclusion, without the inconsistencies and about-faces all too frequent in the Provençal lyric. From various aspects and through various images, the poet expresses all the woes of the lover refused by the lady of his choice, culminating in self-exile. The poem is here printed from Appel's edition,[18] with some of our usual symbols added to indicate the chief figures of repetition.

I   Can vẹi la lauzẹta movẹr
     de joi sAs AlAs contrA·l rAi,
     que s'oblid' e·s laissa chazer
     per la doussor c'al cor li vai,
5 ai! tAn grAns ẹnvẹya m'ẹn vẹ
     de cui qu'eu veya jauzion,
     meravilhas ai, car desse
     lo cor de dezirer nọ·m fọn.

II   Ai, lAs! tAn cuidAvA sAber
10 d'amor, e tAn petit en sAi!
     car eu d'amar no·m posc tener
     celeis dọn ja prọ nọn aurai.
     Tout m'a mo cor, e tout m'a me,
     e sẹ mezẹis e tọt lo mọn;
15 e can se·m tolc, no·m laisset re
     mas dezirer e cor volon.

III   Anc non agui de me poder
     ni no fui meus de l'or' en sai
     que·m laisset en sos olhs vezer,
20 en un mirAlh que mout me plAi.
     Miralhs, pus me mirei en te,
     m'an mort li sospir de preon,
     c'aissi·m perdẹi com perdẹt se
     lo bels Narcisus en la fon.

IV 25 De las domnas me dezesper;
     jA mAis en lor no·m fiArAI;
     c'aissi com las solh chaptener,
     enaissi las deschaptenrai.
     Pois vẹi c'una prọ nọ m'ẹn tẹ
30 vas leis que·m destrui e·m cofon,
     totas las dopt' e las mescre,
     car be sai c'AtretAls se son.

---

[18] Lazar's version is virtually identical to Appel's.

V   D'aisso·s fa bę fęmna parẹr
ma *domna*, per qu'e·lh o retrai,
35 car no *vol so c'om* deu *voler*,
e *so c'om* li deveda, fai.
Chazutz sui en *m*ala *m*erce,
et ai be *f*aih co·l *f*ols en pon;
e no *sai* per que m'esdeve,
40 mas car trop puyei *contra* mon.

VI   *Merces* es perduda, per ver,
(et eu non o *saubi* ᴀɴc mᴀi),
car cilh qui plus en degr' aver,
no·n a ges, et on la querrai?
45 a! cᴀn mᴀl sęmbla, qui la *ve*,
qued aquest *chaitiu deziron*
que ja ses leis non aura be,
laisse morir, que nǫ l'aǫn!

VII   Pus ab mi*dons* no·m *pot* valer
50 pręcs ni *merces* ni·l dręihz qu'eu ai,
ni a leis no vęn a *plazęr*
qu'eu l'*am*, ja mais no·lh o dirai.
aissi·m part de leis *e·m recre;*
mort *m*'a, e per *mort* li respon,
55 e *vau m'ęn*, pus ilh no·m retę,
chaitɪus, en ɪssɪlh, *no sai on*.

VIII   Tristans, gęs no·n aurętz de mę,
qu'eu *m'en vau, chaitius, no sai on.*
de chantar *me* gic e·m recre,
60 e *de* joi *d*'amǫr m'escǫn.

In accordance with our findings in chapters III and IV, we may hypothesize that the best clue allowing us to penetrate the poem's stylistic world or, in Spitzerian terms, its "philological circle," will be the repeated words and roots. Excluding forms of *aver* and *esser*, the poem has twenty-four repeated words or repeated roots of significant semantic content. Of these the most frequent, with seven and five occurrences respectively, are the verbs *saber* and *vezer*, describing the perception and awareness by which the lover takes stock despairingly of his unhappiness.

One form of both verbs is used more than once, appropriately the first person singular, *sai* (lines 10, 32, 39, 56, 58) and *vei* (lines 1, 29). Furthermore, most other uses of these verbs also describe the first person singular, whether in the inflected forms *veya* (6) and *saubi* (42) or the infinitives *vezer* (19) and *saber* (9). Found also in the repetition of *vau* (55, 58), this preponderance of the first person, like the great frequency of the pronouns *e(u)* and *m(e)*, reflects the poet's obsession with his own psychological state.

The poem's next most frequent words or roots, repeated four times each, are *am-* (10, 11, 52, 60), *mort* (22, 48, 54, 54), *cor* (4, 8, 13, 16), and *laiss-* (3, 15, 19, 48). Three of these are not unusual. The themes of love and death are central in the Provençal lyric, though not always in such balance as here (where, for example to the proximate use of *amor* and *amar* early in the poem (10, 11) replies the gloomier pair *mort*, participle and noun, in a single line (54) of the last stanza). And *cor* is also a word to be expected; here, its quadruple repetition [19] helps link the first two stanzas and more particularly the images of the skylark's heart, to which sweetness goes (4), and of the poet's heart, which is apt to melt of desire (8). We begin to see an implied, though never precisely defined, contrastive parallel between the lark and the poet.

The four uses of the verb *laissar*, "to leave, let," are more exceptional. All are in the third person; it is not the poet-lover who performs this action. Rather, his lady *left* him only desire (15-16), *let* him to look into her eyes (19), and seems willing to *let* him die (48). The poet pictures himself very much as a recipient, in accordance with the conventional submission to the lady, while the skylark is not just acted upon, since he at least *lets himself* fall (3). Both verbs describing his fall, *s'oblid'* and *·s laissa* with their repeated pronoun, are reflexive; grammatically the lark, unlike the poet, exercises at least some control over his fate.

The six roots or words occurring four or more times, and the eighteen occurring two or three times, include two very significant semantic groups. One of these groups describes the poet's desires and sensations by *saber, vezer, amar, voler, dezirar, jauzir, plazer, merce, pro,* and their cognates, in a total of thirty-two occurrences. Another more physical group, equally characteristic of this poem, describes conflict, opposition, and privation through *morir, tolre, chazer, perdre,*

---

[19] In three oblique singulars and one nominative singular without flexion; cf. ch. V, n. 129.

vau, contra, recre (plus *mescre*), *(des)chaptener, chaitius,* and their cognates, in a total of twenty-four occurrences.

Some of these roots point out revealing parallels. Repetition of the preposition *contra* allows us to compare the bird who soared *contra·l rai* (2) and the poet who climbed too high, figuratively, *contra mon* (40). Or as the bird lets himself *fall* (3), so the poet has *fallen* into *mala merce* (37). Such distant parallels, like the surprise of homophonous words, suggest fertile comparisons.

Morphemic repetition reveals more closely-knit thought structures than these. Thus the derivative rime *chaptener-deschap-tenrai* (27-28) expresses Bernart's change of attitude toward the opposite sex. The derivative rime *saber-sai* (9-10), in convergence with repeated *tan,* stresses his newly-realized ignorance about love. And, as already mentioned, the pairs *amor-amar* (10-11) and *mort-mort* (54-54) reveal two of the poem's major themes.

But the most remarkable such group occurs in lines 13-15. Repetition of *tout m'a* brings *mo cor* and *me* into a strong parallel, implying that the heart is the most important part of the self — at least for the lover. The enumeration develops polysyndetically (with three *e*'s), from "my heart" and "me" to "herself" and "all the world," the last expression being intensified by the near-homophony *tout-tot.* Thus, to the poet, the lady is more important than himself, and only the entire world is perhaps more valuable than she. But then the more remote and definitive preterite *tolc* takes over, with its direct object again being the lady (*se*), the true center of the poet's universe. And the stanza moves smoothly from the *tolre*-theme back to the first stanza's *laissar-* and *cor*-themes, ending like stanza I on a juxtaposition of *dezirer* and *cor.*

From here, the poet continues to trace back in his memory the course of this love, and the heart image of stanza II leads him now to the image of his lady's eyes, through which the arrow of love supposedly attained his heart. Her eyes suggest a mirror, and Bernart turns to two new and less common stressed roots. The group *miralh-miralhs-mirei,* reinforced by *m*-alliteration, is particularly striking; and the progression from this group to the pair *perdei-perdet* reveals and expresses an association of ideas and of comparisons leading from the lady's eyes to the mirror image to Narcissus, like whom the poet has *lost* himself.

A last dense concentration of figures of repetition comes, fittingly, at the end of the poem. We have already (p. 116) seen how, in the tornada, repetition and reorganization of the words and expressions of the last four lines of the last stanza forms the effect of desolation and despair on which the poet takes leave of his heartless lady and of song, joy, and love, forever.

These have been effects largely of free convergence, which tend to extend over greater areas and to have wider application than enumerative or automatic convergence. But we have also seen enumerative convergence for example in lines 13-15, where four uses of the conjunction *e* cement together the parallel clauses and syntagms dominated by the verb *tolre*. Or in lines 9-10, the two clauses linked by *e* are set parallel by repeated *tan* and by the pair *saber-sai*. And the poem's last lines form a complex polysyndetic network of different figures of repetition.

Moreover, the simpler definition of convergence allows us to see convergences in many enumerations containing a single figure of repetition, especially in verbal pairs like

>Que *s*'oblid' e·*s* laissa chazer (3);
>Totas *las* dopt' e *las* mescre (31);
>De chanter *me* gic e·*m* recre (59).

In each example, the repetition or variation of the direct object or reflexive pronoun reinforces the thought already doubly expressed by the complementary verb. Or, in the more complex structure of lines 35-36, the conjunction links two clauses marked by repetition of the expression *so c'om* in the adversative context of the series *no vol-deu voler-deveda-fai*.

In addition to the sound repetition implicit in the preceding examples of word and root repetition, quite effective alliteration occurs, in indicated in the text above, in lines 14, 20, 22, 25, 32, 33, 37, 38, and 54; while vowel repetition, often in the form of assonance at the cesura and rime, occurs in lines 1, 2, 5, 8, 9, 12, 14, 20, 23, 26, 29, 33, 42, 45, 50, 51, 55, 56, and 60. Assonance with following consonance occur in *tan grans* (5); while *miralh*, at the cesura of line 20, is skillfully integrated into the line by alliteration with *mout* and *me* and by assonance with *plai*, in the rime. Finally, we find near-homophony in *enveya, en ve*, and *eu veya* (5-6) and in *tout, tot,* and *tolc* (13-15), and unaccented *rim fayshuc* in *sas alas* (2) and in *per ver* (41).

Also, the effects of duration treated in section V. I are prominent in the five "delaying" diphthongs of line 58 in *eu, vau, chaitius, sai*. So the poem has quite varied sound effects, yet not generally in convergence with other figures. As is usual with Bernart, sound forms frequent individual figures rather than fitting into the complex patterns typical of Arnaut Daniel or Jaufre Rudel. Sound can here be said to provide a continual harmony, having a direct relation to meaning chiefly where sound repetition and especially alliteration occur by automatic convergence with word or root repetition.

We are now ready to assemble the poem's stylistic parts and to view its continual movement and interpenetration, from the first stanza to the tornada, of themes defined by repeated roots and words, against the harmonious background of many individual figures of sound. Of the twenty-four roots we have found to be thematic, the concentration is thickest in the first, second, and last stanzas, with respectively eleven, fourteen, and twelve occurrences. But the important roots and words occur throughout, for example some form of *saber* in all but two of the poem's eight metrical units. Roots and words carry forward the comparisons and ideas, even through the humble first-person pronouns and negative adverbs which betray the self-centeredness and pessimism of the poetic universe that Bernat creates in this poem. Here word and sound cooperating in interlocking patterns demonstrate, better than any statistic, the ubiquity and the efficacity of the troubadours' figures of repetition, and the esthetic unity of a truly masterful work of art.

CONCLUSION

This general conclusion will not so much summarize the preceding pages — which is already done by a detailed table of contents — as it will discuss the problems posed by troubadour stylistics, in terms of our previous findings, of issues we have not yet been able to raise adequately, and of the assumptions which have underlain much of our work.

First, we have proceeded on an assumption which seems undeniable to anyone who has closely examined the medieval lyric: that we can safely speak of individual and collective styles in the troubadours. Style, usually defined as an artistically motivated choice among the means of expression offered by a language, has certain peculiarities in certain troubadours as it does in certain genres and in the Provençal lyric in general compared to other literatures. Choice among known figures for expressing conventional *topoi* is the essence of the troubadours' work. For them, figures of speech or techniques of expression *are* poetry; and content is incidental to style. Anyone can say: "I love"; it is not the idea but the manner of saying it that sets the troubadours apart from other lovers and poets and one troubadour apart from his rivals. There is indeed a collective "troubadour style" (though not as the eighteenth century saw it), just as any troubadour or any poet has a more or less pronounced individual style.

The "troubadour style," in our view, is a concentrated, cohesive, and "convergent" one, with close cooperation of style, form, music and meaning. Its essential verbal characteristic is the intensification of ideas by the accumulation of sounds and words in what we have called "figures of repetition" and their "convergences." We have followed Zumthor's suggestion that troubadour study should aim to focus on "le concours de plusieurs déterminismes."[1] These "determinisms" are most visibly stylistic, but ultimately linguistic and cultural. For the troubadours, the transitional stage between synthetic and analytic stages of language must have been particularly fertile; and an oral lyric dedicated to slow-moving non-narrative subjects provided impetus for stylistic accumulation, parallelism, contrast and what Hatzfeld calls "symétries asymétriques."[2]

In arriving at this characterization of "troubadour style," we have had to make other assumptions about the two related questions of intent and effect, already raised in the conclusion to chapter V. It has seemed that even sound, the most elusive of poetic elements, in addition to being beautiful or striking in itself, is also often expressive or illustrative of some meaning in its context. For other figures of repetition, expressivity is more evident since roots and words, even most function words, have inherent semantic values. This general link between figures of repetition and meaning has made us suppose that the use of figures of repetition was generally conscious on the troubadours' part. Indeed, how could a troubadour not be at least aware that he had repeated a certain word, root or sound in the process of verbalizing his ideas or of fulfilling a preconceived structural pattern?

Yet we have generally assumed that the poet is more than such a passive observer of the results of his own creativity. Our reasons for believing the troubadours highly conscious of their style — their metaphors for poetry, their self-praise, their recommendations to their jongleurs, their "signatures," their frequent quest for originality — have been given in section I. E. Although it actually makes little difference in describing and interpreting figures of repetition, we have therefore supposed that in general the troubadour consciously chose certain stylistic means which he found appropriate to his subject. For example, if the wanted to stress the idea of love or joy, he might choose to repeat the root *am-* or *jauz-*, in various patterns, positions and frequency according to the desired effect and degree of intensification. Even those critics who would not accept such a high degree of stylistic intentionality must admit a cause-and-effect relation between the poet's mind and the poem it creates; and this alone would suffice to justify a detailed stylistic study of the poem.

---

[1] Zumthor, *Langue et techniques*, p. 75.
[2] Hatzfeld, "Style 'roman,'" pp. 531ff.

Here the new problem of perceptibility is raised. If the effects desired by the poet are unperceived by his audience — whether a single lady, a medieval court, or a modern reader — they are useless. On the other hand, how can we be sure of not reading effects into a text whose author would repudiate them, or at least be surprised to have them pointed out to him? Our discussion of intent and effect helps here. If, as we have assumed, an intentional link between ideas and means of expression produces desired effects, then we can check the effects which we perceive against their ideological context. If an effect of sound or word seems inappropriate to the sense of the words, then something has gone wrong, either in the poet's art or else in our analysis of it. But if perceived effect and expressed meaning correspond, then we are on the track of a profitable stylistic analysis.

Therefore, we have tried to respect Spitzer's dictum that "it is not enough, to notice a remarkable feature in an author; one must also reflect on the meaning which it expresses." [3] This attitude charts a middle course between the idea of the "average reader," for whose perceptions no one, and certainly no critic, can truly speak, and the idea that everything in a poem can be significantly interpreted, with all the attendant dangers of overinterpretation.

These are our assumptions about style, intent, effect and perceptibility. In other cases, we would rather speak of "conclusions" than of "assumptions," though the distinction between the two may be slimmer than one often likes to imagine. It has seemed, first of all, that quantitative statistics may, with due caution, be used as a measure of the importance of different techniques, since in general, the frequency of any repetition corresponds (except where formalism has triumphed) to the intensity of the emotion felt and expressed. It has seemed, with reference to rime word repetition and equivocal rime, that what we have called "melodic identity" allows music to reinforce words in a way which must often be intended by the poet and perceived by his medieval audience. And it has seemed that certain positions of emphasis exist, for figures of repetition, at the beginning and end of the line, stanza, and poem. Hence the special importance of anaphora, of the rime, of the exordium with its habitual nature

---

[3] Leo Spitzer, *Stilstudien*, II (Munich, 1961), 4: "Es genügt nicht, eine auffallende Eigenheit bei einem Schriftsteller zu konstatieren, man muß sich auch nach ihrem Ausdruckssinn fragen."

description and announcement of themes to come, and of the tornada, which so often summarizes the poem and sends it off to its destination.

These conclusions, or demonstrable assumptions if one prefers, suggest a theory of the efectiveness of figures of repetition. Effect depends first on the repeated element's inherent importance, thus on its more or less striking phonetic, lexical, and semantic value. The second factor is the relation between the occurrences of a repeated element, in terms of frequency, proximity, structure, and meaning. Thirdly, the effect of repeated elements depends on their place in larger poetic structures: the verse, the stanza, the poem. These three levels of factors have helped us to describe and appraise the different figures of repetition.

We must still mention, for our stylistic assumptions, methods, and conclusions, the potential applications to which we have been able to address ourselves only occasionally. A "stylistique des genres" would study the techniques, or combinations and proportions of techniques, used in the *canso, sirventes, planh, alba,* and other genres and, in conjunction with study of form and music, would doubtless discover certain generic peculiarities, especially of the *canso* as the "noblest" genre. Stylistic study of individual troubadours would describe the particular traits of each, find evidence of stylistic influence (as has been done for formal influence), and perhaps help to decide if certain *tensos* are real or fictitious, to attribute poems of anonymous or disputed authorship, and to date certain poems by their place in a given poet's stylistic evolution.

Such stylistic study of various troubadours, in which "figures of repetition" would play a large role, would justify a comparison and grouping of troubadours and ultimately would clarify the characteristics of the two or three Provençal "schools" of poetry which are so often talked about and too seldom defined. And comparison of individual troubadours and schools would lead to a chronology of their style and of its evolution imposed by changing taste, the quest for originality and the "erosion" of the effect of conventional techniques. Thus, just as in form the "primitive" long isometric lines are known to give way in general to shorter and more often polymetric lines, so in style one might discover progressively greater alliteration, less assonance, more frequent rime word repetition, approximately constant morphemic repetition, longer and denser enumerations and convergences, or else a cyclical evolution of these factors dependent on the rise and fall of *trobar clus*. Within the chronological schema discovered, dating of individual troubadours like Rigaut de Berbezilh, the subject of much recent debate, could perhaps be facilitated by stylistic criteria.

Finally, such studies could be broadened to include other literatures: the poetry of the Goliards, of Moorish Spain, of the *trouvères*, of the *Minnesänger*, and even of more recent times. We have already discussed the nature and influence of the rhetorical tradition. It would be just as important to trace an unbroken stylistic tradition from early medieval Latin lyric to the vernacular poets of Provençal and other Romance languages, and to investigate whether the Hispano-Arabic theory of the origins of Provençal poetry is founded only on formal and thematic similarities which could be merely coincidental, or else on a fundamental community of those stylistic techniques which, according to our conception, are the essence of the Provençal lyric.

It is true, of course, that different languages have different characteristics. Thus in Provençal, the tendency of the accent toward finality encourages rime and assonance, especially on the most common tonic vowel, *a*; an analytical syntax facilitates repetition of function words; and largely synthetic systems of conjugation and declension encourage frequent repetition of major roots with varying inflection. But the linguistic individuality underlying each literature is no reason that such linguistically-induced stylistic characteristics cannot be passed from one language to another, just as classical French borrowed much from Latin vocabulary and even syntax. Thus we can picture the troubadours being influenced, directly or indirectly, whether from pre-literary Provençal, Vulgar Latin, or Classical Latin, by popular vernacular song, by wandering clerical singers, by the classical and post-classical theoreticians of poetry, and ultimately by Ovid and Vergil, or possibly by other traditions such as those of Moorish Spain.

This literary and linguistic context is the eventual basis for comparing the Provençal lyric to other forms of literary expression, and the troubadours to other artists of the word. But the value of the sort of study we have engaged in is not only historic and scientific. It has well been said that "the only sound reason for examining poetry technically is that this adds to our enjoyment." [4] Technical stylistic examination can in fact add greatly to our enjoyment and appreciation of

---

[4] Marjorie Boulton, *The Anatomy of Poetry* (London, 1953), p. xii.

the troubadours. What might seem insignificant and elusive shades of difference among various troubadours can become important and evident contrasts of personality and of style. Under the supposed monotony and gray areas of Provençal style lie vivid colors of rhetoric and colorful poetic techniques; and close study of the troubadours bears out the importance and the truth of Paul Meyer's statement that "C'est la poésie provençale qui, la première depuis l'antiquité, a réalisé... cet accord parfait de l'idée et de l'expression." [5]

---

[5] Paul Meyer, *Les derniers troubadours de la Provence* (Paris, 1871), p. 1.

BIBLIOGRAPHY OF WORKS CITED

This bibliography includes only those works and editions actually quoted or mentioned in our text or notes. Section A of the bibliography, including critical works and articles, anthologies, dictionaries, etc., is arranged by alphabetical order of authors, of editors, or of abbreviations; section B, including editions of individual troubadours, is arranged by alphabetical order of troubadours' first names and in the section for each troubadour, by the dates of editions.

Short titles are indicated in brackets, except that short titles for editions of troubadours are understood to be the troubadours' name as spelled by the editors.

Section A: all works except editions of individual troubadours

Albalat, Antoine. *Le travail du style enseigné par les corrections manuscrites des grands écrivains.* 3rd ed. Paris, 1905.

Alden, Raymond. *An Introduction to Poetry.* New York, 1909.

Anglade, Joseph. "Onomastique des Leys d'amors." *Revue des Langues Romanes,* LXIII (1925), 69-82.

———, ed. *Las Leys d'amors.* 4 vols. Toulouse, 1919-20.

———, ed. *Las Flors del Gay Saber.* Barcelona, 1926.

Appel, Carl, ed. *Provenzalische Chrestomathie.* 2nd ed. Leipzig, 1902. [*Chrestomathie*]

Aston, S. C. "The Troubadours and the Concept of Style." *Stil- und Formprobleme in der Literatur.* Vorträge des VII. Kongresses der Internationalen Vereinigung für Moderne Sprachen und Literaturen in Heidelberg. Heidelberg, 1959, pp. 142-147.

Barnet, Sylvan; Berman, Morton; and Burto, William. *The Study of Literature: A Handbook of Critical Essays and Terms.* Boston, 1960. [*The Study of Literature*]

Bartsch, Karl, ed. *Denkmäler der provenzalischen Literatur.* Bibliothek des Literarischen Vereins in Stuttgart, XXXIX. Stuttgart, 1856. [*Denkmäler*]

———. "Die Reimkunst der Troubadours." *Jahrbuch für Romanische und Englische Literatur,* I (1859), 171-197. ["*Reimkunst*"]

Bertoni, Giulio, ed. *I trovatori d'Italia.* Modena, 1915.

———. *I trovatori minori de Genova.* Dresden, 1903.

Bezzola, Reto R. *Les origines et la formation de la littérature courtoise en Occident,* pt. III, vol. II. Paris, 1963.

Birch-Hirschfeld, Adolf. "Uber die den provenzalischen Troubadours des XII. und XIII. Jahrhunderts bekannten epischen Stoffe." Diss. Leipzig, 1878.
Bloch, Oscar, and Wartburg, Walther von. *Dictionnaire étymologique de la langue française*. 2nd ed. Paris, 1950.
Boulton, Marjorie. *The Anatomy of Poetry*. London, 1953.
Bourciez, Jean. Review of Marco Boni, *Sordello: le poesie*. *Revue des Langues Romanes*, LXXII (1955), 115-116.
Boutière, Jean, and Schutz, Alexander H., eds. *Biographies des troubadours*. 2nd ed. Les Classiques d'Oc, I. Paris, 1964. (All *vidas* and *razos* are quoted from this edition.) [*Biographies*]
Boyde, Patrick. *Dante's Style in his Lyric Poetry*. Oxford, 1971.
Branciforti, Franco. "Note al testo di Guilhem de Montanhagol." *Filologia e Letteratura*, XIV (1968), 337-405.
Briffault, Robert. *Les troubadours et le sentiment romanesque*. Editions du Chêne, Paris, 1945.
Camproux, Charles. *Le "joy d'amor" des troubadours*. Montpellier, 1965. [*"Joy d'amor"*]
Caplan, Harry. "Rhetorical Invention in Some Medieval Tractates on Preaching," *Speculum*, II (1927), 284-295.
Chambers, Frank M. "The Lady from Plazensa." *Essays Presented to Honor Alexander Herman Schutz*, pp. 196-209. Ed. Urban T. Holmes. Columbus, Ohio, 1964.
―――. *Proper Names in the Lyrics of the Troubadours*. Chapel Hill, N.C., 1971.
Chassé, Charles. *Styles et Physiologie*. Paris, 1928.
Chaytor, H. J. *From Script to Print, An Introduction to Medieval Vernacular Literature*. Cambridge (Eng.), 1945.
Cnyrim, E. *Sprichwörter, sprichwörtliche Redensarten und Sentenzen bei den provenzalischen Lyrikern*. Ausgaben und Abhandlungen, LXXI. Marburg, 1888.
Crescini, Vincenzo. *Manuale per l'avviamento agli studi provenzali*. 3rd ed. Milan, 1926.
Curtius, Ernst Robert. "Neue Dantestudien." *Gesammelte Aufsätze zur romanischen Philologie*, pp. 303-345, part IV: "Die *Commedia*." Bern, 1960.
de Boor, Helmut, and Newald, Richard. *Geschichte der deutschen Literatur*. Munich, 1953.
Delaporte, P. V. *L'art poétique de Boileau, commenté par Boileau et par ses contemporains*. 3 vols. Lille, 1888.
del Monte, Alberto. *Studi sulla poesia ermetica medievale*. Naples, 1953.
Diez, Friedrich. *Die Poesie der Troubadours*. 2nd ed., revised by Karl Bartsch. Leipzig, 1883. [*Poesie*]
Dragonetti, Roger. *La technique poétique des trouvères dans la chanson courtoise*. Bruges, 1960. [*Technique poétique*]
Dronke, Peter. *Medieval Latin and the Rise of the European Love-Lyric*. 2 vols. Oxford, 1965-66. [*Medieval Latin*]
―――. *The Medieval Lyric*. New York, 1969.
Duffy, Charles, and Pettit, Henry. *A Dictionary of Literary Terms*. Denver, 1953.
Erdmannsdörffer, E. *Reimwörterbuch der Trobadors*. Romanische Studien, II. Berlin, 1897.

Faral, Edmond. *Les arts poétiques du XIIe et du XIIIe siècle.* Paris, 1924. [*Arts poétiques*]
Fassbinder, Klara M. "Der Trobador Raimbaut von Vaqueiras: Leben und Dichtung." *ZfRP*, XLVII (1927), 619-643, and XLIX (1929), 129-190, 437-472. ["Raimbaut von Vaqueiras"]
Faulhaber, Charles. *Latin Rhetorical Theory in Thirteenth and Fourteenth Century Castile.* University of California Publications in Modern Philology, vol. 103. Berkeley, Cal., 1972.
FEW. See Wartburg, Walther von, ed.
Frank, István. "*Babariol-Babarian* dans Guillaume IX." *Romania*, LXXIII (1952), 227-234.
———. *Répertoire métrique de la poésie des troubadours.* 2 vols. Paris, 1953 and 1957. [*Répertoire métrique*]
Frye, Northrup. *Anatomy of Criticism: Four Essays.* Princeton, 1957.
Fucilla, Joseph. "*Parole identiche* in the Sonnet and Other Verse Forms." *PMLA*, L (1935), 372-402.
Gamillscheg, Ernst. *Etymologisches Wörterbuch der französischen Sprache.* 2nd ed. Heidelberg, 1969.
Gatien-Arnoult, Adolphe-Félix, *et al.*, eds. and trans. *Las Flors del Gay Saber, estiers dichas Las Leys d'amors.* 3 vols. Paris, 1841-43. (All references to the *Leys d'amors* are to this edition, identified by volume number and page. In quotations, all punctuation and italics are mine.)
Gay-Crosier, Raymond. *Religious Elements in the Secular Lyrics of the Troubadours.* Chapel Hill, N.C., 1971.
Gennrich, Friedrich. *Der musikalische Nachlass der Troubadours.* 3 vols. Summa musicae Medii Aevi, III, IV, XV. Darmstadt (vol. III Langen bei Frankfurt), 1958-65.
Gröber, Gustav. Review of E. Wölfflin, "Uber die allitterirenden Verbindungen der lateinischen Sprache." *ZfRP*, VI (1882), 467-469.
Guiraud, Pierre. *Langue et versification d'après l'œuvre de Paul Valéry.* Paris, 1953.
Hatzfeld, Helmut. "Style 'roman' dans les littératures romanes: essai de synthèse." *Studi in Onore di Italo Siciliano*, I, 525-540. Florence, 1966.
Hill, Raymond T., and Bergin, Thomas G. *Anthology of the Provençal Troubadours.* New Haven, Conn., 1941.
Hoepffner, Ernest, and Alfaric, Prosper, eds. *La chanson de sainte Foy.* 2 vols. Paris, 1926. [*Sainte Foy*]
Holmes, Urban T., ed. *Essays Presented to Honor Alexander Herman Schutz.* Columbus, O., 1964.
Hubert, Merton J., and Porter, Marion, eds. and trans. *The Romance of Flamenca, A Provençal Poem of the 13th Century.* Princeton, 1962. [*Flamenca*]
Jeanroy, Alfred. "Les Leys d'amors." *Histoire Littéraire de la France*, XXXVIII, 139-233. Paris, 1949.
———. *La poésie lyrique des troubadours.* 2 vols. Toulouse and Paris, 1934. [*Poésie lyrique*]
———. "Poésies provençales inédites d'après les manuscrits de Paris." *Annales du Midi*, XVII (1905), 457-489.
Köhler, Erich. "Zum 'trobar clus' der Trobadors." *Romanische Forschungen*, LXIV (1952), 71-101. Also included in next entry.
———. *Trobadorlyrik und höfischer Roman.* Berlin, 1962.

Koehler, Moritz. *Uber alliterierende Verbindungen in der altfranzösischen Literatur.* Diss. Leipzig, Oppeln, 1890.

Kökeritz, Helge, "Rhetorical Word Play in Chaucer." *PMLA,* LXIX (1954), 937-952.

Larousse, Pierre. *Cours de style: livre de l'élève.* 52nd ed. Paris, n.d.

Lausberg, Heinrich. *Elemente der literarischen Rhetorik.* 3rd ed. Munich, 1967. [*Elemente*]

———. *Handbuch der literarischen Rhetorik.* 2 vols. Munich, 1960. [*Handbuch*]

———. "Zur Stellung Malherbes in der Geschichte der französischen Schriftsprache." *Romanische Forschungen,* LXII (1950), 172-200.

Lazar, Moshé. *Amour courtois et "fin' amors" dans la littérature du XIIe siècle.* Paris, 1964.

Leiffholdt, Friedrich. *Etymologische Figuren im Romanischen.* Diss. Göttingen, Hildesheim, 1883. [*Etymologische Figuren*]

Levy, Emil. *Petit dictionnaire Provençal-Français.* 2nd ed. Heidelberg, 1923.

Lewent, Kurt. "Observations on Old Provençal Style and Vocabulary." *Modern Language Quarterly,* II (1941), 203-224.

LEYS. See Gatien-Arnoult.

Louria, Yvette. *La convergence stylistique chez Proust.* Geneva and Paris, 1957.

Mahn, C.A.F., ed. *Die Werke der Troubadours in provenzalischer Sprache.* 4 vols. Berlin, 1846-53. [*Werke*]

Maillard, Jean. *Anthologie de chants de troubadours.* Nice, 1967.

Marouzeau, Jules. *Précis de stylistique française.* Paris, 1946.

Marshall, J. H., ed. *The "Donatz Proensals" of Uc Faidit.* London, 1972.

———. *The "Razos de Trobar" and Associated Texts.* London, 1972. ["*Razos de Trobar*"]

McGarry, Daniel D., trans. *The Metalogicon of John of Salisbury: A Twelfth-Century Defense of the Verbal and Logical Arts of the Trivium.* Berkeley, Cal., 1955, rep. Gloucester, Mass. 1971.

Meillet, Antoine, and Ernout, Alfred. *Dictionnaire étymologique de la langue latine.* 2nd ed. Paris, 1939.

Meyer, Paul. *Les derniers troubadours de la Provence.* Paris, 1871.

Meyer-Lübke, W. *Romanisches etymologisches Wörterbuch.* 3rd ed. Heidelberg, 1935. [REW]

Mölk, Ulrich. *Trobar clus - Trobar leu: Studien zur Dichtungstheorie der Trobadors.* Munich, 1968. [*Trobar clus - Trobar leu*]

Molinier, Guilhem. See Gatien-Arnoult; Anglade.

Morier, Henri. *Dictionnaire de poétique et de rhétorique.* Paris, 1961. [*Dictionnaire*]

Murphy, James J. "Cicero's Rhetoric in the Middle Ages." *The Quarterly Journal of Speech,* LIII (1967), 334-341.

———. "The Scholastic Condemnation of Rhetoric in the Commentary of Giles of Rome on the *Rhetoric* of Aristotle." *Arts libéraux et philosophie au moyen-âge:* Actes du Quatrième Congrès International de Philosophie Médiévale. Paris, 1969, 833-841.

Nelli, Rene. *L'érotique des troubadours.* Toulouse, 1963.

Newton, Robert P. "The First Voice: Vowel Configuration in the German Lyric." *Journal of English and Germanic Philology,* LXVIII (1969), 565-592.

OED. Shorter Oxford English Dictionary. Ed. C. T. Onions. Oxford, 1933. [*Shorter OED*]
Ogle, Marbury Bladen, "Some Aspects of Mediaeval Latin Style." *Speculum,* I (1926), 170-189.
P-C. See A. Pillet and H. Carstens.
Paetow, Louis J. *The Arts Course at Medieval Universities with Special References to Grammar and Rhetoric.* Champaign, Ill., 1910. [*The Arts Course*]
Pätzold, Alfred. *Die individuellen Eigentümlichkeiten einiger hervorragender Trobadors im Minneliede.* Ausgaben und Abhandlungen, XCV. Marburg, 1897. Originally pub. in part as the author's diss., Marburg, 1896.
Panvini, Bruno. *Le biographie provenzali: valore e attendibilità.* Florence, 1952.
———. *Giraldo di Bornelh, trovatore del secolo XII.* Catania, 1949.
Parker, DeWitt H. *The Principles of Aesthetics.* Boston, 1920.
Parr, Roger P., ed. *Geoffrey of Vinsauf, Documentum de Arte Dictandi et Versificandi.* Milwaukee, Wis., 1968.
Patterson, Warner F. *Three Centuries of French Poetic Theory.* 2 vols. Ann Arbor, Mich., 1935.
Pellegrini, Silvio. "Iterazioni sinonimiche nella Canzone di Rolando." *Studi Mediolatini e Volgari,* I (1953), 155-165.
Pillet, Alfred, and Carstens, Henry. *Bibliographie der Troubadours.* Halle/Saale, 1933. [P-C]
PMLA. Proceedings of the Modern Language Association.
Pollmann, Leo. "*Trobar clus*," *Bibelexegese und hispano-arabische Literatur.* Münster/Westfalen, 1965.
Pound, Ezra, "Planh for the Young English King." *Personae,* pp. 36-37. New York, 1926.
———. "Arnaut Daniel." *Make It New,* pp. 43-92. New Haven, Conn., 1935.
Preminger, Alex, ed. *Princeton Encyclopedia of Poetry and Poetics.* Princeton, N.J., 1965. [*Encyclopedia*]
Rickert, Edith. *New Methods for the Study of Literature.* Chicago, 1927.
Ricketts, Peter; Hamlin, Frank; and Hathaway, John, eds. *Introduction à l'étude de l'ancien provençal.* Geneva, 1967.
Riffaterre, Michael. *Le style des "Pléiades" de Gobineau. Essai d'application d'une méthode stylistique.* New York, 1957. [*Pléiades*]
Roncaglia, Aurelio. *La lingua dei trovatori.* Rome, 1965.
Rougement, Denis de. *L'amour et l'Occident.* Paris, 1939.
Ruffini, Mario. *Il trovatore Aimeric de Belenoi.* Turin, 1951. [*Aimeric de Belenoi*]
Rychner, Jean. *La chanson de geste, essai sur l'art épique des jongleurs.* Geneva, 1955.
Sachse, Max. *Über das Leben und die Lieder des Troubadours Wilhelm IX., Graf von Poitou.* Diss. Leipzig, 1882.
Scheludko, Dimitri. "Beiträge zur Entstehungsgeschichte der provenzalischen Lyrik," in 4 parts:

    I. *Archivum Romanicum,* XI (1927), 273-312;
   II. *Ibid.,* XII (1928), 30-127;
  III. *Zeitschrift für Französische Sprache und Literatur,* LII (1929), 1-38, 201-266;
  IV. *Archivum Romanicum,* XV (1931), 137-206.

(All our references are to part IV.) ["Entstehungsgeschichte"]
Schiaffini, Alfredo. *Tradizione e poesia.* 2nd ed. Rome, 1943.
Schirmer, Karl-Heinz. *Stil- und Motivuntersuchungen zur mittelhochdeutschen Versnovelle.* Tübingen, 1969.
Scholz, Martin. *Die Alliteration in der altprovenzalischen Lyrik.* Diss. Halle/Saale, 1913. Expanded under same title in *ZfRP*, XXXVII (1913), 385-426, and XXXVIII (1917), 76-98, 193-210, 311-343; references to the latter will be given in parentheses in our text and designated according to volume of *ZfRP* and page. ["Alliteration"]
Schultz-Gora, Oscar. *Altprovenzalisches Elementarbuch.* 4th ed. Heidelberg, 1924.
Servien, Pius [Pius Servien Cocolescu]. *Lyrisme et structures sonores: nouvelles méthodes d'analyse des rythmes appliquées à "Atala" de Chateaubriand.* Paris, 1930.
Shepard, William P. "Two Derivative Songs by Aimeric de Peguilhan." *Speculum*, II (1927), 296-309.
Spitzer, Leo. "Paronomasie im Spanischen." *Stilstudien*, I, 101-108. Munich, 1928.
―――. "Speech and Language in *Inferno* XIII." *Dante*, pp. 78-101. Ed. John Freccero. Englewood Cliffs, N.J., 1965. [*Inferno XIII*]
―――. *Stilstudien.* 2nd ed. 2 vols. Munich, 1961.
Stendhal [Henri Beyle]. *De l'amour.* Paris, 1822.
Stössel, Christian. *"Die Bilder und Vergleiche der altprovenzalischen Lyrik."* Diss. Marburg, 1886. [*Bilder und Vergleiche*]
Switten, Margaret L. "Raimon de Miraval's 'Be m'agrada' and the Unrhymed Refrain in Troubadour Poetry." *Romance Philology*, XXII (1969), 432-448.
―――. "Text and Melody in Peirol's Cansos." *PMLA*, LXXVI (1961), 320-325.
Tauli, Valter. *Introduction to a Theory of Language Planning.* Uppsala, 1968. [*Language Planning*]
van der Werf, Hendrik. *The Chansons of the Troubadours and Trouvères.* Utrecht, 1972. [*Chansons*]
Waddell, Helen. *Medieval Latin Lyrics.* Baltimore, 1952.
Warren, F. M. "Some Features of Style in Early French Narrative Poetry (1150-1170)," parts I-II. *Modern Philology*, III (1905-06), no. 2, pp. 1-31; no. 4, pp. 1-27.
Wartburg, Walther von, ed. *Französisches etymologisches Wörterbuch.* 25 vols., not all complete to date; 3 supplements. Basel (some vols. elsewhere), 1928- . [*FEW*]
Wieruszowski, Helene. *The Medieval University.* Princeton, N.J., 1966.
Wimsatt, William K., Jr. *The Verbal Icon: Studies in the Meaning of Poetry.* Lexington, Ky., 1967.
ZfRP. Zeitschrift für Romanische Philologie.
Ziegler, Vickie. "Reinmar von Hagenau and His School: A Study in Leitword Technique." Diss. Yale University. German Department, 1970.
Zumthor, Paul. *Essai de poétique médiévale.* Paris, 1972.
―――. *Langue et techniques poétiques à l'époque romane (XIe-XIIIe siècles).* Paris, 1963. [*Langue et techniques*]
―――. "'Roman' et 'Gothique': deux aspects de la poésie médiévale." *Studi in Onore di Italo Siciliano*, II, 1223-34. Florence, 1966.

Section B: editions of individual troubadours

The editions of the troubadours are arranged alphabetically by their first names, and under each troubadour by dates of editions. The starred (*) editions are those which we quote, except where otherwise indicated, and whose numbering we adopt. Quotations from other troubadours are from the editions given here, or from the anthologies indicated in section A, etc.

Aimeric de Belenoi

*Dumitrescu, Maria. *Poésies du troubadour Aimeric de Belenoi.* Paris, 1935.

Aimeric de Peguilhan

*Shepard, William P., and Chambers, Frank M. *The Poems of Aimeric de Peguilhan.* Evanston, Ill., 1950.

Albertet de Sestaro

*Boutière, Jean. "Les poésies du troubadour Albertet." *Studi Medievali,* nuova serie, X (1937), 1-129.

Arnaut Daniel

Canello, U. A. *La vita e le opere del trovatore Arnaldo Daniello.* Halle/Saale, 1883.
*Toja, Gianluigi. *Arnaut Daniel: canzoni.* Florence, 1960.

Bernart Marti

*Hoepffner, Ernest. *Les poésies de Bernart Marti.* Paris, 1929.

Bernart de Ventadorn

Appel, Carl. *Bernart von Ventadorn: seine Lieder.* Halle/Saale, 1915.
*Lazar, Moshé. *Bernard de Ventadour, troubadour du XIIe siècle: chansons d'amour.* Paris, 1966.

Bertran de Born

Stimming, Albert. *Bertran de Born.* 1st ed. Halle/Saale, 1879.

Cercamon

*Jeanroy, Alfred. *Les poésies de Cercamon.* Paris, 1922.

Cerverí de Girona

*Riquer, Martín de. *Obras completas de Cerverí de Girona.* Barcelona, 1947.

Folquet de Marselha

*Strónski, Stanislas. *Le troubadour Folquet de Marseille.* Cracow, 1910.

Guilhem IX (William IX of Aquitaine)

*Jeanroy, Alfred. *Les chansons de Guillaume IX, duc d'Aquitaine (1071-1127).* 2nd ed. Paris, 1927.

Guilhem Ademar

*Almqvist, Kurt. *Poésies du troubadour Guilhem Adémar.* Uppsala, 1951.

Guilhem de Montanhagol
Coulet, Jules. *Le troubadour Guilhem Montanhagol*. Toulouse, 1898.
*Ricketts, Peter T. *Les poésies de Guilhem de Montanhagol, troubadour provençal du XIIIᵉ siècle*. Toronto, 1964.

Guiraut de Bornelh
*Kolsen, Adolf. *Sämtliche Lieder des Trobadors Giraut de Bornelh*. 2 vols. Halle/Saale, 1910 and 1935.

Guiraut d'Espanha
*Hoby, Otto. *Die Lieder des Trobadors Guiraut d'Espanha*. Diss. Freibourg (Switz.), 1915.

Guiraut Riquier
Mann, C. A. F. *Werke*, IV. 1853. Ed. S.L.H. Pfaff.

Jaufre Rudel
Stimming, Albert. *Der Troubadour Jaufre Rudel*. Kiel, 1873.
*Jeanroy, Alfred. *Les chansons de Jaufré Rudel*. 2nd ed. Paris, 1924.

Lanfranc Cigala
*Branciforti, Francesco. *Il canzoniere di Lanfranco Cigala*. Florence, 1954.

Marcabru
Dejeanne, J.-M.-L. *Poésies complètes du troubadour Marcabru*. Toulouse, 1909.

Monge de Montaudo (the Monk of Montaudon)
*Klein, Otto. *Die Dichtungen des Mönchs von Montaudon*. Ausgaben und Abhandlungen, VII. Marburg, 1885.

Peire d'Alvernhe
*Zenker, Rudolf. *Die Lieder Peires von Auvergne*. Erlangen, 1900. Also in *Romanische Forschungen*, XII (1900), 653-924.
Del Monte, Alberto. *Peire d'Alvernha: liriche*. Turin, 1955.

Peire Bremon Ricas Novas
*Boutière, Jean. *Les poésies du troubadour Peire Bremon Ricas Novas*. Toulouse, 1930.

Peire Cardenal
*Lavaud, René. *Poésies complètes du troubadour Peire Cardenal (1180-1278)*. Toulouse, 1957.

Peire Raimon de Tolosa
*Cavaliere, Alfredo. *Le poesie de Peire Raimon de Tolosa*. Florence, 1935.

Peire Rogier
*Appel, Carl. *Das Leben und die Lieder des Trobadors Peire Rogier*. Diss. Berlin, 1882.

Peire Vidal
Bartsch, Karl. *Peire Vidal's Lieder*. Berlin, 1857.

*Anglade, Joseph. *Les poésies de Peire Vidal.* 2nd ed. Paris, 1923.
Avalle, D'Arco Silvio. *Peire Vidal: poesie.* 2 vols. Milan and Naples, 1960.

Pons de Capduolh

*Napolski, Max von. *Leben und Werke des Trobadors Ponz de Capduoill.* Halle/Saale, 1879.

Raimbaut d'Aurenga

*Pattison, Walter T. *The Life and Works of the Troubadour Raimbaut d'Orange.* Minneapolis, Minn., 1952.

Raimbaut de Vaqueiras

*Linskill, Joseph. *The Poems of the Troubadour Raimbaut de Vaqueiras.* The Hague, 1964.

Raimon de Miraval

Topsfield, L. T. *Les poésies du troubadour Raimon de Miraval.* Les Classiques d'Oc, IV. Paris, 1971.

Rigaut de Berbezilh

Anglade, Jean. "Les chansons du troubadour Rigaut de Barbezieux." *Revue des Langues Romanes,* LX (1920), 201-310.
Braccini, Mauro. *Rigaut de Barbezieux: le canzoni.* Florence, 1960.
*Varvaro, Alberto. *Rigaut de Berbezilh: liriche.* Bari, 1960.

Sordel

de Lollis, Cesare. *Vita e poesie di Sordello di Goito.* Halle/Saale, 1896.
*Boni, Marco. *Sordello, le poesie.* Bologna, 1954.

Uc de Saint Circ

*Jeanroy, Alfred, and Salverda de Grave, J.-J. *Poésies de Uc de Saint-Circ.* Toulouse, 1913.

William IX of Aquitaine. See Guilhem IX

INDEXES

INDEX 1: SUBJECTS AND TERMS

This selective index is intended to complement the table of contents by helping the reader to find all pages which take up a given idea or term which he has found either in the book or in other works. It aims to include all references to stylistic features, to the various figures of repetition, and to the English, Provençal, and Latin technical terms used. For reasons of space, this index excludes other items: names of critics, genres, and non-Provençal writers, and also a few terms which are constantly alluded to: figures of repetition in general, repetition, rime, style, troubadour, etc. Terms such as *cobla capfinida* or *mot accentual* are cited under the adjective (in the oblique singular), hence permitting easier comparison of figures of repetition based on the same principle. Occasionally terms of equivalent or closely related meaning have been grouped (e.g., alliteration and *replicatio;* tornat (*mot, bordo*); etc.).

accentual (mot, rim), 255
adjectio, 127
affectuosa (cobla), 76
alliteration, *replicatio,* initial sound repetition [see also 2 following entries], 32, 35, 42, 51, 65, 67-9, 74, 117, 119, 130, 132, 150, 155, 162, 172-3, 183-6, 189-191, 195, 201, 204-6, 209-28, 230-1, 237, 241, 245-7, 250, 262, 271-2, 274-5, 279, 281, 283-5, 290-2, 296
alliteration of consonants, initial consonance, 51, 183, 187, 192, 203-5, 232, 234, 236, 243-4
alliteration of vowels, initial vocalism, 140, 192-3, 198, 201-3, 205, 209, 225, 232-4, 238
allomorphs, 138-41, 152, 154, 280, 282
ambiguitas, amphibolia, 259, 262
amplificatio, 75
anadiplosis, anadyplozi, 75-6

anaphora, *anafora,* word repetition initial in the line, 19, 73, 75-6, 78-84, 86, 88-90, 93, 97, 99, 101-6, 108-9, 111-2, 116, 118, 121, 125-6, 150, 163, 295
annominatio, agnominatio, 65-66, 126-7, 129-30, 164, 193, 255, 262
antanaclasis, 263
antonyms, antonymy, 80, 85, 87, 121, 132, 134, 138, 151, 154, 162-3, 178, 180, 217, 230, 252, 260, 276-7, 284
"architectural" ("structural") figures of repetition, 42, 81-3, 90-1, 97, 99-101, 122, 125, 130, 150, 156-7, 179
artisan metaphors, "craft" of poetry, 25, 54-7, 61, 90
ascensus, 75
assonance, tonic vocalism, 23, 65, 69, 183, 185-6, 193, 198, 202-5, 207-

INDEXES 309

10, 218, 221, 229, 232-48, 250-1, 271-2, 279, 283-4, 291, 296-7
asyndeton, asyndetic, 91, 217, 223, 251, 276-7, 280-1
audience, listeners, public, 22-3, 28-9, 57-8, 77, 90, 93, 111, 131, 286, 295.

biaysshat (mot), 127
biography, see *vida, razo*
borda (consonansa or *sonansa),* 205

cacenphaton, cacemphaton, 230, 259-60, 267
cacophony, 266
cacosyntheton, 195, 211, 267
capcaudada (cobla), see *capfinida*
capdenal (cobla), 76-7
capfinida, capcaudada (cobla), 73, 76-7, 96-7, 106-7, 109, 121-2, 156-7, 174, 179, 215, 283
catena, 75
cesura (figures of repetition at) [see also *tornat*], 76-7, 92, 138, 208, 223-4, 233, 236, 238-9, 242, 244, 247, 251, 253-5, 291
chiasmus, chiastic, 82, 146, 149, 163, 176, 219, 238, 278
climax, 75
cobla, see accompanying adjective
collizio, conlisio, 194, 267-9, 271
"colors" of rhetoric, 30, 44-5, 48-9, 75, 126, 254, 298
comparison, 37-8, 87, 159, 172, 254
complexio, 66, 75-6, 105, 122
complexity, see difficulty
composition, *compositio,* compounds, 65-6, 124, 127, 131, 134, 175, 177-9, 205, 211, 255
concentration of sounds, density, duration, 184, 194, 197, 212, 219-20, 231, 244-6, 258, 266-71, 292
conduplicatio, 66, 74-7, 109, 122
conexio, 75
coniunctio, 273
consciousness of style, etc., intentionality, 32, 35-6, 59-61, 72-3, 76-7, 294-5
Consistori del Gay Saber, 30, 33
consonance, *consonansa,* repetition of consonants [see also alliteration], 151, 183, 188-9, 192-5, 200-1, 207-9, 211-33, 239, 241, 245, 247, 250, 279, 291
consonance (final), 154, 205, 228-30, 235, 242-5, 248, 251-2, 258, 271, 278, 284
convergence, conjunction of figures of repetition, 67-8, 70, 85, 93, 111, 122, 179, 220, 231, 241, 247, 273-93, 296
conversio, 75-6, 92, 105
"coordinated" figures of repetition, see enumeration

declinatio, 126
deffrenada (cobla), 76
deformitas, 259
density of sounds, see concentration
derivatio, 126
derivativa, derivans, entretracha (cobla), 128, 182
derivative rime, *rim derivatiu,* see rime (morphemic repetition in)
descriptio, 78, 118, 218, 237
diakote, 75
"dialectical" morphemic repetition, 147, 162, 284
diastole, 75
difficulty, complexity (of style), 20, 40-1, 212, 228
"direct" grammatical relation, 132, 143, 145, 221, 225, 239, 252
dissolut (rim), 97
distance factor, 95, 125
duplicativa (cobla), 76, 260
duration of sounds, see concentration
dyaliton, 276
dysprophoron, 266

enpeutat (vers), 253-5
enpost liamen, mot enpost, 254-5, 260, 267
entier (mot), 260
entretincha (cobla), 212
entretrach (rim), see rime (morphemic repetition in)
entretracha (cobla), see *derivativa*
enumeration, *enumeratio,* "coordinated" figures of repetition, 68, 80, 84-6, 90-1, 93, 114, 117-22, 125, 135, 139-40, 142-3, 145, 150, 152-3, 161, 176, 205, 207, 209-10, 214, 216-20, 223-5, 227, 233, 238,

240, 244-5, 250, 252, 275-83, 285, 290-1, 296
epanadiplosis, 75
epanalepsis, epinalensi, 75-6, 105
epanastrophe, 75
epinalensi, see *epanalepsis*
epiphora, 75
epiploke, 75
epistrophe, 75, 92
epitheton, 276
epizeuxis, epizeuzi, 66, 75-6, 91-2
epymone, 76, 92, 127, 156
equivoc(a) (mot, cobla), equivocatio, equivocal rime, 66, 127, 255, 259-62, 265, 295
esthetics, taste, judgment, 23, 25-9, 33, 35, 37, 61, 73
estramp (rim), 97, 195, 207
etymological figure [see also morphemic repetition], 65, 80, 90-1, 106, 124, 126, 130-4, 140-1, 143, 147, 150-1, 159, 165, 173, 175-6, 205, 208, 212, 219, 228, 254, 256, 274
exordium, 51, 111-2, 125, 146, 160, 169, 175-6, 209-10, 216-9, 221, 280, 283-4, 295
expolitio, 120-1, 160, 273

fayshuc, faysshuc (rim), internal rime, 68, 125, 151-2, 195, 205, 224, 229, 238-9, 242, 244, 248-255, 270-1, 283, 291
figures of rhetoric in general, 18-19, 30-2, 34, 40, 48, 62-4, 75-7, 194, 211, 249, 254-6, 273-4, 293
flowers of rhetoric, *flors, flores*, 30-2, 44, 49, 55, 76-7, 248-9, 254, 260
form, formal, 19-22, 29, 37, 50, 61, 63, 77, 122, 182, 292, 296-7
formalism, 21, 34, 77, 99, 295
fre, 195

geminatio, 75-6, 92

homoeoprophoron, 188, 193-4, 211
homoeoptoton, omoptoton, 124, 248-53, 278
homoeoteleuton, omotheleuton, 124, 128, 193, 205, 248-53
homophony [see also *equivoc*], 65-6, 114, 126, 156, 199, 201-2, 255-66, 271, 290

hyat, 195

inclusio, 75
interiectio, 75
interpretatio, 126
interpretatio per etymologiam, 264-5
inventio, invenire, 43
iothacisme, iotacismus, 195
iteratio, 75

jongleurs, 22, 36, 52-3, 58, 82

kyklos, 75

lambdacismus, laudacisme, 173, 195
lexical repetition, see words (repetition of)

"major" parts of speech, 69-70, 86, 117, 119-22, 125, 131, 135, 139, 141-50, 152, 154, 166, 205, 279
manuscripts, 22, 36-38
melody, music, so, melodic repetition or identity, 21, 26-8, 41-3, 50, 58, 60-1, 63, 83-4, 97, 100, 102, 104, 108-11, 113-4, 123, 149, 177-8, 206, 209-10, 260-1, 285-6, 293, 295-6
methacisme, 195
"minor" parts of speech, function words, 69-70, 84-6, 117-9, 122, 125, 135, 139, 150-4, 166, 181, 278-9, 294, 297
morphemic repetition in general, repetition of roots [see also morphological figure; etymological figure; rime (morphemic repetition in)], 23, 65-9, 72, 74, 76, 84, 90, 100, 103, 117, 122, 124-82, 251-3, 255, 273, 275, 279, 283-6, 288-90, 292, 294, 296-7
morphological figure, 65, 103-5, 116, 118, 131, 134-43, 137-8, 152-5, 164-7, 175, 186, 230, 258, 260, 280
multiple figures of repetition, 88-91, 99, 103, 113, 118, 125, 145, 164-74, 179-81, 199, 205, 209, 218, 223, 226-7, 230, 237, 245-8, 255, 277-8, 283
music, see melody
mytacismus, 195

INDEXES 311

near-homophony, 126, 173, 186, 202, 209, 218, 231, 235, 255-9, 262, 265, 285, 290-1

obscuritas, 259
obscurity, obscure style, see *trobar clus*
omoptoton, see *homoeoptoton*
omotheleuton, see *homoeoteleuton*
onomatopoeia, *onomothopeia*, see sound symbolism
oral literature, 22-3, 294
originality, individuality, novelty, 20-2, 59-61, 103, 105, 219, 224, 294, 296
ornamentation, *ornatus*, *ornamen*, 20-1, 39-40, 44, 47, 75-6, 126, 249

pallillogia, 75
paramoeosis, 254
paranomeon, 35, 212-3
parody, see satire
paronomasia, *paronomazia*, paronomastic [see also morphemic repetition], 65, 68, 127-9, 212, 255, 263
pezan (mot), 66, 76, 90, 122
plenisonan (vocal), 267
pleonasmum, 126, 143, 182
poliptoton, 126-8, 182
polysyndeton, polysyndetic, *polissintheton*, 89, 111, 217, 276, 278, 280, 290-1
prosapodosis, 75
pun, 173, 254-5, 262-6

quays(h)-replicatio, 35, 211-2

rare rimes, see *rimas caras*
razo [see also *vida*], 17, 26, 36-7, 53, 59, 192, 210
recordativa (cobla), 76
redditio, 75, 105
reduplicatio, 75
reforsada (cobla), 249
refrain, refrain word or refrain expression, 73, 84, 99-101, 108, 122, 158, 169-74, 179, 280, 283
refrancha (cobla), 67-8, 167
repetitio, 65, 74-6

replicatiu (dictat), *replicativa (dictio, cobla)*, 212, 215
retardiu (mot), *retardiva (dictio)*, 267, 269-70
retronchada (cobla), 76-7
rhetoric, rhetoricians, 22, 25, 30-2, 35, 38-45, 47-9, 54, 56, 71, 74-6, 92, 107, 122, 124-7, 129, 182, 188-9, 193-5, 211-2, 235, 248-9, 259-60, 262-4, 266-7, 269, 271, 273, 276, 282, 297-8
rimas caras, rare rimes, 27, 55, 57, 59, 94, 228, 268
rime, *rim*, see accompanying adjective
rime (internal), see *rim fayshuc*
rime (morphemic repetition in), derivative rime, *rim derivatiu*, *rim entretrach*, 63, 95, 102, 125, 128-30, 134, 138, 147, 151, 155, 164, 174-82, 285, 290
rime (repetition of words in), 63, 69, 73, 76, 86, 88, 90, 92-116, 121-2, 125, 130, 176-7, 210, 221, 260-2, 295-6

satire (literary), parody, 41-3, 50, 57, 61, 170, 215, 226, 254, 256, 258-9, 265
schools, universities, 47-9, 53
semisonan (vocal), 267
separatio, 75
serpenti (rim), 254
similiter cadens, 248
similiter desinens, 248
singing, singer, 22, 26-7, 41, 53, 58, 61, 101, 210, 254
sonansa, sonansa borda, 183, 195, 235, 271
sounds (repetition of, in general) [see also alliteration, assonance], 23, 64-8, 105, 125-6, 149, 154, 183-272, 275, 278-9, 283, 286, 291-2
sound repetition (rich), 202, 221, 230, 232, 245
sound repetition (weak), 117, 201-2, 204, 212, 218, 232, 238, 241, 246, 284
sound symbolism, onomatopoeia, *onomothopeia*, 185, 188, 194, 198-9, 227, 234, 245, 266, 272
structura aspera, 266
synaloephe, 267

synonyms, synonymy, near-synonymy, 87, 118, 121, 160, 192, 199, 209, 217, 219, 224, 236, 242, 275-7, 285

taste, see esthetics
"thematic" figures of repetition, 74, 81-2, 88, 90, 94, 104-5, 108, 113, 115, 122-3, 125, 141-2, 157-9, 162, 165, 168, 171, 173, 177-8, 209, 217, 242, 244, 258, 283-4, 286, 289-90, 292
tornada, 83, 98-9, 102, 106-16, 120-1, 123, 125, 165, 178, 209, 215-7, 220, 223, 252, 260-1, 263, 286, 290, 292, 296
tornat (bordo, mot), tornada (pauza), 76, 93, 122
Toulouse (School of), see Consistori del Gay Saber
traductio, 66, 126-8, 260
trencat (mot), 255, 260
trobar clus, obscurity, 18, 26-7, 38-9, 41, 57, 69, 126, 228, 268, 296-7
trobar leu, 18, 38-9, 42, 69, 127, 296

trobar ric, prim, 39
trope, tropus, tropare, 40, 43, 62

utrissonan (a; mot, rim), 201, 255

variation, variatio, varietas, variety, 76, 83, 87, 102, 139-40, 143, 146, 153-4, 156, 160, 162, 182, 216, 252, 274-6, 279, 281-2, 291
"vice" of style, vici, vitium, 30-2, 34-5, 76-7, 113, 122, 128, 189, 194-5, 211, 230, 235, 248, 250, 254-5, 260, 267, 271
vida, biography, 17, 25-9, 36-7, 46-7, 53, 61, 187
vocalism, vowel repetition [see also sonansa], 193-5, 200-1, 207-8, 231-55, 271-2, 278-9, 284, 291

words (repetition of), lexical repetition, 23, 42, 65-6, 68-9, 71-126, 128-9, 146, 149, 153, 156, 158, 164, 167, 169, 174, 179-80, 182, 183, 201, 205-6, 209, 212, 217-8, 237-8, 273, 275, 278-81, 283-6, 288-92, 294, 297

INDEX 2: TROUBADOURS AND POEMS

This index includes all references to any troubadour or other Old Provençal literary figure and to any specific poem or other literary work. Poems are identified by the number in the "standard" edition (if any) indicated in the Bibliography, section B; by the Pillet-Carstens numbers; and by the abbreviated first line. Thus, the reader will be able to identify any poem mentioned even if he does not have access to the edition I have used, and will be able to assemble all references to a given poem in order to gain a more integrated picture of its figures of repetition, as has been done in section VI.E for a poem of Jaufre Rudel. In alphabetizing names of troubadours, *de* is here ignored.

Ademar de Rocaficha
  5.1 Ges per freg, 103-4
Aimeric de Belenoi, 19, 130, 215, 276
  9.21 Tant es d'amor, 51
Aimeric de Peguilhan, 26, 54, 130, 181
  VI, 10.6 Amics Albertz, 51-2
  XLVII, 10.47 Ses mon apleich, 54-5, 57, 180

Albertet de Sestaro, 27
  IV, 16.13 En amar trop, 51
  VII, 16.8 Bo chantar, 58
  XIX, 16.5, see Aimeric de Peguilhan, VI
Amanieu des Escas
  21a.— El temps, 44-5
Anfos d'Aragon, 52
anonymous
  461.202 Quand lo pels, 43

INDEXES

Arnaut Daniel, 19, 26, 29, 45-6, 50-2, 55, 59, 69, 86, 131, 181, 187-8, 192, 207-8, 216, 219-20, 225-6, 228, 234, 240, 264, 266, 268, 274, 278-9, 292
   I, 29.15 Pois Raimons, 95, 156-7, 173-4, 216, 254, 258, 264
   II, 29.6 Chanson do·ill mot, 56, 157, 209, 219, 221, 223, 231, 246-7
   III, 29.16 Quan chai, 135, 147, 219, 231
   IV, 29.11 Lancan son passat, 139, 219, 251
   V, 29.12 Lanquan vei fueill', 145, 209, 216, 219
   VI, 29.7 D'autra guiz', 222, 237
   VII, 29.2 Anc ieu, 138, 141, 147, 209, 222, 277-8
   VIII, 29.5 Autet e bas, 188, 219, 237
   IX, 29.13 L'aur' amara, 88, 161, 206, 208-9, 216, 243, 246, 268
   X, 29.10 En cest sonet, 56-7, 59, 121, 198
   XI, 29.9 En breu, 188, 209, 216, 222, 258, 264
   XII, 29.8 Doutz brais, 146-7, 219, 252
   XIII, 29.4 Er vei, 44, 166, 209, 216, 219, 227, 245-6, 252, 254, 262-3, 269, 277, 280
   XIV, 29.1 Amors e iois, 88, 137, 148, 168, 209, 251
   XV, 29.18 Sols sui, 88, 133, 209-10, 216, 219, 222
   XVI, 29.3 Ans qe·l cim, 219, 246
   XVII, 29.17 Si·m fos, 50, 88, 138, 143, 219, 222, 259
   XVIII, 29.14 Lo ferm voler, 42, 50, 88, 97, 133-4, 150, 161, 175, 208
Arnaut de Maruelh, 46, 53
   30.22 Si com li peis, 38
Arnaut Plagues, 61
Ath de Mons, 33, 212

Berenguer de Noya, *Mirall de trobar*, 30
Bernadet (?), *Flamenca*, 49
Bernart Marti, 39
   IV, 63.5 Companho, 60
   V, 63.6 D'entier vers, 56
   VI, 63.7 Farai un vers, 60
Bernart de Ventadorn, 29, 36-7, 50, 68, 86, 90, 94-5, 115-6, 131, 181, 217, 220, 225, 246, 266
   I, 70.31 Non es meravelha, 58, 136, 160, 175-6, 218, 223, 260, 263, 284-5
   II, 70.15 Chantars no pot, 60, 133, 137-8, 166, 218, 284
   III, 70.1 Ab joi mou, 133, 137, 180
   IV, 70.44 Tant ai, 159, 208
   V, 70.7 Ara no vei, 153, 180, 285-6
   VI, 70.24 Lancan folhon, 137, 142, 169-70, 176, 223
   VII, 70.42 Can vei, 134, 145, 151, 166, 174, 218, 247
   VIII, 70.18 E mainh genh, 207, 217
   IX, 70.12 Be m'an perdut, 133, 146, 151, 159
   X, 70.33 Pel doutz chan, 144, 153, 166, 283-4
   XI, 70.21 Ges de chantar, 263
   XIII, 70.13 Be·m cuidei, 270
   XIV, 70.5 Anc no gardei, 36
   XVII, 70.28 Lo gens tems, 223
   XVIII, 70.36 Pois preyatz me, 222
   XIX, 70.27 Lonc temps a, 256
   XX, 70.39 Can l'erba fresch', 132, 149
   XXI, 70.35 Per melhs cobrir, 198, 237
   XXV, 70.6 Era·m cosselhatz, 133, 143, 166
   XXVI, 70.37 Can la freid' aura, 42-3, 132, 134, 137, 159, 166, 220-1
   XXIX, 70.26 Lancan vei, 208, 257-8
   XXXI, 70.43 Can vei la lauzeta, 36, 116, 122, 132, 150, 223, 256-7, 270, 286-92
   XXXIV, 70.23 La dousa votz, 237
   XXXVII, 70.37 Gent estera, 36
   XXXIX, 70.9 Bel m'es, 106-7
   XLII, 70.40 Can lo boschatges, 36, 229

XLIV, 70.30 Lo tems vai, 46, 217, 227
Bertoleme Zorzi
  74.4 En tal dezir, 50
Bertran d'Alamanon
  76.12 Mout m'es greu, 50-1
Bertran de Born, 36, 50, 69, 215, 226, 228, 272
  80.1 Ai, Lemozis, 276, 278
  80.7 Bel m'es, 82-4, 164, 223
  80.8a Be·m platz, 88-9, 92, 142, 155, 222-4
  80.12 Domna, pos de mi, 138
  80.13 D'un sirventes, 61
  80.15 Ieu m'escondisc, 149, 223
  80.25 Mieg sirventes, 120-1, 138, 140, 223-4, 227, 277
  80.41 Si tuit li dol, 101, 108, 169, 227, 258
Bertran de Paris de Rouergue
  85.1, Gordo, 53
Boeci, 193, 235

Cercamon, 68, 115, 220, 225, 234, 240
  I, 112.4 Quant l'aura, 59, 111, 148, 150-1, 197, 202, 207, 220-1, 230, 237, 239-41, 243-4, 252, 268
  II, 112.1b Ab lo temps, 220, 240, 257
  III, 112.1c Assatz es, 45, 55, 220, 244
  IV, 112.1a Ab lo pascor, 220-1, 224, 236, 244, 247
  V, 112.3a Puois nostre temps, 59, 198, 240-1
  VI, 112.2a Lo plaing, 59, 108-9, 156, 169, 251, 260
  VII, 112.1 Car vei fenir, 55
Cerveri de Girona, 226
  XIV, 434.9a Pres d'un jardi, 218
  LXXXVII, 434a.43, Obra sobtil, 57

Daude de Pradas, 46

Eble de Ventadorn, 46, 52
Elias Cairel, 27
Elias d'Ussel
  136.1, see Gui d'Ussel 194.2

Ferrari de Ferrara, 47
Flamenca, see Bernadet
Folquet de Marselha, 37
  II, 155.22 Tan m'abellis, 52

Gaucelm Faidit, 37
Gausbert Amiel, 27-8
Gausbert de Poicibot, 46
Girart de Rossillon, 235
Gui d'Ussel
  194.2, Ara·m digatz, 262
Guilhalmi
  200a.1, see Cercamon, VII
Guilhem IX, 69, 86, 132, 161, 191, 220, 225, 234, 240
  I, 183.3 Companho, faray, 84, 133, 148, 165, 220, 233, 247, 252
  II, 183.4 Compaigno, non puosc, 84, 236
  III, 183.5 Companho, tant ai, 84, 114-5, 206, 229, 247
  IV, 183.7 Farai un vers de dreyt nien, 80, 85, 90, 155, 165-6, 220, 236, 252, 259
  V, 183.7 Farai un vers, pos mi sonelh, 78, 114-5, 142, 190, 193, 207, 220, 228-9, 253, 281
  VI, 183.2 Ben vuelh, 44-6, 55-6, 114, 169, 223
  VII, 183.11 Pus vezem, 91, 114, 160, 165, 229
  VIII, 183.6 Farai chansoneta, 60, 83-4, 99, 104, 132, 238-9, 246
  IX, 183.8 Mout jauzens, 79, 151, 160, 162-3, 206, 208, 256
  X, 183.1 Ab la dolchor, 78, 95-6, 144, 220-1, 229, 231, 236
  XI, 183.10 Pos de chantar, 102, 114, 116, 149, 220, 237, 253, 257
Guilhem Ademar, 187
  IX, 202.11 Quan la bruna, 227
  XIII, 9.5 Al prim pres, 51, 180, 185, 215, 221, 223
  XIV, 202.4 Comensamen, 215
Guilhem Anelier de Tolosa, 226
Guilhem de Cabestany, 37
Guilhem de Durfort, 50
Guilhem Fabre, 185-7, 256
Guilhem de la Tor
  236.5a Pos n'Aimerics, 51

Guilhem Molinier, *Las Leys d'amors*, 25, 29-35, 44, 53, 61, 66-7, 74-7, 90, 92-3, 97, 104-7, 113, 122, 124, 127-8, 156, 164, 171, 175, 182-3, 194-5, 201, 211-2, 222, 235, 248-50, 253, 255-6, 259-60, 262-3, 266-7, 269, 271, 273
Guilhem de Montanhagol, 265
  II, 225.1 A Lunel, 66-7, 172-3, 226, 275
Guilhem de Saint Gregori
  233.2 Ben grans avoleza, 42, 50
Guiraut de Bornelh, 28-9, 36-7, 45-7, 55, 69, 226, 228
  I, 242.13 Er ai, 99
  XII, 242.60 Can lo glatz, 146, 153-4
  XXV, 242.16 Ar si·m fos, 56
  XXIX, 242.37 Ges de sobrevoler, 46
  XXX, 242.17 Ar auziretz, 57
  LIV, 242.64 Reis glorios, 84, 148, 158, 160
  LVIII, 242.14, see Raimbaut d'Aurenga, XXXI
  LXIX, 242.69 Si·us quer, 61, 132, 136
Guiraut de Cabreira
  242a.1 Cabra joglar, 52-3
Guiraut de Calanso, 27, 46
  243.7a Fadet joglar, 53
Guiraut d'Espanha, 213
Guiraut Riquier, 226, 228

Jaufre Rudel, 27, 36, 52, 68, 159, 213, 220, 225, 234, 240, 292
  I, 262.6 Quan lo rossinhols, 160-1, 209, 252, 280
  II, 262.5 Quan lo rius 139, 152, 242-3, 251, 263-4
  III, 262.4 Pro ai, 91, 161, 166, 175-6, 198, 206, 227, 237, 241-6, 256, 276, 281
  IV, 262.1 Belhs m'es, 58, 96, 119-20, 161, 202, 238, 253
  V, 262.2 Lanquan li jorn, 100, 115, 142, 157-8, 160-2, 241-3, 250, 257
  VI, 262.3 No sap, 58, 90, 107-8, 115, 155, 162, 247, 253, 281-2
Joan de Castelnou, 30

Jofre de Foixà, *Regles de trobar*

Lanfranc Cigala, 19, 55, 130, 276
  VI, 282.12 Joios d'amor, 252
  XII, 282.5 Escur prim, 39, 55-6
  XXI, 282.6 Estier mon grat, 265
  XXVI, 282.9 Ges no sui, 90-1, 100, 284
  XXVII, 282.18 Pensius, 100
Las Leys d'amors, see Guilhem Molinier
Lluis d'Aversó, *Torcimany*, 30

Manfred Lancia
  285.1, see Peire Vidal, XXI
Marcabru, 27, 36, 52, 69, 226, 228
  293.1 A la fontana, 140, 224
  293.4 Al prim, 179
  293.6, see Uc Catola, 451.1
  293.30 L'autrier, 91, 132, 144-5, 163, 264
  293.35 Pax!, 60, 100, 167
Miquel de la Tor, 26, 53
Monge de Montaudo (Monk of Montaudon), 36
  305.15 Mout mi platz, 81
  305.16 Pois Peire, 41-2

Peire d'Alvernhe, 19, 28-9, 39, 46, 214-5, 226, 228
  I, 323.20, L'airs clars, 208
  III, 323.24 Sobre·l vielh, 39
  IXa/b, 323.23 Rossinhol, 142, 144, 161, 176
  XII, 323.11 Chantarai, 28, 41-2, 166, 246, 252
Peire de Blai
  328.1 En est son, 60, 105
Peire Bremon Ricas Novas, 264
  330.14 Pos partit, 51
Peire Cardenal, 46, 189, 191, 226, 264
  I, 335.7 Ar me puesc, 42, 215, 222, 226
Peire de Cols, d'Aorlac
  337.1 Si co·l soleilhs, 38, 251
Peire Guilhem de Luserna, 264
Peire Raimon de Tolosa, 187
  III, 355.4 Ara pos, 55
  IV, 355.5 Atressi com la candela, 38

XII, 355.14 Pos vezem boscs, 55
Peire Rogier, 46, 208, 213, 250, 270
Peire de Valeira, 27
Peire Vidal, 26, 33, 36-7, 51, 69, 97-8, 109-13, 115, 117-9, 130, 176-7, 181, 213, 219-20, 225-6, 234, 260-1, 264, 278-9
I, 364.25 La lauzet', 99-100, 153
II, 364.6 Atressi co·l perilhans, 113, 118-9, 145, 177
IV, 364.9 Bels amics, 113
VIII, 364.20 En una terra, 118-9, 177, 233, 247
IX, 364.27 Mos cors, 119
X, 364.36 Tant ai, 152-3, 155, 263
XI, 364.7 Baros, 133
XII, 364.50 Una chanso, 118, 140, 152
XIII, 364.40 Quant hom honratz, 86-7, 98, 118
XIV, 364.18 Drogoman, 103, 105, 120, 145
XVI, 364.11 Be·m pac, 113-4, 177, 257
XVII, 364.29 Mout m'es, 51, 96-7, 117-9, 121-2, 177
XVIII, 364.36 Plus que·l paubres, 87, 113, 118, 120, 154, 156
XIX, 364.1 Ab l'alen, 119, 233
XX, 364.2 Ajostar e lassar, 94, 178, 261
XXI, 364.19 Emperador, 265
XXII, 364.43 Si·m laissava, 94, 178
XXIII, 364.24 Ges pel temps, 177
XXIV, 364.4 Anc no mori, 83, 91, 118, 261
XXV, 364.31 Nuls hom, 133, 178-9
XXVII, 364.10 Be m'agrada, 81-2, 119
XXIX, 364.22 Ges car estius, 144, 168-9
XXX, 364.49 Tart mi veiran, 119
XXXI, 364.3 Amors, 97, 100
XXXII, 364.35 A per pauc, 138, 150
XXXIII, 364.16 De chantar, 113, 261-2
XXXIV, 364.21 Estat ai, 113
XXXV, 364.47 Tant an, 118, 264
XXXVI, 364.34 Per ces, 119
XXXVII, 364.14 Bon' aventura, 121, 178
XXXIX, 364.39 Quant hom es, 154, 177-8, 278
XLI, 364.33 Per melhs, 51, 94
XLIII, 364.30 Neus ni gels, 80, 88, 103, 178
XLIV, 364.30a Non es savis, 177
XLV, 364.38 Pos ubert, 219, 265, 277
XLVIII, 461.197 Pos vezem, 98
Avalle XLVII, 364.12 Ben aja ieu, 82, 101, 150
Peirol
366.2 Atressi co·l cignes, 38
Pons de Capduolh, 213
Pons Fabre d'Uzes
376.2 Quan pes, 50
Raimbaut d'Aurenga, 19-20, 26-7, 46, 48, 226, 228
I, 389.22 Car, dous, 56-7
IV, 389.10 Apres mon vers, 41
XXIV, 389.28 Escotatz, 52, 166, 231
XXXI, 389.10a Era·m platz, 39
XXXVI, 389.14 Ar no sui, 42, 170
XXXIX, 389.16 Ar resplan, 102-3, 147, 161, 180, 283
Raimbaut de Vaqueiras, 19, 33, 37, 130, 226, 276
VII, 392.23 Leu pot hom, 23, 144, 159, 223
XIII, 392.18 Guerras, 166-7
XVIII, 392.32 Truan, mala guerra, 51
Epic letter, 392.I Senher marques, 151
Raimon de Cornet, 30
Raimon de Durfort
397.1 Turc Malec, 173, 264
Raimon de Miraval
XI, 406.13 Be m'agrada, 171
Raimon Vidal de Besalù, *Las Razos de trobar*, 30, 33, 53
Razos de trobar, see Raimon Vidal
Rigaut de Berbezilh, 26, 33, 37-8, 297
II, 421.2 Atressi con l'orifanz, 231, 237

III, 421.3 Atressi con Persavaus, 84, 99
V, 421.5 Ben volria, 104
VI, 421.6 Lo nous mes, 84, 99
dubbia I, 461.102 Eissamen com la pantera, 38
dubbia II, 5.1, see Ademar de Rocaficha
dubbia V, 337.1, see Peire de Cols
30.22, see Arnaut de Maruelh
355.5, see Peire Raimon, IV
366.2, see Peirol

Sordel, 51, 127, 226
  IV, 437.7 Bel m'es, 41
  XXVI, 437.24 Plaigner voill, 50

Terramagnino da Pisa, *Doctrina d'acort*, 30
Torcafol, 264
Turc Malec, 173

Uc de la Bacalaria, 27
Uc Brunet, 46, 105

Uc Catola
  451.1 Amics Marchabrun, 46
Uc Faidit, 30, 53
Uc de Lescura
  452.1 De motz ricos, 42
Uc de Saint Circ, 26, 46, 50, 53
  X, 457.18 Longamen, 60
  XVII, 457.39 Totz fis amics, 282
  XVIII, 457.22 Na Maria, 280
  XIX, 457.38 Tant es de paubr', 283
  XX, 457.8 Chanzos q'es leus, 42
  XXII, 457.21 Messonget, 61
  XXIII, 457.42 Un sirventes, 61
  XXIV, 457.41 Una danseta
  XXVI, 457.43 Valor ni prez, 169, 177
  XXVII, 457.27 Pei Ramonz, 42
  XXVIII, 457.17 Guillelms Fabres, 42, 185-7, 256
  XXIX, 457.32 Raimonz, 42
  XLIV, 457.— Bella donna, 282

William IX, see Guilhem IX

NORTH CAROLINA STUDIES IN THE ROMANCE LANGUAGES AND LITERATURES

I.S.B.N. Prefix 0-88438

Recent Titles

CHARLES NODIER: HIS LIFE AND WORKS, by Sarah Fore Bell. 1971. (No. 95). -895-6.

RACINE AND SENECA, by Ronald W. Tobin. 1971. (No. 96). -896-4.

LOPE DE VEGA. "EL PEREGRINO EN SU PATRIA," edición de Myron A. Peyton. 1971. (No. 97), -897-2.

CRITICAL REACTIONS AND THE CHRISTIAN ELEMENT IN THE POETRY OF PIERRE DE RONSARD, by Mark S. Whitney. 1971. (No. 98). -898-0.

THE REV. JOHN BOWLE. THE GENESIS OF CERVANTEAN CRITICISM, by Ralph Merritt Cox. 1971. (No. 99). -899-9.

THE FOUR INTERPOLATED STORIES IN THE "ROMAN COMIQUE": THEIR SOURCES AND UNIFYING FUNCTION, by Frederick Alfed De Armas. 1971. (No. 100). -900-6.

LE CHASTOIEMENT D'UN PERE A SON FILS, A CRITICAL EDITION, edited by Edward D. Montgomery, Jr. 1971. (No. 101). -901-4.

LE ROMMANT DE "GUY DE WARWIK" ET DE "HEROLT D'ARDENNE," edited by D. J. Conlon. 1971. (No. 102). -902-2.

THE OLD PORTUGUESE "VIDA DE SAM BERNARDO," EDITED FROM ALCOBAÇA MANUSCRIPT ccxci/200, WITH INTRODUCTION, LINGUISTIC STUDY, NOTES, TABLE OF PROPER NAMES, AND GLOSSARY, by Lawrence A. Sharpe. 1971. (No. 103). -903-0.

A CRITICAL AND ANNOTATED EDITION OF LOPE DE VEGA'S "LAS ALMENAS DE TORO," by Thomas E. Case. 1971. (No. 104). -904-9.

LOPE DE VEGA'S "LO QUE PASA EN UNA TARDE," A CRITICAL, ANNOTATED EDITION OF THE AUTOGRAPH MANUSCRIPT, by Richard Angelo Picerno. 1971. (No. 105). -905-7.

OBJECTIVE METHODS FOR TESTING AUTHENTICITY AND THE STUDY OF TEN DOUBTFUL "COMEDIAS" ATTRIBUTED TO LOPE DE VEGA, by Fred M. Clark. 1971. (No. 106). -906-5.

THE ITALIAN VERB. A MORPHOLOGICAL STUDY, by Frede Jensen. 1971. (No. 107). -907-3.

A CRITICAL EDITION OF THE OLD PROVENÇAL EPIC "DAUREL ET BETON," WITH NOTES AND PROLEGOMENA, by Arthur S. Kimmel. 1971. (No. 108). -908-1.

FRANCISCO RODRIGUES LOBO: DIALOGUE AND COURTLY LORE IN RENAISSANCE PORTUGAL, by Richard A. Preto-Rodas. 1971. (No. 109). 909-X.

RAIMOND VIDAL: POETRY AND PROSE, edited by W. H. W. Field. 1971. (No. 110). -910-3.

RELIGIOUS ELEMENTS IN THE SECULAR LYRICS OF THE TROUBADOURS, by Raymond Gay-Crosier. 1971. (No. 111). -911-1.

THE SIGNIFICANCE OF DIDEROT'S "ESSAI SUR LE MERITE ET LA VERTU," by Gordon B. Walters. 1971. (No. 112). -912-X.

PROPER NAMES IN THE LYRICS OF THE TROUBADOURS, by Frank M. Chambers. 1971. (No. 113). -913-8.

STUDIES IN HONOR OF MARIO A. PEI, edited by John Fisher and Paul A. Gaeng. 1971. (No. 114). -914-6.

DON MANUEL CAÑETE, CRONISTA LITERARIO DEL ROMANTICISMO Y DEL POSROMANTICISMO EN ESPAÑA, por Donald Allen Randolph. 1972. (No. 115). -915-4.

When ordering please cite the *ISBN Prefix* plus the last four digits for each title.

Send orders to: University of North Carolina Press
                 Chapel Hill
                 North Carolina 27514

NORTH CAROLINA STUDIES IN THE ROMANCE LANGUAGES AND LITERATURES

I.S.B.N. Prefix 0-88438

Recent Titles

THE TEACHINGS OF SAINT LOUIS. A CRITICAL TEXT, by David O'Connell. 1972. (No. 116). -916-2.
HIGHER, HIDDEN ORDER: DESIGN AND MEANING IN THE ODES OF MALHERBE, by David Lee Rubin. 1972. (No. 117). -917-0.
JEAN DE LE MOTE "LE PARFAIT DU PAON," édition critique par Richard J. Carey. 1972. (No. 118). -918-9.
CAMUS' HELLENIC SOURCES, by Paul Archambault. 1972. (No. 119). -919-7.
FROM VULGAR LATIN TO OLD PROVENÇAL, by Frede Jensen. 1972. (No. 120). -920-0.
GOLDEN AGE DRAMA IN SPAIN: GENERAL CONSIDERATION AND UNUSUAL FEATURES, by Sturgis E. Leavitt. 1972. (No. 121). -921-9.
THE LEGEND OF THE "SIETE INFANTES DE LARA" (Refundición toledana de la crónica de 1344 versión), study and edition by Thomas A. Lathrop. 1972. (No. 122). -922-7.
STRUCTURE AND IDEOLOGY IN BOIARDO'S "ORLANDO INNAMORATO," by Andrea di Tommaso. 1972. (No. 123). -923-5.
STUDIES IN HONOR OF ALFRED G. ENGSTROM, edited by Robert T. Cargo and Emmanuel J. Mickel, Jr. 1972. (No. 124). -924-3.
A CRITICAL EDITION WITH INTRODUCTION AND NOTES OF GIL VICENTE'S "FLORESTA DE ENGANOS," by Constantine Christopher Stathatos. 1972. (No. 125). -925-1.
LI ROMANS DE WITASSE LE MOINE. Roman du treizième siècle. Édité d'après le manuscrit, fonds français 1553, de la Bibliothèque Nationale, Paris, par Denis Joseph Conlon. 1972. (No. 126). -926-X.
EL CRONISTA PEDRO DE ESCAVIAS. Una vida del Siglo XV, por Juan Bautista Avalle-Arce. 1972. (No. 127). -927-8.
AN EDITION OF THE FIRST ITALIAN TRANSLATION OF THE "CELESTINA," by Kathleen V. Kish. 1973. (No. 128). -928-6.
MOLIÈRE MOCKED. THREE CONTEMPORARY HOSTILE COMEDIES: Zélinde, Le portrait du peintre, Elomire Hypocondre, by Frederick Wright Vogler. 1973. (No. 129). -929-4.
C.-A. SAINTE-BEUVE. Chateaubriand et son groupe littéraire sous l'empire. Index alphabétique et analytique établi par Lorin A. Uffenbeck. 1973. (No. 130). -930-8.
THE ORIGINS OF THE BAROQUE CONCEPT OF "PEREGRINATIO," by Juergen Hahn. 1973. (No. 131). -931-6.
THE "AUTO SACRAMENTAL" AND THE PARABLE IN SPANISH GOLDEN AGE LITERATURE, by Donald Thaddeus Dietz. 1973. (No. 132). -932-4.
FRANCISCO DE OSUNA AND THE SPIRIT OF THE LETTER, by Laura Calvert. 1973. (No. 133). -933-2.
ITINERARIO DI AMORE: DIALETTICA DI AMORE E MORTE NELLA VITA NUOVA, by Margherita de Bonfils Templer. 1973. (No. 134). -934-0.
L'IMAGINATION POETIQUE CHEZ DU BARTAS: ELEMENTS DE SENSIBILITE BAROQUE DANS LA "CREATION DU MONDE," by Bruno Braunrot. 1973. (No. 135). -934-0.
ARTUS DESIRE: PRIEST AND PAMPHLETEER OF THE SIXTEENTH CENTURY, by Frank S. Giese. 1973. (No. 136). -936-7.
JARDIN DE NOBLES DONZELLAS, FRAY MARTIN DE CORDOBA, by Harriet Goldberg. 1974. (No. 137). -937-5.

When ordering please cite the *ISBN Prefix* plus the last four digits for each title.

Send orders to: University of North Carolina Press
                 Chapel Hill
                 North Carolina 27514

NORTH CAROLINA STUDIES IN THE ROMANCE LANGUAGES AND LITERATURES

I.S.B.N. Prefix 0-88438

Recent Titles

MYTHE ET PSYCHOLOGIE CHEZ MARIE DE FRANCE DANS "GUIGEMAR", par Antoinette Knapton. 1975. (No. 142). *-942-1.*
THE LYRIC POEMS OF JEHAN FROISSART: A CRITICAL EDITION, by Rob Roy McGregor, Jr. 1975. (No. 143). *-943-X.*
HISTORIA Y BIBLIOGRAFÍA DE LA CRÍTICA SOBRE EL "POEMA DE MÍO CID" (1750-1971), por Miguel Magnotta. 1976. (No. 145). *-945-6.*
THE DRAMATIC WORKS OF ÁLVARO CUBILLO DE ARAGÓN, by Shirley B. Whitaker. 1975. (No. 149). *-949-9.*
POETRY AND ANTIPOETRY: A STUDY OF SELECTED ASPECTS OF MAX JACOB'S POETIC STYLE, by Annette Thau. 1976. (No. 158). *-005-X.*
STYLE AND STRUCTURE IN GRACIÁN'S "EL CRITICÓN", by Marcia L. Welles, 1976. (No. 160). *-007-6.*
MOLIERE: TRADITIONS IN CRITICISM, by Laurence Romero. 1974 (Essays, No. 1). *-001-7.*
CHRÉTIEN'S JEWISH GRAIL. A NEW INVESTIGATION OF THE IMAGERY AND SIGNIFICANCE OF CHRÉTIEN DE TROYES'S GRAIL EPISODE BASED UPON MEDIEVAL HEBRAIC SOURCES, by Eugene J. Weinraub. 1976. (Essays, No. 2). *-002-5.*
STUDIES IN TIRSO, I, by Ruth Lee Kennedy. 1974. (Essays, No. 3). *-003-3.*
VOLTAIRE AND THE FRENCH ACADEMY, by Karlis Racevskis. 1975. (Essays, No. 4). *-004-1.*
THE NOVELS OF MME RICCOBONI, by Joan Hinde Stewart. 1976. (Essays, No. 8). *-008-4.*
FIRE AND ICE: THE POETRY OF XAVIER VILLAURRUTIA, by Merlin H. Forster. 1976. (Essays, No. 11). *-011-4.*
THE THEATER OF ARTHUR ADAMOV, by John J. McCann. 1975. (Essays, No. 13). *-013-0.*
AN ANATOMY OF POESIS: THE PROSE POEMS OF STÉPHANE MALLARMÉ, by Ursula Franklin. 1976. (Essays, No. 16). *-016-5.*
LAS MEMORIAS DE GONZALO FERNÁNDEZ DE OVIEDO, Vols. I and II, by Juan Bautista Avalle-Arce. 1974. (Texts, Textual Studies, and Translations, Nos. 1 and 2). *-401-2; 402-0.*
GIACOMO LEOPARDI: THE WAR OF THE MICE AND THE CRABS, translated, introduced and annotated by Ernesto G. Caserta. 1976. (Texts, Textual Studies, and Translations, No. 4). *-404-7.*
LUIS VÉLEZ DE GUEVARA: A CRITICAL BIBLIOGRAPHY, by Mary G. Hauer. 1975. (Texts, Textual Studies, and Translations, No. 5). *-405-5.*
UN TRÍPTICO DEL PERÚ VIRREINAL: "EL VIRREY AMAT, EL MARQUÉS DE SOTO FLORIDO Y LA PERRICHOLI". EL "DRAMA DE DOS PALANGANAS" Y SU CIRCUNSTANCIA, estudio preliminar, reedición y notas por Guillermo Lohmann Villena. 1976. (Texts, Textual Studies, and Translation, No. 15). *-415-2.*
LOS NARRADORES HISPANOAMERICANOS DE HOY, edited by Juan Bautista Avalle-Arce. 1973. (Symposia, No. 1). *-951-0.*
ESTUDIOS DE LITERATURA HISPANOAMERICANA EN HONOR A JOSÉ J. ARROM, edited by Andrew P. Debicki and Enrique Pupo-Walker. 1975. (Symposia, No. 2). *-952-9.*
MEDIEVAL MANUSCRIPTS AND TEXTUAL CRITICISM, edited by Christopher Kleinhenz. 1976. (Symposia, No. 4). *-954-5.*
SAMUEL BECKETT. THE ART OF RHETORIC, edited by Edouard Morot-Sir, Howard Harper, and Dougald McMillan III. 1976. (Symposia, No. 5). *-955-3.*

When ordering please cite the *ISBN Prefix* plus the last four digits for each title.

Send orders to: University of North Carolina Press
Chapel Hill
North Carolina 27514
U. S. A.

The Department of Romance Studies Digital Arts and Collaboration Lab at the University of North Carolina at Chapel Hill is proud to support the digitization of the North Carolina Studies in the Romance Languages and Literatures series.

www.ingramcontent.com/pod-product-compliance
Lightning Source LLC
Chambersburg PA
CBHW030607230426
43661CB00053B/1883